KEY CONCEPTS IN MEDIEVAL LITERATURE

Palgrave Key Concepts provide an accessible and comprehensive range of subjects at undergraduate level. The ... are the ideal companion to a standard textbook ... making them invaluable reading to students ...

Palgrave Key Concepts

Key Concepts in ... and Finance

Key Concepts in International Business

Key Concepts in Information and Communication Technology

Key Concepts in International Business

Key Concepts in Language and Linguistics (second edition)

Key Concepts in Politics

Key Concepts in Management

Key Concepts in Marketing

Key Concepts in Human Resource Management

Key Concepts in Operations Management

Key Concepts in Psychology

Key Concepts in Strategic Management

Key Concepts in e-Commerce

Palgrave Key Concepts: Literature

General Editors: John Peck and Martin Coyle

Key Concepts in Contemporary Literature

Key Concepts in Medieval Literature

Key Concepts in Renaissance Literature

Key Concepts in Victorian Literature

Literary Terms and Criticism (third edition)

Further titles are in preparation

Palgrave Key Concepts
Series Standing Order
ISBN 1-4039-3210-7
(outside North America only)

You can receive future titles in this series as they are published by placing a standing order. Please contact your bookseller or, in the case of difficulty, write to us at the address below with your name and address, the title of the series and the ISBN quoted above.

Customer Services Department, Macmillan Distribution Ltd,
Houndmills, Basingstoke, Hampshire RG21 6XS, England

Palgrave Key Concepts

Palgrave Key Concepts provide an accessible and comprehensive range of subject glossaries at undergraduate level. They are the ideal companion to a standard textbook, making them invaluable reading to students throughout their course of study and especially useful as a revision aid.

Key Concepts in Accounting and Finance
Key Concepts in Business Practice
Key Concepts in Drama and Performance
Key Concepts in e-commerce
Key Concepts in Human Resource Management
Key Concepts in Information and Communication Technology
Key Concepts in International Business
Key Concepts in Language and Linguistics (second edition)
Key Concepts in Law
Key Concepts in Management
Key Concepts in Marketing
Key Concepts in Operations Management
Key Concepts in Politics
Key Concepts in Psychology
Key Concepts in Strategic Management
Key Concepts in Tourism

Palgrave Key Concepts: Literature
General Editors: John Peck and Martin Coyle

Key Concepts in Contemporary Literature
Key Concepts in Medieval Literature
Key Concepts in Postcolonial Literature
Key Concepts in Victorian Literature
Literary Terms and Criticism (third edition)

Further titles are in preparation

www.palgravekeyconcepts.com

Palgrave Key Concepts
Series Standing Order
ISBN 1–4039–3210–7
(*outside North America only*)

You can receive future titles in this series as they are published by placing a standing order. Please contact your bookseller or, in the case of difficulty, write to us at the address below with your name and address, the title of the series and the ISBN quoted above.

Customer Services Department, Macmillan Distribution Ltd
Houndmills, Basingstoke, Hampshire RG21 6XS, England

Key Concepts in Medieval Literature

Elizabeth Solopova and Stuart D. Lee

palgrave
macmillan

First published 2007 by
PALGRAVE MACMILLAN
Houndmills, Basingstoke, Hampshire RG21 6XS and
175 Fifth Avenue, New York, N.Y. 10010
Companies and representatives throughout the world

PALGRAVE MACMILLAN is the global academic imprint of the Palgrave Macmillan division of St. Martin's Press, LLC and of Palgrave Macmillan Ltd. Macmillan® is a registered trademark in the United States, United Kingdom and other countries. Palgrave is a registered trademark in the European Union and other countries.

ISBN-13: 978–1–4039–9723–4
ISBN 10: 1–4039–9723–3

This book is printed on paper suitable for recycling and made from fully managed and sustained forest sources.

A catalogue record for this book is available from the British Library.

A catalog record for this book is available from the Library of Congress.

10   9   8   7   6   5   4   3   2   1
16   15   14   13   12   11   10   09   08   07

Printed in China

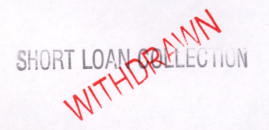

To Anastasia, Michael, Maurice, and Truda

Contents

General Editors' Preface

The purpose of Palgrave Key Concepts in Literature is to provide students with key critical and historical ideas about the texts they are studying as part of their literature courses. These ideas include information about the historical and cultural contexts of literature as well as the theoretical approaches current in the subject today. Behind the series lies a recognition of the need nowadays for students to be familiar with a range of concepts and contextual material to inform their reading and writing about literature.

But behind the series there also lies a recognition of the changes that have transformed degree courses in Literature in recent years. Central to these changes has been the impact of critical theory together with a renewed interest in the way in which texts intersect with their immediate context and historical circumstances. The result has been an opening up of new ways of reading texts and a new understanding of what the study of literature involves together with the introduction of a wide set of new critical issues that demand our attention. An important aim of Palgrave Key Concepts in Literature is to provide brief, accessible introductions to these new ways of reading and new issues.

Each volume in Palgrave Key Concepts in Literature follows a similar broad structure. Here, an initial chapter introducing the major key concepts is followed by three sections – Old English, Middle English and Approaches, Theory and Practice – each containing a sequence of brief entries on a series of topics. Alongside entries focussing on the works themselves, other entries provide an impression of the historical, social and cultural environment in which these literary texts were produced. In the final chapter, entries outline the manner in which approaches, theory and practice have affected the ways in which we discuss the texts featured in the present volume. The informing intention throughout is to help the reader create something new in the process of combining context, text and criticism.

John Peck
Martin Coyle

List of Abbreviations

c.	*circa*
EETS e.s.	Early English Text Society, Extra Series
EETS o.s.	Early English Text Society, Original Series
EETS s.s.	Early English Text Society, Second Series
ELN	*English Language Notes*
ES	*English Studies*
JEGP	*Journal of English and Germanic Philology*
MA	*Medium Aevum*
MnE	Modern English
OE	Old English
PMLA	*Publications of the Modern Languages Association*
SP	*Studies in Philology*
SAC	*Studies in the Age of Chaucer*

Introduction

This book sets out to present key themes, texts, terminologies, and methods related to a period of English literature we broadly term 'medieval'. In short, this covers the dates from some time in the mid-5th century to the third quarter of the 15th century – a period of over 1,000 years. The length of this time-span should not be forgotten, nor underestimated. It covers from the beginnings of English to the start of the Tudor dynasty. Any generalisations about the literature, people, or culture of the period should be avoided. To say there is complete commonality between the first settlers in the 5th century and the men and women who lived in the 15th century is akin to saying we ourselves have the same ideas and values as the people who lived around the year 1000.

Before this period England did not exist, but by the end of the medieval period it had become one of the most powerful nations in the world. Moreover, before the period, the notions of 'English' and 'the English' did not exist.

The *Oxford English Dictionary* defines 'medieval' as:

> Of or relating to a period of time intervening between (periods designated as) ancient and modern; *spec.* of, relating to, or characteristic of the Middle Ages.

This definition is interesting as it illustrates one of the problems besetting the medieval period. It is often seen purely as a time 'in between', i.e. one between the glory of the ancient world of Rome and Greece, and the enlightenment of the Renaissance. This in turn can lead to a ready willingness to dismiss the period as somehow irrelevant; a cultural blot on the history of humanity. Yet, as we will see throughout this book, the achievements and legacy of the medieval period are of crucial importance to the study of the English language and its literature.

Taking the history of England alone, we can see a pivotal event occurring in the year 1066 which seems to neatly divide the period. This was the Norman Conquest, in which the throne of England passed from the Anglo-Saxons to the Normans under William the Conqueror. This again, however, causes problems. The date 1066 presents scholars and students with an all-too-easy point to 'begin from', i.e. ignoring the earlier period up to the arrival of William. Yet we must not fall into the trap of seeing important historical dates as openings and closings of chapters. Instead, as is seen in this book and others (e.g. Treharne, 2004), we strongly advocate an approach of looking at the entire medieval period and beyond to see continuity in texts, language, and cultural themes.

To begin with, the terminology adopted in this book needs some explanation:

Medieval: this is used to refer to the historical period, occasionally to the people who lived there ('medieval women'), the language (e.g. Medieval English), and the literature. It is subdivided into the Early Medieval Period (5th to 11th century) and the Later Medieval Period (11th century to the third quarter of the 15th century).

Anglo-Saxon: this term refers to the races that ruled England from the mid-5th century until the Norman Conquest. It can also be used to refer to that historical period (e.g. 'Anglo-Saxon history'), but decreasingly now to the language and literature of the time (e.g. 'I am studying Anglo-Saxon'). The term has been much abused nowadays as it can stand as a collective adjective referring to Britain, Australia, New Zealand, Canada, and the USA; or it can be used by right-wing political groups to refer to some nonsensical common Germanic ancestry.

Old English: this is the preferred term in literary and linguistic studies and describes the language and literature of the Anglo-Saxons. This is used nowadays as it immediately illustrates its place and continuity in the history of English.

Middle English: this refers to the period from the Norman Conquest until approximately the third quarter of the 15th century, and to the literature of this period. The date which is often taken to be the borderline between the Middle English and Early Modern periods is 1476, when William Caxton set up the first printing press in England.

As pointed out already, the borderlines between the periods in the history of English language and literature, marked by political rather than cultural events, can be only conventional, because the development of language and literary evolution are gradual processes and happen continuously. The traditional division into periods, adopted in this book, is not meaningless, but is best understood with reference to what precedes and what follows each historical period. The Norman Conquest resulted in important cultural changes, such as the temporary loss of prestige which English, and the English, enjoyed during the Anglo-Saxon period. The end of the Old English period was also a time of significant linguistic changes many of which we can observe only in later post-Conquest texts, again making the Norman Conquest an artificial but nevertheless convenient borderline. The introduction of printing in the 15th century started a major change in how texts were produced, transmitted, and received. The end of the 15th century was also the time when the influence of the Italian Renaissance started to be felt in England, introducing new ideas and new trends in the development of literature and art.

1 Introductory Key Concepts

(a)   The Anglo-Saxon Period

Before we begin to discuss Old English literature it is essential to have a basic understanding of the historical events of the period, and the nature of Anglo-Saxon culture. This 'context-based' approach is one that is common to medieval literary studies. Linked to the study of the cultural aspects is the need for an understanding of the religion of the period, which, as will become increasingly clear, is essential to the discussions of its poetry and prose. It was, after all, the Christian monks of Anglo-Saxon England that copied, or were actually responsible for the composition of, much of Old English literature and therefore an awareness of the context in which they lived and worked is required.

The term 'Anglo-Saxon' is used generically to describe the period of English history from around the mid-5th century when the Angles and others arrived, to the year 1066, the beginning of the Norman Conquest, at which point the rule of England passed to the new invaders. 'Anglo-Saxon' is also used to refer to the people who occupied and ruled the land for those 600 years (i.e. *the* Anglo-Saxons). This apparently neat bracketing of history, however, belies a more complicated story. Britain was obviously inhabited before the Anglo-Saxons came, and these indigenous people were assimilated into Anglo-Saxon England (see below) or were driven to other lands. Moreover, even after the Norman Conquest the country was still predominantly occupied by Anglo-Saxons,[1] but by then they had become subservient to Norman rule. 'Anglo-Saxon' is also used occasionally to refer to the language and literature of the period (more so by earlier scholars) but the term 'Old English' is favoured now as it conveys the continuity of the language, i.e. from Old

---

[1] Sir Walter Scott's *Ivanhoe*, for example, tells of a Saxon noble living in a much later period, and the equally fictional Robin Hood is also, according to some legends, a Saxon nobleman.

English to Middle English to Modern English. However, even this categorisation by chronological period is misleading, and indeed should perhaps be abandoned (see Frantzen, 1990, p. 19) since it breaks up the real ebb and flow of language across time.

The Anglo-Saxons arrived in Britain sometime in the mid-5th century with the collapse of Roman rule. They found there the indigenous Celts (or 'Brittonic') and the remnants of Romano-British society. Their original homeland was in the area of modern-day mainland Denmark and northern Germany. Economic necessity[2] and military ambitions no doubt sparked the migration. However, the legendary tale of a British chief called Vortigern hiring Saxon mercenaries who in turn rebel against him and seize lands, is one which clearly held an attraction for Anglo-Saxon writers themselves.

The early centuries, known as the 'migration period', involved gradual influxes and military incursions by people from three main tribes (according to Bede) – the Angles, Saxons, and Jutes; but other evidence points to settlements by other races such as the Franks and Frisians. It would appear the early incursions were on the east and south-east coasts of England. The complexity and chaos of the migration period can only be guessed at, but these warrior tribes eventually began to settle, forming dozens of kingdoms, at first either assimilating the locals or pushing them westwards and northwards to the traditional modern-day Celtic lands of Wales, Scotland, Cornwall, Brittany, and Ireland. The savagery of this period must also be assumed though archaeology has, as yet, failed to produce evidence of mass graves to imply many major pitched battles or genocide. There clearly was some British resistance to these incursions (it is in this period, for example, that the legendary name of Arthur first appears as a leader combating the invaders), but this seems more akin to a lengthy rearguard action, especially successful in delaying the Saxon advance into Cornwall.

Overall, though, the 'migration period' poses many questions, which may never be answered. Most crucially, as one scholar suggests, we are completely unclear as to whether this was 'a huge influx of settlers over the sea from the east' or 'a total cultural and ethnic shift whereby the descendants of the Roman-period native population became English' (Hines, 2004, p. 39).

As the invading tribes battled the indigenous population and fought among themselves, larger kingdoms began to form, so that by

---

[2] Archaeological evidence at places such as Feddersen Wierde in Northern Germany indicates that settlements around that time were abandoned.

the 7th century the famous Anglo-Saxon Heptarchy emerged. This consisted of seven major kingdoms: Northumbria, Mercia, East Anglia, Essex, Kent, Sussex, and Wessex. War between the kingdoms was clearly common, with power bases shifting back and forth; but this was all to change in the 8th century when the first Viking invasions began. The increasing attacks of the Vikings brought many of the kingdoms to their knees and led to a wave of migration from Scandinavia and the subsequent settlement of areas of England by these new invaders (mainly in the north of England). So much so that by the end of the 9th century only the kingdom of Wessex, under King Alfred 'the Great' (871–99),[3] remained independent. After a series of near catastrophic setbacks Alfred 'defeated' the Vikings and began the refortification, re-education, and rebuilding of Wessex. Once the truce he had signed was broken (in which Alfred had ceded northern England to Viking control – the so-called 'Danelaw'), the king began the reconquest of England, gradually pushing northwards. This was continued by his sons and grandsons so successfully that by the mid-10th century all of England had been reclaimed and came under the single rule of King Athelstan of Wessex (924–39), who properly deserves the title of the first King of England.

With this reconquest came a sense of national unity, and the notion of the *Angelcynn* ('race of the English') as used by Alfred, and *Engla lond* ('England' – a term which came into existence by 1000). Interestingly both were named after the Angles (the race that settled Mercia, Northumbria, and East Anglia) but accepted and adopted by the Saxons. Yet this unity would always be tested, and the rise of the power of the Church at the expense of the nobility (thus leading to a lack of loyalty on the latter's part), coupled with the now permanent Danish population in the north, weakened national security. This was most evident under the reign of Æthelred the Unready (979–1016), where renewed Viking invasions (more organised and disciplined this time) brought England to defeat, so much so that by 1016 the throne was handed to the Viking king, Cnut (1016–35), becoming part of his wider Scandinavian empire. Although the English regained the throne under Edward the Confessor (1042–66), Anglo-Saxon rule ended in 1066 in a flurry of political intrigue over the right of succession. The successful claim to the throne by William the Conqueror, backed with military might and papal approval, brought the Normans to power after the defeat of Harold at Hastings.

[3] Dates for kings refer to the time they ruled, not their lifespan. Alfred was in fact born in 849.

In summary then, the history of Anglo-Saxon England is a complicated story. Yet it is important to take away some key observations:

- the Anglo-Saxons started to migrate to an already occupied
  Britain in the mid-5th century from the area we now term
  northern Germany and Denmark;
- according to Bede (see Chapter 2(a) and (d)) they consisted of
  three tribes – the Angles, Saxons, and Jutes – but we know that
  other races were also represented;
- it is assumed that originally they continued their warrior tribe
  structure, but gradually these tribes formed into larger kingdoms, eventually becoming the famous seven kingdoms or
  Heptarchy;
- Viking attacks in the 8th and 9th centuries nearly destroyed
  Anglo-Saxon rule, but under Alfred the Great the reconquest
  began and England was unified in the 10th century under
  Athelstan;
- Anglo-Saxon rule finally came to an end with the Norman
  Conquest in 1066.

See also   Chapter 1(e), Chapter 2(d), (e), (g), and Chapter 4(k).

Further Reading

Throughout this book we refer to many monographs and series that will reinforce the
study of Old English from a literary, linguistic, and historical perspective. For a gentle
introduction to the events of the period we recommend Blair (2000), John (1996), the
Short Oxford Histories of the British Isles (Charles-Edwards, 2003, and Davies, 2003),
and Campbell et al. (1991). If you are interested in the cartography and geographical
development of Anglo-Saxon England then see Hill (1981). For more information on
Anglo-Saxon society, see Chapter 1(b), (e), (f), and (d).

(b) Anglo-Saxon Society

The legacy of the Anglo-Saxon period (outlined in Chapter 1(a)) was
remarkable. Not only did the English language rise to a dominant
position as the language of court, and to a certain degree the church,
but the boundaries of England as a country and its administrative
system were also set. We will touch on these issues many times in
this book, but for now it is worth capturing a few of the general
points.

The period began with the migration of tribes from mainland

Europe to Britain. These small groupings, or war bands, were probably built primarily around family ties and led by war leaders. They survived according to a harsh code, based on violence, feuding, and vengeance. Original settlements in the east and south of the country were basic, with huts made of timber, and wattle and daub, smaller craft huts, and a large – probably communal – hall. This latter building seems to have been a place where the local populace gathered, feasted, and told tales or were told tales by the *scop* ('poet', see Donoghue, 2004a, pp. 24–55). The hall was so important to the people that it became symbolic in their literature of a well-ordered society (for example, various halls, and thus the kingdoms they represent, are contrasted in the heroic poem *Beowulf*).

As time progressed these tribes grew, and the settlements grew with them. Mergers and conflict gradually saw some of these gain supremacy over their neighbours and thus small kingdoms began to form. These fought each other, and via conquest and political mergers (we assume) formed larger countries until the formation of the Heptarchy. These seven kingdoms were subdivided into shires (many of which survived until their boundaries were restructured in 1974) and these in turn, into smaller land areas called 'hundreds' (or 'wapentakes' in the Danelaw – an area of northern England controlled by the Danes in the early 10th century).

A kingdom was ruled by a king who was chosen by the group (so not necessarily by succession). Occasionally in this early period kings were recognised as being the dominant power by other kings, hence the term *bretwalda* or 'overlord'. Beneath the king were his *gesithas* or 'companions' made up of thegns and ealdormen. These were divided into the *duguth* – the trusted/proven companions; and the *geoguth* – the young warriors. The relationship between the king and his nobles, the so-called *comitatus*, was key to early Anglo-Saxon society and was based on a system of loyalty and reward. Beneath the nobility were the *ceorls* or freemen, and then finally the slaves. This tightly structured society was based on mutual dependencies and we can detect in their writing a clear fear of exile from the community (see Chapter 2(i), 'Elegies and Transience').

The place of women in society is also noteworthy. Although it would be inaccurate to say they enjoyed equal status to men, they were certainly not as disenfranchised as they were in later medieval society (Fell, 1984). In Anglo-Saxon England, for example, they could hold property, bestow it, run joint religious houses, and lead armies into battle.

Eventually, a single nation was formed: England. However,

although this was a new nation, often troubled by internal difficulties and external attackers, it was also a country that continually remembered its roots. Bede, for example, called the other Germanic tribes on the Continent *gens nostra* or 'our people', and this is probably linked to the efforts made by Anglo-Saxon missionaries to convert the Germanic tribes on mainland Europe. They were aware also of the mythological beliefs they held in the past, and celebrated many of the ideals that we can assume were prized in their early history, such as heroism, loyalty, the reliance on kinship and family bonds, and the *comitatus* relationship between the warrior and the lord. All of these hearken back to the original tribal societies and structures. Even when towns and cities emerged and systems of administration more akin to modern society formed, their understanding and fondness for the past was still evident. This is clear in the famous 'elegies' where the problems of the present are set against a eulogised the past.

See also   Chapter 1(a), (c), (e), (f), and Chapter 2(c), (i) and (j).

Further Reading

For approachable introductions to life in Anglo-Saxon England one should look to Page (1970), and Lacey and Danziger (1999). Pollington (2003) provides a specific study of the hall in Anglo-Saxon society, to which one should add general books on the history and archaeology of the Anglo-Saxons. For a more detailed study of the development of the role of kings, see Chaney (1970), and for an introductory study of the role of women in the period, see Fell (1984), and the notes on feminist criticism in Chapter 4(k).

(c)   The Norman Conquest and the Later Medieval Period

Normandy as a principality was founded *c*.911 when King Charles the Simple of France granted the province to the Scandinavians who settled there in the 9th and 10th centuries. Norse settlers, who gave Normandy its name (e.g. 'Northmen/Norsemen'), quickly assimilated and became French-speaking. In the 11th century the civilisation in Normandy was essentially French but it had close economic, cultural, and political ties with Anglo-Saxon England. In 1002 King Æthelred the Unready married Emma, daughter of the Duke of Normandy. Throughout Æthelred's reign England was under threat from Viking invaders, and it was natural for Æthelred to seek an alliance with a strong neighbouring state (Norman ports had also been used safely by the Vikings). Moreover in 1013–14 England was invaded by the Danish king, Swein Forkbeard and his son Cnut, and Æthelred was forced into exile in Normandy. In 1016 Æthelred died, and Cnut led a more successful invasion, becoming the king of all England (after the death of Æthelred's son Edmund Ironside), which he ruled until 1035. However, in 1042, when the Danish line died out, Edward the Confessor (the son of Emma and Æthelred) became king, so restoring Anglo-Saxon rule. After a 24-year reign he died childless in January 1066.

One of the claimants to the English throne before 1066 was William the Conqueror, Duke of Normandy. He was Emma's great-nephew and considered himself next in line to the throne after the death of Edward the Confessor. Moreover, Edward was brought up in Normandy where he had lived in exile after Cnut became king, and according to Norman chroniclers promised his throne to William in the event of his childless death.

However, only a few days after Edward's death his brother-in-law, Harold Godwineson, was crowned King of England. He was the Earl of Essex, and brother of Edith who Edward the Confessor had married in 1045 (probably more down to pressure than by choice). Because of Harold's wealth, political influence, and successful campaigns against the Welsh, he was the second most powerful man in England after the king, and by the 1060s was probably responsible for much of its administration. Allegedly Edward nominated him on his deathbed as his successor.[4] William's supporters, however, claimed that during an earlier visit to Normandy Harold had sworn to uphold Edward's promise of succession to William and was therefore guilty of perjury. Through this, William was also able to gain papal backing for his claim to the throne.

As a result, William invaded England in September 1066, while Harold was away fighting another campaign in the north of England against his own brother – Tostig – and the King of Norway, another claimant to the throne. Harold defeated both at the Battle of Stamford Bridge but was forced to march south to meet William's marauding armies. As is commonly known, Harold was defeated at the Battle of Hastings on 14 October 1066 and killed on the battlefield. William was crowned in London on Christmas Day 1066 and the rule of

---

[4] Nearly all the events leading up to the Battle of Hastings are detailed in the Bayeux Tapestry, though how these should be interpreted is open to debate. Nevertheless, the tapestry demonstrates the important interconnection between art and history (and by extension, literature) which we promote throughout this book (see Chapter 4(i)).

England immediately passed from the Anglo-Saxons, who had been in power for nearly five centuries, to the new invaders.

The effects of the Norman Conquest and how much it changed English history are a matter of scholarly debate. What is clear, however, is that many of the English nobility were killed at Hastings, and many of those who survived were gradually replaced by William's followers. In a similar way Norman clergymen were introduced into all the important positions in the Church (this was a slower process but had actually begun under Edward the Confessor). Many other Normans – soldiers, merchants, and craftsmen – gradually settled in England after the Conquest. Though they were still only a small minority, their influence was considerable because of their position as the ruling class. In the 12th and the first half of the 13th centuries Norman French was thus the language of the nobility and to some extent the clergy and the middle classes. Moreover a considerable body of French literature was produced in England from the beginning of the 12th century onwards.

William the Conqueror's two sons reigned after him – William II ('Rufus') from 1087 to 1100 and then Henry I (1100–35). Then followed the disastrous reign of King Stephen (1135–54), the Conqueror's grandson by his daughter Adela, in which England was plunged into civil war. In 1154, Henry II, son of Matilda (the daughter of Henry I) and Geoffrey Plantagenet, took the throne after Stephen's death. Henry's family came in part from Anjou in France, hence the term given to him and his successors – the 'Angevin' kings – with the Plantagenets being the specific Angevin dynasty that ruled England (so-called after adopting the broom flower – *planta genista* – as their emblem).

Henry II's reign is representative of the Norman and Plantagenet kings (though he is probably best known for his part in the murder of Thomas à Becket). Firstly he spent only a third of his reign in England, the rest of his time was spent in mainland Europe. Secondly, there was the problem of rebellious heirs and the right of succession. Henry had envisaged that on his death his dominions would be divided amongst his three sons Henry, Richard, and Geoffrey – with his fourth son, John, being given the conquered territories of Ireland (a recent acquisition). The fact that Henry and Geoffrey failed to outlive their father should have simplified things, and indeed in 1189 on the death of the king, Richard I (the 'Lionheart' 1189–99) seized the throne. Yet Richard's attention lay elsewhere and he took part in the Third Crusade, being captured on his way back and imprisoned in Germany for over a year. In his absence John ruled England, and on Richard's death John was chosen by the barons to be King of England and Normandy.

John (1199–1216) has been popularised as a bad king by the legends surrounding Robin Hood, but it is true to say that his reign was not successful. He lost his lands on the Continent and was forced to withdraw to England, raising money for his military campaigns via excessive taxation. He was also excommunicated from the Church. A rebellion in England ensued which sought to implement reform, resulting in the signing of the Magna Carta at Runnymede (1215), which set out to establish certain rights of the king and his subjects. John's son, Henry III (1216–72), also had to contend with dwindling fortunes on the Continent, and the rise of the power of the barons (such as Simon de Montfort), which culminated in turn in the rise of Parliament.

Although France was to occupy English thoughts again in the fourteenth century, Edward I (1272–1307), who succeeded Henry, looked elsewhere to his Celtic neighbours to expand his kingdom. He led the conquest of Wales, turned his attentions to the lowlands of Scotland, and drained Ireland of its resources. His mixed success was not enough for his son Edward II (1307–27) to build on and the latter not only suffered defeat to the Scots at the Battle of Bannockburn in 1314, but also saw his kingdom in Ireland reduced to a small enclave (the 'pale') around Dublin.

The Plantagenets had not given up on regaining their land in France however (especially as they noted that the French had assisted the Scots in their struggle). In 1337, Edward III (1327–77) claimed the French throne, thus beginning a series of campaigns that were to last until 1453 and have become known as the Hundred Years War. This was even to spread to the Low Countries, and to Spain and Portugal.

The financing of the war, and the outbreak of plague in 1348 (the so-called 'Black Death'), caused unprecedented changes and social disruption in England. The plague reduced the country's population by a third and labourers became especially scarce. The peasants suddenly became an economic power able to demand higher wages and lower rents. Yet this did not tally with the need to divert revenues towards financing the wars. On the death of Edward, his ten-year-old son Richard II (1377–99) took the throne, but the power lay in the governing council that 'supported' Richard. A series of poll taxes and attempts to impose maximum wage levels led to the ultimately unsuccessful Peasants' Revolt of 1381, which brought together a range of grievances against the new taxes, political mismanagement, and dissatisfaction with the Church.

Richard II's reign ended in tyranny and he was deposed in 1399 (and probably murdered), to be replaced by Henry Bolingbroke of the House of Lancaster, who became Henry IV (1399–1413). The Lancastrian dynasty and Henry's kingdom became established, so much so that his son Henry V (1413–22) could renew the war in France with some vigour, scoring notable successes at Agincourt (1415). Yet the drain on England's finances meant that the continued fighting in France could not be sustained.

Henry VI, a well intentioned king, sought peace and consolidation but in 1453 (the notional end of the Hundred Years War) he lost Gascony, and the English empire in France was reduced to Calais. Faced with this disaster, and Henry VI's own ill-health, the time was ripe for rival dynasties to seek power. None more so than the House of York: in 1460 Richard (previous protector of England) claimed the throne, and in the following year (on Richard's death) his son declared himself king – Edward IV (1461–70). Yet Edward never commanded the support he needed; in 1470 he was forced to flee, and Henry VI was restored – thus giving Henry the claim to fame of two separate reigns (1422–61 and 1470–1). Yet the dynastic warfare (which is now commonly known as the War of the Roses after the flower emblems of the Houses of York and Lancaster) did not end there. Edward IV returned with a military force in 1471, and managed to succeed in battle (and through luck), to secure the throne again. This time the Lancastrian line of succession had been removed, and the Yorkist claim seemed to be unshakeable. The final denouement, however, has led to much debate over the years. When Edward IV died (1483), his son, Edward V (but never crowned), was only 12. The way was open for Richard of Gloucester, Edward IV's brother, to take the throne. After the death of the 'Princes in the Tower' (Edward V and his brother) Richard became King – Richard III (1483–5). Yet it was to be shortlived. In 1485, Henry Tudor, whose claim to the throne was tenuous to say the least, invaded England and defeated and killed Richard at the Battle of Bosworth. The Tudor dynasty thus began, which was to rule throughout the sixteenth century.

Throughout the period England's attention was drawn in multiple directions over the centuries; far more than had been the case under the Anglo-Saxons. There were the Crusades to the Holy Land, which ran through the 11th to13th centuries; the continued war to protect England's holdings in mainland France; and conflicts with its Celtic neighbours in Wales, Ireland and Scotland. The changes of fortune in France, the impact of the plague, and the continued warfare led to numerous changes in the social order. Moreover the rivalry between

England and France was key, and this led to the growth of national-istic feeling which helped to raise the prestige of English. The figure who perhaps most represents this new status for the language is, as might be expected, Chaucer.

See also   Chapter 1(d) and Chapter 3(b) and (k).

Further Reading

For the accounts of post-Conquest England and later Middle English history, see Chibnall (1987), Clanchy (1998 and 1993), Gillingham and Griffiths (2000), Keats-Rohan (1997, 1999–2002, and 2002), Loyn (1991), McKisack (1959), Morris (1972), Poole (1955), Powicke (1962), and Tuck (1985).

(d)   Middle English Society

The social structure of post-Conquest England up until the end of the Middle English period is extremely complicated and went through several changes. We can only present here a basic summary, written purely from the stance of informing literary analysis.

After his success at Hastings William needed to reward the 6,000 or so men who fought for him. The most obvious way to do this was with land taken from the conquered Saxon lords, and thus, at a stroke the ruling class and power shifted to the Normans. This happened so quickly that by the time of the Domesday Book (1086) only a few of the king's leading tenants were English. In return the landowners swore fealty to the king and promised to fight for him and pay dues.

In a sense this is the basic premise of the so-called feudal society. A lord would reward the vassal (or liege) with land (the 'fief') and in return the vassal would perform military service for the lord. This is very much a development of the Anglo-Saxon *comitatus* relationship, but historians often dispute how widely uniform the notion of a feudal society was. Nevertheless, this relationship does appear to be a common factor in post-Conquest society.

At the time of the Conquest, Anglo-Saxon society was made up of a king, who was served by earls, ealdormen, thegns ('thanes' – mainly in Scottish territories), administrative posts, the *ceorls* ('free men'), and then the slaves. With the Normans came the *barones regis*, the 'King's Barons', a new term and class for the landowning rulers. Barons were vassals to the king, but at the same time were given the responsibility for maintaining their lands (which were often spread out over the country to avoid concentration of power). Barons, in return, would also have to provide the king with fighting men, trained in cavalry warfare – or as they were known, 'Knights'. Originally knights were just mercenaries, or hired warriors, but they developed into a class of their own, so much so that by the thirteenth century they had established their own code of conduct – 'chivalry' (from the French *chevalier*, i.e. 'someone who fights on horseback').[5]

The rights were cascaded so that there were lesser barons, or minor 'lords', who might owe fealty to their superiors, and in turn demanded duty from those beneath them. This extended right down to the *ceorls*, a term gradually used for anyone 'common' as opposed to noble, who would work the land for their lord (usually grouped under manors), paying their tribute through their labour or produce. They were also occasionally referred to as *rustics* or *villeins* (though not, at the time, as 'peasants'). A 'sub-class' of the *ceorl* were serfs, who were legally bound to their lord in terms of what they could do, but enjoyed more freedom than slaves. It should be remembered also that the landholders were not solely secular, and the abbots and bishops could easily exert manorial control over the local population.

As only a few thousand foreigners were in charge of approximately four million Anglo-Saxons at the time of the Conquest, expressions of power needed to be made evident, the most obvious of these being the building of castles. These were governed by a constable, and held a standing garrison, ready to suppress any problems. The barons and their knights and foot soldiers controlled key areas of the country, and used administrative staff such as the sheriff (from the Anglo-Saxon 'shire reeve') to collect taxes, and to maintain the law.

Tensions between the barons and the king often ran high, notably in the disastrous reign of King Stephen (1135–54), the pressure on King John (1199–1216) to recognise the rights of others in the *Magna Carta* (1215), and the barons' revolt of 1258–65. The most lasting effect of this was the rise of power of the Great Council, to which the barons were summoned to discuss national affairs. It was from the French word for 'discussion' that the council came to be known by its more familiar term – Parliament.

As noted above, land was divided into manors (hence the term used to describe the period, 'manorialism'). Each manor was divided

---

[5] It is worth noting that groups of knights, known as the Christian warrior class, are also evident throughout the period – such as the Knights Templar.

into the 'demesne', where the lord's farm was worked, and the remainder, which was leased to tenants. Manors are important also as they form the basis of part of the law, in that manorial courts could be held (a right of the manorial lord). Over the period we see further developments of the legal system, including the tripartite split between common law, customary law, and canon law (this has precedents in the Old English period – see Chapter 2(c)); and the emergence of borough courts, and Justices of the Peace.

The power of landholding began to shift noticeably, over the period, to the power of finance. Taxes were imposed and collected by the sheriffs, and twice a year accounted for to the king's ministers (e.g. the Treasurer) at an office known as the Exchequer (because counting was literally conducted in the early days on an oblong exchequer table). Overseeing this was the office of the Chancellor and his clerks, who worked in the Chancery. They had responsibility also for drawing up various royal documents. This shift to commerce also saw a rise in towns, and centres of population. Cities were small: the population of London and Westminster was around 40,000, whereas the population of most other towns was between 1,000 and 5,000. However, throughout the period the towns continued to grow. They were independent self-governing communities that elected their own administration. Most of their population were merchants and artisans, who established professional fraternities or guilds for their protection, regulation, organization, and expansion of trade. Some guilds became very wealthy and powerful in the 14th century and, being a source of income for the government, could influence royal policies (as noted earlier). The growth of trade and the decline of the feudal order (feudal communities were self-sufficient and did not depend on trade) resulted in the rise of the middle class: merchants, craftsmen, and professionals who were becoming wealthier, more educated, emancipated, and politically influential. These provided many of the characters that form the background to Chaucer's pilgrims, for example.

The political and economic climate in the 14th century was also influenced by the Black Death (1348–50), which killed around one-third of the population in England. This resulted in a shortage of labour, followed by a rise in wages and greater social mobility. Agricultural workers discovered that they could bargain with land-lords and travel to wherever the wages were highest. In response Parliament passed a number of measures, including the Statute of Labourers in 1351, which aimed to stop workers breaking their contracts and to freeze the wages at their pre-plague level.

Resentment against such laws and unprecedented levels of taxation demanded by the government resulted in the Peasants' Revolt of 1381. During this uprising armed bands of peasants and townsmen attacked manors and religious houses. They stormed London, burned the palace of John of Gaunt (the uncle of Richard II), opened prisons, destroyed legal records, and executed the Archbishop of Canterbury and the Chancellor. The decline of the feudal order and serfdom, the growth of towns and trade, and the effects of the Black Death, all led to an increase in the importance of the middle and labouring classes and consequently the importance of the language they spoke. The use of English as the language of writing continued to expand therefore.

The 13th century also saw the development of commercial book production. If earlier books were copied mostly in the monasteries, in the 13th century secular scribes started to form their own guilds and workshops. Such workshops were required because of the development of trade and the emergence of the merchant class, who required documents to be written and copied for personal and business use. In addition to this, secular books increased in number and the demand for all kinds of books grew with the growth of literacy (particularly among the laity and the middle class). Throughout the Middle English period the importance of the laity in education and as patrons and audience for literature in English continued to increase, and their role in the production and dissemination of texts became more prominent.

A major cultural concern of the Middle English period was translation and making historical, religious, philosophical, and scientific texts available in the vernacular. This coincided with the development of literature in English, which involved adaptation of European literary models and forms, and expansion of the use of English into new areas, especially as a language of different kinds of literary discourse.

Throughout the period, then, we can observe the following key points:

- William the Conqueror rewarded his followers (the barons) with landholdings, and in return they would provide him with knights;
- the rights of the lord cascaded down in the so-called 'feudal' system;
- tensions between the barons and the king eventually led to the rise of the power of Parliament;

- during the Middle Ages, England was a largely agricultural society, but the late medieval period saw the development of trade, the rise of guilds (professional fraternities of merchants and artisans), and the growth of towns and the middle classes;
- the importance of English as a written language grew as the middle classes and laity became more educated, and politically and economically influential.

Further Reading

A standard account of the feudal society is Bloch (1961); see also Stenton (1961). Various aspects of Middle English society are described in Given-Wilson (1987), Goldberg (2004), McFarlane (1972 and 1973), Keen (1973 and 1984), Thrupp (1948), Pantin (1955), Scattergood and Sherbourne (1983), and Ziegler (1969). The cultural role of institutions and social groups is explored in Barr (2001), Cannon (1999), and Leclercq (1982). See also the 'Prosopography of Anglo-Saxon England' project (www.pase.ac.uk).

(e)   Religion: Pagan and Christian

In this section we will attempt to summarise the development and supremacy of the Christian religion in the Middle Ages. However, before concentrating on the changes in the practices and organisation of Christian worship in England, we should begin with a recognition that this was not the only set of beliefs evident during the period.

Germanic paganism vs Christianity

To the Anglo-Saxons (in keeping with the general belief at the time) the world was flat, and surrounded by *garsecg* or 'spear man', a clearly defined barrier at the edge of the sea (*garsecg* was also used as a poetic word for the oceans – see the Old English poem *The Seafarer*, ll. 27–38). The world, or *middangeard* ('middle-earth/ enclosure') as they called it, was suspended between heaven and hell in the Christian model, but again this may have close links to the pagan concept of *miðgarð* mostly known from Scandinavian mythology.

This simple opening illustrates two key issues we need to face if we are to understand the beliefs and practices of the Anglo-Saxons. This can prove to be fascinating as we begin to discover a range of new legends, deities, and codes of practice. Secondly, we can observe two perspectives – that of Christianity,[6] and that of the Germanic pagan world. This is fundamental to the study of Old English and is a running thread throughout the following chapters – namely the continued tension between the old beliefs and legends and the new religion of the Christians, or the 'endless project of identifying the precise blend of Christian and Germanic' (Lees, 1999, p. 4). Indeed as one book remarks:

> Perhaps the study of Old English literature still finds that its primary question is the same one Alcuin asked nearly twelve hundred years ago: Quid Hinieldus cum Christo? 'What has Ingeld[7] to do with Christ?' . . . the encounter between an unlettered Germanic tribal aesthetic and the remnants of the classical tradition, itself transformed by the Christian religion. (Greenfield and Calder, 1986, p. 3)

In this section we will begin to explore this.

Even taking into account the military conflicts and nation building by the Anglo-Saxons, perhaps the most important event of the period was the conversion of the English to Christianity that took place with the arrival of St Augustine in 597. The key word to note here is 'conversion', i.e. changing from one state to another. If the Anglo-Saxons *became* Christian what can we say they were before this? In short, we do not know exactly as the evidence for their earlier beliefs is minimal, but the generic term 'pagan' is often used. Many scholars have attempted to re-create the beliefs of the pre-Christian Anglo-Saxons but this is all regarded as incredibly tenuous (see Wilson, 1992, and Stanley, 2000). At best we can only pick up glimpses. As they were closely associated with other Germanic tribes, one could conclude that the Anglo-Saxons that arrived in the migration period brought with them something akin to the Norse mythology with its pantheon of gods and goddesses. These probably included Odin (also called Woden), Tiw, Thor, Freya and many others; and there is evidence pointing to the fact that these gods were worshipped at

---

[6] Christianity is the only organised religion we know of. Although the Anglo-Saxons knew of Judaism no Jews are recorded as living in England during the period, and in the entire vernacular Old English corpus there is not a single reference to Islam (though 'pagan Saracens', i.e. muslims, are mentioned in Huneberc's 8th-century Latin *Vita Willibaldi* – or *Life of Willibald*). This was to change in the Middle English period as Jews began to settle in England, and the impact of the Crusades against the muslims was felt.

[7] Ingeld is a figure of Germanic history/legend, mentioned in *Beowulf*, l. 2064.

some point by the English. We have the survival of the names of these deities in our weekdays (Tuesday – Tiw's day, Wednesday – Woden's/Odin's day, Thursday – Thor's day, and Friday – Freya's day). There are also pagan elements in some place names, and names which appear in genealogies of English kings (who traced their roots back to Woden and beyond to such Old Testament figures as Noah). Finally there is the direct condemnation of these 'gods' in texts by the later Old English writers Ælfric and Wulfstan, who both wrote a version of a text entitled *De falsiis diis* – 'On false gods'. Furthermore, the influx of the Vikings from the 8th century onwards must also have led to a resurgence in pagan worship.

Loosely coupled with this are the Norse legends, though it has to be remembered that these may not necessarily reflect religious beliefs. Old English literature, often allusively, refers to such legendary characters as Weland the Smith for example, or characters from pseudo-history, attesting to the survival of these legends after the migration period. The interest in these stories, moreover, did not seem to abate with the establishment of Christianity, as Alcuin noted with his 'Quid Hinieldus' question. Therefore the survival of these stories, however brief the reference to them is, goes some way to providing evidence for pre-Christian beliefs.

We must also consider the small corpus of what one could call 'magical' writings (although the boundary between religion, science, and magic is contentious). The series of charms (or spells perhaps) presented to us in collections such as those edited by Storms (1948) and Griffiths (1996) place before us an array of fantastical creatures and beliefs. We have mentions of elves and demons (to supplement mentions elsewhere in the literature of dragons, trolls, giants, and orcs), references to 'Erce, mother of earth' (Storms, charm number 8) and emphasis placed on moonlight, plants, earth, and water. With the latter we must also remember that the indigenous Celtic people had their own beliefs, and their worship of natural places (such as springs, wells, etc.) may have influenced the English. Many of the charms, though occasionally infused with Christian elements, also make mention of a single figure responsible for enacting the spell, possibly a shaman or wizard (a *wicca*), a practitioner of *wiccecræft* or 'witchcraft'.

A problematic issue which often appears when discussing pagan beliefs centres around the Old English concept of *wyrd*, meaning 'fate' or 'providence'. This is mentioned often in Old English literature as some form of guiding force which directs the lives of men, but its true meaning has caused problems for scholars. Whereas it is tempting to ascribe to *wyrd* some form of personification, i.e. another entity that the pagan Anglo-Saxons worshipped (and there is some evidence for this in the poetry), its appearance in many late texts seems to imply it had simply entered the realm of common expression (such as 'count your lucky stars') and was not symbolic of any religious practices. Furthermore, in poetry more than half the references to *wyrd* occur in verse devoted to the Old Testament so it was clearly acceptable to Christian poets.

This battle between the old religious beliefs of the Germanic tribes and the new Christianity is a fundamental one to the study of Old English literature, as noted at the outset (see also Chapter 3). Evidence for the conflict seems to underpin many of the texts that survive, if not explicitly, then implicitly. The Anglo-Saxons undoubtedly held a strong interest in the history of Christianity and the Church, and even felt an affinity between the oppression of the Israelites in the Old Testament and their own fate at the hands of the heathen Vikings. Yet they also sought to bring this in line with their own beliefs, notably the high esteem they attached to heroism and loyalty. Christian scholars did not attempt to dismiss these earlier practices, but as we will see they often incorporated them. This is a very complicated, but fascinating aspect of Anglo-Saxon culture.

The conversion of the Anglo-Saxons from their old beliefs to Christianity was a slow process, beset by problems. We should remember that when St Augustine arrived in 597, he was in fact bringing Christianity back to England (that is to say, the later Roman Empire, of which Britain was a part, was Christianised under Constantine). Faced with the warlike Anglo-Saxons, St Augustine and his followers adopted a traditional tactic of the Church when attempting conversion: namely appropriation of existing beliefs and modifying them to fit the new religion. Thus the date for Christmas was fixed as the old Roman winter solstice, and Easter itself is named after the feast of *Eostre* (seemingly a pagan goddess worshipped by the Germanic tribes, and alluded to by Bede).

The importance of the arrival of Christianity cannot be overstated. Not only did it bring new beliefs, it also brought a new wave of literacy based originally around Latin. It had an impact on architecture, art, education, scholarship, the law, the structure of society, the balance of power, landholdings, and much more. Anglo-Saxon England also, as a consequence, became part of the wider fold of the Church, which led to increased ties with the Continent. As Fulk states (1991, p. 10):

Conversion represents a fundamental shift in the society, something far greater than simply a change in faith. It created a new class of citizens, churchmen who stood outside any family structure.

As well as facing competition from the pagan beliefs of the resident Saxon tribes, the mission of St Augustine and his subsequent followers also had to accommodate the Celtic Christian Church. With the collapse of Roman rule and the arrival of the Germanic tribes, Christianity was pushed westwards to Wales and Cornwall, and most notably Ireland. Somewhat cut off from mainland Europe the practices of the Celtic Church understandably diverged from Roman Christianity, and although this was never on a par with the violence of later theological clashes (such as Protestantism versus Catholicism), it did lead to differences of opinion and practice. These were not settled (in terms of which would be the dominant force in English Christianity) until the famous Synod of Whitby in 664. Here, the argument centred primarily over the dating of Easter (the two Churches differed in their practice), but the debate was more important than that as it was about which practice – that of Ireland or Rome – would hold sway. Understandably the Roman school won.

The Anglo-Saxon Church

The administration and support of Christianity needs further explanation, though, as it has direct relevance for students of the literature. To begin with there was an early split in the structure of the Church between those we may call 'secular' clergy (dealing primarily with pastoral duties) and the monks or 'regular' clergy (i.e. living according to a rule). The secular clergy were allowed to marry, and were divided into major roles such as bishops, priests, and deacons; and minor roles such as doorkeepers, readers, exorcists, and acolytes. Monks, on the other hand, led a much stricter and more insulated life. They were either 'eremitic', i.e. living as hermits (such as St Guthlac), or 'cenobitic', which implied living as part of a community, or order, under an abbot or abbess. The dominant order in the later Anglo-Saxon period was the Benedictines.

Monks were originally not defined as clergy, but over time they started to receive ordination (i.e. they could become a priest, usually at the age of 30), partook in pastoral duties, and took up major clerical positions. The major repositioning of power with a shift away from the secular clergy to the monasteries came during the so-called Benedictine Revival of the mid-10th century. This was led by Saints

Oswald, Dunstan, and Æthelwold and saw a re-establishment of the Benedictine order (so-called because it lived according to the rules defined by St Benedict of Nursia) in the vacuum left by the Viking wars of the ninth and early tenth centuries. We know that St Benedict's ideas were first studied in the late seventh century in England, but it is from 950 onwards that we see the true rise to power of the Benedictine order. So much so that in 970 a revision of the *Rule of St Benedict* called the *Regularis Concordia* was drawn up by St Æthelwold as a version specifically for English monks.

The influence of this on literature was profound. Notably monasteries needed scriptoriums, scribes, and libraries; and in those libraries they collected together key patristic and biblical texts, which acted as source material for much of their own writing. A fundamental part of monastic life was the Divine Office, a series of timed periods throughout the day set aside for prayer and study (such as Matins, Lauds, Prime, etc.). During these, when Mass was said, the monks would listen to a set text (called the 'pericope'), which would then be explained and interpreted (a practice known as 'exegesis'). There would also be an opportunity for other liturgical readings, notices, and other prayers. But why is this key? In short, these offices required texts for the monks to use – not just the original set texts, but also guides on how to interpret them. It is not surprising therefore that the bulk of religious prose that survives to us from the period were aimed at satisfying these monastic needs.

Post-Conquest Christianity

After the Norman Conquest the Church continued to play a major role in society and education, and remained an important patron of literature. Monasteries preserved their position as cultural centres and powerful landowners, directly involved in the social and economic lives of all strata of society. This was partly due to the fact that they were economically stable institutions: their lands were never broken up, reorganised or confiscated, and unlike lay properties they remained intact after the Conquest (Cannon, 1999, pp. 320–3). This was important for the preservation of texts and literacy. A direct outcome of such economic and institutional stability was the continuation of the *Anglo-Saxon Chronicle* until 1070 at Christ Church Cathedral priory, until 1080 at Worcester Cathedral priory, and until 1154 at Peterborough. Post-Conquest monastic libraries held a variety of religious and secular works in English, Latin, and French, and were centres of education, research, and literary activity. Monasteries also formed part of an international network which supported cultural, political, and ideological exchanges. Medieval English monasteries had close links with monasteries on the Continent since the 8th century and certainly since the Benedictine Revival in the 10th century.

During the Middle English period a variety of new religious orders established themselves in England. We have already noted the Benedictine order, which was dominant during the Anglo-Saxon period and continued to be influential after the Conquest. Benedictine monasticism, introduced to England by Augustine of Canterbury, was the main form of monastic life in western Europe until the 11th century. In the 11th century, however, new orders were formed, partly out of a desire for reform caused by successive relaxation of Benedictine discipline and the lack of centralised policy and control (Benedictine abbeys were entirely autonomous).

From the beginning of the 12th century the new orders started to arrive in England from the Continent. The order of the Augustinian Canons, governed by the Rule of St Augustine (the second of the two major medieval monastic rules, based on the writings of Augustine of Hippo), originated in Italy in the 11th century and established itself in England early in the 12th century. Its rule was quite flexible and allowed members of the order to have responsibilities outside their monastic house in parishes, hospitals, schools, and almshouses. The Cistercian order was founded c.1100 in France and established its first monastery in England in the first quarter of the 12th century. The Cistercians wanted to return to a stricter and more 'authentic' form of Benedictine monasticism. They insisted on a literal observance of St Benedict's rule, including a return to strict asceticism, manual labour (particularly agricultural work), and using a purer version of the Divine Office stripped of later accretions. Another highly austere new order, the Carthusians, was founded at the end of the 11th century in France. It was a strictly contemplative order where monks were vowed to silence and practised contemplation and mental prayer. It combined the eremitic and cenobitic forms of monasticism because its members lived as a community of hermits. They spent most of their life in solitude in individual cells, but came together for some services and meals on Sundays and feast days.

The 13th century saw the coming of the fraternal orders to England: the Dominicans, the Franciscans, the Carmelites, and the Augustinian friars (the latter was a separate order, different from Augustinian Canons). The Dominicans, the Franciscans, and the Carmelites were also known respectively as the Black Friars, the Grey Friars, and the White Friars, distinguished by the colour of their mantles. The two largest orders, the Dominican and Franciscan friars, arrived correspondingly in 1221 and 1224, and became well established by the middle of the 13th century. Whereas monastic religious orders avoided contact with secular society, and had their foundations in remote regions away from towns, the friars saw their mission as bringing the teachings of the Church to 'the world'. In contrast to monks who lived a cloistered life in a specific community, friars lived as individuals in the secular world, travelled, and engaged in preaching and pastoral work among the laity chiefly in towns. Fraternal orders were also known as 'mendicant' (from Latin *mendicare* – 'to beg') because they were required to live in absolute poverty, begging for food and being dependent on the charity of their listeners. Unlike monastic orders they applied the requirements of poverty and not owning any property both to individual friars and corporately to the whole order. The Franciscans, also known as Friars Minor, emphasised poverty, helping the poor, and providing a ministry among ordinary people. The Dominicans, also known as the Order of Preachers, emphasised preaching and theological study, which was seen as a necessary preparation for ministry. As a result of this the Dominicans played an active role in universities and schools, and during the Middle Ages established their foundations in most university towns.

Fraternal orders spread rapidly in England and their piety initially won them a strong following. Friars produced many famous scholars and teachers, and because of their mission among the laity contributed to the development of penitential literature, sermons, and lyrical poetry in English. As fraternal orders grew, however, the ideal of poverty proved to be impossible to sustain if taken literally. In the 14th and 15th centuries the orders became large and wealthy, which in many cases led to a considerable relaxation of discipline. After the Black Death particular resentment arose against the practice of using 'limites' as a source of income to support the life of luxury. These were districts licensed to individual friars by their order where they had exclusive rights of preaching and hearing confessions. Thus Chaucer's Friar, one of the pilgrims in *The Canterbury Tales*, is a 'lymytour' characterised as 'wantowne' ('pleasure-loving') and 'merye'. In the General Prologue to *The Canterbury Tales* Chaucer described the Friar's lifestyle and 'ministry' in some detail, focusing his satire on life among the laity and its temptations, confessions and absolutions, and begging and preaching. His description reflects a view widely held in the 14th century that the friars were failing in their pastoral duty to laity. Referring to the four fraternal orders described above, Chaucer says about his Friar that:

In alle the ordres foure is noon that kan
So muchel of daliaunce and fair langage.   (ll. 210–11).

('In all the four orders [of friars] there is no one who knows
As much about socialising and fair language'.)

Friars roused hostility among secular clergy and bishops because of their privileges, such as exemption from episcopal jurisdiction, and their role as preachers and confessors to the laity. The relationship between friars and monks also often involved rivalry and mutual suspicion. Thus *The Land of Cokaygn*, a 13th-century satire of monastic life, is preserved in a single manuscript believed by some scholars to have been put together by a Franciscan friar.

In addition to the monastic communities and the mendicant orders, there were the 'solitaries' – those who left the secular world and lived a life of seclusion in order to practise asceticism, silence, prayer, and contemplation. Anchorites and anchoresses are especially notable (see the *Ancrene Wisse* or 'Guide for Anchoresses' in Chapter 3(d)) as they were literally walled up in a small cell, frequently attached to a parish church. The practice was recognised and supported by the Church and an anchorite was often 'enclosed' by a bishop.

A major event of religious life in the 13th century was the Fourth Lateran Council, convened by Pope Innocent III in 1215. This was one of a series of important councils which took place in the Lateran Palace at Rome from the 7th to the 18th centuries. The Fourth Lateran Council sought to reduce the proliferation of religious orders and to consolidate the church's teaching on various matters. Among other things it forbade the foundation of new religious orders, gave an official definition of the doctrine of the Eucharist, and made annual confession compulsory for all Christians. It encouraged religious education of the laity and because of this had an important impact on the development of vernacular literature.

The late medieval period was also the time of a great flourishing of scholarship and theology, and saw many developments in religious thinking, including the emergence and development of theories relating to purgatory, confession, and transubstantiation; and of a celebration of the Corpus Christi ('the Body of Christ'). Shrines and pilgrimages maintained their popularity, and with the increase in overall wealth the latter in particular were in vogue in the fourteenth century (hence Chaucer's basis for *The Canterbury Tales*).

The 12th and 13th centuries were the time when universities

appeared and established themselves in Europe and England. They became rivals to the monasteries in terms of religious thought and education, and indeed some of the great critics of the Church emerged from such surroundings. Hand in hand with this we witness the emergence of grammar schools (ostensibly to teach Latin grammar) and parochial schooling by local clergy.

Finally, the 14th century saw the rise of the Lollard movement. The Lollards attacked many doctrines and practices of the Church and emphasised personal faith and the role of lay believers. Their programme of reform and the belief that people should have access to the Bible in their own language anticipated the ideas of the Reformation. The movement was largely academic until the end of the 14th century, but became increasingly popular in the 15th century and its social teaching became more pronounced.

In summary then, the history of religion in medieval England is complicated:

- although illiterate, when the Anglo-Saxons arrived they brought with them their myths, legends, and religious beliefs;
- Britain had been Christian under the Romans, but the Anglo-Saxon settlers were pagan; this all began to change, however, with the arrival of St Augustine in 597;
- the conversion utilised the common approach of appropriation, and evidence for earlier pagan beliefs is scant but still remains;
- with Christianity came a rise in literacy and education;
- two Christian practices emerge – the secular clergy, and the monastic clergy – with the latter eventually gaining dominance under the Benedictines in the 10th century;
- the requirements of the Divine Office adhered to by the monks necessitated a series of texts such as homilies and sermons;
- the Benedictines were the dominant order in Anglo-Saxon England and contemporary Europe but after the Conquest new orders emerged, including Augustinians, Cistercians, Carthusians, fraternal orders, and others;
- the Church was an important patron of literature throughout the Middle Ages;
- the importance of monasteries as cultural centres diminished during the late medieval period with the establishment of universities, fraternal orders and commercial book production.

See also   Chapter 1(d), Chapter 2(d), (f), (g), (j), Chapter 3(d), (i), and (k).

Further Reading

Concise explanations of institutions, concepts, and practices of the Christian Church can be found in Livingstone (2005). Historical surveys by Lynch (1992) and Oakley (1979) offer a good introduction to the medieval Christian Church. For information on Anglo-Saxon pagan beliefs see Frank (1991), Griffiths (1996), Niles (1991), North (1997), Stanley (2000), Storms (1948), and Wilson (1992). The history of Anglo-Saxon Christianity is covered in most general history books of the period but see especially Blair (2005); for information on the Divine Office see Gatch (1985). For information on monasticism and religious orders see Burton (1994), Knowles (1963 and 1969), Lawrence (2003), and Leclercq (1982); for fraternal orders see Brooke (1975) and Lawrence (1994). See also Sumption (2002) for an account of pilgrimages in the Middle Ages.

(f)   Philosophy and Political Thought

What follows is an indicator of some of the main philosophical discussions that students encounter when studying the literature of the period.

Old English philosophy

As previously stated, the literature of the period was (almost without exception) written in monasteries, and thus enveloped in the Christian world (we must remember that there were no universities in England before the foundation of Oxford in the 12th century). It is not surprising, therefore, to see a summary of medieval philosophy as being aimed primarily at 'the understanding of Christian faith and its defence against those who attacked it' (Gracia, 2003, p. 3).

However, as we have also observed, the period is noted for the clash of religions and ideologies – pagan Germanic and Christian – and the appropriation of the former by the latter. Evidence that survives therefore of Germanic philosophy is negligible. Perhaps the most striking concept is that of *wyrd* ('fate'), which appears consistently in Old English literature. This has been discussed earlier, and cannot be taken as any proof of a pagan belief in a deified Fate, but clearly has links with discussions of predestination and free will: e.g. did God control all fate (as Alfred seemed to think), was it some unknown force termed *wyrd*; or did man have an entirely free choice in how he behaved (as Ælfric argues)?

The Anglo-Saxons also displayed a clear interest in eschatology (from the Greek ἔσχατος 'last' and λόγος 'discourse'), which was mirrored in their fixation on transience and as the millennium approached, the possible impending apocalypse. Although this tone decreases in the mid-11th century it is clearly noticeable in the early writings of Ælfric and the sermons of Wulfstan. They saw the world as being one in decline (no doubt influenced by the backdrop of continued Viking aggression), as witnessed in Ælfric's homily *De die iudicii*. With this impending doom (hence *domesdæg* or 'judgement day') they viewed their worldly surroundings as temporary, and their primary concern was salvation (Gatch, 1991, p. 187).

It should also be remembered that the Anglo-Saxons did not write in isolation. We know that they drew on others (notably the Carolingians) as inspiration for their literature, art, science and so on; and thus it is not surprising that influential figures emerge from the past as shaping their philosophy. A key group is that of the patristic writers, or the Fathers of the Church, who provided spiritual guidance for medieval scholars replacing the guidance of the pagan philosophers. The patristic period is often dated as being from the time of St Augustine of Hippo (354–430) to the death of St Isidore of Seville in AD 636; but it extends earlier than that. The works of such important patristic authors as St Jerome and others were used again and again by Anglo-Saxon writers in shaping their own views – most notably their exegesis of biblical texts. Ælfric, for example, notes his indebtedness to Augustine, Jerome, Bede, Gregory, and Smaragdus in the preface to his *First Series of Catholic Homilies*.

St Augustine of Hippo

Of these the most dominant figure is that of St Augustine of Hippo (354–430 AD).[8] Indeed along with Boethius (below) he could be described as one of the cornerstones of Old English philosophy. Augustine was a prolific writer and his works were widely copied, distributed, and read by early medieval authors (his reflection on the soul, for example, the *Soliloquia*, was 'translated' by King Alfred – see Chapter 2(e)). His impact on medieval Christianity cannot be underestimated, but more important for the purposes of this discussion is his influence on writers from the Old English period. Scholars have for some time now discerned strong links (occasionally attributed directly) between the writings of Augustine and homilists such as Ælfric and Wulfstan, including similarities in style and the use of rhetorical devices. In addition, casting such poems as *Beowulf*

[8] Not to be confused with St Augustine who led Gregory's mission to England in 597 to begin the conversion of the Anglo-Saxons to Christianity.

against a patristic Augustinian background has also been a focus of academic attention.

Augustinian philosophy proposes several arguments of interest evident in key texts such as the *Confessiones*, *De doctrina Christiana*, and *De civitate dei*. These include:

- That sin is evident in *the choice* made by the individual to commit a certain action, and therefore not in the action itself or the object of the action. This ties in with the choices presented to individual Christians in Old English prose and poetry, and also possibly in the choices made by heroes.
- That evil is a corruption of good, and not a substance in itself. It stems from sin or is a result of a sin, and in this we have free choice (and thus must take responsibility for our action). This was to change in St Augustine's later writings, however, when he emphasised much more the power of predestination.
- That there is a distinction between what we do, and what is done to us that is beyond our control. In the former we have control, and must take responsibility; with the latter we are innocent but must live through it in a Christian manner.
- That we must recognise the flaws of worldly life and joys (linking to the Old English notion of transience in the elegies – Chapter 2(i)) and the permanence of heavenly glory.
- That sinners will be damned and salvation is reserved for the righteous few who will enter the City of God (*De civitate dei*).
- That a clear path to understanding is the study of scriptural exegesis.

Boethius

Anicius Manlius Severinus Boethius (*c*.480–*c*.525), who lived slightly after Augustine, was a lay person, and not a patristic writer. Yet his influence on medieval philosophy is undeniable. He was a Roman consul and a leading counsellor to the Ostrogothic king Theoderic, the then ruler of Italy. At the height of his career he was accused of treason, sent into exile and possibly imprisonment in Pavia, and executed a year later. While in Pavia he wrote the famous treatise *De consolatione philosophiae* or *The Consolation of Philosophy*,[9] in which he explores the nature of fortune and happiness, and the problems of

[9] Boethius wrote many other works including treatises on logic, astronomy, geometry, maths, and music; plus a range of philosophical translations and commentaries.

evil and free will. It is written in Latin prose, interspersed with passages of verse, and presents the philosophical argument in the form of a discussion with 'Lady Philosophy'. She attempts to answer the main issue facing Boethius of why evil is allowed sway in the world. In her argument she points to two key concepts – fortune and providence – the former being that of the human world and the latter, of the divine. Fortune is likened to a wheel that turns bringing good and ill to humans, demonstrating the transient nature of worldly joy. Yet within men, they can always find solace in their mind; true happiness comes from within the person but not from external pleasures and is something which fortune cannot take away. In the discussion of providence, Boethius questions aspects of fate and predestination, wondering openly whether men really have free will or whether everything is predestined. He concludes that there is freedom of choice, and that evil only happens when men choose to allow it. The book is not overtly Christian but obviously deals with key issues of Christian debate.

The impact of the *Consolation* on medieval thought cannot be underestimated. It was one of the most widely translated books of the period and in Old English was one of the four texts translated by King Alfred. The attraction of Boethian philosophy to the Anglo-Saxon mind can be seen in three key areas:

- the discussion of fortune, which in turn may link to the Old English concept of *wyrd* or fate;
- following on from this is the discussion of free will – a tenet of the heroic ideal in that heroes are free to choose their course of action but must be seen to adhere to it steadfastly (see also above, under the discussion of Augustine);
- insistence on the transience of worldly goods and glory, which is also clearly evident in many Old English poems, especially the so-called 'elegies' (see Chapter 2(i), 'Elegies and Transience').

Old English political thought

In Chapter 1(b) we discussed the basic format of Anglo-Saxon society in that it hinged on a hierarchical structure, starting with the king, and moving down through the thegns/ealdormen, civil servants such as the Reeve, to the *ceorls* (free men), and eventually to the slaves. Although this only presents a snapshot of society at one point, we can assume that throughout the period there would always have been some form of stratification of the rights and privileges of people and their obligations and 'worth' to society (as witnessed in the law codes – see Chapter 2(c)).

Although much can be gleamed from historical and legal texts from the period, the views presented to us on political structures and the obligations of those in power are sparse in comparison. The key texts one should look to are:

- King Alfred the Great's translations – notably his version of Boethius's *The Consolation of Philosophy*;
- the *Regularis Concordia* – a reworking of the Rule of St Benedict in 973, outlining the duties and responsibilities of monks;
- Ælfric's *Colloquy*, which outlines the roles and responsibilities of various 'professions';
- Wulfstan's *Institutes of Polity* – a detailed analysis of the roles and duties of secular and clergy.

This is far from complete but what this indicates collectively is:

- an understanding of the complicated structure of society and the interdependence of its members;
- an attempt to define, in an ordered manner, the duties and responsibilities of each;
- an almost equal weighting between the duties and profile (possibly even the power) of Church and State;
- a split between the spiritual world and the physical world with each requiring actions by different members of society (but with an element of interdependence).

The latter point is clearly identifiable in the repeated discussion of the 'three orders of society' or 'estates'. This appears in Alfred's translation of Boethius, Ælfric's *Homily on the Books of the Maccabees*, and Wulfstan's *Institutes of Polity*. In short, this states that there are three key roles that need to be filled, in any society – people who work to bring in food (*laboratores*), people who fight to protect society (*bellatores*), and people who pray to protect spiritual matters (*oratores*). Any king or kingdom needs all three to stand, and by implication without any one of them a kingdom will fall. At first this may seem to suggest a separation of Church and State but instead it presents the opposite. Without the Church fighting the spiritual fight the people would be damned, and without the State fighting the military fight or engaging in the fight against hunger, the Church could not continue. Both, then, were interdependent, or more importantly this placed the Church and its well-being at the heart of the body politic.

Middle English philosophy

After the early Christian writers and Boethius there was a period of dormancy in European philosophy until it re-emerged in the later Middle Ages in the monastic milieu (see McGrade, 2003, pp. 10–50). Between the years 900 and 1200 Europe experienced economic growth which led to an increase in population, the emergence of towns and commerce, and the revival in education. Monasteries were centres of literary activity, teaching, and scholarship crossing international boundaries. Thus Archbishop Anselm of Canterbury (1033–1109), an outstanding Christian philosopher and theologian, received his education and spent much of his career at the monastic school at the Benedictine abbey at Bec in Normandy. He is most famous for proposing what later became known as 'ontological argument', a reason-based proof of the existence of God. Anselm insisted that the use of reason did not undermine faith, but was entirely compatible with it, and in his works theology started to develop into a systematic discipline.

Anselm's work gave impulse to the development of the academic and educational tradition known as 'scholasticism'. This was a method of philosophical and theological speculation aimed at achieving a better understanding of Christian doctrine through the application of intellectual, reason-based inquiry. Scholasticism relied on the earlier work of Boethius and St Augustine, who introduced medieval scholars to Greek philosophy, logic and dialectic, and demonstrated how methods and ideas of philosophy can be applied to theological study. Scholasticism also had foundations in the work of medieval scholars such as John Scotus Erigena (c.800–c.877), an Irishman who may have lived and taught for part of his life in England, though this is uncertain. His important contributions, among others, were his translations of writings of Greek philosophers and commentaries on the works of Boethius.

The development of scholastic philosophy and theology continued in the works of the 12th-century thinkers, such as Peter Abelard (1079–1142). They saw the universe as rationally ordered and accessible to analysis, and increased the use of reasoning and argumentation in theology and philosophy. If early medieval philosophical writings, as witnessed in the works by Boethius and St Augustine, were addressed to, and could be understood by, any educated person, the 12th-century philosophy became a highly specialised academic discipline. It developed sophisticated methods of investigation and complex technical jargon which could be difficult for a non-specialist reader. Late medieval philosophy already included all the main areas which it has today as an academic discipline.

In the 12th and 13th centuries new translations of major philosophical works by Greek and Arabic thinkers were also produced. In the 13th century most of Aristotle's works which are known today were translated and integrated into the academic curriculum. The 12th and 13th centuries also marked the foundation of the major European universities, including Oxford and Cambridge, which became centres of teaching and research. Paris was also the site of a pre-eminent university in the 13th century which brought together an international comunity of scholars. Many of the best known late medieval thinkers studied or taught there.

Influential philosophers who spent some part of their career in England (mostly at Oxford) included John Duns Scotus (1265/66–1308), William of Ockham (*c*.1287–1347), Walter Burley (*c*.1275–1344), Robert Grosseteste (*c*.1175–1253), Roger Bacon (*c*.1214–94), John Wyclif (*c*.1330–84), and Johannes Sharpe (*c*.1360–after 1415). Their greatest achievements were in logic, ontology, metaphysics, natural philosophy and philosophy of science, and epistemology. William of Ockham, a Franciscan and a native of Ockham in Surrey, is best known for formulating the principle of economy in explanation and theory-building known as 'Ockham's razor' (i.e. reducing any hypothesis or theory to its key assumptions).

There are only a few texts of philosophical instruction in Middle English. These include translations of Cicero's *De amicitia* ('On friendship') and *De senectute* ('On old age') dating from the second half of the 15th century (see Raymo, 1986, pp. 2372–3). *De amicitia* was translated by John Tiptoft, Earl of Worcester, and *De senectute* by William Worcester, who used an early 15th-century French version as the basis for his translation. Both works were published by Caxton in 1481. *The Consolation of Philosophy* by Boethius was translated by Chaucer, and *c*.1410 by John Walton, an Augustinian Canon of Oseney (see Science, 1999). Walton worked from the Latin original, but also made extensive use of Chaucer's translation. A unique commentary on Book 1 of the *Consolation*, based on Chaucer's translation, survives in a 15th-century manuscript (Oxford, Bodleian Library MS. Auct. F. 3. 5). *The Consolation of Philosophy* also influenced literary works of many Middle English authors, including Chaucer, Gower, Lydgate, Henryson, and King James I.

A range of philosophical ideas is discussed in Middle English literary texts. The following, by no means a complete list, offers some examples:

- The problems of free will, predestination, and fortune are very prominent in several of Chaucer's works, including *Troilus and Criseyde* and *The Knight's Tale* in *The Canterbury Tales*. Their characters debate the existence of predestination, and they have a structure of astrological references to the state of the heavens and the positions and movements of planets which may imply that these influence human actions.
- The problem of evil and its nature is prominent in *A Revelation of Love* by Julian of Norwich.
- The limitations of human reason are explored in *Pearl* (see Chapter 3(p);
- The problems of eschatology and the meaning of human history are present in Langland's *Piers Plowman*.
- The problems of authority, experience, and language are discussed in Chaucer's *The House of Fame*.

Middle English political thought

Late medieval thinkers were interested in the analysis and rationalisation of society. The themes of the ideal society and of the failings of contemporary society are common in Middle English literature. Several poets, including Chaucer, Langland, and Gower, used the model of the 'three estates' (see above) in their description and criticism of social structure. Other political and social ideas explored by Middle English authors included the following:

- Good kingship and the qualities and responsibilities of a ruler. This was a very widely discussed subject, and the main theme of works within the tradition of the 'mirror for princes', such as Hoccleve's *The Regement of Princes*, or John of Trevisa's translation of *De regimine principum* of Aegidius Romanus.[10]
- Corruption in society and the need for its moral reform. This was again an immensely popular subject. Langland gives it the form of an internal and external quest in *Piers Plowman*, and explores the possibility of the reform of society side-by-side with the problems of the reform of the individual. It was also a running theme in Wulfstan's sermons.

[10] This was also a concern of King Alfred in his translation of Gregory's *Pastoral Care* – which was used by the Carolingian rulers as a manual for kingship. Ælfric also discusses and presents 'model kings' in his writings (notably St Edmund).

- The proper use of wealth. This question is debated by allegorical characters in the alliterative poem *Wynnere and Wastoure*. Langland's *Piers Plowman* portrays a complex allegorical character Lady Meed, who embodies the morally ambiguous nature of 'treasure'. The question of 'evangelical poverty' and disendowment of the Church was debated throughout the 14th century, and received a particularly radical expression in the teachings of John Wyclif.
- Responsibilities of different classes of society. This question is present in all works influenced by the three-estates model. A number of authors also discuss it with reference to the 14th-century Peasants' Revolt and the Statutes of Labourers (see, for example, Helen Barr's discussion of the use of the Parable of the Labourers in the Vineyard in *Pearl* (2001, pp. 40–62)).
- Personal responsibility of the members of society. In *The Parliament of Fowls*, Chaucer linked the idea of harmonious society to the need for moderate and responsible behaviour by its members.
- Criticism of the way of life and moral standards among the clergy and the need to reform the Church. This was a very widely discussed subject particularly prominent in *Piers Plowman* and the Lollard texts.
- Greater lay participation in religion. In the 13th century, concrete steps were made towards involving the laity in the life of the Church. In 1215 the Fourth Lateran Council, assembled by Pope Innocent III, authorised the statement of faith for all Christians, and made a call for personal confession and the reception of the Eucharist at least once a year by all members of the Church. The early 13th century marked the foundation of the first two orders of mendicant friars, the Franciscans and the Dominicans, who emphasised the pastoral mission among the laity. There was also an ongoing debate about lay access to theological knowledge and lay authority in matters of religion. These issues are explored in *Piers Plowman* and were central to the Lollard movement.

See also   Chapter 1(d) and (e), Chapter 2(c)–(f), (i), (j), (n), and Chapter 3(d), (e), (g), (k), (m), and (o)–(u).

Further Reading

On eschatology, see Old English poems such as *Judgement Day II*, *Christ III*, and *Domesday*. The core collections of patristic source material are J.-P. Migne's *Patrologia*

Latina (1844–65), commonly referenced as *PL*, followed by the volume number, and Brepols's *Cetedoc Library of Christian Latin Texts* (both available on CD, and the latter at www.brepolis.net/ by subscription). Gracia and Noone (2003) and McGrade (2003) offer a good introduction to medieval philosophy. See also Bolton (1986), Gatch (1991), and J. J. O'Donnell, *Augustine of Hippo* (http://ccat.sas.upenn.edu/jod/augustine.html).

(a)   Old English Literature: An Overview

Old English literature could be initially defined as the texts created in England, and in English, by the Anglo-Saxons (see Chapter 1(a) for a summary of the Anglo-Saxon period). It represents a relatively small collection of texts in comparison with other periods (e.g. Victorian literature), though chronologically it covers approximately one-third of the history of English, from the 5th century to the 11th century. A rough estimate suggests that there are around 3 million words surviving in Old English. These are extant in various manuscripts held around the world, but predominantly in the major collections in the British Library, Oxford's Bodleian Library, Exeter Cathedral's Library, and Corpus Christi College's Library in Cambridge. These manuscripts have been studied by scholars for centuries, and editions of the texts they contain have been appearing since the 16th century. Three million words may sound a large amount but we must recognise these are not unique words (many, for example, are repeated). Furthermore, when one considers that Charles Dickens's *Bleak House* alone, with its more than 300,000 words, would account for around 10 per cent of the entire Old English corpus, we can see the parsity of the collection. However, contextually, compared with other languages from the early medieval period (with the exception of Latin), this is one of the largest extant corpora from that period. As Greenfield and Calder note:

> Anglo-Saxon prose and poetry are the major literary achievement of the early Middle Ages. In no other medieval vernacular language does such a hoard of verbal treasures exist for such an extended period (c.700–1100). (Greenfield and Calder, 1986, p. 1)

Yet we must recall that this is just what survives to us, nearly a thousand years after the close of the Anglo-Saxon period. Thus we need to make two assertions:

(1) The surviving manuscripts must represent a fraction of what was originally recorded.
(2) The manuscripts themselves, if they had all survived, still would only have covered a small amount of the 'literature' *created* by the Anglo-Saxons.

Let us consider the first statement. According to our current knowledge there are over 400 'manuscripts' surviving that contain Old English material (whole codices and fragments). Most of these were compiled before the Norman Conquest but we also know that some scribes were still recording Old English material well into the 13th-century. Yet we can easily surmise that over the years many manuscripts have been lost or destroyed. Contemporary evidence from such writers as Alcuin (*c*.735–804) indicates that the great libraries of Anglo-Saxon England (such as that at York) could have originally held as many as 2,000 books. It is true that many of these would have contained material in Latin, but nevertheless the indications are that throughout the Anglo-Saxon period there were considerably more manuscripts available in the vernacular (i.e. the 'common language of the people' – Old English) than survive today. We can list the reasons why this might be so:

- Viking raids during the period, which destroyed monasteries and their collections;
- ill-treatment of Anglo-Saxon manuscripts after the Norman Conquest (e.g. manuscript pages were scrubbed and cleaned for re-use later);
- theft or accidental loss;
- natural damage (wear and tear, water damage);
- man-made damage (early use of chemicals to enhance legibility).

One major catastrophe (post-Conquest, that is) that befell Old English was the fire of 1731 in Ashburnham House, in which many of the manuscripts collected by Sir Robert Cotton in the previous century were destroyed or damaged. We know from catalogues and descriptions of the holdings of the library that several were lost, and looking at some of the manuscripts that survived (e.g. the *Beowulf* manuscript) one can still see the damage caused by the heat.

Let us now consider the second statement made earlier. In the Anglo-Saxon period the rate of literacy was very low and was confined, we assume, to the monasteries, clergy, and some of the nobility. Indeed literacy itself only came to the English with the arrival of Christianity in the 6th century – and even then we are still talking about the educated elite, not the bulk of the population of England. Our understanding is that it was predominantly monks who recorded material, and undoubtedly they would have been mainly interested in religious writing (though not always, as we can see in such manuscripts as the Exeter Book, see Chapter 2(k)). It is again very possible, therefore, that much of the literature of the Anglo-Saxons existed only in oral form, i.e. it was spoken, performed, and handed down through word-of-mouth from generation to generation by lay people (see below). Over the years, unless these texts were recorded in manuscripts, they would have been lost.

Nevertheless, as noted above, there are many manuscripts surviving that do contain Old English material; but it is open to discussion how these manuscripts would have been used. For the most part we believe that texts would have been read out from the manuscript to an assembled audience. This is understandable; as already noted earlier, most of the population was illiterate. However, some texts (such as those by the poet Cynewulf where he inserts a runic cryptogram at the end) are clearly intended to be seen on the page (you cannot solve Cynewulf's puzzle without actually seeing the individual runes), and the numerous manuscript images and marginalia which appear in Anglo-Saxon manuscripts indicate their visible value.

Furthermore we must recognise the way texts were disseminated. A single manuscript copy was only of use to one institution, and therefore scribes copied these into other manuscripts for wider distribution. In the case of poetry the distinction between author and scribe is one that causes much discussion, but the general assumption is that the manuscripts that survive today are not written by the hand of the author but by a copyist. This separation of the text from the author, and indeed the whole discussion about the identity of the original author or authors of a text, are clearly different from the accepted norms in modern literature, and challenge many 'author-based' theories. In most cases we simply do not know who composed or wrote the original texts, and how far removed they were from the copies that survive. In addition, the notion of the fixed authorial text is a more modern concept and scribes clearly felt at liberty to alter the text they were copying. The problems associated with this were clearly understood at the time – Ælfric, for example, urged future copyists not to make too many alterations to his text.

The material that does survive was recorded mainly during the period from the mid-10th century to early 11th century. Indeed, the four main Old English poetical manuscripts (the Exeter Book, the *Beowulf* manuscript, the Junius manuscript, and the Vercelli manuscript) all were written in a 50-year period around the year AD 1000. Earlier material is much rarer, probably lost in the Viking wars of the late 8th and 9th centuries. It is only after the reconquest of England, initiated by Alfred the Great towards the end of the 9th century, that there was an opportunity for the scriptoriums (i.e. the parts of the monastery charged with copying manuscripts) to flourish in safety, and for documents to be widely distributed and preserved. Later (post-Conquest) material in Old English does survive as well, notably in the *Anglo-Saxon Chronicle*, which was still being maintained in the mid-12th century.

Now let us consider what actually does survive. Old English literature can be divided quite simply into prose and poetry. Drama, as something written for a stage to be performed by actors, does not survive in Old English. However, there are indications that certain religious ceremonies were elaborately choreographed, involving numerous participants, for an audience (e.g. processions and dedications – see Raw, 1991, pp. 230–1), and some elements of the surviving literature (such as those taking the form of a dialogue) could have involved more than one orator. However, this is a far cry from the later mystery plays or the theatre of Shakespeare, and thus when we talk of medieval drama we generally refer to material appearing well after the Conquest.

Old English texts themselves are usually presented to the student in modern editions, or textbooks. Old English poetry is typeset as short lines, with a caesura (metrical pause) marked by a gap in the middle of them, thus producing two half-lines. Prose, on the other hand, runs continuously across the page, in common with modern practice. However, in the manuscripts the text is continuous for both prose and poetry.[1]

Only a small fraction of what survives would be considered poetry (*c*.30,000 lines); the vast majority is prose (and we must remember that vernacular prose is outweighed by Latin writing from the period). It is also accepted that poetry 'came first'. This may seem a strange thing to say. Clearly, in everyday speech the Anglo-Saxons would have spoken as we do now, in something roughly equivalent to what

---

[1] We refer to the literature (both prose and poetry) by lines: l. 7 means 'line 7', ll. 4–56 means 'lines 4 to 56'. In the case of poetry we also refer to the half-lines (as 'a' and 'b'), e.g. l. 56a, or l. 56b, means 'line 56a' (the first half of line 56), and 'line 56b' (the second half).

we would call prose, that is language with the prosody of everyday speech, without specialised metrical patterns. Therefore, in defence of the statement 'poetry came first', what we are really saying is that poetry was the first *literary* form in English, i.e. something that is designed to entertain or exact an emotional response.

In the earliest days of the Anglo-Saxons, both before and after the migration, this poetry would have been learnt by the poet (or *scop*, to use the Old English term) and then performed from memory; probably early on this consisted mainly of 'lays', shorter poems of a narrative nature. Oral performance was in effect the only option open to the poet, as apart from a few runic inscriptions, it appears that illiteracy was almost universal. We would describe early Anglo-Saxon England therefore as an 'oral society', where the spoken word was the predominant form. With the coming of literacy brought by the Christian missionaries in the 6th century, and the subsequent rise of the monasteries, this was to change. The word and rule of God had to be recorded, interpreted, and disseminated and that required a literate society. In the course of events, some of the monks also recorded secular texts, such as prose documents (see below) and apparently non-religious poems.

In other entries in this collection we will look more closely at the nature of Old English verse, and at some of the major texts. But for now, a few introductory details are worth noting:

- most of the poems are anonymous;
- the names of only two poets are known to us – Cædmon and Cynewulf;
- most of the poetry that survives is contained in four manuscripts, and thus in general only one extant version of each survives;
- although we can date these four manuscripts, we cannot with any certainty date the original composition of many of the poems.

Old English prose, as we noted above, outweighs poetry by a factor of over 10:1. Elements that distinguish prose from poetry are the lack of metrical patterns (Old English poetry has very strict rules), and a simplified syntax (especially word-order) and vocabulary. The earliest prose that survives is very straightforward in its structure, consisting of short simple sentences. However, later on in the period the prose becomes much more elaborate with developed use of clause structures, and with writers such as Alfred the Great, Ælfric, and Wulfstan, we see it elevated to a true literary form.

The range of prose material that survives is extremely impressive. As Janet Bately notes:

> One of the most significant literary achievements of the Anglo-Saxons was the establishment of vernacular prose as an acceptable medium both for the dissemination of knowledge on a wide range of subjects and for the provision of moral instruction and entertainment. (Bately, 1991, p. 71)

Bately also outlines some of the lost prose texts of the period; but even taking this into account, compared with other contemporary cultures in western Europe, the Anglo-Saxons are unrivalled in the amount of material they recorded in their own language. We have law codes (the earliest from around 600, though surviving solely in a post-Conquest manuscript), historical texts (such as the *Anglo-Saxon Chronicle*), scientific and medical texts, charms, proverbs, homilies, saints' lives, liturgical texts, history books, genealogies, catalogues, wills, writs, charters, letters, glosses to Latin texts, and translations of classical texts and the Old and New Testaments. In addition, as noted earlier, a lot of material (both prose and verse) exists in Latin written by Anglo-Saxons, and this survives in many manuscripts. But even then they occasionally provided translations of these Anglo-Latin texts in English, the most obvious example being the Venerable Bede's early history of England, which originally was composed in Latin (appearing in 731), but was translated into English at the end of the 9th century.

The rise of prose is generally attributed to the educational policy of Alfred the Great (849–99). Faced with the destruction left behind by the Vikings, Alfred launched a learning programme, at the root of which was a series of key texts that he had widely disseminated. Most importantly, recognising the needs of his countrymen, Alfred chose to produce these texts in English, the language that most people could understand. This laid the foundations of English literary prose, and established English as an acceptable language in which to write material of value to court and clergy, thus rivalling Latin.

In summary, we can also make a few introductory remarks about Old English prose:

- it is used mainly for factual information – and consequently it is often hard to argue that all of Anglo-Saxon prose has a literary appeal;
- the range of material recorded is extensive;

- many Anglo-Saxons (such as Bede, Alcuin, and Aldhelm) composed prose in Latin;
- English (or vernacular) prose really only begins as a literary form under Alfred the Great;
- a single prose text can survive in many versions in different manuscripts.

With such a large collection of prose and poetry (compared with other vernacular languages from the period) it is impossible to generalise about the nature of Old English literature. Therefore in subsequent sections we have singled out the main styles and collections. Sometimes these groupings are self-evident, sometimes they seem forced. Yet these are the standard categories under which Old English is studied, taught, and written about in scholarly texts. Throughout this book we also adopt a range of approaches, but in keeping with most studies, we are advocating a 'context-based' approach, namely looking at the text or writer in terms of the possible historical and social context. To this end then, one should not ignore the introductory essays on Anglo-Saxon history and culture; one should consider Old English as part of the evolving story of English language and literature (as this book attempts to show), and look at their relationship to other contemporary languages and literature (especially with Old Norse literature – see McTurk, 2005; and O'Donoghue, 2004).

See also   Chapter 2(b), (d)–(g), (h), (k), Chapter 3(a) and (c), and Chapter 4(a), (d), (e), (j), and (k).

Further Reading

Although Old English first appeared in print in the 16th century, the majority of texts were only properly edited for the first time in the 19th century. Two series stand out from this period: the German editions by Christian Grein et al. entitled *Bibliothek der Angelsachsischen Prosa* and *Bibliothek der Angelsachsischen Poesie*, and in Britain, the publications of the Early English Text Society. The latter has survived to become the dominant series, and runs into several hundred editions. These in turn are divided into the 'Original Series' (abbreviated OS), the 'Extra Series' (ES), and the 'Supplementary Series' (SS). In the late 19th and 20th centuries, editions of individual texts proliferated, often via University Presses; but also, teaching texts appeared, which anthologised key poems or prose extracts. Such primers and teaching collections (some of the earliest coming from 19th-century scholars such as Henry Sweet, e.g. Sweet (1965 and 1975)) were designed to meet the needs of emerging English departments, as Old English became incorporated into the syllabus. Nowadays there are plenty of teaching texts to choose from which bring together editions of Old English literature. We have listed the major textbooks used, in Chapter 4(a) on the 'Old English Language', and in addition other key reference works such as dictionaries, thesauri, and online resources.

In keeping with its academic nature, most studies of Old English literature appear in academic monographs and research journals. The key journals in this field are: *Anglo-Saxon England* (abbreviated *ASE*), the *Old English Newsletter* (abbreviated *OEN*), *The Year's Work in English Studies* (*YWES*), *Anglia*, the *Journal of English and Germanic Philology*, *Medium Ævum*, and *Neuphilologische Mitteilungen*. The latter are often diffi-cult to access outside of major university libraries, so for this book we have tended to concentrate on works that are readily available. There are some key introductions to the period which one should try to get access to, and these are referenced throughout this book. Notably these include: Donoghue (2004b), Fulk and Cain (2003), Godden and Lapidge (1991), Lambdin and Lambdin (2002), Liuzza (2002), and Pulsiano and Treharne (2001, especially pp. 3–10 for a general overview). It is also strongly advis-able that one invests in a copy of *The Blackwell Encyclopaedia of Anglo-Saxon England* (ed. Lapidge et al., 1999). When attempting to find secondary material of interest, students could look to the online bibliography at www.oenewsletter.org/OENDB/index.php; and the annual listings in *ASE* and *YWES*.

When researching a subject in Old English the introductory guides and bibliogra-phies of the journals noted above are good starting points, plus some of the various routes suggested elsewhere in this book (i.e. under specific areas, or through the language reference works and online sources listed in Chapter 4(a)). To this we should add key texts like Greenfield and Robinson (1980), Hollis and Wright (1992), Poole (1998), and Waite (2000). Students should also consult the *International Medieval Bibliography 1967–2001* (www.brepolis.net/imb_en.html), and generic titles such as the *Modern Languages Association (MLA) Bibliography*, or journal contents listings under such resources as the ISI Web of Knowledge, OCLC FirstSearch, JSTOR, or PCI Contents Index. See also Swan and Treharne (2000), and www.le.ac.uk/ee/em1060to1220 for the transition during the 12th and 13th centuries.

(b)   Anglo-Latin Writing

Although the major focus of this book is material written in the vernacular (i.e. the native language of a country, in this instance English), it is fitting to begin with a discussion of the large and impor-tant corpus of Anglo-Latin material from the period, that is Latin texts written by Anglo-Saxons (for post-Conquest texts in Latin see Chapter 3(b)). It is in England, for example, that the *Codex Amiatinus* appears; dating from the late 7th and early 8th centuries and origi-nating from Monkwearmouth and Jarrow, it is one of the most impor-tant extant copies of the complete Latin Bible.

We have explored elsewhere that the rise in English literacy goes hand in hand with the growth of Christianity in England, and as Orchard observes (2003a), 'Christianity has always been (like Islam and Judaism) a religion of the book' (p. 207). The *lingua franca*[2] of Christianity by the 6th century onwards was Latin; so it is not surprising that many writers from Anglo-Saxon England adopted this. Indeed, when viewing the collection of material emanating from England during the early period (7th and 8th centuries) the overwhelming majority of writing is in Latin. As McGowan observes:

> The use of Latin in Anglo-Saxon England was essential to its intellectual development. The far better-known and better-studied vernacular literature of Anglo-Saxon England is only part of the picture (and constitutes a smaller surviving corpus). (McGowan, 2001, p. 43)

We know also that words were 'borrowed' from Latin throughout the early Anglo-Saxon period by the English. These so-called 'loan words' include such things as *strǣt* 'street' (Latin *strata*), *weall* 'wall' (Latin *vallum*), *win* 'wine' (Latin *vinum*), etc. This can be explained by the increased amount of interchange between the Germanic tribes and the Romans in the latter stages of the Empire, fuelled no doubt by increased commercial links, but also through a policy of using Germanic mercenaries in the Imperial army.

As with English, Latin also has historical periods. These are broken into Early Latin (240–70BC); the Golden Age (70BC–AD14); the Silver Age (AD14–130); Late Latin (2nd–6th century); and then Medieval Latin or Low Latin (6th–15th centuries). The last two periods are possibly the most important for the study of Old English in that many of the texts the Saxons read or used for source material were written by the early Church (or patristic) writers and originated in the Late Latin period. The texts they themselves composed (e.g. writers such as Bede or Alcuin – see below) are in what we would call Medieval Latin. The differences between Late Latin and Medieval Latin are noteworthy but not as dramatic as the changes experienced in the history of English. Medieval Latin is fairly similar to the Latin of Virgil, for example, but is notable for introducing new vocabulary, changes in meaning of words, and a more simplified syntax.

Latin writing is evident across the British Isles prior to and throughout the Anglo-Saxon period but with some key variations. 'British Latin', i.e. texts written by indigenous British writers, survives from the early part of the Saxon invasions. It declines notably after

---

[2] *Lingua franca* is a term for the common language used by people of different nationalities.

the time of Gildas (mid-6th century) with only a few later examples such as the *Historia Brittonum*, written in the early 9th century, and occasionally referred to as the 'Nennius'. 'Hiberno-Latin', i.e. texts written by Irish monks, is much more widespread and several texts survive from throughout the period that were written either in Ireland or by Irish missionaries living elsewhere.

Concentrating on the Anglo-Saxons, though, the student new to this area should consider:

(1)   the influence of Latin writers on vernacular authors;
(2)   the re-use of Latin texts;
(3)   the main Anglo-Latin writers (i.e. writers from the Anglo-Saxon period who wrote almost entirely in Latin);
(4)   the demise of Latin in Anglo-Saxon England.

With the first we have already noted that Latin texts were read, studied, and used by Anglo-Saxon writers (when writing either in Latin or in English). This is important to understand as it places Anglo-Saxon literacy in the context of its predecessors, and presents us with an argument for seeing a continuation of many philosophical and religious ideas. A major attempt to catalogue these and other sources for extant Old English texts can be seen with the *Fontes Anglo-Saxonici* project (http://fontes.english.ox.ac.uk/). Using this, one can search under a specific Old English work and see what possible source texts were used (see Chapter 4(f) for a discussion of 'source studies').

We must also recall the re-use of Latin texts written by English writers in the later Anglo-Saxon period (such as an Old English version of Bede's *Historia ecclesiastica gentis Anglorum* – 'Ecclesiastical History of the English Nation' – originally written in Latin and appearing in 731, which emerges in the late 9th century). Similarly we must also remember that many interlinear English glosses are inserted into existing Latin manuscripts, possibly indicating the range of texts used for educational purposes. Here the translator or glossator writes the equivalent Old English word above the Latin word, between the lines of the original text.

Finally there are the Anglo-Saxon writers themselves, who created new, original texts in Latin. Nearly all of these are drawn from the clergy, who would have learnt their Latin at school in the monasteries. Latin, it should be noted, was a key part of the educational process for monks as it allowed them to engage with the important texts used by the Church. Not only would this have exposed them to the earlier patristic and philosophical writers, but they would also have had a thorough grounding in Latin grammar and vocabulary. Several authors emerge as key figures in Anglo-Latin writing, all living around the same time. First there is Aldhelm of Malmesbury (died *c.*709), who was educated at Theodore's monastic school at Canterbury, and wrote extensively in prose and verse. Second there is the 'Venerable' Bede (*c.*673–735), who contributed his famous history of the early English period as well as numerous religious and scientific texts. Finally, there is Alcuin (*c.*735–804), who again worked in the mediums of prose and verse, and whose importance is recognised by the fact that he was invited to reside at the court of Charlemagne, and eventually became abbot of the important religious establishment at Tours. This demonstrates the level to which Anglo-Latin scholarship had risen, in that English scholars were recognised on the Continent for their expertise. In addition we have writers such as Boniface (675–754), whose contributions may not have been as prolific but whose importance cannot be understated. Throughout the remaining chapters many of these writers will be referenced. Between them their contributions and influence are undeniable, but a key point to note is that they lived, wrote, and died within 150 years of each other. This indeed was the golden age of Anglo-Latin writing.

The passing of this age comes with the Viking attacks of the late 8th and throughout the 9th century. Indeed it is common to divide the corpus of Anglo-Latin writing into 'pre-Viking' and 'the Viking Age' (or 'post-Viking') as in the latter the number of Latin texts greatly diminishes. With the risk of over simplification, English could be said at this point to become the language of written communication. To understand this we must recall Alfred the Great's rearguard action at the end of the 9th century that only just saved the English state. In the lead-up to this the continued raiding and destruction throughout that period had resulted in the demise of numerous monastic establishments, so much so that in Alfred's *Preface to the Pastoral Care* the king bemoans the almost complete loss of Latin scholarship in England. The direct result of this was the elevation of English as an accepted language of writing. Alfred stated that this was a decision brought about by the situation he faced. If he was to rebuild the country he needed to rebuild its education, and the easiest and most practical way to do this was to increase literacy levels in the language of the people, i.e. English. The effect of this decision was to elevate English to the language of the court, and in part the church. Throughout the 10th century therefore English writers began to produce English texts. Although Latin witnessed a revival under the Benedictines in the mid-10th century, it is notable that two of the major writers from the period – Ælfric and Wulfstan – wrote predominantly in English (though they clearly re-used Latin texts from the earlier period).

Looking at the corpus of Anglo-Latin writing that does survive to us from the earlier period, it is interesting to observe the types of texts available. Predominantly these are religious and didactic. There are educational texts of direct use in the curriculum, e.g. grammars, or texts on Latin metre. There are scientific texts (such as Bede's *De natura rerum* – now lost); bibles or commentaries on the Bible; *enigmata* (or riddles); treatises on religious doctrine; letters; and so on. The range of material is extensive.

What then should we take from this discussion? In summary the key points are:

- there is an extensive corpus of material written in Latin by English writers from the Anglo-Saxon period;
- major figures that stand out for particular further study are Bede, Aldhelm, and Alcuin; but several others also deserve attention;
- earlier Latin texts written by non-English writers were used by the Anglo-Saxons throughout the period for inspiration, and as direct sources;
- Latin texts written by Saxon writers were also translated into English or re-used later on in the period (e.g. the Latin works of Bede);
- the history of Anglo-Latin writing tends to be divided into two periods: the pre-Viking period (when the bulk of texts that survive originated, and the main known Anglo-Latin writers lived); and the Viking period up until the Conquest, when English became the main language of writing, following on from Alfred's educational programme beginning at the end of the 9th century.

See also Chapter 1(f), Chapter 2(d), (e), (g), and Chapter 4(d).

Further Reading

For an introduction to the corpus of Anglo-Latin writing and its main scholars, see Lapidge (1986), McGowan (2001), and Orchard (2003a). For a comprehensive look at the whole range of writings and texts, see Lapidge (1993 and 1996). For discussions of the Latin texts available to the English, see Chapter 4(d) and (f), Gneuss (2001), Lapidge (1985), and Ogilvy (1967 and 1984–5). On Aldhelm, see Lapidge and Herren (1979), Lapidge and Rosier (1984), and Orchard (1994). On Alcuin, see Allott (1974),

Gaskoin (1966), and Godman (1982). On Bede, see Hunter Blair (1990), Marsden (1989), Sherley-Price (1968), and Wallace-Hadrill (1988).

(c)   Legal Texts

One of the more remarkable accomplishments of the Anglo-Saxon period was the elevation of English as an acceptable language of court and clergy (as opposed to the more common practice of using only Latin). In particular a range of legal documents survive from the period that attest to its recognition as the main language in which to conduct business and legal matters. Moreover, these documents provide us with invaluable information about the nature of Anglo-Saxon society, its development, and the level of sophistication it had reached by the time of the Conquest. Such a seemingly 'non-literary' subject base can provide us with considerable material for literary studies. The range of Old English legal material is extensive: law codes of kings, charters, writs, wills, manumissions (a document freeing a slave from servitude), and treaties. Before progressing to these, however, we need to understand how the law was maintained, originated, and judged.

In the early history of Anglo-Saxon England undoubtedly the law was maintained orally at a tribal level and the main penalty and weapon of the law was force. Yet even then we can ascertain from early law recordings that systems were in place to attempt to maintain some form of balance. At the root of this was the blood-feud, in which it was acceptable to exact revenge for harm done to a member of your family or tribe (see Fletcher, 2003).

Although this may seem extreme by modern-day standards it need not be viewed as so. First, revenge could be replaced with remuneration in the form of the *wergild* ('man-money') – some form of financial compensation for the injury performed to the victim or the victim's family, paid for by the perpetrator. *Wergild* in effect reflects the monetary value of a life, or by extension a part of the body, e.g.:

If anyone kills a freeman, 50 shillings shall be due to the king as a sum for the loss of a subject

If a big toe is struck off, the aggressor shall pay over 10 shillings

(Law Code of Æthelberht of Kent, 560–616)

Failure to pay could result in banishment (and thus the surrounding problems of exile), physical punishment, or death (but not imprisonment). This was such a powerful notion that *wergild* and compensation form the base of many law codes of the Anglo-Saxon kings. Indeed, these were developed to such an extent that fines for all manner of crimes are listed (murder, manslaughter, rape, bestiality, slander, to name but a few). Moreover, some historians (e.g. John, 1996) argue that the blood-feud was in fact a stabilising device as both sides realised that if it was allowed to spiral out of control it could lead to mutual destruction.

The first law code we have surviving is that of Æthelberht, King of Kent, an extract of which is quoted above. This originated around the year AD602 (Fulk and Cain, 2003, p. 150). Throughout the code we can see the gradual emergence of the role of the king in Anglo-Saxon society, and in particular as a protector of those without kin. It is not surprising therefore that many people see a connection between the conversion of Kent to Christianity (St Augustine arrived in 597) and the appearance of a law code: priests after all needed protecting as they had no tribe to call on to threaten the blood-feud. Æthelberht's laws are not extensive, and were not entirely original as they bear signs of Continental influence (notably Frankish), but they are the earliest datable document we have in English,[3] and set several precedents:

(1) they were drawn up in English, by the English, and for the English;
(2) they show the emerging power and role of the king;
(3) they show the continuation of practices: *wergild*, blood-feuds, compensation;
(4) they offer protection to the clergy.

This pattern was repeated with later law codes (e.g. those of Ine of Wessex AD688–94, and Wihtræd of Kent AD695–6), so that by the time of Alfred's law codes (*c.*AD880) many principles were firmly established. We can see the rise in the power of the king (in receiving payment for law breaking), the concept of a unified nation, and the ascendancy of the Church in terms of its involvement in secular activities. Moreover, it was possibly also, under Alfred, that the notion of a crime being a direct affront to the king himself began to emerge (i.e.

---

[3] It should be noted, however, that the only surviving copy we have of Æthelberht's codes is in a post-Conquest manuscript.

the start of the 'crime against society'). Alfred, we must recall, made it a requirement that everyone at the age of 12 had to take an oath of allegiance to him and swear that they would not break the law. Alfred's law codes were strengthened by a direct link to the Ten Commandments (they open with them), which not only tied his law to that of God, but also utilised a common ploy of linking the plight of the Anglo-Saxons, beset by the heathen Vikings, to that of the persecuted Israelites.

Another aspect of Anglo-Saxon law that developed with the rise of the Church was trial by ordeal. This may have originated in pagan times, as in Ine's early codes it is a secular law, but it was fully appropriated by the Church by the end of the period. Trial by ordeal was administered by the clergy (hence the fact that the details are preserved in several pontificals), and attempted to show a person's guilt or innocence through divine action. There were four types of ordeal: fire, boiling water, immersion in cold water, and the eating of consecrated bread and cheese (the latter reserved for the clergy). Ordeal by battle, however, appears to have come to England after the Conquest.[4]

As law codes became more complicated and the protection and power of the Church grew, they were often split into those covering ecclesiastical matters and those relating to secular crimes (given the nomenclature *'Roman Numeral / King's Name'*, e.g. II Edgar, or III Edgar). The last law code drawn up in the Anglo-Saxon period was under the reign of Cnut and was drafted by Wulfstan, Archbishop of York. That the king decided to delegate his legal matters to an Archbishop is worth noting, but not surprising as Wulfstan was constantly engaged in political affairs of state. Yet the impact of the Old English laws did not rest there. Many of them were re-used in a Latin version of the laws entitled the *Quadripartitus*, drafted under the reign of Henry I, and five centuries later these in turn were re-used by Parliamentary lawyers at the time of the English Civil War to promote their views on the legal rights and practices of the English (see Fulk and Cain, 2003, p. 227).

As the Anglo-Saxon kingdoms emerged and the power of the relevant kings rose, systems of jurisdiction were also needed. By the later period there had developed an elaborate system consisting of hundreds' courts,[5] dealing with low-level jurisdiction and tax affairs

---

[4] The ordeal eventually disappeared in England after the Fourth Lateran Council of 1215 had forbidden clergy to take part in this practice.

[5] A 'hundred' was a unit of land.

(these met every four weeks, possibly emerging from original tribal gatherings or 'moots'); shire courts (which met twice a year), dealing with serious criminal cases; and borough courts and special local methods of jurisdiction, such as the court of the Riding in Yorkshire. Accompanying this was a range of administrative roles, most notably the various offices of the Reeve (a local official under the King), who as part of his duties oversaw legal gatherings.

In addition to the law codes, the other main body of legal texts that survives consists of writs and charters. A writ is a short document, usually with a seal of authority by the king, that contains administrative instructions or appointments to office. A charter, on the other hand, usually focuses on the bestowal of land (*bōcland* or 'bookland', i.e. land granted in perpetuity and recorded in written documents). These are more numerous than writs. Although many charters exist solely in Latin, and a lot of them are open to question in terms of their authenticity (that is to say many were forged in later times), from 930 onwards the boundary-clause of the charter, namely the section which defines the perimeter of the land held, was recorded in English. Boundary-clauses provide us with information about the formation of the landscape of early England, and were considered so important in Anglo-Saxon times that at Rogationtide[6] local children were taken around the bounds to familiarise them with the borders, and beaten if they failed to remember them (hence the phrase 'beating the bounds'). A key study of these charters was performed by Sawyer in 1968. This is cited so often that charters are now known by their 'Sawyer number', e.g. S1, S33, etc.

As noted above, many other types of legal documents survive (e.g. treaties, wills, diplomas, etc.), but for now we should consider the importance of these documents to our study of literature:

- Students of literature should look to legal material for contextual information. They should also consider the re-use of source material (i.e. in the copying of law codes) and some literary extracts, such as the Preface to Alfred's law codes, that draw on the Ten Commandments for inspiration (thus establishing the authority and continuity of the code).
- The survival of so much factual material in English further attests to the importance the Anglo-Saxons attached to their

---

[6] Days of prayer highly esteemed by the Anglo-Saxons, concentrating on good harvests. Major Rogation Day was 25 April, and three minor ones were celebrated in the run up to Ascension Day (40 days after Easter Sunday).

own language as the communication vehicle of the court, the law, and the Church. Latin was used (notably in the charters), but the amount of material surviving in the vernacular is noteworthy.

- Collected together these documents give us a greater understanding of Anglo-Saxon history, and more notably the changes in the Anglo-Saxons' political and social attitudes. In the law codes, for example, we can see the rise of the power of centralised institutions such as the monarchy and the Church, and the interdependence of both.
- Combined also, these legal documents attest to what Wormald described as 'a stratified society' (1991, p. 11), i.e. one with structures and authority across all sectors.

See also Chapter 1(e) and (f).

Further Reading

For general introductions to legal practices and texts, see Donoghue (2004a), Fulk and Cain (2003), Griffiths (1995), Hough (2001), and Wormald (1991). For more detailed studies see Wormald (1999a and 1999b). For access to the texts, and examples, see Whitelock (1996). See Griffiths (1995, pp. 23–8) for a concise list of the law codes of the Anglo-Saxons and their possible sources. An 'Electronic Sawyer', with details of land charters and other types of documents, is available at www.trin.cam.ac.uk/chartwww/charthome.html.

(d)   Historical Texts

There are numerous books and articles written on the Anglo-Saxon period, describing the major historical events and social changes. Yet it should be remembered that during the period the English also made concerted, and in context unparalleled, attempts to record their own history. These texts are obviously key documents giving us an invaluable insight into the events themselves, of course, but they are also important as they capture the attitudes of the people at the time to the surrounding changes (for post-Conquest historical writing see Chapter 3(e)).

Taking a chronological approach, the first important text regularly cited is the *Germania* by the Roman writer Tacitus, which appeared between AD90 and 100. This was written over 300 years before the migration period during which the Anglo-Saxons came to Britain, but it is regarded as an important insight into the early Germanic customs which can be still gleaned from later Old English texts. Tacitus described a multitude of nations at war in the area akin to modern-day Germany. Most importantly he attempts to describe their customs and beliefs. For example, for the Germanic warriors 'it is an infamy and a reproach for life to have survived the chief [in battle], and returned from the field' (visible also in the idealised Anglo-Saxon society, as depicted at the end of *The Battle of Maldon*, see Chapter 2(j)).[7]

The problem with Tacitus is one that is common to many historical texts of the period: namely that he was writing with a clear political agenda, and this influenced his interpretation of events (which, it should also be remembered, he did not witness first-hand). So much so that as one study of Tacitus has observed 'little . . . can be taken at face value' (Toswell, 1996, p. 501). More interesting, perhaps, is what his aim was. Mainly he was using the examples of the barbarian Germans to illustrate failings in Rome, i.e. he was writing a purportedly historical book with the sole purpose of influencing things locally. This is a thread that runs through much historical writing of the medieval period – Gildas, as we will see, was attempting to educate the British to change their lifestyle; Bede was attempting to show to the local population the unifying strength of the Church; Alfred's educational programme was attempting to show the history of a 'unified nation', and so on (see Chapter 3(b) and (e) for examples of political and ideological approaches of post-Conquest historians).

When it comes to the migration period itself (*c*.410 onwards), apart from the texts written by the English (see below) we have a few non-English sources. The *Notitia Dignitatum* ('List of Dignitaries') is a Roman document, written in the 4th century, which importantly outlines the construction and size of the 'Saxon Shore Forts' in Britain; a series of coastal defences which were designed, many think, to repel the Germanic invaders. Supplementing this is the *Historia nova* ('The New History'), written by the early 6th-century Greek historian Zosimus, who wrote (in part) about the collapse of Roman rule in Britain. Yet it should be remembered that Zosimus was far removed from the events of the migrationary period in both time and distance (he was an official in the eastern Roman Empire), and, as with Tacitus's account, we must view his conclusions with some scepticism.

---

[7] Similar attempts to look at the characteristics of the Germanic tribes are made with *De origine actibusque Getarum* ('Of the origin and history of the Goths'), written by the 6th-century historian Jordanes.

Before looking at texts written in English we must also consider three noteworthy commentaries written from the other perspective, namely by the indigenous population of Britain – the Romano-British and Celts. The first is the *De excidio Britanniae* ('On the Ruin of Britain') written by the British monk Gildas around the middle part of the 6th century. Gildas's text is an attack on the rulers of Britain, whom he sees as immoral and corrupt, and puts the successful incursions by the Anglo-Saxons down to God's retribution on the sinful leaders and their people.[8] Although the text reads as a polemic it contains valuable, albeit biased, insights into the establishment of the early Saxon kingdoms and the retreat of the British. Similar insights and perspectives can be found in the 6th-century Welsh poet Aneirin's *Y Gododdin* ('The Gododdin') about the destruction of the British warriors of the Gododdin tribe at the hands of the Anglo-Saxons, a turning point in the battle for supremacy over the north of England and south-eastern Scotland. Finally there is the *Historia Brittonum* written in the early 9th-century and often attributed to the British monk Nennius (hence the alternative name the *Nennian*). All three present to us the views of the victims of the Anglo-Saxons, and thus the disinherited, or the conquered. Aneirin and the *Historia Brittonum* ('History of the Britons') also mention a British leader called Arthur who successfully made a stance against the Saxons (Gildas only refers to the Battle of Mons Badonicus – Mount Badon – which the *Historia Brittonum* states was one of Arthur's victories).

Concentrating on the English perspective, two major texts emerge as our primary reference documents. The first is the Venerable Bede's *Historia ecclesiastica gentis Anglorum* ('Ecclesiastical History of the English Nation'), which was completed in 731, and the second is the series of annals we commonly term the *Anglo-Saxon Chronicle*. Bede's history supplies us with much information about the early period of Anglo-Saxon rule, and established many names, dates, and events that were repeated in later texts. Yet although most people are ready to accept that the events he records for the 7th century are accurate (if somewhat biased), early material is often open to debate. Bede wrote his history in Latin, but it was translated into English during the reign of King Alfred. It is also at the time of Alfred that the second great historical text by the English was initiated, namely the *Anglo-Saxon*

---

[8] This idea is mirrored several hundred years later by Wulfstan, Archbishop of York, in his famous *Sermo Lupi ad Anglos*. In this, Wulfstan refers to Gildas, stating that the renewed Viking onslaught at the turn of the millennium is a direct result of a collapse in English morals.

Chronicle. The several manuscripts which come under this title collectively cover the period AD1–1154, but there are many variations between them in terms of what they record and how far they continue. With the *Chronicle*, for example, we recognise a 'common stock' of entries from the 9th century and earlier (e.g. annals which are shared more or less by the versions) but variations enter after that period as the texts were distributed and compiled in different regions.

Supplementing these two important works is material written after the conquest. Norman writers such as Guy of Amiens, William of Jumièges, and William of Poitiers present us with the perspective of the victors at Hastings. However, later writers (Florence of Worcester's *Chronicon ex chronicis* – 'Chronicle from Chronicles', *c*.1130–40; William of Malmesbury's *Gesta regum Anglorum* – 'Deeds of the English Kings', 1126; and Geoffrey of Monmouth's *Historia regum Britanniae* – 'History of the Kings of Britain', 1138), plus a series of other anonymous texts, present a more balanced view of the period (though they are, in the case of Geoffrey of Monmouth, somewhat far-fetched at times).

We must also not forget that the history of England was intertwined heavily with the history of other nations (as indeed is the case with language and literature development). The two major external influences are the Normans (see above), and the Scandinavians. For the latter then, the *Gesta Danorum* ('Deeds of the Danes') by Saxo Grammaticus (1150–1220) is an invaluable source document, covering Danish history up to the 12th century. Students, therefore, should not be wary of looking at general histories of medieval Europe (e.g. Holmes, 1988) to supplement their knowledge of Anglo-Saxon England.

Although the above provides a sample listing of the main historical texts, information about the events of the period can be drawn from a range of other sources. Administrative documents such as the Mercian *Tribal Hidage* (7th century) and the later *Burghal Hidage* (*c*.917) give us information about the landscape, 'taxation', development of population centres, etc. Miscellaneous annals, wills, charters, law codes, and writs can also provide us with information. Isolated examples such as Asser's Latin *Life of King Alfred* present us with details about events from the latter part of the 9th century and must also be taken into account. There are also the more 'literary texts', such as Alfred's *Preface to the Pastoral Care*, which gives us a glimpse of the structure of government and learning in his kingdom (albeit an exaggerated one), as do later writers such as Ælfric or Wulfstan when they comment on contemporary events.

We must remember that Old English poetry often contains historical references. In the case of such poems as *The Battle of Maldon* or *The Battle of Brunanburgh* it is fairly obvious. However, we also get somewhat allusive references to ancient tales, myths, and events in poems such as *Deor*, *Widsith* (which contains over 180 named characters alone), and *Beowulf*. The fact that these are only obliquely referenced suggests to many that the details of the events were well-known. There are also other artefacts, such as the Bayeux Tapestry, outside of the written word, which present us with further information.

Finally we must be wary of the blurred distinction between fact and fiction. Thus, when the writer of the entry for the year 793 in the *Anglo-Saxon Chronicle* chose to record that 'fiery dragons were seen flying in the air' we cannot say for certain whether this was simply for dramatic effect or would have been truly believed by him and his readers.

It would be amiss, however, not to say anything about the other major disciplines that present us with details of the Anglo-Saxon period. Elsewhere, we discuss the disciplines of palaeography and codicology, both of which give us important information about the workings of the monastery, the dissemination of literature, and the influence of Continental practices. To this we must add the disciplines of archaeology and art history. Combined, these present us with information that is often lacking in the literature, or support or even change our perceptions of texts (see Chapter 4(i)).

There are some key points to take from all of this and to remember when approaching any of these historical texts.

- All of these were written with a purpose in mind and are rarely objective. The British writers were either castigating or praising their own leaders; Bede was trying to establish a unified vision of the Christian church; the Normans were presenting their view of the Conquest, and so on. Even the annalists of the *Anglo-Saxon Chronicles* occasionally digress from simple recording of the facts to making value judgements.

- The further an author is away from the period being written about, the more suspicious one has to be about the work's accuracy. Bede's statement, often widely cited, that the Anglo-Saxons arrived in AD449 (the *adventus Saxonum*) is to be taken lightly. As is the story, for example, of the rebellion by the Anglo-Saxons against the British chief Vortigern which started the conquest of Britain.

- Writers were willing to copy material from previous texts, and thus many of these original errors were perpetuated or elaborated on. A simple example of this reliance on previous writers can be seen with a comparison of the opening of Bede's history and that of the *Anglo-Saxon Chronicle*:

> BRITAIN, formerly known as Albion, is an island in the ocean, lying towards the north west at a considerable distance from the coasts of Germany, Gaul, and Spain, which together form the greater part of Europe. It extends 800 miles northwards, and is 200 miles in breadth, except where a number of the promontories stretch further, so that the total coastline extends to 3600 miles. . . . At the present time there are in Britain, in harmony with the five books of the divine law, five languages and four nations – English, British, Scots, and Picts. Each of these have their own language; but all are united in the study of God's truth by the fifth – Latin.   (Sherley-Price (1968), *Bede*, Book I)

> The island Britain is eight hundred miles long and two hundred broad; and here in this island are five languages: English and British and Welsh and Scottish and Pictish and Book-Latin.   (Swanton (1996), Preface to the *Anglo-Saxon Chronicle*, p. 3)

Clearly the latter, written some 150 years later or more, draws its opening from either the Latin Bede or the Old English translation in the 9th century. Bede, in turn, drew some of the material elsewhere in his history from Gildas.

See also   Chapter 1(a), Chapter 2(b), (e), (f), (j), Chapter 3(b), (e), (h), and Chapter 4(d) and (i).

Further Reading

For general historical overviews of the Anglo-Saxon period see Campbell, John, and Wormald (1991), John (1996), Pelteret (2000), and Stenton (1971). For an atlas of the period see Hill (1981). To widen one's study to cover medieval Europe look at Holmes (1988). Editions of the *Anglo-Saxon Chronicle* abound but Garmonsway (1972) or Swanton (1996) offer good introductions. For Gildas see Winterbottom (2002). For Bede see Colgrave and Mynors (1969), Miller (1997), Sherley-Price (1968), and Chapter 2(b).

(e) Prose

In the section introducing Old English literature we noted that prose (from the Latin *prosa* or *proversa oratio*, meaning 'straightforward discourse') was a later literary medium compared with poetry. We assume that verse was being composed and performed orally for many centuries. The first prose that survives to us dates from the early 7th century (Æthleberht of Kent's law codes) and the first non-legal prose text we have is the *Old English Martyrology* (which is generally placed in the 9th century). Neither though could be said to be especially emotive or literary, and it is not until the prose of King Alfred that we can see a flourishing in this area.

When we survey the range of material surviving in vernacular prose it covers such things as:

- law codes, writs, charters, treaties, manumissions, etc.;
- historical texts;
- scientific, medical, and other educational texts;
- homilies, sermons, and saints' lives;
- translations of classical texts and the Old and New Testaments;
- some other miscellaneous texts.

In the case of the first three, an interesting debate is to be had as to whether these would be considered literature as such, though their value to the study of the language, history, geography, politics, and society of Anglo-Saxon England is undeniable. Moreover, if we do adopt a context-based approach to literary studies even this factual material may be of assistance. Yet with the religious texts and the translations of classical, patristic, and biblical material we are approaching something more akin to a work of 'superior quality' or 'artistic merit'.

Early use of prose was simple and straightforward. However, as practice and confidence in the medium grew (undoubtedly influenced by prose writers in Latin), we see the development of clause structures, syntax, and an expansion of the vocabulary. Towards the latter part of the Anglo-Saxon period writers felt at ease to engage in complicated philosophical, scientific, and religious debates, and employed a full range of rhetorical skills. This development can be seen with three simple examples:

(a) In this year there occurred a great slaughter at Woden's barrow. (*Anglo-Saxon Chronicle* entry for AD592).

(b)   All those disasters befell us through bad policy, in that they [the Vikings] were never offered tribute in time nor fought against; but when they had done most to our injury, were peace and truce made with them.   (*Anglo-Saxon Chronicle* entry, AD1011).

(c)   The holy mother Mary fed that child and it grew, just as other children do without any sins.   (Ælfric's *De initio creaturae*)

Entry 'a' was written towards the end of 9th century when the chroniclers began to compile the entries. It is typical of material from that period, where short, straightforward single-clause sentences prevail.[9] Yet only a hundred or so years later we can see just how far things had developed in entries 'b' and 'c'. The second entry from the *Chronicle* builds up an argument for the need to resist the Vikings in a timely manner, and Ælfric ('c'), writing a few years earlier, deals with the innocence of children and compares it to the early life of Christ.

Another device available to writers of prose, freed from the tight metrical constraints of poetry, was a more developed use of conjunctions, which enabled explanatory clauses to be included. They also had a greater ability to explore parallelisms (such as repetition of word-stems and endings), phonetic correspondences, similes, and so on. Writers such as Ælfric and Wulfstan even felt free to use the devices of poetry (e.g. alliteration, stress, and metre), and these were utilised to such an extent that the boundaries between prose and verse became blurred.

Even at its most developed, however, modern readers may still find some of the syntax troublesome. For example, when translating closely from Latin originals earlier writers (such as Alfred or the translator of Bede's *History* into English) found difficulty in replicating the structures of the original in the embryonic prose of Old English. At times this can cause considerable difficulty when attempting to translate into Modern English. There is also the frequency of parataxis, whereby clauses are not subordinated and are often joined together by a series of conjunctions (known as syndetic parataxis). For example:

And then King Æthered and his brother Alfred fought against the army at Meretown and they were in two armies and there was

---

[9] The obvious exception to this is the entry for the year 755, commonly entitled 'Cynewulf and Cyneheard', which is a lengthy piece akin to a short story.

great slaughter on either side and there Bishop Heahmund was killed.   (*Anglo-Saxon Chronicle*, AD871).

This sentence alone (accepting that it can start with a conjunction) contains five clauses, none subordinated, and all linked sequentially with 'and'. Although this may seem clumsy it should not be forgotten that occasionally this is a deliberate device used by the writer for emphasis.

There are two main highlights in the history of Old English prose, which saw, with the first, its establishment as a literary medium; and with the second, a major outpouring of texts and further refinement and expansion of prose style. The first comes with Alfred the Great, towards the end of the 9th century; and the second is a direct result of the Benedictine Revival of the mid-10th century and evident in the works of writers such as Ælfric and Wulfstan.

Historically, Alfred's important role in the defence and development of England as a nation is undeniable (much of the information about the king is derived from the 'biography' written by his advisor Asser). Born in 849 in Wantage, of the Wessex royal family, he lived through the most devastating series of Viking raids. In 865–71 this had become a full-scale invasion when the Great Viking Army wintered in England. By the time Alfred reached the throne in 871, Wessex was the only kingdom standing in the path of the Vikings, and was on the verge of defeat. Having been reduced to a stronghold in the Athelney marshes in Somerset, Alfred led the fight back at the Battle of Edington in 878. This led to the treaty between Alfred and Guthrum the Viking leader, with the establishment of the Danelaw (effectively dividing England in half – with the Danes holding the land to the north-east and the English to the south-west). This had important implications for the development of the English language, especially in northern England, where Danish influence is evident in vocabulary, place names, and possibly changes in language structure.

Although later years saw renewed conflict, with Alfred winning a series of victories that further pushed back Viking control, the post-treaty peace (albeit short-lived) allowed him to concentrate on rebuilding the nation militarily, spiritually, and most important for this topic, educationally. It is within this educational programme that Alfred commissioned a series of prose texts translating major works into English for the education of his subjects. This cemented the vernacular as the main language of discourse. More importantly, the king himself translated four major texts: Gregory the Great's *Cura*

Pastoralis (the 'Pastoral Care'), Boethius's *De consolatione philosophiae* ('The Consolation of Philosophy'), St Augustine's *Soliloquia* ('Soliloquies'), and the first fifty Psalms of the Bible. This core collection provided Alfred's subjects with a handbook on leadership, one of the most influential philosophical works of the early medieval period, a treatise on the soul and the afterlife, and a linking between the troubles experienced by the Anglo-Saxons and the biblical Israelites. Moreover, they were all written in English so that they could be widely disseminated and his subjects could understand them. Alfred declares his intentions openly in his *Preface to the Pastoral Care*, bemoaning (perhaps to the point of exaggeration) the loss of learning in the country, especially that of Latin. This, he concluded, necessitated the use of English.

Supplementing these, several other works were seemingly commissioned at around the same time. We have a translation of Orosius's *Historia adversus paganos* ('History against the Pagans'), Bede's *Historia ecclesiastica gentis Anglorum* ('Ecclesiastical History of the English Nation'), and the beginning of the *Anglo-Saxon Chronicle*. Combined, all three presented the Saxons with a core history reaching back before the migration, and established (perhaps politically motivated as well) the concept of a unified people and nation. In addition there was a translation of Gregory the Great's *Dialogues* by Bishop Werferth of Worcester, and a new and extensive set of Law Codes.

In terms of Old English prose, this sudden flowering is remarkable but at the same time understandable. The devastation of the Viking attacks and the virtual destruction of society's structures meant that education, literacy, and the knowledge of Latin via the monasteries had been seriously disrupted (as Alfred noted). To assist in this rebuilding Alfred wisely chose a policy of selecting key texts, having them translated into the vernacular (i.e. a language which he knew would be more widely understood by his subjects), and disseminated through the remaining (and new) monastic houses. Thus not only did Alfred lay the foundations for the reconquest of England in the early to mid-10th century, he also lay the foundations of English prose, a policy which was to flourish so notably in the later 10th century under the Benedictine Revival.

When approaching Old English prose then, there are some key principles and questions one must bear in mind:

- Vernacular prose (as opposed to Latin) developed later than poetry as a literary form, beginning to flower under Alfred in the late 9th century.

- Alfred, presented with a kingdom that needed both protecting and rebuilding, chose a two-pronged strategy: fortify the towns, and strengthen the educational system. With reference to the latter he did so by promoting, commissioning, and actually translating works of prose. He declared in the *Preface to the Pastoral Care* that these would all be presented in English as this would allow for a greater impact amongst his subjects.
- When looking at Old English prose texts themselves there are some key questions one might consider:

  - How well structured is the text? Does it use any common rhetorical devices (see especially the discussion on Sermons and Homilies in the next section)?
  - How advanced is the prose in terms of syntax and use of vocabulary?
  - When dealing with a translation of a text, at what point does it stray into a paraphrase, and could it even be defined as a unique work by the Anglo-Saxon author?
  - Are there any known sources for the prose work (see Chapter 4(f))? This is often more common and more identifiable in prose than in poetry.

See also   Chapter 2(a)–(d), (f), and (g) and Chapter 4(f).

Further Reading

For introductions to Old English prose see Bately (1991), Fulk and Cain (2003, pp. 48–69), Scragg (2001), and Szarmach (1986 and 2000). For access to a range of prose texts in translation see Swanton (1993). For an introduction to the texts of King Alfred see Keynes and Lapidge (1983), and Discenza (2005).

(f)   Homilies, Sermons, and Saints' Lives

A wealth of religious prose survives from the Anglo-Saxon period. Much of this is written in Latin, of course (we have fifty homilies from Bede alone, for example). However, a considerable amount survives in the vernacular (in keeping with the profile English held as the main language of written discourse after the Viking wars of the 9th century). In Chapter 2(l) we note the treatment of religious themes and stories in Old English poetry but here we will concentrate solely on prose.

There are numerous types of prose texts that could be catalogued under the heading 'religious'. The most obvious starting point is the Bible itself. The Latin Bible of the Anglo-Saxons was St Jerome's *Vulgate* version, though we know that manuscripts of the earlier Latin version known as *Vetus Latina* were also circulated in Northumbria in the 7th century. The Anglo-Saxons did not have a single established text of the Bible: manuscripts presented somewhat different versions of the Latin text and books now generally considered apocryphal, such as the Gospel of Nicodemus, were also used. The earliest manuscripts of the Bible were imported, but Anglo-Saxons made their own copies of the Latin biblical texts. Complete bibles, such as the famous *Codex Amiatinus*, were rare; more common were collections of individual books, particularly the Gospels. Anglo-Saxon writers also produced biblical commentaries,[10] such as that by Bede, and more importantly, vernacular translations. A translation ('gloss') into English, added in the second half of the 10th century, runs through the Lindisfarne Gospels (which originally date from the late 7th or early 8th century). We have Alfred's translation of the Psalms, the *Old English Hexateuch* (the first six books of the Old Testament),[11] and Ælfric's translations of the books of Kings, Judith, the Maccabees, Esther, etc.; plus verse treatments of Old and New Testament stories. To these we can also add such texts as vernacular versions of the Lord's Prayer or *Pater Noster*; penitentials, confessionals, ecclesiastic letters, monastic rules, 'scientific texts';[12] and above all, texts to assist with the liturgy (i.e. the worship of God through a prescribed ceremony, most commonly the celebration of the Holy Eucharist[13] through Mass). However, three categories of texts stand out as worth pursuing further – mainly because of their proliferation. These are: homilies, sermons, and saints' lives.

The distinction between a homily and a sermon is often difficult to grasp. Strictly speaking a homily will be based around a set scriptural reading for the day (called the 'pericope') and will analyse, interpret,

---

[10] Like other religious writers of the time, the Anglo-Saxons were interested in interpreting key events in the Bible, and in particular how the events in the Old Testament prefigured those in the New Testament.

[11] An illustrated version of which survives in London, British Library, Cotton MS. Claudius B. IV.

[12] For example, Byrhtferth of Ramsey's *Enchiridion* ('A Concise Handbook'), written to accompany his *Computus* ('computation'), which outlined how to calculate the date of Easter.

[13] Eucharist itself means 'thanksgiving', and in the Catholic Church, specifically the celebration of the body and blood of Christ.

and seek to explain the text (an activity we call 'exegesis'). The text or reading will be dictated according to a defined calendar, which changes each year as it is based around the moveable feast of Easter. We term this timetable the 'temporale'. This immediately explains why titles of homilies are generally linked to their place in that calendar (e.g. 'Second Sunday in Advent', etc.). For example, if we were to look at the table of contents of Godden's edition of *Ælfric's Catholic Homilies II* we can see titles such as:

IV   Dominica II post Aepiphania Domini
V   Dominica in Septuagesima
VI   Dominica in Sexagesima.[14]

However, on closer inspection this is not as straightforward as it seems. Some texts that we define as homilies are not linked to the temporale, and instead are associated with the feast day of a saint (see below).

How did they analyse the reading? The answer here lies in the accepted practice and training that is evident in the school curriculum that operated within the monasteries. This demonstrates that it was common to work on a four-fold analysis or exegesis of the text: literal, typological (i.e. the text's symbolic meaning, and an explanation of the allegory if appropriate), tropological (the moral meaning of the story), and anagogical (the spiritual message) – in a sense the basis for literary criticism. This may need some explaining to those new to the concept. Simply put, it means that each story or text could be interpreted in four ways of increasing abstraction. Donoghue (2004b, p. 43) presents a good example based on the story of the exodus of the Israelites from captivity in Egypt. Donoghue (basing his analysis on Dante's interpretation) notes that this could be interpreted as:

1. the departure of the Israelites from Egypt (literal);
2. redemption of the individual through Christ (typological/ allegorical);
3. conversion of the soul from sin to grace (troplogical/moral);
4. departure of the soul from the slavery and corruption of the world to freedom in heaven (anagogical/spiritual).

---

[14] *Dominica* means 'Sunday', *Septuagesima* and *Sexagesima* are terms used for the third and second from last Sundays before Lent (respectively).

A sermon, on the other hand, is not tied to any set reading. Instead it tends to be based around a theme or topic, with direct moral instruction in basic Christian ideas or principles (such as chastity). We call this 'catechesis'; and in terms of style, sermons tend to be much more encouraging or persuasive (or 'hortatory'), whereas homilies are more analytical and explanatory. Homilies were designed for preaching in part of the Divine Office (i.e. purely for a monastic audience) or at a Mass (for a monastic audience or for lay people), but there are also indications that they were used for private study. Sermons, on the other hand, were designed solely for oral presentation as part of the Mass.

Major collections of homilies, and to a lesser extent sermons, survive from the period. We have the large anonymous collections known as the Vercelli Homilies and the Blickling Homilies to begin with (both named after the places where the manuscripts of the homilies are now held, or were held at one point – Vercelli in Italy, and Blickling Hall in Norfolk). Indeed, compared with mainland Europe the number of surviving homilies from Anglo-Saxon England is outstanding. We also have two named writers to thank for the bulk of the extant collection, and we have considerable biographical information about these two men. They are Ælfric (eventual Abbot of Eynsham) and Wulfstan (Archbishop of York) – see below.

The third genre of texts centres on saints (we call this 'hagiographical' writing). Lapidge (1991, p. 247) notes that there were over 300 saints created in England alone, and each had a feast day, which in turn potentially spawned celebrations, church services devoted to the saints, and relics with miraculous powers. The popularity of saints, and of the stories about them, is understandable for two further reasons. First, they helped promote the conversion to Christianity, giving the new religion a tradition and a range of prominent noble characters. Secondly, saints and their relics were big business in the early medieval period as they attracted pilgrims and donations. For example, the translation (moving) of relics from one site to another is well attested to in Anglo-Saxon England (and may even have been the motive behind the composition of some of the saints' lives themselves).

Names of saints were recorded in a liturgical calendar or, in the case of those killed for their faith, a martyrology (hence the *Old English Martyrology*, which lists 238 martyrs). We also have surviving litanies – a text that includes a prayer to Christ and then a list of saints. Combined, all of these present us with a wealth of information about the individuals revered by the English.

Yet these are only lists in a sense, and what was needed was longer biographical outlines – hence 'saints' lives' or hagiographies. These are based on a classical tradition for saints' lives, and over 100 of these survive in Old English and in Anglo-Latin writing, many composed by Ælfric. We distinguish the ordering of saints' lives as being based around the calendar known as the 'sanctorale', which dictates set dates for particular feasts that do not change with the dating of Easter (e.g. St Valentine's Day will always be 14 February). If we look at the table of contents of Skeat's edition of Ælfric's *Lives of Saints* we can see this clearly:

I.   Dec. 25. The Nativity of our Lord Jesus Christ
II.   Dec. 25. St Eugenia, Virgin
III.   Jan. 1. St Basilius, Bishop
IV.   Jan. 9. St Julian and his wife Basilissa,
etc.

Here the actual date is given, as opposed to the chronological position in relation to Easter, Advent, etc.

Considering these lengthy tales in more detail we can discern that they tend to fall into two distinct categories: a *passio* or passion, in which the saint is tortured and martyred; and a *vita* or 'life', in which the saint leads a model life (occasionally also profiled as the life of a confessor, in which the saint converts to Christianity). Hence titles such as *Vita Sancti Cuthberti* or *Passio Sancti Eadmundi*. These are all prose texts though, but we should not forget that we also have verse saints' lives (e.g. *Juliana*, or *Guthlac A* and *Guthlac B* – see Chapter 2(l)).

Eventually these lives of saints began to be gathered into legendaries (such as the 'Cotton Corpus Legendary') or passionals, a practice which began in, or around, the 8th-century. Although they were undoubtedly used for private study there is sufficient evidence to suggest they were also used as readings in the Divine Office (e.g. at Nocturns, the Night Office, or in the refectory) for the education of the monks.

Having discussed the major types of religious prose, let us consider two often studied writers – Ælfric and Wulfstan. Taking Ælfric first: he was born around the mid-part of the 10th century, and educated at Winchester under St Æthelwold; he worked at the Cerne Abbas monastery where he developed his skills as a teacher (hence his 'nickname' – Grammaticus), and finally became Abbot of the new monastery at Eynsham, where he died around 1010 (hence the other common nomenclature – Ælfric of Eynsham). During that period, however, Ælfric's output was prodigious covering a wide range of texts. With particular reference to the above he singularly accounts for nearly half of all the homilies that survive from the period. He wrote his homilies in two series (termed *Catholic Homilies I* and *II*, often abbreviated *CHI* and *CHII*) that provided a reading for nearly every week of the year. These could be rotated on a two-yearly cycle. In the latter stages of his life he supplemented these with 40 further homilies. Although we usually call these 'homilies', and most of them clearly are (i.e. they are based on a set reading and perform an exegesis of each), Ælfric also included texts we might more correctly call sermons, plus some saints' lives in *CHI* and *CHII*. This appears to be because some Sundays and feasts which would have been important to his 10th-century Benedictine audience were not just related to the temporale but drew also from the sanctorale.

In addition to these he provides a series of around 35 hagiographical texts commonly termed the *Lives of Saints*. These are still generally numbered and referenced according to the late 19th-century editions produced by Skeat for the Early English Text Society (e.g. 'Skeat III' is the *Life of St Basil*, see above). Ælfric stated that his selection was based on those saints honoured by the monks, and showed a preference for passions, but he did include the details of some confessors. It is clear from the texts that this collection was also suitable for the laity.

As already noted, when analysing Old English prose we should look for possible sources for the texts. We know that Ælfric drew his tales from earlier writers (e.g. his famous *Life of St Edmund* is drawn from the version by Abbo of Fleury), and following on from a pioneering study by Patrick Zettel we can even identify the original collection he was using (the so-called Cotton Corpus Legendary).

Ælfric also produced translations of the early books of the Old Testament; and a series of teaching texts. He is noteworthy for the breadth of source material he employed, and more importantly, his development of the prose style. Influenced by patristic writers and presumably also by Old English poetry, Ælfric employed many standard rhetorical formulas, as well as creating what is called 'rhythmical prose'. This, like poetry, employs alliteration linking 'half-lines', rhyme and wordplay, but with a syntax and vocabulary more akin to prose (see also Chapter 3(c) on the blurring between prose and poetry in early Middle English texts).

Wulfstan was a near contemporary of Ælfric (they corresponded and Wulfstan re-uses some of Ælfric's work) but although he was not as prolific, his sphere of influence was equally wide. Wulfstan was Bishop of London from 996 to 1002, then held plurally the Archbishoprics of York and Worcester. He advised kings directly and helped them draft their law codes (notably Æthelræd and Cnut). He also wrote a major political treatise (the *Institutes of Polity*), and assisted in entries to the *Anglo-Saxon Chronicle*. For the purposes of this section, however, it is his surviving sermons that are more note-worthy. These were published by Dorothy Bethurum and this is still the main edition. A much-used example of these is the famous *Sermo Lupi ad Anglos* ('Sermon of the Wolf to the English').[15] This forceful diatribe denouncing the vices of the English made a direct link to the moral collapse of the nation and the new Viking invasions. It demon-strates extensive use of rhetorical devices, and a variation of the rhythmical prose style. Wulfstan also based his rhetoric on the guide-lines contained in St Augustine's *De doctrina Christiana* ('On Christian Doctrine'), employing a mixture of tones (*tenue, medium*, and *grande* – mild, medium, strong) for teaching, encouragement, and demand-ing obedience respectively.

This lengthy section covers much important ground. In summary we can see that:

- The corpus of Old English 'religious prose' is extensive.
- Three major types of texts emerge as being very common: homilies, sermons, and saints' lives.
- All three have distinctive characteristics and purposes. Homilies are generally tied to a pericope or set text, and are ordered according to the temporale. Sermons are more cate-chetical, based around the instruction of key Christian princi-ples. Saints' lives, or hagiography, can be divided into *passiones* and *vitae* and record the biographical details of a saint in dramatic fashion. These are ordered in the collections that survive according to the calendar known as the sanctorale.
- Two writers of note contribute much to our collection of Old English prose, namely Ælfric and Wulfstan. Both are studied extensively in Old English courses.
- Ælfric's major collections include his *Catholic Homilies I* and *II* and his *Lives of Saints*. Wulfstan is noted mainly for his sermons, but also for his political writings. Both writers make extensive use of common rhetorical devices that they would

---

[15] Wulfstan had adopted the pen-name 'lupus' while Bishop of London.

have learnt in their monastic education, and both develop and utilise what is known as the 'rhythmical prose' style.

See also Chapter 1(e) and (f), Chapter 2(b), (g), and (l), and Chapter 3(c).

Further Reading

For introductions of Old English religious prose, see Bately (1991), Fulk and Cain (2003), Godden (1991), Hall (2005), Liuzza (2001), and Raw (1991). For studies directly relating to saints' lives, see Anderson (2005), Damon (2003), and Lapidge (1991). On Ælfric, see Clemoes (1966) and Hurt (1972); and with reference to his texts see Godden (2000 and 1979), Pope (1967–8), and Skeat (1966). For Wulfstan, see Bethurum (1971) and Jost (1959 – but available only in German). On preaching and the Divine Office, see Gatch (1977) but also preliminary notes in Chapter 1(e). For the closest translation of the Vulgate consult the Douay–Rheims version of the *Biblia Sacra*. For further discussion of the influence of St Augustine see Chapter 1(f).

(g)   Scientific and Educational Texts

Two issues complicate any discussion of the scientific and educational texts surviving in the vernacular from the Anglo-Saxon period. The first is the modern-day divide between science and religion in that we see the former as something which is supported by facts, and the latter, by faith. Yet to the Saxons this distinction would be difficult to comprehend. Certainly to the writers of Old English texts (religious men predominantly) it was as truthful and useful to analyse the physiology of the human body, and to record the findings, as it was to critically discuss the meanings of an episode in the Bible. Both were factual, both were beyond questioning, both were important. Indeed the analysis of the natural world around them was utilised mainly as a tool to further understand God's plan. The separation therefore that we are so keen to make in modern times between religion and science is something we must recall does not apply to the English writers.

Secondly there is the definition of an educational text. In a sense all material written down in the period appears to have been 'educational' in some way or other. The fact that it was recorded in an age when the construction of a manuscript was so expensive attests to its importance at the very least. From the historical records in the *Anglo-Saxon Chronicle* to the gnomic statements in the wisdom poems, the audience is presented with something which either informs, instils knowledge, questions, debates, or reflects – in other words, 'educates'. For the purposes of this discussion, however, we will limit ourselves to factual books that were designed to be used directly in the classroom or by those readers wishing to pursue a scientific or medical exploration.

Although an element of education would have existed in the early tribes of Anglo-Saxon England (we conjecture that legends, beliefs, ancestral history, herblore, etc., were all 'passed down' orally), what we would describe as 'formal education' came from the clergy and in particular the monasteries. That is to say, there was no formal education witnessed in Anglo-Saxon England until the arrival of St Augustine and the gradual conversion to Christianity; and in particular the formation of the monastic schools, notably at Canterbury under Theodore of Tarsus (668–90) and Abbot Hadrian (earlier of Nisida). Schools were linked to the monasteries for the training of new monks (see below), and in particular for the scribes needed by the Church and other professions. At the core, then, was the need for a literate body of workers to read and write manuscripts. Women, we should note, also had the same access to education opportunities, as witnessed in the Abbess Hild's joint monastery or 'double house' (i.e. it held both nuns and monks) in Whitby in the 7th century.

The level of education and the subjects taught had a profound effect on the literature of the period. It also feeds directly into discussions of the levels of literacy in England and what this implies for 'reader-centred' theoretical approaches. If we accept that only a small minority of people could read (let alone write, see Kelly, 1990), then 'reading' as such may have been much more of a communal activity.

The core purpose of education was to further the understanding (and in so doing, the dissemination) of the word and the work of God (the *opus Dei*). As Lendinara observes (1991, p. 270), the interest lay 'not with Latin learning as an end in itself, but as a means of serving God'. The monks would have been trained in their duties and responsibilities, particularly with concern to the Divine Office, but also in subjects which had wider application. We know most about the practices of the Benedictine monasteries in this respect, but we also have information about earlier practices. In summary, boys entered the monastery as young as seven[16] and were called *oblates*. They would begin to learn Latin to assist in their prayers, especially useful when working with psalters and hymnals. In the beginning this would be by

---

[16] Bede states that this was the age he entered the monastery (*Eccleslasticl History*, V. 24).

rote learning, i.e. the teacher would dictate passages to them, which they would transcribe onto wax tablets and learn by heart. This would be recited back in the classroom (an example of this can be found in Ælfric's *Colloquy*, see below). Once they had learned the basics they would move on to grammar, metre, and orthography, using prose and verse versions of scriptures, grammars, and other texts such as *enigmata* (riddles). They would also be trained in how to interpret texts at various levels.

Our evidence for this knowledge is widespread. Alcuin, for example, tells us that he learnt grammar, rhetoric, music, metrics, astronomy, nature, and 'computus' under his teacher Ælberht of York. We also know of a common European curriculum used in monastic schools elsewhere, and by various clues surviving from the period we can tell that the Anglo-Saxons used that and added to it. It seems clear, for example, that they certainly concentrated on the disciplines of grammar, logic, and rhetoric (known as the *trivium*), with grammar appearing to be the dominant subject. We have surviving Latin grammars from Anglo-Saxon scholars of the 8th century such as Tatwine, Boniface, and Alcuin, and then after a gap (brought about by the Viking wars), a grammar and glossary by Ælfric from the late 10th century. These allow us to begin to get a glimpse of the set texts that would have been widely needed by the schools. Further evidence for this comes from the number of surviving Latin texts that have been glossed into Old English – the glossing, we assume, has an educational purpose. We also have texts by Bede (e.g. *De orthographia*), Alcuin, Boniface, and Aldhelm illustrating that orthography and metrics were taught as well. Bede also composed books such as *De natura rerum*, *De temporibus*, and *De temporum ratione* which deal with Christian cosmology, computus, and chronology. The other formal syllabus of the medieval period (known as the *quadrivium*, covering such things as arithmetic, geometry, music, and astronomy) seems to only have been fully adopted by the Anglo-Saxons in the 11th century.

Glimpses of the educational process can also be found in other texts such as Asser's *Life of King Alfred*, and in Alfred's own *Preface to the Pastoral Care*. In the former there is the famous tale of Alfred memorising a set of poems in order to win a competition, but it also outlines the education the king sought in the latter part of his life. In the *Preface* he decrees that the children of nobility should learn to read English and some Latin, and even (according to Asser) established a court school. Indeed the *Preface* can be seen as a policy document launching a new educational programme for England, to counteract the loss of learning experienced during the Viking wars.

However, in the later period the figure of Ælfric looms large over the field of education. As well as being one of the most prolific (known) writers of Anglo-Saxon England, he also provided a set of key educational texts which give us an insight into the practices of the classroom. These included a Latin *Grammar*, *Glossary*, and what has become known as the *Colloquy*. The latter is worth further comment as it is often studied. As the name suggests, it is a teaching text based around a conversation or 'colloquia', in which the master asked a set of questions and the young monks would be expected to recite back the answers that they had memorised previously (a model common to classical education). In Ælfric's text, written in Latin, the conversation is between the master (the *magister scholae*) and individuals representing a range of professions (a ploughman, a hunter, a merchant, etc.); with the young boys playing the tradesmen. Three key issues emerge from this. First it illustrates a familiar teaching method which sets out basic sentences and then builds on them with a range of progressively more complicated responses that the boys were required to learn (i.e. the grammatical skills and knowledge of vocabulary expected of the students become more difficult). Secondly it shows the emphasis both on the need to know Latin, but also on the ability to remember it. This is a different concept from our present-day teaching methods that rely heavily on the textbook and the reading, writing, and conversational skills of the students. In Anglo-Saxon times education, like so many other things, relied more heavily on memory and oral delivery than on written communication. Finally, the *Colloquy* presents us with glimpses of everyday life through the practices of these various craftsmen. Ælfric's *Colloquy* was then glossed into Old English by one of his pupils (Ælfric Bata) and it is this later version (usually edited and adapted by scholars) that appears in modern-day anthologies of Old English.

The later careers of monks also provided further opportunities for education and erudition. As we can see from such writers as Ælfric and Wulfstan, the formal education outlined above directly influenced the way these writers approached their subject matter and the way they delivered their material. Some writers, however, concentrated more on what we might loosely term 'scientific' texts as opposed to religious texts, but as Fulk notes (Fulk and Cain, 2003, p. 156), 'the categories that one distinguishes as folklore, theology, and science tend to overlap in Old English'. For example, the body of literature surrounding the field of 'computus' – the chief purpose of which is the calculation of the date of Easter – is extensive. We have over 15 manuscripts alone which outline this area of study, the most notable being Byrhtferth of Ramsey's 11th-century *Computus* and his accompanying *Enchiridion* (a manual in English to assists in the interpretation of the former).

Yet the fields of study extend beyond such curricula. The Anglo-Saxons showed interest in the creatures and the peoples that inhabited other countries, as can be attested to by *The Letter of Alexander to Aristotle*, which describes the journeys of Alexander the Great; *The Wonders of the East*, a catalogue of strange and curious beasts and men; and the earlier *Liber monstrorum* ('Book of Monsters'), which focuses on mythical beasts. We also see further interest in the natural world and medical matters through books such as herbariums, lapidaries, lists of charms, cures (*Lacnunga*), and an extensive analysis of human diseases, ailments, and anatomy known as Bald's *Leechbook*.

The key facts and discussion points that arise from the above are as follows:

- the modern-day distinction between fact and faith is not so clear cut in the medieval period;
- although some form of education undoubtedly existed, literacy and formal education were introduced to the Anglo-Saxons (and co-ordinated) by the Church, according to established curricula;
- the subjects studied matched the requirements of the Church (it needed scribes for both Latin and English) but also reflect the interests shown by Anglo-Saxon writers in certain disciplines;
- the driving force behind most scientific investigation was to meet the needs of the Church in the sense of further understanding of the Divine plan;
- the range of scientific texts demonstrates the extent of interest shown by the Anglo-Saxons in their surroundings; covering mythology, flora, fauna, medicine, astronomy, and so on.

See also Chapter 1(e) and (f), Chapter 2(d)–(f), and (m), and Chapter 4(k).

Further Reading

For general discussions of educational and scientific texts see Fulk and Cain (2003, pp. 155–63), Hollis (2001), and Lendinara (1991). For more information on schools and schoolmasters see Lutz (1977). For a list of 'set texts', there is a mid-11th-century manuscript held in Cambridge University Library (Gg.5.35). See Anderson (2002) on the *Colloquy* providing an interesting observation of everyday life and social classes in Anglo-Saxon England.

(h)   Poetry

As noted in previous sections, surviving Old English literature includes both prose and poetry. We have discussed prose elsewhere and have also looked at the main types of text produced, and the known authors. Now we shall turn to the more studied of the two mediums – poetry – and to some of the more famous texts from the period.

To begin with there are a few key points we need to observe about Old English poetry.

Titles

First, the poems that survive to us are all untitled. The names we give them (e.g. *Beowulf, The Dream of the Rood*) are inventions of later scholars – and no such headings appear in the manuscripts. Occasionally this can lead to some confusion with different editors over time having different names for the same poems. However, nowadays the titles tend to be settled on especially after the appearance of Krapp and Dobie's *Anglo-Saxon Poetic Records* (*ASPR*). This presented a series of six volumes during the period 1931 to 1953, and these are commonly abbreviated to *ASPR I*, *ASPR II*, etc. This is also often used as a standard to judge other editions by.

Manuscripts

For the most part the poems survive only in single extant witnesses, i.e. there is only one surviving copy of each poem. This is different from prose, of course, where we often find several versions of the same text. There are four major manuscripts that contain Old English poetry and these are:

(1)   The 'Beowulf Manuscript' (London, British Library, Cotton MS. Vitellius A. XV)
(2)   The 'Junius Manuscript' (Oxford, Bodleian Library MS. Junius 11)
(3)   The 'Vercelli Book' (Vercelli, Biblioteca Capitolare cxvii)
(4)   The 'Exeter Book' (Exeter, Exeter Cathedral MS. 3501)

Here we give the common title of the manuscript, and then in brackets the correct shelfmark (i.e. the official catalogue reference in the hosting library). However, this is somewhat misleading, as although it is true that the bulk of Old English poetry survives in these codices (all dating from around the end of the 10th to the early 11th centuries) a few other poems survive in other manuscripts (e.g. *Maxims*), in other texts (e.g. *The Battle of Brunanburgh* appears as part of the *Anglo-Saxon Chronicle*), or in later transcripts where no medieval manuscript survives (e.g. *The Battle of Maldon*).

The texts in the manuscripts are written out continuously and to the casual observer may appear as prose – at the very least very different from the way they appear in printed editions. Yet on closer inspection they are clearly verse, following the rules we outline below.

Authorship

There has been much debate over the years as to the nature of authorship in relationship to Old English poetry. The 'liedertheorists',[17] for example, approached Old English poems from the stance that they were in fact collations of earlier lays, and thus the focal point of study should be the separate stories that went into such longer poems as *Beowulf*. To them, the search was not for the poet of *Beowulf* but for the stories that lay behind the poem. A similar effect (but for different reasons) was achieved by the oral-formulaic theorists (see below). They argued that what was presented in the manuscripts was simply a recording of one of many versions of that text, and in performance the poem could change dramatically from event to event, and from *scop* to *scop*. In effect this again made the discussion of the 'poet', i.e. a single author of the text, redundant.

Discussing authorship when it comes to poetry is undoubtedly problematic. As with the lack of titles, there is no signature at the end of poems, and no attribution anywhere. For the most part, then, all the Old English poems are anonymous – we simply have no idea who composed them. The two exceptions to this are the poets Cædmon and Cynewulf.[18] Bede tells us the tale of Cædmon, and provides a Latin paraphrase of the first poem Cædmon wrote as a lowly herdsman at Abbess Hild's Abbey in Whitby (the Old English text of this poem, known as *Cædmon's Hymn* – see below – was circulated in the margins of *Ecclesiastical History*). Although Bede states that Cædmon also wrote many other poems it is generally assumed that these have

---

[17] A critical approach adopted by 19th-century German scholars (literally 'ballad theory').

[18] A third possibility is King Alfred, who may have been responsible for the *Metres of Boethius*.

been lost. Cynewulf is a different matter. We have no knowledge of who he was or where or when he lived, but we do have his name. In the closing lines of four poems (*Elene*, *The Fates of the Apostles*, *Christ II*, and *Juliana*) we have a series of runes, intertwined successfully with the text, which spell out 'CYNEWULF' (or a form of this). These seem to be an appeal by the poet for prayers from the audience for his soul. This is interesting for many reasons, not least of which being that one can only work out the puzzle by viewing the runes on the page – thus showing that Cynewulf clearly knew that some people would read his poems (as opposed to simple hearing them).

Dating

When it comes to dating Old English poems there are three dates one may have to consider:

(1)   If possible, the date of the events depicted in the poem (e.g. *The Battle of Maldon* tells of a battle in AD991).
(2)   The date the poem was written down, i.e. the date of the manuscript (when it comes to the four major codices we clearly are looking at dates around the year AD1000 give or take 25 years).
(3)   The date the poem was composed.

The latter is by far and away the most contentious. With so little evidence to go on, and indeed against a background of discussion around whether the poem is actually a unified text from a single author or not, for the most part it is impossible to date with any certainty the original period of composition. For example, scholars have argued for dating the composition of *Beowulf* from the 7th century to the 11th century and the discussion still continues.

Structure

Old English poetry is highly structured and adheres to strict metrical patterns. A single line from *Beowulf* will illustrate this effectively:

> grimre gūðe,   gif þū Grendles dearst   (l. 527)
> 'at the grim battle, if you (of) Grendel dare . . .'

This is typeset in the accepted manner for editions of Old English poetry. The line is short, divided into two halves with a space in the middle indicating the metrical pause (the caesura). Here we note this as line 527, but in most modern editions poetry is numbered only every five or ten lines in the margin (e.g. 520, 525, 530, etc.).

Every metrically regular line in Old English poetry can be broken into two half-lines as above. We term these two halves 'a' and 'b' so *grimre gūðe* would be line 527a, for example. These half-lines are often short, but have a minimum of four syllables. Each half-line also tends to have two stresses and these fall on 'meaningful' elements in the verse. Most importantly the half-lines are linked by alliteration (in 'a' one or both of the stresses alliterate with the first stress of 'b').

Let us look at this line again:

/ X / X (stress pattern)

grimre gūðe, gif þū Grendles dearst

1 2 3 4 (syllables)

For line 527a we have numbered the syllables underneath the line, but above it we have marked the stress patterns. The common way to do this is / = stress, X = unstress. Finally we have shown the alliteration on the hard 'G' sound by bold type. One may wonder why the 'g' in *gif* has not been underlined. This is because it means 'if' and thus it is an unstressed function word and not one of the 'meaningful elements', i.e. words with a full lexical meaning, such as nouns or adjectives, which are stressed in sentences and alliterate in verse.

The stress patterns in Old English poetry are notable because they tend to fall into five major types (the above one of '/X/X' or 'stress/unstress/stress/unstress' is very common). This was first systematically described by Eduard Sievers in 1885 and he termed these five patterns A, B, C, D, and E (see further explanation in Chapter 4(g)). Students will often come across reference to 'Sievers' five types', and mention of 'stress pattern C'. A lot of material has been published in this area, analysing the possible application of Sievers five-types and how comprehensive they are. However, for a good overview see Scragg (1991), including a discussion of how the stress patterns can be used for poetic effect.

The poetry also employs complex syntactic structures (certainly compared with the relatively simple word order evidenced in prose). This can present many problems to the student when attempting to translate the text, especially when coupled with variation (see below and Chapter 4(c)). We must remember, however, that this complicated syntax would also have heightened the attention of the audience, allowing the poet to employ plays on words.

Poetic devices

There are several devices we can identify as being common to Old English poetry (we will look at the use of formulas in more detail below). First there is 'variation'. This is where an object, person, or idea is described repeatedly but with some variation over a short span of lines. For example, in the opening of *Cædmon's Hymn* below (ll. 1–4a),[19] the Lord is described in 6 instances (underlined) but they are all slightly different:

> Nū sculon herigean   heofonrīces Weard,
> Meotodes meahte   ond His mōdgeþanc,
> weorc Wuldorfæder,   swā Hē wundra gehwæs,
> ēce Drihten . . .

> Now we must praise the Guardian of heaven,
> the Creator's might and His purpose,
> the work of the Father of glory, as He each of the wonders,
> the eternal Lord . . .

Next there is repetition or parallelism (the two are often used synonymously). Here, a grammatical structure or idea is repeated or paralleled elsewhere in the poem (whereas variation is the repeated description of the same object or concept). This can work over a few lines, or over a whole poem; thus the burials that begin and end *Beowulf* can be seen as parallels or repetitions at a macro-level. Orchard (1997) also notes that parallelisms are used in prose.

We already know that alliteration is used to link half-lines but it can also link two lines – 'double alliteration'; or the same alliterative pattern can be employed over several lines – 'ornamental alliteration'.

Rhyme, or assonance, is also occasionally used as in *The Ruin* (ll. 5–8):

> scearde scūrbeorge   scorene, gedrorene,   5
> ældo undereotone.   Eorðgrāp hafað
> waldend wyrhtan,   forweorone, geleorene

---

[19] The *Hymn* appears in Bede's *Ecclesiastical History* – a prose text from AD731. It appears in many anthologies, often complete with the surrounding story as Bede records it.

the broken protectors from the showers, [are] shorn, fallen,   5
undermined by age. Earth's grip has
the master builders, withered, departed . . .'

Here we can see rhyme employed in the words *scorene /gedrorene / undereotene / forweorone /geleorene*. The scheme though is internal to the line (or lines), and is sporadic. End-rhyme, where the rhyme falls repeatedly on the last word in the line, is rare (certainly in comparison with later verse) but was occasionally employed (as in the aptly termed *The Rhyming Poem*).

There is undoubtedly a poetic diction, i.e. a notable difference in the words and sentence structure used in poetry from those used in prose. A glance at the *Historical Thesaurus of Old English* (see Roberts et al., 1995, and http://leo.englang.arts.gla.ac.uk/oethesaurus/) shows repeated examples of words that only ever appear in poetry. One example is the use of compound words and especially 'kennings' (where two separate words are brought together to mean a third thing, e.g. 'whale + road = the whale's road = the sea'). There is also a notable lack of definite articles, prepositions, and conjunctions, undoubtedly due to the fact that the metrical rules of verse restrained the poets considerably (compared with the freedom of prose). They needed tight constructions and dispensed with superfluous words. We must remember that an Old English noun did not need a definite or indefinite article and meanings expressed by articles in Modern English were often rendered in other ways, such as through context. The poet in addition would also choose terms that contained multiple meanings or ambiguities.

The internal structure of Old English verse is also notable. On a smaller scale there are so-called 'envelope patterns' (where a section of lines is enveloped by a phrase or word used at the beginning and end – i.e. opening and closing the envelope); or so-called ring compositions, a chiastic device that repeats ideas or phrases along the pattern of '*abcba*'. For example, an idea or phrase that appears in the first line is repeated at the end, the idea or phrase that appears in the second line is repeated in the second from last section, and so on, with a single unique idea at the middle – the so-called 'kernel'.

There are other poetic devices that are used in Old English verse, but the above examples illustrate the key features and its complex artistry.

Formulas

Special mention should be given to the use of formulas in Old English poetry. In short it has long been observed that the same phrases, often covering a half-line, appear again and again across various poems. These we term a 'formula'. Two stances can be taken to explain this phenomenon. First, it could show borrowing by poets (e.g. with the poems *Beowulf* and *Andreas* there is notable overlap in the repeated use of formulas, which may imply the poets were aware of the other works and borrowed from them, or indeed were the same poet). The second approach is that taken by those supporting the 'oral-formulaic' theory. This was notably applied to Old English poetry by Magoun in 1953. In a very important article Magoun argued that the repeated use of formulas that one can observe in Old English poetry is nothing to do with poets borrowing from other poems, or to do with common authorship, but instead stems from the nature of their composition. Magoun, basing his work on that of Milan Parry and Albert Lord, argued that Old English poetry was orally composed and performed, and passed down orally from generation to generation. Understandably then, the poetry that was transmitted in this way changed, and existed in multiple versions. In their unique performance poets may have kept to the general plot or theme but they would have drawn from their repertoire and collections of formulas as they saw fit, to satisfy the immediate demands of a live recitation. In short, the use of formulas showed clearly that Old English poetry was composed orally by illiterate poets and passed down orally.

Although there is undoubtedly an attraction to the oral-formulaic theory, in that it explains some aspects of Old English poetic diction, it has lost much of its prominence since the 1960s. Mainly this is due to the fact that it was shown that some poets who we know were literate (such as Alcuin or Cynewulf) also employed formulas, and in the case of Cynewulf were writing for the reader (see above). Therefore, Magoun's assertion that the presence of formulas immediately indicated oral composition and performance does not stand scrutiny. Yet at the same time it is undoubtedly true that many poems would have been performed and composed orally, certainly during the pre-literate period, but also probably later in Christian Anglo-Saxon England. Oral-formulaic theory explains the origin of formulaic style in oral pre-literate culture, but not its persistence in later learned and written poetry.

The study of formulas is similar to the analysis of 'type-scenes'. A 'type-scene' is a theme, event, or situation that appears again and again in Old English poetry. 'Type-scenes' were associated with their own vocabulary and formulas and tell us about the ideas that interested audiences in the period and how the poets introduced these. Common 'type-scenes' that are often mentioned are 'the arming of the warrior', 'the beasts of battle', 'the hero on the beach' (a scene where the hero arrives by sea and appears on the beach with his retainers), and many others.

This extremely brief introduction to the basics of Old English poetry has pointed to several areas for investigation. In short, the poetry from the Anglo-Saxon period is highly structured. Drawing all the above together we can see:

- the poems that survive (mainly in the four poetical codices) are untitled, undated, and for the most part anonymous (with the exception of Cynewulf and Cædmon);
- verse lines are divided into two halves linked together by alliteration;
- each half-line generally adheres to one of five stress patterns and their variants;
- other poetic devices employed include rhyme, special vocabulary, synonyms, special metaphors such as kennings, variation, and repetition/parallels;
- the use of formulas (phrases that are repeated from poem to poem) was taken by the oral-formulaic theorists as proof that the poetry was composed, performed, and disseminated orally by illiterate poets; but it has since been shown that the appearance of formulas is not sufficient proof of this.

See also Chapter 2(d) and (j) and Chapter 4(c)–(e) and (g).

Further Reading

Getting access to Old English poems is relatively easy. In addition to the texts we recommend in Chapter 2(a) and Chapter 4(a), readers could also look at Alexander (1966), Bradley (1982), Crossley-Holland (2002), Hamer (2006), and Muir (2000). Crossley-Holland presents only translations but mixes this with some prose. Bradley provides the most complete collections of poems (again only in translation), and interestingly chooses to sequence them in the order they survive in the manuscripts. For introductory articles on the nature of Old English verse see Calder (1979), O'Brien O'Keeffe (1994), Robinson (2001), and Scragg (1991). Concerning oral-formulaic theory readers should look to Acker (1998), Olsen (1988), and Orchard (1997). For material specific to Cynewulf, see Bjork (2001) and Calder (1981). For a multimedia version of *Cædmon's Hymn*, see O'Donnell (2005). See also Chapter 4(c) on translating Old English, Chapter 4(g) on metre, and Chapter 4(j) on editorial practices.

(i)   Elegies and Transience

A number of Old English poems are often grouped together under the title 'elegies'. These are: *The Ruin*, *The Wanderer*, *The Seafarer*, *Resignation*, *The Rhyming Poem*, *Wulf and Eadwacer*, *The Wife's Lament*, *The Husband's Message*, and *Deor*. However, the differences between these poems are widely recognised and the single term 'elegy' is often dismissed as insufficient to encapsulate all of them. Furthermore, elegiac episodes also appear in other poems (notably in wisdom poems – see Chapter 2(m); and consistently in *Beowulf*, see Chapter 2(n)) and thus the list presented above is far from conclusive. Nevertheless, the category has become so much ingrained into medieval scholarship that students will consistently come across the term and the group, and thus it requires exploration (see also a discussion of post-Conquest lyrical poetry and its relationship to Old English elegies in Chapter 3(f)).

In classical literature the term 'elegy' was used for any poem in dactylic hexameter and pentameter, commonly known as the elegiac metre. Yet in English literature, certainly since the 17th century, the term refers to a poem discussing personal or general loss, often in a pastoral setting (a much-used example being Thomas Gray's *Elegy Written in a Country Churchyard* from 1751). The Old English poems tend to fall under this latter definition for several reasons:

- they focus on both individual loss and themes of general loss;
- they recognise the transience of life and earthly glory;
- they often concentrate on themes of separation or exile; occasionally using the sea as a boundary;
- they balance the present (cold, wintry, deprived of joy) with the past (warmth, happiness).

A good example of this is a poem called *The Ruin*. This survives in one of the four major codices of Anglo-Saxon poetry, known as 'The Exeter Book'. It describes a ruined city (probably Bath) complete with crumbling roofs and walls, linking the decay directly to the men and women who had built the buildings and occupied them but now have passed away. This builds on the *'de excidio'* ('about ruination') tradition as seen in such texts as Gildas's *De excidio Britanniae*, and Venantius's *De excidio Thoringiæ* (*The Destruction of Thuringia* – a region in modern-day Germany). In this, Venantius describes how:

> The palace which once flourished with courtly elegance is now roofed with gloomy embers instead of arches. A pale ash has smothered the lofty buildings which used to gleam and shine, adorned with gold'. (Allen and Calder, 1976, p. 137)

This is strikingly similar to the description in *The Ruin*.

The Old English poet also chooses to set the present day in wintry grey surroundings, comparing this directly with the warmth and colour of the past. The poem thus centres on the theme of transience – the passing of worldly glory – which is a major topic in Old English literature. Indeed a common phrase used is *lif is lǣne* or 'life is transitory' (literally 'life is on loan'). Simply put, this refers to the transient nature of worldly joys and possessions, i.e. they will pass to dust and will not last. Instead importance is attached to the way one behaves in preparation for what is to come – namely the eternal afterlife (in keeping, to a certain extent, with the Germanic heroic ideal of reputation). In Christian terms it is the heavenly life that is important, and how easily you get there depends upon your actions on earth. The only glory that is permanent is God's. As Alcuin explained *'amemus eternal et non peritara'* ('let us love the eternal not the transient' – see Chapter 1(f) for how this relates to general philosophical beliefs).

This concentration on transience is not surprising, perhaps, when one considers the harshness of life in the period; and is witnessed also in the preoccupation in homilies with eschatological themes (eschatology concentrates on the end of things, or the apocalypse). The evidence of worldly transience was all around the Anglo-Saxons – there was the collapse of the Roman Empire in the early period, and then the destruction of their own kingdoms by the Vikings.

Two elegies which are often anthologised and are worth studying in more detail are *The Wanderer* and *The Seafarer*. Both poems, like *The Ruin*, also survive in single copies in the Exeter Book. Beginning with *The Wanderer*, this is a powerful poem detailing an individual's exile from society and their lonely wanderings. We must recall that exile in Anglo-Saxon England, i.e. being without family ties or the protection of the *comitatus*, could well have proved fatal. At the same time the poem touches on themes of general loss. In this sense then, it conforms to the standard elements of an elegy noted above.

The poem opens with an image of a lonely individual suffering hardship (ll. 1–4). This is the wanderer of the title, who we discover to be an outcast, pacing the earth without the solace of friends, relations, or a lord (ll. 8–10). The poet then proceeds to explore a range of ideas and topics familiar to other Old English poems, opening up from a single incident (the exiled wanderer of the poem's title) to explore wider issues about the nature of suffering, and the transitory nature of existence. Thus the personal loss becomes a general loss.

As it stands it is a Christian poem. Yet on the face of it, it is not concerned with any great theological debate, instead concentrating on the plight and personal loss of one human being – the wanderer. They tell us of their loss, and exile, and how they wander the lands seeking comfort and friendship. They dream of the past and contrast it with the harsh present (as happened in *The Ruin*). In their mind they can summon up images of past joys and friends but they cannot capture them forever. On wakening, such images simply disappear and 'swim away' (ll. 41–8). The wanderer is lonely because they have outlived all of their friends. They extrapolate from their own situation the observation that all worldly glory and comforts seem transitory.

In a famous passage, known as the *ubi sunt* section (i.e. 'where are'), because it is based on a device employed by earlier Latin poets, the wanderer asks:

'Hwǣr cwōm mearg? Hwǣr cwōm mago?   Hwǣr cwōm
  māþþumgyfa?
Hwǣr cwōm symbla gesetu?   Hwǣr sindon seledrēamas?
Ēalā, beorht bune!   Ēalā, byrnwiga!
Ēalā, þēodnes þrym!   Hū sēo þrāg gewāt,   95
genāp under nihthelm,   swā hēo nō wǣre.

Where has gone the horse? Where has gone the young man?
  Where has gone the giver of treasure?
Where has gone the dwellings of the feasts? Where are the
  joys of the hall?
Alas, the bright cup! Alas, the mailed warrior!
Alas, the glory of the prince! How the time went,   95
grew dark under night's helm, as if it never were.

But the wanderer then reminds us that everything passes, and all is on loan (ll. 108–10). Yet at the same time a person must not bemoan their loss and instead must hold resolute (or 'keep a stiff upper lip', ll. 112–13). Fortitude, to the wanderer, is seen as a distinct virtue, for suffering can in itself lead to wisdom (ll. 64–5), as if to say that it is necessary to bear a loss in order to get things into perspective and understand true values. This offers *consolatio* (or 'consolation'). The poet appeals, therefore, to all lonely voyagers and wanderers in exile – which to a Christian outlook is everyone, as we are all exiled from Eden and, temporarily, from Heaven.

The Seafarer also survives in the Exeter Book. It deals with personal grievance, but the loss, expected in an elegy, is difficult to identify. It starts with a vivid picture of the hardship of life at sea (ll. 1–33), and the loneliness experienced by the subject of the poem, a seafarer (ll. 14–16). He tells of the harsh conditions he had to endure, and the cold and the desolate lifestyle (ll. 8–10, etc.). As in *The Wanderer* the separation experienced by the exile (this time on the sea) from the comforts offered on land is accentuated, and familiar motifs, such as the sea-birds replacing the companionship of friends, are repeated (ll. 19b–26). Yet the seafarer seems compelled to go back to the sea, time and time again, even though he knows he will experience hardship there (ll. 33–8, and 58–64). This allows the poet to broaden out to wider themes, contrasting the life at sea with the joys on land (ll. 27–30, and 44–5, etc.), but pointing out that the man who does not undergo the trials of the sea cannot reach true wisdom (ll. 12, 27, and 55). The poet considers the wisdom one can receive through suffering, and the inevitably transient nature of worldly joys and glory (ll. 80–96). The seafarer is saying that although we may surround ourselves with comforts and luxuries, these do not last, and instead we should be preparing ourselves for the real journey, the one after death when we journey to God (ll. 117–24). As Treharne states (2004, p. 48), the poem 'evolves into a universal debate on the mortality of mankind, the futility of earthly wealth, the morality of Christian living, and the need to be judged worthy of *lof* ("praise")'.

The main discussions around *The Seafarer* concentrate on two things. First its tripartite structure, with the personal account at the beginning, the widening out to consider broader themes, and the final Christian didactic ending. In the past some scholars considered this as a clear sign that the Christian elements are later, somewhat forceful additions; but most now believe the extant version to have been a complete composition from the beginning, and that the final exposition is in keeping with the earlier personal journey. Secondly, there is the question of whether it is an allegory of a person's life, or a literal representation of seafaring. Many scholars agree with Dorothy Whitelock that the poem is more of a symbolic journey rather than a real nautical experience. Whitelock suggested that the poem specifically referenced the medieval concept of the *peregrinus pro amore Dei* ('pilgrim for the love of God'), in which the practice was to wander or set sail without any true direction, in an attempt to understand further God's plan. However, others see the allegory to be tied more to the natural journey of life, through old age, death, and to the afterlife.

Most courses in Old English will cover the 'elegies' at some point, and therefore it is worth repeating some of the important issues raised above:

- There is a common list of poems that come under the term 'Old English elegies', but this is constantly open to discussion, as: (a) this list is far from complete; (b) it implies a uniformity under the definition 'elegy' which is clearly not evident.
- The common features that we see in most of these poems are: separation, loss, exile, hardship, comparison of the past (generally good) with the present (harsh).
- Most important, in keeping with other Old English texts, is the concentration on the concept of transience (embodied by the Old English word *lǣne*). This states that worldly joys and possessions will fade and vanish (and thus by extension are meaningless), and that true importance should be attached to spiritual virtues, which will prepare the Christian soul for the afterlife.
- The elegies draw on Anglo-Saxon literary tradition, as can be seen in their close integration with other genres and the occurrence of elegiac passages in other types of poetry, but also on themes and ideas which were common in medieval Christian literature as a whole.

See also   Chapter 1(b), Chapter 2(d), (h), (j), (m) and (n), and Chapter 3(f).

Further Reading

For introductory studies on the elegies, see Conner (2005), Fell (1991), Green (1983), and Klinck (1992). For Alcuin's view of the relative value of earthly and heavenly glory, see his *De clade Lindisfarnensis monasterii* ('On the Destruction of the Monastery at Lindisfarne').

(j)   Battle Poetry and Concepts of Heroism

Bearing in mind the bellicose image of the early medieval period, and the Anglo-Saxon/Viking wars, it is surprising to see just how little

Old English battle poetry there is. Only a few Old English poems stand out as directly relating to a specific battle, e.g. *The Battle of Brunanburgh*, *The Battle of Maldon*, or *The Fight at Finnsburgh* (all three are commonly referred to by their shortened titles – *Brunanburgh*, *Maldon*, and *Finnsburgh*). Yet at the same time we should be aware of poems that may not at first suggest they detail an armed conflict, but:

- have battles included as part of wider story (e.g. *Beowulf*, *Judith*);
- allude to battles or past conflicts (*Widsith*, *Deor*);
- are incomplete and thus may have originally contained a battle (*Waldere*); or
- use the imagery of battles and heroic conflict in new and interesting ways (*Exodus*, *Genesis*, *The Dream of the Rood* – see Chapter 3).

A battle itself needs no real explanation – it is simply the coming together of two opposing forces in armed combat. However, underlying much battle poetry, and indeed other poems, including directly Christian verse, is the concept of heroism. This perhaps does need some elaboration as it is often referred to.

The 'Germanic' heroic ideal (so-called because it is witnessed in other Germanic texts, such as the Norse sagas) is problematic. As Toswell states:

The heroic code of Anglo-Saxon society continues to be a commonplace of the subject. Such a code is, however, based much in the reader's preconception of what is honourable and noble. It is also a code remade in each generation, for each war, according to the sociocultural necessities of that environment. (Toswell, 1996, p. 503)

Yet it is referenced so often that a few of the key concepts need to be outlined. In short, the heroic ideal can be summed up as extolling:

- bravery in the face of overwhelming/impossible odds;
- acceptance of a (usually harsh) situation;
- the resolve to carry out declared intentions willingly;
- a desire to forge a reputation for yourself (posthumously if need be) – encapsulated by the Old English word *lof* ('praise, glory');

- desire to be judged favourably by your companions – *dōm* ('judgement', hence 'Doomsday' or 'Judgement day');
- loyalty to one's superiors.

For example in *Maldon* (ll. 312–13) towards the end of the poem, the remaining English warriors are encircled by the Viking armies, and the aging warrior Byrhtwold declares:

> Hige sceal þē heardra,   heorte þē cēnre,
> Mōd sceal þē māre,   þē ūre mægen lȳtlað

> Resolve must be firmer, heart the braver,
> courage the greater, though our strength diminishes.

Furthermore in *Beowulf* (ll. 1384b–1389), the hero, in attempting to comfort the distraught King Hrothgar, states:

> Sēlre bið æghwæm
> þæt hē his frēond wrece   þonne hē fela murne.   1385
> Ūre æghwylc sceal   ende gebīdan
> worolde līfes;   wyrce sē þe mōte
> dōmes ær dēaþe;   þæt bið drihtguman
> unlifigendum   æfter sēlest.

> Better it is for each one
> that he avenge his friend than mourn greatly.   1385
> Each of us must experience the end
> of worldly life; he who might achieve
> favourable judgement before death; that is the best
> afterwards to the unliving warrior.

Here Beowulf concentrates on the concepts of glory and judgement. These are praised so often in Old English verse that they must have been key tenets of the heroic ethos (e.g. see *Maxims I*, l. 80, where it declares *Dōm biþ selast* or 'esteem is the best').

Kaske (1958) added two more aspects to an Old English hero – *sapientia* ('wisdom') and *fortitudo* ('bravery'), drawing on models outlined in earlier patristic writers[20] (thus fusing the two). He argued that the model hero from a Christian perspective would also have to have both of these, and applied his theory to the characters in *Beowulf*.

[20] For example, Isidore of Seville (*Etymologiae*, I, xxxix, 9).

Added to the above characteristics of the hero, is their relationship to the rest of society. The concept of the individual, roaming at will in a nomadic fashion (much beloved of Western films for example), is not evident in Old English literature. Indeed to be outside of society and thus to be without the support of your tribe, lord, friends, and family, was one of the bleakest prospects that could be faced by someone in the Anglo-Saxon period (as is evident in *The Wanderer* and *Deor* – see Chapter 1(b) and Chapter 2(i)). Undoubtedly as legal structures came into place, partly, it is suggested, to protect the clergy who were without tribal support, the problems of exile may have lessened. However, in the early social structures each person depended on the other and the hero was no exception. Specifically he was interwoven into the *comitatus* ('following' or 'band') either as a retainer (i.e. he served his lord and was thus part of the lord's *comitatus*) or as a leader of his own retinue (when the hero was the ruler and thus enjoyed the loyalty of his followers). The hero could be part of the *duguð* (tried and tested warriors) or the *geoguð* (young warriors eager to achieve glory). Beowulf, in the poem, goes through all of these – at the beginning of the poem he is a young member of Hygelac's *comitatus*, and eager for fame; in the middle we are told he has become the most trusted warrior of Hygelac's retainers; and at the end, by the time he is king, he commands his own band of followers. The relationship of the *comitatus* to the leader is also crucial to understanding some concepts in heroic literature. In summary, the members of the *comitatus* are loyal to their lord, defending him in battle.[21] He, in return, rewards them with land, property, and/or treasure, often gained from the expansion of the kingdom. Or, as Wormald describes it (1991, p. 11):

> The fundamental principle was that the warrior owed loyalty (in theory to the point of death[22]) in return for his lord's generous reward.

---

[21] Many studies refer, at this point, to the Roman historian Tacitus who, in his 1st-century book *Germania*, which described Germanic tribal practices, stated: 'When they go into battle, it is a disgrace for the chief to be surpassed in valour, a disgrace for his followers not to equal the valour of the chief. And it is an infamy and a reproach for life to have survived the chief, and returned from the field. To defend, to protect him, to ascribe one's own brave deeds to his renown, is the height of loyalty.' However see Chapter 2(d) for the historical accuracy of Tacitus.

[22] This means that the warriors should not leave the battlefield if their lord has died, and should fight to the death.

How far we can take this is debatable as much of it is based on preconceptions derived from sources which are not necessarily historically accurate. For two takes on this subject see Woolf (1976) and Frank (1990). Neveretheless we can certainly say that the ideal warrior is often defined as 'loyal', and a common term for a lord is a 'ring-giver', showing the relationship the other way (see *Beowulf*, ll. 64–86, for an idealised description of a good king).

One should not assume, however, that this encapsulates the Anglo-Saxon philosophy entirely. As the period progressed, and perhaps as a result of the increased stability within the nation, a more developed view emerged. We begin to see the tripartite categorisation of society into those who fought, those who prayed, and those who worked. Each is important for society, but increasingly we see reference to, and elevation of, the spiritual struggle (waged by the clergy) in conjunction with the physical battles such as those waged against the Vikings.

Yet returning to the notion of heroism let us now look at the battle poems and consider two of these – *The Battle of Maldon* and *The Battle of Brunanburgh* – to see some common themes and devices. Both are possibly pieces of propaganda it should be noted, stirring the English into unity and action. The former, though, tells the tale of an English defeat; where, led by their leader Byrhtnoth, the English fight a pitched battle against the Viking invaders in the year 991. *Brunanburgh*, on the other hand, outlines the victory in the year 937 by King Æthelstan over a combined army of Vikings, Welsh, and Scots. *Maldon* survives in a later transcript (the original manuscript was lost), and is incomplete; whereas *Brunanburgh* is one of a selection of poems that survives in the prose *Anglo-Saxon Chronicle*.

Taking the latter first, *Brunanburgh* is a simpler poem briefly outlining the details of the battle, praising the victors, i.e. the English. Although it is not a particularly good poem, it does contain some typical elements of battle verse:

- The main protagonists are named (Æthelstan, Eadward, Eadmund, Anlaf, etc.).
- Geographical details are given (in this case place names – Brunanburgh, Dingesmere, Dublin).
- Realistic details of the fighting are given such as types of weapons, shields, and troop formations.
- The poem follows the chronology of the battle (i.e. up until the departure of the defeated Vikings and their allies).

- The slaughter of the warriors is described in realistic terms. To accentuate this carnage the poet uses the common 'beasts of battle' type-scene, in which carrion creatures (commonly a raven, eagle, and wolf) are listed to either report the forthcoming slaughter, or in this case, highlight the bloodshed.
- The poet is undoubtedly biased, extolling the virtues of the English and using negative terminology for the enemy.

Combined, all of these create an effect of realism, and thus suggest that the details described, however heroic, are factual; witnessed by the poet or by somebody he knew.

Maldon uses similar devices but is a much more developed poem. As mentioned earlier it tells of a defeat in 991. It should be noted that it is incomplete, but when we join the battle the leader of the English (Byrhtnoth) is marshalling his troops on the river bank whilst the Vikings are positioned on an island opposite. A narrow causeway separates the two. We know this to be geographically accurate, and indeed the island (Northey) and the causeway are still visible at Maldon (in northern Essex). The Vikings attempt to force their way across the causeway, but fail to make an impression, and ask for permission to come across to the mainland to engage in full battle. In a hotly debated piece, Byrhtnoth allows them passage and is said to do so *for his ofermōde*, commonly translated as 'because of his pride' (l. 89). The question of whether this is a criticism of Byrhtnoth (*ofermōde* can be translated in other ways), and whether it was a tactical necessity to face the Vikings in the field at that moment (rather than allowing them to harass the coast at will), has been discussed at length (see Chapter 4(a) for a suggestion as to how one might answer this). Nevertheless the facts of the battle thereafter are straightforward. The Vikings are allowed across and the full battle ensues. After initial successes the English lose the momentum especially when Byrhtnoth himself is killed. Some of the English take this as a signal to escape, much to the poet's criticism, and thereafter the result is without question. The final part of the poem details individual English warriors who successively make heroic speeches before going to their death.

There are many comparisons to *Brunanburgh* but also to the earlier portrayals of heroism.

- The main English protagonists are named (Byrhtnoth, Wulfmær, Ælfnoth, etc.); however, the Vikings are anonymous figures, described in negative general terms such as 'heathens'.

- Geographical details are given. The Maldon countryside is described accurately (Northey Island, the river, the nearby woods, etc.).
- Realistic details of the fighting are given; such as the types of weapons, shields, and troop formations.
- The poem follows the chronology of the battle (up until the monologues by the individual English warriors).
- The slaughter of the warriors is described in realistic terms. Again, to accentuate this, the poet uses the 'beasts of battle' type-scene (ll. 106–7), this, time the raven and eagle.
- The poet is undoubtedly biased, extolling the virtues of the English and using negative terminology for the enemy.
- This time the *comitatus* is emphasised. Byrhtnoth continually makes reference to his allegiance to his ruler King Æthelræd, and the retainers at the end fight to defend their fallen lord.
- The poet openly criticises the warriors who flee on Byrhtnoth's horse (Godric, Godwin, and Godwig, ll. 186–201). They break the oath of the *comitatus* by leaving the field of battle alive when their lord lies dead. A common theme also, of young warriors boasting in the mead hall of their prowess but failing to live up to this in battle, is picked up by the poet (ll. 188–201).
- The depth of the *comitatus* relationship is also emphasised by the poet through the selection of the individual warriors he focuses on. We have a warrior Leofsunu (l. 244), a peasant Dunnerer (l. 255), Æscferth a Northumbrian hostage (l. 265), and so on. All fulfil their side of the relationship by fighting to the death, and their speeches, almost resembling maxims at times, encapsulate the ideals of heroism.
- The final speech by Byrhtwold (ll. 312–19), partly quoted above, is a model of bravery and resolve.

The poet also presents an interesting mixture of perspectives on the battle. At times he concentrates on the actions of individuals, then shifts his point of view to a more global perspective describing troop movements, and then returns to the individual. This device, typical of modern war films, allows one to understand the events of the battle as well as seeing the personal struggles and sacrifices.

One could consider that many of the heroic ideals outlined above go some way to describing the Anglo-Saxon view of masculinity. It is certainly true that in most cases these virtues are discussed, encouraged, or demonstrated by male characters; but that is not always the case. In some instances we can see these also centring on heroic female characters such as saints or the poetic Judith.

There are several key concepts surrounding the notion of heroism and the depiction of battles in Old English. These include:

- There is a well-defined, and probably ancestral set of principles surrounding the notion of heroism – most notably the elevation of *dōm* ('judgement') and *lof* ('praise').
- The heroes are usually placed in the wider context of the *comitatus* relationship. As well as being gauged by *dōm* and *lof*, therefore, their actions according to the rules of the *comitatus* also serve as measures by which the audience would have judged them.
- Battles in Old English poetry seem to follow accepted patterns. They also use set type-scenes such as the famous 'beasts of battle'.
- Anglo-Saxon attitudes to war and warfare developed during the period, moving to concepts of spiritual warfare.
- There is a tension between Germanic heroic ideals and those espoused by Christianity, but the poets attempted to accommodate both to further the cause of conversion (see Chapter 3).

See also   Chapter 1(b) and (f), and Chapter 2(b) and (c).

Further Reading

For further studies of heroism see Bremmer (2005), Hill (2000), and O'Brien O'Keeffe (1991). For a female perspective see Chance (1986). If you are interested in kingship and the structure of society, see Chapter 1(c).

(k)   Riddles

In terms of the number of individual poems, a very common type found in Old English are the so-called 'riddles'. These are short poems which set out to describe aspects of everyday life but in the form of a puzzle. These riddles are contained in the Exeter Book in three continuous sequences.[23] Around 95 survive there but scholars debate the exact number as the scribe is not clear at times when one poem finishes and a new one starts. We should also remember that

---

[23] One riddle from the Exeter Book also survives in another manuscript now residing in Leiden.

other Old English texts, such as the *Solomon and Saturn* series (see Chapter 2(m)) or the puzzling *Wulf and Eadwacer*, also contain elements of riddles. This indicates to many scholars that this form of intricate verbal puzzling appealed greatly to the Anglo-Saxons.

The riddles are usually referred to by a number, e.g. *Riddle 5* (see, for example, Treharne, 2004, pp. 66–74), but this is problematic bearing in mind the discussions around the exact number of individual poems. Occasionally riddles are given a title based on their solution (e.g. The *'Moth'* Riddle). All conform more or less to the accepted rules of Old English poetry.

The Old English riddles are closely linked to earlier Latin *enigmata* ('mysteries'), which often numbered 100 per collection, suggesting that a few have been lost from the Exeter Book. Several Anglo-Latin writers (such as Aldhelm, Boniface, and Tatwine) wrote Latin *enigmata*, possibly for teaching purposes, which at times are the source of the Old English texts.

Riddles commonly employ the following devices:

- *prosopopoeia* – in which an inanimate object is given a voice, thus we often find the riddle written in the 1st person;
- *ambiguity* – the object of the riddle will describe itself and its actions in an obscure way to deliberately confuse the audience;
- *direct questioning* – the object personified in the riddle will often present a final question such as 'What am I?' to the listener.

Williamson (1983) attempted a taxonomy for the riddles, suggesting they fell under one of the following categories:

biomorphic – the subject is compared to a living creature or given body parts;

zoomorphic – the subject is actually presented as a living creature (very common);

anthropomorphic – the subject is presented as a human being (very common);

phytomorphic – the subject is compared to a plant;

inanimate – the subject is presented as an inanimate object;

multiple – the subject is described using a series of unrelated comparisons;

selected details – detailed descriptions of the subject are given but in a deliberately ambiguous way;

'neck-riddle' – a riddle that is simply impossible to solve;

arithmetical – the subject is described in arithmetical terms, i.e. by indicating key numbers one would associate with the object;

family relations – the subject is presented in terms of its relationship to other objects or people;

cryptomorphic – the name of the subject is presented through an unfamiliar spelling (e.g. the letters are reversed);

homonymic – the riddle has a possible double meaning;

erotic – the riddle is based on a *double entendre*;

non-riddles – a category where the standard riddle form is ignored, and instead one is presented with a set of direct questions.

Of these, in the surviving Old English riddles the most common forms are the zoomorphic and anthropomorphic, but nearly all the others are represented.

As with all Old English poems, none of the riddles are titled, nor do they provide solutions (unlike their Latin counterparts, which often came with a title). Thus modern scholars have been left to provide the answers themselves; which is especially problematic when multiple solutions present themselves. Pollington (2003, p. 213) makes an interesting suggestion by noting that the wisdom poems, such as *Maxims I*, may possibly be explained if looked at in the light of the riddles. These poems, more akin to catalogues, are 'just the kind of immediate mental associations the solvers would have to use to crack the paradoxes of riddles'.

Some of the riddles use a form of *double entendre* in addition to the above (Wilcox, 2005, numbers these as eight in total). This earthy humour, which clearly must have appealed to the scribe in addition to the audience, bears all the trademarks of British seaside comedy. An everyday object (such as a key or onion) is described in such a way as to imply another interpretation (in both cases a penis). Yet at the other extreme we are presented with a devout riddle on the Gospels describing the construction of the codex and the salvation the text offers (see Chapter 4(d)).

Although riddles may at first seem simplistic it is occasionally possible to reveal deeper meanings within the text. A good example of this is the 'Moth' riddle. We can see this below with a translation facing.

Moððe word fræt. Mē þæt þūhte	A moth ate words. This seemed to me
wrætlicu wyrd, þā ic þæt wundor gefrægn,	a strange event, when I heard of that wonder,

þæt se wyrm forswealg wera gied sumes,	that the worm utterly swallowed the speech of a certain one of men,
þēof in þȳstro, þrymfæstne cwide	the thief in the darkness, the glorious saying
ond þæs strangan staþol. Stælgiest ne wæs 5	and the foundation of the strong one. The thieving guest was not 5
wihte þȳ glēawra, þē hē þām wordum swealg.	at all the wiser, though he swallowed those words.

At first the riddle seems simple enough. A moth (or bookworm) eats words, i.e. devours the manuscript page. Yet the observer notes the paradox that even though the bookworm swallows the words on the page (literally), it is not at all the wiser for it.

However, a deeper analysis of the poem possibly leads to a further interpretation. If we look at the original poem again and single out the subjects and objects, we can observe something interesting. In the version below, the key subjects are underlined, and the objects are in italics.

Moððe *word* fræt.   Mē þæt þūhte

wrǣtlicu wyrd,   þā ic þæt wundor gefrægn,

þæt se wyrm forswealg   *wera gied sumes*,

þēof in þȳstro,   *þrymfæstne cwide*

ond *þæs strangan staþol*.   Stælgiest ne wæs   5

wihte þȳ glēawra,   þē hē þām *wordum* swealg.

Beginning with the subject of the poem – the bookworm – we can see a widening of the terms used to describe it. At first it is a 'moth' (line 1a), then 'the worm' (line 3a), 'the thief in the darkness' (line 4a), 'the thieving guest' (line 5b), and finally 'he' (line 6b). We move from the specific to the general and it could be argued this is intentional, not simple variation of description. To a modern reader a 'bookworm' can also refer to a human being who reads extensively, and although this may not have had the same connotations in the Anglo-Saxon period, it is possible that this generalisation of the subject is a deliberate attempt to describe anyone who reads ('devours' a book). The criticism being levelled at them is that it is not enough just to read a book, one must attempt to understand it to gain wisdom. But what book? Looking at the objects this time (in italics) we can again see something interesting. We start with 'words' (line 1a, repeated on line 6b), but in the middle the text being 'eaten' is described as 'the speech of a certain one of men' (line 3b), 'the glorious saying' (line 4b), and the 'foundation of the strong one' (line 5a). It is possible that this is simple variation, but the choice of terminology indicates otherwise. The *staþol* or 'foundation', of line 5, can also refer to the 'law', and when placed alongside 'the glorious saying' this could mean religious law. Indeed, by extension one could then argue that the 'certain one of men' in line 3 is Christ, and thus the law is the New Testament. If this is accepted then, a simple riddle suddenly yields an allegorical, moral, and spiritual message; namely that it is not enough just to read the sayings of Christ; instead one must understand them and live by them.

In summary then:

- a considerable quantity of riddles survive in the single Exeter Book manuscript;
- these range from bawdy *double entendres*, through observations on nature, to religious subject matter;
- the riddles are untitled but are usually given a number or a name based around the proposed solution; occasionally some riddles still remain unanswerable;
- many Old English riddles draw on Latin *enigmata* for their sources, which originally were possibly used for educational purposes.

See also   Chapter 2(b), (g), (h), and (m), and Chapter 4(d).

Further Reading

The riddles are often included in general anthologies of Old English poetry (see Chapter 2(h)). For specific studies see Crossley-Holland (1978), Tigges (1994), Tupper (1968), Williamson (1977 and 1983), and Wilcox (2005). See also the Kalamazoo Riddle Group (www2.kenyon.edu/AngloSaxonRiddles/).

(l)   Christian Verse

It is clear that the Christian stories (as contained in the Old and New Testaments) and the subsequent history of the Church held considerable interest for the Anglo-Saxons, which manifested itself in poetry (for religious prose see Chapter 2(f)). This is evident even with

Cædmon's Hymn, the first recorded poem in Old English which appears in Bede's *History*. According to the story in Bede, Cædmon was a lowly herdsman at the abbey of Whitby in the late 7th century. In the story, Cædmon leaves the main refectory because he is embarrassed that he is unable to 'sing' a poem. Sleeping in a nearby shed he is woken by a vision, probably of an angel, who tells him to sing something. Despite his protestations Cædmon is suddenly able to sing and recites his hymn, a short poem about the creation of the world, praising the Lord's power. Importantly therefore for this section it is a Christian poem, based (albeit very loosely) on the Book of Genesis. Bede tells us that Cædmon composed other poems based on the Old Testament, but although many scholars in the past have attempted to attribute some of the poems that do survive to Cædmon, this is generally considered to be impossible to prove. The hymn consequently represents Cædmon's only known surviving work.

Nevertheless there is a sizeable corpus of Christian verse from the Anglo-Saxon period that does survive, in addition to the much larger corpus of Christian prose writing. A list of these poems might include:

Old Testament
Azarias
Cædmon's Hymn
Daniel
Exodus
Genesis A
Genesis B
Judith
Psalms

New Testament (and Apocryphal)
Christ I
Christ II
Christ III
Christ and Satan
The Dream of the Rood
The Descent into Hell

Later Church history
Andreas
Elene
The Fates of the Apostles

Guthlac A
Guthlac B
Juliana
Menologium

These appear in a variety of manuscripts but only one copy of each survives. The 'Junius' manuscript, however, notably only contains religious verse (see Chapter 4(d)). As we can see from the above there is a spread over the Old and New Testaments, as well as an interest in the history of the Church after the death of Christ. This is reflected in prose writings also, with writers such as Ælfric providing us with translations of several Old Testament books, and commentaries via his homilies on New Testament episodes. The Christian story, from Genesis to the New Testament, provided the Anglo-Saxons with a clear simple narrative of the beginning of the world.

Such a highly structured history may have appealed to the Anglo-Saxons as they formed their new kingdoms in a foreign land. This suggests they were looking for a sense of, and place in, history (as seen by the fact that Old Testament characters find their way into the genealogies of Anglo-Saxon kings). On top of this there was the detailed narrative of the Church year, based primarily around a celebration of Christ's life, further instilling a sense of order and purpose but allowing the audience to partake in, and be reminded of, the Christian story on an annual basis.

There is also a unity of instruction that the Anglo-Saxons (in keeping with standard practice) explored by demonstrating how the Old Testament prefigured the New Testament. In other words events in the former could be seen to mirror or prophesy events in the life of Christ, and thus the latter was the fulfilment of the Old Testament. As Keefer (2005, p. 17) notes with reference to the poems based on the Old Testament:

> These poems are not true translations . . . but interpretations made of those sources from a Christian viewpoint, assuming the New Testament as an absolute point of departure.

In addition to the titles listed above, there are hagiographical poems such as *Elene, Juliana, Andreas, Guthlac A* and *Guthlac B*. There are also didactic texts such as *Soul and Body I* and *II, Judgement Day I* and *II*; all of which deal with Christian themes and messages. We also have liturgical and devotional poems (see Raw, 1991, pp. 233–5) such as *Alms-Giving, Resignation A* and *Resignation B*, the *Kentish Hymn*, and *Homiletic Fragment I* and *Homiletic Fragment II*. To this already impressive list we could add allegorical poems with clear Christian messages, such as *The Phoenix*, and the poems of the 'Old English Physiologus' – *The Panther*, *The Whale*, and *The Partridge*. Finally we must not forget the Christian elements in the Old English elegies and *Beowulf*.

However, a few key points emerge from these poems:

(1) an acceptance of what are now considered to be apocryphal stories such as Christ's harrowing of hell;

(2) a concentration on good narratives (seen also in prose texts);

(3) an identification by the Anglo-Saxons with the oppression of the Israelites in the Old Testament, and the early Christians (again this is also seen in prose texts);

(4) a willingness to modify stories to include elements that would appeal to Anglo-Saxon audiences, notably heroic ideals.

Point (4) is perhaps the most interesting to note. As O'Brien O'Keeffe remarks, 'the ethos of heroic life pervades Old English literature' (1991, p. 107), so one should not be surprised that it also finds its way into Christian verse.

The re-use of the Germanic ideals in Christian verse served a clear purpose, namely to appeal to the audience these poems were directed at. Christians (and by extension Christian poems) in the early period needed to do three things: educate, promote Christian beliefs, and entertain. By using or 'appropriating' ideas and motifs from existing beliefs the poems would have greater reference and association. Two examples will suffice to illustrate this. The first is the poem based on the Old Testament Book of Judith (which survives in the *Beowulf* manuscript). In this the standard story of Judith and Holofernes is told (though its complexities are reduced and the stereotypes accentuated). However, at the end of the poem, unlike in the biblical version, a 'battle' is inserted complete with common type-scenes such as the 'beasts of battle'. The excitement of a battle would have appealed to the English audience, making the poem suitable for public recitation and entertainment, and the re-use of common devices would have allowed the audience to relate to the poetry.

Another good example is *The Dream of the Rood*. This highly regarded poem is a dream vision (like parts of *Elene*, see also Chapter 3(n)) in which the poet sees the cross on which Christ was crucified.

In the dream the cross recounts its fate, and the events at Calvary. Most notably, Christ, in this story, is presented as a heroic warrior readying himself for battle (i.e. the struggle on the cross), and after his death is treated exactly like a Germanic hero with his *comitatus* singing dirges, and burying him in a mound. The emphasis on the suffering of Christ found in later Middle English Christian narratives and poetry would not have appealed so much to an Anglo-Saxon audience, who looked for strong heroes. Similarly in Cynewulf's *Christ I* he is transformed into a military leader who marches his troops into heaven. Faced with the pantheon of Norse Gods or similar (one can assume), Christian figures, and notably Christ himself, had to match or even better the exploits of Germanic heroes.

In addition we must remember the possible changes in the audience for this poetry. Even if it was not intended to be performed in front of lay people (which is open to debate), in the 7th and 8th centuries monastic houses were populated by members of the aristocracy (and throughout the period received their patronage). We can assume that they would have welcomed stories affirming the heroic ideal, therefore (see Wormald, 1991, p. 10).

However, even if one recognises the need, the tenets of Christianity did not always sit easily with the old ideals. Poets and prose writers both struggled in balancing the need for heroism with the message of Christian mercy; or the will of God with the pre-Christian concept of *wyrd* or 'fate'. The old Germanic virtues of heroism, loyalty, fame, and treasure, and the apparent interest in these older tales, was seemingly a cause of tension in the Anglo-Saxon period. As noted above, the policy of appropriating pagan beliefs and practices meant that the two genres were intertwined, and the need to present tales and messages to the Anglo-Saxons that would appeal to them, to assist in their conversion, strengthened this intermingling even more. Yet as Alcuin famously remarked: *Quid Hinieldus cum Christi?* ('What has Ingeld to do with Christ?'),[24] seemingly despairing at the fact that ancient tales of the pagan past were still being told in monasteries.

At times, in such poems as *The Wanderer*, *The Seafarer*, or *Beowulf*, the appearance of Christian elements can even seem obtrusive, almost like interpolations. Yet modern scholarship recognises the unity of these texts and sees the original composition and the

---

[24] Ingeld is a character from Germanic history/myth, mentioned, for example, in *Beowulf*.

Christian elements as sympathetic, and thus probably taking place at the same time. Importantly, therefore, this means that such poems must be interpreted as Christian poems written by Christians for Christians.

What can we take from the above? In summary:

- there is an extensive corpus of Christian verse covering both Old and New Testament subjects, and the later history of the Church;
- Christian ideas and concepts are also explored in poems that we list under other categories such as the elegies;
- in keeping with the requirements of conversion, the Christian poets concentrated on key narratives, and felt free to modify the stories, or alter perceptions of figures to make them more in keeping with Germanic heroic ideals;
- although this seems to have been a successful policy (Anglo-Saxon England was, after all, converted to Christianity) certain writers, such as Alcuin, display a concern about the apparent interest in the older tales;
- Alcuin's concern may also have stemmed from the seeming contradiction between the values of the heroic ethos and the teachings of Christ.

See also   Chapter 2(b), (d), (f), (i), (j), and (n), Chapter 3(n), and Chapter 4(d).

Further Reading

For further studies of religious verse in the Old English period, see Conner (2001), Godden (1991), Keefer (2005), and Raw (1991). For issues relating to the tension between heroism and Christianity, see O'Brien O'Keeffe (1991), and discussions in Chapter 2(j). For the poetic saints' lives, see Bjork (1985).

(m)   Wisdom Poetry

Like the category 'elegy', 'wisdom poetry' is a problematic term as it implies that there is a defined set of texts that can be identified under such a heading. Undoubtedly poems like *Solomon and Saturn I* and *II*, *Maxims I* and *II*, *Precepts*, *The Gifts of Men*, *The Fortunes of Men*, and so on, have a seemingly familiar sense of purpose in that they 'share a common concern with the fundamentals of human existence and experience' (Lapidge et al., 1999, p. 484). However, similar sentiments can be discerned also in the so-called elegies – *The Ruin*, *The Wanderer*, *The Seafarer*, etc. – with their contemplation of the transient nature of worldly glory. To this we could add 'list' poems such as the *Menologium*, *Widsith*, or *Deor*; and the inherent wisdom in shorter poems such as *Bede's Death Song*, or *Pharaoh*. *Beowulf*, which continually defies any attempt to categorise it, also has elements in common with all these texts.

Is there any commonality though? A good starting point is to look at the usual descriptive terms that appear in studies of wisdom literature; namely 'gnomic', 'maxims', or 'aphorisms'. The former implies a general concern with wisdom, and comes from the Greek γνώμη meaning 'mind, judgement'. A 'maxim', according to the *Oxford English Dictionary*, is:

> A rule or principle of conduct. Also: a pithily expressed precept of morality or prudence (*spec*. occurring in Old English verse); such a precept as a literary form.

And an 'aphorism' is:

> Any principle or precept expressed in few words; a short pithy sentence containing a truth of general import.

From all three, we can see agreement with a focus on wisdom, rules, or a short pithy statement. This then provides us with an answer. The poems we could group under this heading outline a set of rules and short statements that present basic facts or wise sayings with an air of certainty. This may seem banal, patronising, or just completely unfamiliar to a modern audience in our uncertain world. Yet clearly it held a fascination for the Anglo-Saxons.

A good example is the poem *Maxims II*. It is found in a single British Library manuscript (Cotton MS. Tiberius B. I, ff. 115r–v), and not surprisingly is of a similar vein to the poem we term *Maxims I*. It consists of a series of short observances on the nature of things (thus following the features noted above that might be common to wisdom poetry). Marsden (2004, p. 296) observes: 'The OE maxims present an intimate view of the world in literal terms. Indeed, on the face of it, they may seem to state the obvious . . . but that is the point.' Indeed, when one reads the poem it does consist of a series of generally uncontestable statements. At the beginning of the poem, for example, we have the following:

Wind byð on lyfte swiftust,
þunar byð þrāgum hlūdast.

Wind is the swiftest in the sky,
thunder is sometimes loudest.

(ll. 3b–4a)

Here we have two maxims or aphorisms, linked by the common theme of the weather or nature. The wind, to the medieval mind, was the swiftest thing in the sky, and thunder (sometimes) could create a terrifyingly loud noise. It is questionable as to how much wisdom could be derived from memorising these statements though, and they seem somewhat trite taken out of context. Yet the poem continues for 66 lines covering various themes and topics in a similar manner, and intertwined throughout this are statements about the power of the Lord (e.g. *þrymmas syndan Cristes myccle*, 'Christ's glories are great', line 4b). Shippey (1976, p. 12) described the whole thing as having 'barely imaginable purpose' (yet at the same time 'undeniable charm'); but perhaps at times one tries to look too deeply for a meaning. A confirmed list of certainties could be reassuring, but more important, to a Christian audience, it places their religious beliefs alongside irrefutable facts. The poem, for example, builds up effectively to a discussion of the afterlife, concluding:

Meotod āna wāt
hwyder sēo sāwul sceal   syððan hweorfan,
and ealle þā gāstas   þe for Gode hweorfað
æfter dēaðdæge,   dōmes bīdað   60
on Fæder fæðme.   Is sēo forðgesceaft
dīgol and dyrne;   Drihten āna wāt,
nergende Fæder.   Næni eft cymeð
hider under hrōfas,   þe þæt hēr, for sōð,
mannum secge   hwylc sȳ Meotodes gesceaft,   65
sigefolca gesetu,   þær Hē sylfa wunað.

The Creator alone knows
whither the soul must journey afterwards,
and all the spirits which journey before God
after the day of death, wait for judgement   60
in the embrace of the Father. The future is
secret and hidden; the Lord, the saving Father,

alone knows. No-one comes back
hither under the roofs, who here, in truth,
might tell men what the Creator's decree is,   65
[or] the dwelling of the victorious people, where He Himself lives.

Here then, following the previous aphorisms, this will seem as factual as the earlier statement that thunder makes a loud noise.

Let us consider another example. The poem *Solomon and Saturn II* takes on the model of a riddling contest. It is 336 lines long, and presents a lengthy dialogue between Solomon, the wise king of the Old Testament, and Saturn, a prince of Chaldea who travels widely seeking wisdom. Four 'versions' of this story exist in Old English. Two of these are in verse form and are given the titles *Solomon and Saturn I* (a shorter poem which survives partly in two manuscripts – Cambridge Corpus Christi College MSS 41 and 422), and *Solomon and Saturn II* (which exists solely in MS 422).

The core scenario is that of a discussion between Saturn and Solomon, with the former asking the latter a series of questions in order to achieve wisdom. *Solomon and Saturn II* is generally regarded as the superior poem of the two. Again, contained therein, we can see examples of maxims or gnomes:

Salomon cwað: 'Dol bið sē ðe gæð   on dēop wæter,
                 sē ðe sund nafað,   ne gesegled scip,
                 ne fugles flyht,   ne hē mid fōtum ne mæg
                 grund geræcan.   50

Solomon said: 'Foolish is he who goes in the deep water,
                 (he) who cannot swim, nor [has] a ship with sails,
                 nor the bird's flight, nor he with [his] feet might
                 reach the ground.   50
                           (*Solomon and Saturn II*, ll. 47–50)

But elsewhere in the poem we see a more lengthy analysis of the *Pater Noster*, thus bringing the factual, almost folk-wisdom together with religious precepts (as with *Maxims II* above). We can only deduce that this was a deliberate policy on the part of the Christian poet.

In conclusion then, using the two examples above, we can summarise the key facts as:

- The term 'wisdom' or 'gnomic' poetry is used extensively to cover a specific collection of poems, and also running themes that occur in other Old English texts. However, like the attempt to bracket a series of poems under the term 'elegy' this can be problematic.
- The poems use maxims or aphorisms, i.e. short, often moralising statements of fact and belief.
- There is a general concern with the state of human existence, and the order of society and the natural world.
- Alongside these statements about the natural world are often declarations on religious matters, thus by association implying that the Lord's might and creation is as indisputable as the speed of the wind or the running of the sea. In other words they assert the 'inevitability and rightness of all of God's creation' (Fulk and Cain, 2003, p. 172).
- The maxims commonly use verbs such as *sculan* ('must'), e.g. *Cyning sceal on healle bēagas dælan*, 'The king must in the hall deal out rings' (*Maxims II*, ll. 28–9). This enforces the idea of 'what must be'.
- Collectively wisdom poems give us valuable insight into Anglo-Saxon priorities, attitudes, and beliefs. In the previous example it is clear, for instance, that ring-giving by a king was expected.

See also   Chapter 2(i).

Further Reading

For further studies of wisdom poems see Fulk and Cain (2003, pp. 164–92), Hill (2005), Howe (1985), Larrington (1983), Rodrigues (1995), and Shippey (1976).

(n)   *Beowulf*

The Anglo-Saxon poem *Beowulf*, stretching to 3,182 lines, seemingly overshadows all of Old English studies. It has appeared in numerous editions and translations, and is the most 'studied' of Old English texts judging by the amount of scholarly articles and books published on it. However, it was not the first Old English text to be published – that accolade belongs to a homily by Ælfric which appeared in the 16th century, whereas *Beowulf* did not appear in print until 1815. Yet its popularity now is undeniable. It is evident in major anthologies, was 'translated' by Seamus Heaney, and more recently it has also attracted several film versions of the text.[25] The surrounding work therefore is extensive, indeed Orchard (2003b, p. 3) suggested that attempting to manage the 'secondary material has become a near-impossible task'. Faced with this daunting prospect, where should the reader of Old English begin?

Plot

The first task is to familiarise oneself with the text, the plot, and the characters. The poem is undoubtedly long, at times moving quickly (almost too quickly for some critics, who observe that a period of fifty years goes by in a couple of lines); but at other times it seems to progress slowly, and is filled with digressions and asides which can often prove difficult for the modern reader. In short, the story centres on the character Beowulf, his life, and possibly the contrast between his youth and rise to fame, and his old age and death. The story begins by establishing the history of the Danes, who are central to the first part of the tale. It starts by detailing the arrival of Scyld Scefing, a mysterious character possibly based on ancient fertility legends, who leads the Danes to glory by expanding their kingdom and attracting power and treasure. We then move swiftly to the story of one of his descendants – Hrothgar – a powerful king who expands the powerbase, and as a sign of this builds a great hall called Heorot. This, however, attracts the wrath of a nearby creature called Grendel, who attacks the hall and over the next twelve years reduces the Danes to fear and misery. News of this reaches the attention of Beowulf of the Geats (a nation that occupied modern-day southern Sweden). Beowulf is a young man at this point and journeys to Denmark with his band of followers. He promises Hrothgar that he will defeat the monster Grendel, which he duly does in hand-to-hand combat, forcing Grendel to flee back to his lair to die. But the troubles do not end there as Grendel's mother, angered by what has happened to her son, renews the feud by attacking the hall the next night, taking off and killing one of the retainers. Beowulf once again aids Hrothgar. He journeys to the mere where the monsters reside and in an underwater *mêlée* kills the mother and completes the slaying of Grendel. Hrothgar rewards Beowulf but warns him that his

---

[25] Kulakov's *Beowulf* (1998 – TV version); Baker's *Beowulf* (1999); Gunnarsson's *Beowulf and Grendel* (2005), and Zemeckis's *Beowulf* (2007). In addition one could add McTiernan's *The 13th Warrior* (1999) based on Michael Crichton's *Eaters of the Dead*, itself inspired by *Beowulf*.

strength will go with old age and he should not become the victim of pride.

Beowulf returns home and recounts his adventures to his lord Hygelac. The story then rapidly progresses fifty years and by that time Beowulf is King of the Geats. We are told that a dragon, disturbed by a thief stealing treasure from his hoard, attacks the Geats. Beowulf, despite his age, resolves to fight the dragon. He does so, but is mortally wounded and only defeats the monster with the aid of one of his retainers – Wiglaf. The poem ends with Beowulf's funeral and indications that the Geats faced a new threat from their warlike neighbours now that their leader was dead. Interspersed throughout the text are several notable digressions, bringing in stories from mythology and history.

Scholarship

Having become familiar with the general plot (via a translation or through the original text)[26] the reader of Old English should then attempt to come to terms with some of the major articles and studies of the poem. A good start would be to read Andrew Orchard's excellent *A Critical Companion to Beowulf* (2003), and to also look at R. E. Bjork and J. D. Niles (eds), *A Beowulf Handbook* (1997). Together, as well as offering new insights, these two summarise the major discussions of the poem over the past 200 years. Looking through these one will see that several key articles are referenced again and again (such as J. R. R. Tolkien's famous lecture from 1936 entitled *Beowulf: The Monsters and the Critics*), and although these can be found in the original journals, of course, many have been anthologised in readily available collections of Beowulfian articles.[27]

Date, authorship, provenance, structure

Looking at these, some key areas of discussion arise. First there is the debate concerning the date and provenance of the poem. Details within the text can be linked to known historical events for example,

[26] There are several excellent editions of *Beowulf* available. Possibly the most famous is Klaeber (1950), but see also Jack (1994), Mitchell and Robinson (1998), and Wrenn (1973). For translations see Clark Hall (1950), Heaney (1999), and Liuzza (2000).

[27] Tolkien's famous article was actually his Sir Israel Gollancz Memorial Lecture of 1936. It appeared in the *Proceedings of the British Academy*, vol. 22, pp. 245–95. For anthologies of *Beowulf* criticism (many of them contain a reprint of Tolkien's article) see Baker (2000), Fry (1968), Fulk (1991), and Nicholson (1963).

which indicate that the action takes place in the first half of the 6th century; whereas the single manuscript witness to the poem (London, British Library, Cotton MS. Vitellius A. XV) was written either late in the 10th century, or possibly in the first decade of the 11th century. The key questions that remain unanswered, however, centre on the actual composition of the poem – namely when it was 'authored', who by, and where they were from.

In scholarly discussions this question is often linked to the stance one takes on the structure of the poem. In the synopsis presented above, a bipartite structure presents itself immediately (namely the events in Denmark when Beowulf was a young man, and those fifty years later in Geatland when he is much older and faces the dragon); but one could equally well argue for a tripartite structure based around the three fights with the monsters, or Beowulf's adventures at King Hrothgar's court, his home-coming, and finally the dragon episode. Either stance, however, indicates a unified structure. Yet towards the end of the 19th century, German scholars promoted the *Liedertheorie* ('ballad theory'). This proposed that the poem developed as a result of amalgamation of a series of shorter lays and it was the origin of these that needed to be pursued. In this sense then, the poem cannot be assigned a single date, author or provenance. On the other hand, research into oral composition and formulaic style conducted in the 1950s and 1960s has been used to argue that the poem that survives was simply one version of an orally performed text. This, again, dismissed the notion of a date of composition or a single author.

Though many modern scholars recognise the complexity of the question about the poem's authorship and origin (at the very least one has to accept that *Beowulf* shares style and formulaic phraseology with other Old English poems, and that these cannot be attributed to a single author), there is one point of almost universal agreement: *Beowulf* is a unified work, in its style, content, and structure. Among others this was convincingly argued by Tolkien in his famous 1936 lecture (possibly the most influential article ever written on *Beowulf*). Scholars looking at the poem from different perspectives have been able to demonstrate exceptional sophistication and harmony of all its elements: its style, vocabulary, and metre are motivated by its content, its structure is deliberate and effective.

And yet it can be argued that the question of the poem's unity is essentially separate from the question of its origin and authorship. Thus the poem's sophistication, integrity, and artistry are not compromised by its use of the traditional poetic phraseology and epic themes which originated in a pre-literate past, and which it shares with the rest of Old English poetry. *Beowulf*'s unity does not rule out that its transmission was lengthy and complex and may have involved reinterpretation and change that have nothing to do with corruption or trivialisation. It is perhaps telling that in spite of a concentrated effort and the use of all available methods and evidence, scholars have not been able to achieve consensus as to the poem's date or provenance. Suggested dates for its composition have ranged from the 7th to the 11th centuries, with 'most' scholars arguing for the early 8th century. As to provenance, there appears to be no general agreement, with strong cases to be made for the area of composition being Northumbria, Mercia, Wessex, Kent, or East Anglia.

Christian elements

The readers must decide which theory they subscribe to concerning date, provenance, and authorship; or even if the discussion is worth having, as, with so little information to go on, a definitive answer is probably impossible. It would be fair to say, however, that most scholars now believe that *Beowulf* as we have it is a work of a Christian poet addressed to a Christian audience. Thus to quote the editor of *Beowulf*, Klaeber: 'The Christian elements are almost without exception so deeply ingrained in the very fabric of the poem that they cannot be explained away as the work of a reviser or later interpolator' (1950, p. l). The poem is set in the pagan past and describes various pagan practices and customs, but nevertheless there is a sense that its action takes place in Christian surroundings: numerous references show that the poet was familiar with Christian teaching and expected the same from the audience.

It would be no exaggeration to say that the poem can be interpreted as a profoundly Christian work, with full justification within the text. For example, its principal characters, Hrothgar and Beowulf, are virtuous monotheists possessing many Christian qualities. Thus Beowulf is described as 'mild' and 'kind' (ll. 3181–2); he is a good king, a protector of his people, and a hero who fights against the enemies of God as His agent in a human world. The poem's tragic ending, and Beowulf's desire to win the treasure bearing the curse, seem to also suggest his blindness to his own fate and the fate of his nation. From the Christian perspective this can be seen as the failure of the pagan hero to achieve the perfection required by the poet's Christian ideals.

On the other hand, however, some of the same characters, events, and references, can be interpreted in a different way. The Germanic heroic code with its notions of *lof* and *dōm* (see Chapter 2(j)) is very strongly present throughout the poem. For example, Hrothgar's and Beowulf's references to God are sometimes almost indistinguishable from references to the pagan *wyrd* ('fate'). The poem's tragic ending may reflect the sense of unyielding fate, and the idea of cursed gold causing a hero's death is found in other Germanic legends and does not necessarily reflect Christian influence. Even the lines describing Beowulf's death at the end of the poem famously contain ambiguity about his fate and the poet's attitude to him. The soul of the dying Beowulf is said to depart to seek *sōðfæstra dōm* (l. 2820). If the word *dōm* has the meaning 'God's judgement' which it acquired in Anglo-Saxon Christian texts (as in modern 'Doomsday'), then the poet is saying that Beowulf's soul departed to seek the 'favourable judgement of God received by the righteous (*sōðfæst*)' as opposed to damnation, which could have been his fate as a pagan. If, however, it is the *dōm* of the Germanic heroic code, then the meaning of *sōðfæstra dōm* could be the 'esteem of the righteous'. Beowulf wanted this as a young man, which points only to his fate in this world, but says nothing about what happened to him after his death.

Such 'ambiguity' is pervasive in *Beowulf* and should not be seen as an imperfection or as necessarily resulting from our inability to understand what the poet meant. It is a genuine characteristic of the text as we have it, possibly reflecting its complex history, and should be taken into account in any serious reading or interpretation of the poem. Multiple layers of meaning can be seen in poetic formulas such as *sōðfæstra dōm*, which were reinterpreted in the course of their long history, as they came to be used in different texts. *Beowulf*'s simultaneous existence in 'both worlds', heroic and Christian, gives it the quality of being timeless and above ideological concerns, which may partly explain its appeal to many contemporary readers.

Purpose and background

To this end then, one must begin to question what *Beowulf* meant to its contemporary audience – what was its purpose? Again the possible answers to this are manifold – ranging from the literal (it is purely entertainment), through the symbolic (the poem is about human frailties, the realities of keeping to the heroic ideals, or the responsibilities of kingship), to the allegorical (e.g. that Beowulf is in fact a symbolic representation of Christ).

Christian interpretations of the poem are taken to excess some-times (the allegory of 'Beowulf = Christ', for example, is generally disregarded now). Yet interesting work has been performed in link-ing the text to key works by patristic writers such as St Augustine. The following Augustinian topics have all been used to analyse *Beowulf*:

- *rex iustus* – the exploration of the concept of a 'just king' (Hrothgar and Beowulf);
- *the city of God* – the mortal transient world and the eternal heavenly city (which ties in with the overall elegiac tone of the poem); linked also to *caritas* and *cupiditas* (mortal desire and spiritual love);
- *sapientia et fortitudo* – 'wisdom and courage' (the key attributes of a hero, e.g. Beowulf).

Key studies have also appeared on the digressions that run through the poem, and the links to archaeology (especially after the discover-ies at Sutton Hoo – see Chapter 4(i)).

Style

As mentioned already, what is indisputable is the artistry of the poem. Its structure is balanced, and internally the poet makes exten-sive use of numerous devices (such as variation, repetition, ring composition, envelope patterns, rhyme, echo words, and so on). This at times may seem excessive (especially the use of variation and repetition), so much so that the progression of the plot can seem stilted; yet the complexity and density of use on top of the standard rules of Old English poetry is at times astonishing. The intertextuality of *Beowulf* has also drawn attention. Its links and possible indebted-ness to other biblical tales, Old Norse sagas, classical literature, and other Old English poems have all been explored.

This briefest of essays can only begin to scratch the surface of *Beowulfian* scholarship. However, if one is approaching the poem for the first time, the key steps might be:

- first, familiarise yourself with the plot and structure of the poem;
- read Orchard's *Companion* and Bjork and Niles's *Handbook*;
- look at some of the major articles on *Beowulf* in one of the series of anthologies of the criticism;

- in particular try to become familiar with the arguments, looking at the date and provenance of the poem, the structure, the
  links to other texts, some of the major themes, and the religious elements.

See also Chapter 1(e) and (f), Chapter 2(j), and Chapter 4(e) and (i).

Further Reading

As mentioned above, there are many editions of *Beowulf*, and translations. For key
introductory studies, as well as Orchard, and Bjork and Niles, see Baker (2000), Fry
(1968), Fulk (1991), Fulk and Cain (2003, pp. 193–224), Liuzza (2005), Nicholson
(1963), and Robinson (1991). For material analogous to *Beowulf* see Garmonsway and
Simpson (1980). The ambiguity about Beowulf's fate and the poet's attitude to him is
discussed by Tolkien in *The Monsters and the Critics* (1997, pp. 36–42). For poetic
devices, see Orchard (2003b).

(o)   *Apollonius of Tyre*

The Old English anonymous prose version of the story of Apollonius
is a fitting end to this section as in many ways it acts as a bridge to
Middle English. It is a text that attracts many elaborate claims among
Old English scholars, though surprisingly little attention. It has been
described as the 'first English novel', conveying a world of 'real
human beings' and the first English contribution to 'the literature of
escape' (Wrenn, 1967, pp. 255–6). It is also regularly called 'a
romance' (Treharne and Pulsiano, 2001, p. 6) and the first example of
this 'genre in English' that denies 'a comfortable thematization' (Hill,
2001, p. 164). The original story behind the Old English text gained
importance in early medieval literature due to its mention by
Venantius Fortunatus, the Bishop of Poitiers, in the 6th century. Later
on though, it became one of the more popular stories of the medieval
period and beyond, appearing in Gower's *Confessio Amantis*, for
example, as well as mainland European texts. Notably it also forms
the basis for Shakespeare's *Pericles* and *The Comedy of Errors*. The
Anglo-Saxon text, however, is the earliest surviving vernacular
version of the tale.

The Old English text is one of the longest pieces of prose from the
period, and thus often earns the highly debatable description as a
novel. It survives in a single copy (Cambridge, Corpus Christi College
MS 201) and in its present form it is over 400 lines long (Treharne,
2004), divided into 51 'chapters'. Of these, owing to manuscript

damage, 25 chapters are missing, which means the full text could have been nearer 800 lines in length (akin more to the length of a 50-page modern novella). Its source, it is assumed, is a Latin adaptation of the tale (the *Historia Apollonii Regis Tyri*), but the exact version has not been traced. It also used to be conjectured that this in turn dated back to a (now lost) Greek original. Putting the Old English version alongside the Latin texts that do survive we can see that the Anglo-Saxon translator was faithful to the source, providing a 'close translation of a corrupt Latin text' (Hollis and Wright, 1992, p. 95). He employed only minor corrections in an attempt to make it more intelligible to the English (Goolden, 1958, p. xx; Scragg, 2001, p. 270);[28] or in the case of omitting a scene in a brothel, more palatable, perhaps, to a monastic audience.

Most importantly, its bridging role between Old and Middle English arises from the subject matter that it deals with and the manner in which it treats it. It is full of dialogue and developed characters, with notable injections of humour and feeling. In terms of its story it clearly is a tale of 'adventure, thwarted love, mysterious circumstances' (Murfin and Ray, 2003, p. 414). Its main interest is in family, love, and the fortune and emotional life of an individual, but also in intelligent and virtuous behaviour, which is duly rewarded at the end. *Apollonius of Tyre* has a happy ending, aristocratic settings, and portrays travel in exotic lands. Its purpose is clearly to entertain, but also to teach about the world and human behaviour, and present examples of virtues and sins. All these features provide clear parallels with later medieval romance, albeit in a different setting from the more familiar world of chivalry and courtly love.

The story begins when Apollonius is a young, wealthy man. We are introduced to King Antioch, a clearly wicked man, who is having an incestuous relationship with his beautiful daughter. He is so jealous of her that he sets a riddle saying that no man may take her as his wife unless they solve the riddle. Failure to do so would lead to their execution. After some time Apollonius comes to court and asks for the daughter's hand in marriage. When he hears the riddle he realises that the answer points to the King's act of incest. When Apollonius gives his solution, however, the King falsely claims that the answer is incorrect, but fearful of discovery allows Apollonius thirty days grace

---

[28] The most argued over alteration comes in chapter 20 when Appollonius declares to the King's daughter '*næs git yfel wīf!*' ('you are not yet a wicked woman!'), with disputes over what this might tell us about attitudes to women in the text.

to come up with another answer. Secretly however, he sends an assassin to kill Apollonius.

What follows then is Apollonius's flight from the King's persecution to Tyre, and further. Through a succession of events (shipwrecks, destitution, chance meetings, etc.) and over a period of years Apollonius finds his true love, has a child, is separated from his wife, but eventually through good fortune is reunited with her and reclaims his rightful position. The key balance here between grief and joy, fortune and misfortune, is one which intrigued many medieval writers. As mentioned above, there is also a happy ending. Apollonius succeeds partly through luck and chance occurrences, but also through his wisdom (in solving the original riddle), skill (which befriends him to the King of Pentapolis), and eventual kindness (to the fisherman).

The text concludes with a memorable codicil:

> Here ends both the grief and the happiness of Apollonius the Tyrenian. Read it whoever wishes to. And if anyone does read it, I ask that he might not speak ill of the translation, but that he will keep quiet about whatever may be derided from it.   (Treharne, 2004, p. 253)

This indicates to Scragg (2001, p. 269) that clearly the translator was expecting this to be read by a literate, and thus monastic audience, who would be used to criticising translations. But why would a monastic audience be interested in such a romantic tale of adventure, and why is it included in a manuscript that otherwise contains homiletic pieces or legal texts? Here we have a highly literate and lengthy prose tale which primarily seeks to entertain via a story of adventure. Elsewhere in Old English, as we have seen, the longest continuous adventure tale is the poem *Beowulf* but its subject matter is a fusion of Germanic and Christian. The *Apollonius*, however, is prose, but more importantly its source material is classical, its subject matter is love and adventure (as opposed to heroism), and there are no obvious Christian messages contained therein. Perhaps this simply indicates the direction Old English literature was heading in towards the end of the period, and shows an interesting continuity in the themes, sources, and topics that later writers were to engage in more fully. As Goolden remarked, it possibly demonstrated that:

> The Anglo-Saxons did not always wish to be reminded of the world around them or the one to come. There was then, too, a

demand for escape entertainment, a taste for the imaginative world of fantasy, excitement, and sensationalism. The break in taste between our pre-Conquest ancestors and ourselves was evidently not so radical as the bulk of the surviving records would lead us to suppose.   (Goolden, 1958, p. xxv)

However, another potential (and not necessarily contradictory) explanation suggests itself. The wisdom and virtuous love of Apollonius and his coming to terms with the vagaries of worldly fortune is entirely in keeping with themes explored elsewhere in Old English. It is only the subject matter and medium here, not the message, that is notably different.

The Old English *Apollonius of Tyre* presents us with:

- a 'bridging text' between the two periods (Old and Middle English);
- a text that deals with developed characterisation, a love story, and classical settings rather than the Christian–Germanic themes common elsewhere in Old English;
- a possible indication of a shift in literary tastes, but we should be cautious as to how much meaning we can take from a single text.

See also   Chapter 3(h) and (q).

Further Reading

The main edition of the *Apollonius* is Goolden (1958), but see also Cathy Ball's online version www.georgetown.edu/faculty/balle/apt/apt.html (1995).

3 Middle English

(a) Old English Literary Tradition after the Norman Conquest

The fortunes of Old English prose and poetry after the Norman Conquest varied because of their different origin, nature, and roles. Old English poetry, though literate and learned at the end of the period, had its roots in a pre-Christian oral past. It inherited from this a number of technical features which influenced its development during the Anglo-Saxon period and at its end. Old English literary prose, however, developed in a learned Christian context and during the Old English period played a central role in the transmission of Christian teaching and learning. This role influenced its development and transmission during the Anglo-Saxon period and contributed to its subsequent survival. Thus Old English prose is preserved in a much larger number of manuscripts than poetry, its written presentation is more sophisticated, and it was read and copied for much longer after the Conquest than its verse counterpart. The key issues in the development of poetry and prose at the end of the Old English and beginning of the Middle English period are outlined below.

Old English poetic tradition was conservative and changed little over the centuries of its existence. Old English poetry was composed using a special literary language which differed from everyday language and the language of literary prose in terms of vocabulary, grammar, syntax, and even phonology. This poetic language, both as a linguistic system and as a corpus of formulas, could develop and respond to new subjects only slowly and depended on the continuity of the literary tradition. It evolved to express the traditional subject matter of Germanic historical, mythological and other poetry, and was later successfully extended to Christian subjects. However, cultural changes at the end of the Old English period, new interests of poets and audiences, and corresponding changes in the subject matter of poetry (such as, among other things, a greater interest in the portrayal of contemporary reality, see below), put an end to its development. Poetry preserved from the end of the 12th and the beginning of the 13th centuries is influenced by Continental literary models and is cosmopolitan in its content and form. Whereas Old English poets employed a single metrical form, and language inseparable from the traditional subject matter, early Middle English poets treated a wide range of subjects using a variety of styles and metrical forms which they shared with poets from other European countries.

The decline of traditional Old English poetry started before the Norman Conquest. This can be seen in poems which appear in 10th- and 11th-century entries in the *Anglo-Saxon Chronicle*. In these poems, datable unlike most of the rest of Old English poetry, an attempt is made to extend the traditional style and metre to the treatment of contemporary subjects, such as recent battles and political events, which is again generally uncharacteristic of Anglo-Saxon verse. The earliest of these is *The Battle of Brunanburgh* of 937, and the last is a poem on the death of Edward the Confessor in 1065. In the more traditional of these poems, which are also relatively metrically correct and use poetic language in a relatively conservative way, contemporary events are described using standard themes and formulas. This makes them similar, in style and approach, to the descriptions of ancient heroic adventures in *Beowulf*.[1] In other *Chronicle* poems the language is no longer formulaic, poetic vocabulary and syntax are not used, and the traditional alliterative verse is replaced by its free approximation. Such is the entry for the year 1036 describing the arrest and death of Prince Alfred, son of King Æthelred. The loss of the traditional metre happened because it simply did not exist on its own, without poetic grammar, vocabulary, and formulaic phraseology, all associated with the traditional subject matter; i.e. when these were abandoned, traditional metre was abandoned as well. Expansion of poetry to new subjects which required new ways of expression led to the loss of the traditional metre and style and opened the way to a gradual adoption of Continental verse forms.

There is hardly any poetry in the classical alliterative metre and style after the Norman Conquest. Perhaps the closest approximation and the last poem in what still resembles the traditional style is *Durham*, a praise of the city of Durham and its Christian relics. It was

---

[1] Tom Shippey observed that another late Old English poem, *The Battle of Maldon*, describing English defeat in 991, could have been written any time during the Old English period, because it uses a traditional style and approach and does not attempt to adapt them to suit contemporary late 10th-century attitudes and events (1972, pp. 188–9).

written soon after the translation of the remains of St Cuthbert to Durham in 1104. Other early Middle English poems, such as *The Grave* and the Worcester Fragments, use alliteration and some features of the alliterative technique, but are not in classical Old English metre or style.

Old English prose was a major achievement of the Old English period, and the Anglo-Saxons developed vernacular literary prose much earlier than other European nations. It was written using a literary language based, in the case of most of the surviving Old English prose, on the West Saxon dialect. After the Norman Conquest the works of Old English prose continued to be copied until the middle of the 13th century, and post-Conquest Old English texts survive in about fifty manuscripts. Though much fewer in number than Latin and Anglo-Norman manuscripts produced during the same period, they contain an impressive variety of important texts. Their production was not an antiquarian exercise: texts were read and copied in order to be used (see essays in Swan and Treharne, 2000). Texts surviving in post-Conquest manuscripts include translations produced during the reign of King Alfred, saints' lives, and parts of the Old English translation of the Bible (the Old English Heptateuch, Gospels, and Psalter). Homilies, including those by Ælfric and Wulfstan, continued to be copied, annotated, and reworked. There is evidence that some 12th-century homiletic manuscripts are not simply copies of earlier exemplars, but new compilations, put together from different sources. Old English charters and law codices also continued to be copied and used after the Conquest, and some Anglo-Saxon laws are known only in post-Conquest manuscripts.

The West Saxon literary standard continued to be used for new compositions and developed as a written language for some time after the Conquest. In Peterborough the *Anglo-Saxon Chronicle* was kept going until 1154. Its 12th-century entries are written in traditional literary language, though somewhat modernised through the inclusion of later linguistic forms. The loss of an Old English literary standard, however, can be clearly seen in the last entry, which describes the reign of King Stephen using a local dialect with an advanced loss of Old English inflections, and other linguistic changes characteristic of early Middle English. West Saxon literary language is found in another 12th-century manuscript of the *Chronicle*, a single leaf containing annals for the years 1113 and 1114 (a fragment from the Cotton library). Its place of origin is uncertain, but it may have been written in Winchester. Its language is a very pure West Saxon, more conservative than the later parts of the *Peterborough Chronicle*.

Important centres of Old English learning after the Conquest included Worcester, Canterbury, Rochester, and Exeter. A number of post-Conquest manuscripts of Old English texts have been located to these centres and may have been produced in the towns' cathedral scriptoria, though much is unclear about the circumstances of their production, and the intended audience and use. At Worcester the library had a collection of Old English manuscripts, and the scriptorium continued to copy Old English liturgical and homiletic texts. A 13th-century scribe, known as the 'Tremulous Hand' of Worcester because of his recognisable handwriting, copied some texts and added Latin glosses to at least nineteen manuscripts in Old English, including translations of Bede's *Ecclesiastical History*, the *Pastoral Care*, homilies of Ælfric, and the Old English *Rule of St Benedict*. The 'Tremulous Hand' also copied some verse, known as the 'Worcester Fragments', which praise Old English learning and the achievements of the Anglo-Saxon church. The scribe's need for glosses shows, however, that in the 13th century written Old English was becoming more and more difficult to understand.

Thinking about the 'afterlife' of Old English literature following the Norman Conquest we should not forget its stylistic influence on Middle English poetry and prose. Though classical Old English metre and poetic language disappeared at the end of the Old English period, poetry continued to use alliteration, and Middle English writers, such as Laȝamon, imitated various stylistic and prosodic features of Old English verse, displaying a detailed knowledge of its conventions. Alliterative poetry, which flourished in the 14th and 15th centuries, shared a number of features with Old English poetry and used some of its vocabulary. Middle English prose writers, such as the authors of the 'Katherine Group' of texts (see Chapter 3(d)), used rhythmical prose with alliteration reminiscent of the style developed in the works of Ælfric and Wulfstan. It is not entirely clear which literary models were used by Middle English writers employing alliterative technique, or how these models were transmitted, but there is no doubt that Old English literary tradition continued to be influential for centuries after the Conquest.

To summarise we should consider the following points:

- the fortunes of Old English prose and poetry were different after the Norman Conquest;
- traditional Old English alliterative verse disappeared at the end of the Old English period and was replaced by Continental verse forms when the traditional subject matter was abandoned;

- Old English prose continued to be copied, studied, and used in the 12th and 13th centuries;
- the style of Old English verse and literary prose influenced the style of Middle English prose and verse.

See also   Chapter 2(c), (e), (f), (h), and (j), Chapter 3(c) and (d), and Chapter 4(g).

Further Reading

For accounts of the copying and use of Old English after the Norman Conquest, see Franzen (1991), Lerer (1999a), Swan and Treharne (2000), Treharne (2001), and *The Production and Use of English Manuscripts 1060 to 1220* (www.le.ac.uk/ee/em1060to1220/index.htm). For a discussion of Old English verse at the end of the Old English period see Shippey (1972), and Solopova (2006).

(b)   Latin and Anglo-Norman Literature

In Anglo-Saxon England the vernacular was used in a much wider range of functions than elsewhere in Europe during this period: as demonstrated earlier, it was the language of literature, learning, church, law, and administration. After the Norman Conquest English temporarily assumed a more limited role: Latin became the language of the Church, of legal and administrative documents, and literature. Somewhat later Anglo-Norman established itself as a prestigious native language of the social elite and its culture.

The earliest major Latin works after the Conquest were chronicles. Latin historiography replaced the *Anglo-Saxon Chronicle* (which had been translated into Latin) and flourished in the 12th and 13th centuries. The works of William of Malmesbury (*c*.1090–*c*.1143), a monk and a librarian at the Benedictine monastery of Malmesbury in Wiltshire, were popular throughout the Middle Ages. The best known are three complementary histories: the *Gesta regum Anglorum* ('Deeds of the English Kings' – a history of England from the Anglo-Saxon invasions to the 1220s), the *Gesta pontificum Anglorum* ('Deeds of the English Bishops' – an early ecclesiastical history of England), and the *Historia novella* ('The Contemporary History' – a history dealing with contemporary events from 1225 to 1142 and covering the reign of King Stephen). Another influential 12th-century historian was Geoffrey of Monmouth (*c*.1100–*c*.1155), a Welshman, Archdeacon of Llandaff, and later Bishop of St Asaph. His *Historia regum Britanniae* tells the 'History of the kings of Britain' from the legendary Brutus, great-grandson of Aeneas of Troy, to Cadwallader, the last king before the Saxons. Geoffrey of Monmouth's *Historia* was based on the works of Latin historians, Welsh sources, and probably to a large extent on legend and oral tradition. He was the first writer to tell stories about King Arthur, only briefly referred to by earlier historians. Arthur is presented as the greatest of British kings and about one quarter of the *Historia* is devoted to his birth, career, and death. When describing events of the distant past the *Historia* addressed major political concerns of its day. It established a connection between the rulers of Britain and the rulers of the ancient world, providing examples of good kingship and lending legitimacy to Norman kings by presenting the history of Britain as a series of conquests. The subsequent flourishing of Arthurian historiography and literature in England, associated with the royal court and benefiting from the royal patronage, was partly due to the same political and cultural needs. Geoffrey's works enjoyed tremendous popularity throughout the medieval period and influenced literature not only as a source of Arthurian material, but also as a source of other stories, such as those of King Lear and Cymbeline.

Another important 12th-century work, the *Chronica maiora* ('Greater chronicles') by Mathew Paris (*c*.1200–59), a monk at the Abbey of St Albans, covers the history of the world from the Creation to the author's time.[2] Its earlier part is based on a chronicle by Roger of Wendover, a previous historian of St Albans. This is followed by an original detailed account of contemporary events in England and Europe. Matthew Paris is best known for writing the *Chronica maiora*, but he was the author of a wide range of historical works and biographies, and was also a diplomat, an expert scribe and a talented artist whose illustrations survive in the margins of his works preserved in autograph manuscripts. Several other 12th- and 13th-century histories focused on the life of a religious community. Such are the chronicle written *c*.1188 by Gervase, a monk of Canterbury, describing the history of his monastery with a detailed account of contemporary events; or the chronicle of the Abbey of Bury St Edmunds by Jocelin de Brakelond (*fl.* 1186–1215).

The works of Giraldus Cambrensis (*c*.1146–*c*.1220) are an important source of our knowledge about Ireland and Wales during the Middle Ages. He was chaplain to Henry II and accompanied Henry's son John (King of England from 1199 to 1216) on an expedition to

---

[2] The tradition of historical writings at St Albans continues with Thomas of Walsingham (d. 1422), who wrote a series of chronicles covering various aspects of English history from the late 13th to the early 15th century.

Ireland in 1184. Shortly afterwards he wrote *Topographia Hibernica* ('Topography of Ireland') and *Expugnatio Hibernica* ('The Conquest of Ireland'), an account of Henry's conquest of Ireland. In 1188 he accompanied the Archbishop of Canterbury, Baldwin of Exeter, on a tour of Wales and wrote an account of this journey, the *Itinerarium Cambriae* ('A Journey through Wales') in 1991, and the *Descriptio Cambriae* ('Description of Wales') in 1194. These works focus on the history and geography of Ireland and Wales, but also include a description of local customs, a record of legends and folklore, and various observations made by an educated and curious traveller.

During the Middle English period important scientific, philosophical, and theological works were written in Latin. Robert Grosseteste, Bishop of Lincoln (*c*.1170–1253), composed theological and philosophical works; commentaries on the Bible; treatises on astronomy, cosmology, mathematics, and optics; translations and commentary on the works of Aristotle; as well as translations of other Greek scientific and theological works. Among his best known contributions to philosophy and science are his commentary on Aristotle's *Posterior Analytics*, and translation of Aristotle's *Ethics* together with its Greek commentators. Grosseteste's student Roger Bacon (1214–92), an outstanding scholar, focused on theology, Aristotelian philosophy and science, optics, mathematics, and alchemy.

Throughout the Middle Ages, Latin was also a language of religious and secular poetry. The so-called 'Goliardic poetry' consisted of anonymous lyrical and satirical verse composed in Latin in Europe, including England, in the 12th and 13th centuries. Much of the 'Goliardic' satire on the clergy is attributed to Walter Map, who lived at the court of Henry II, and held various church positions, eventually becoming Archdeacon of Oxford. The only surviving work which can be attributed to him with certainty, however, is *De nugis curialium* ('Courtiers' Trifles'), which contains in its five books a large number of stories collected from various sources. It comprises legends, folklore, historical material, a satire of the court, a series of anecdotes and gossip, and attacks aimed at corruption in the Church (including the Pope and his court) and various other faults of the time.

Anglo-Norman was originally the language of the French settlers in England after the Norman Conquest. It was not uniform, but derived the largest number of its characteristics from the dialect spoken in Normandy around the time of the Conquest. In England it developed independently and acquired differences from Continental French dialects by the middle of the 12th century. In the 12th century

Anglo-Norman was a living language in England, in the sense that it was the first native language of a particular part of the society: mostly members of the aristocracy, clergy, and professional classes. The same wealthier and more educated classes were probably often bilingual, with a knowledge of English and French, or trilingual, i.e. English, Latin, and French.

Already in the 12th century important works were produced in England in Anglo-Norman, although the largest number of Anglo-French texts come from the 13th and early 14th centuries. These included chronicles and historical works, such as the verse histories of England written by Geoffrey Gaimar and Wace in the 12th century; but also lives of saints, preaching texts, biblical translations, legal texts, and works on medicine, agriculture, and hunting. Most Anglo-Norman romances were created between 1150 and 1230. Among them is *Tristan* by Thomas of Britain (Thomas d'Angleterre), an early version of the story of Tristan and Iseult composed around the middle of the 12th century. These romances also became sources for Middle English adaptations. Thus the *Romance of Horn* by 'mestre Thomas' written around 1170 exists in two Middle English versions. There are three Middle English versions of *Protheselaus*, written by Hue de Rotelande before 1189, a sequel to his earlier romance *Ipomedon*. The *Roman de Toute Chevalerie* ('The Anglo-Norman Alexander') by 'Thomas of Kent', dating from the last quarter of the 12th century, is a predecessor of the English 13th-century *King Alisaunder*. Two late 12th-century Anglo-Norman romances have an English setting: *Boeve de Haumtone* ('Bevis of Hampton') is set in Southampton, and *Waldef* in East Anglia. According to Rosalind Field, Anglo-Norman romances reflected the concerns of local barons (1999, pp. 161–2). They rarely use Arthurian material with its interest in centralised kingship, and in some the hero challenges the royal power. They also display little interest in romantic love, but focus on local setting, family, dynasty, and inheritance.

In the 12th and 13th centuries Anglo-Norman was particularly associated with women: ladies of Anglo-Norman nobility were often patrons, and literary works were addressed and dedicated to them. It appears that French was seen as particularly suitable for compositions by women or addressed to women, as a language of culture and aristocracy devoid of associations with clerical learning, science, and theology. One of the most important Anglo-Norman writers was Marie de France, who probably lived in England in the second half of the 12th century, and wrote for the royal court. Her *Lais* ('Lays'), a collection of short romances in verse, were highly influential and inspired numerous imitations and adaptations.

The decline of Anglo-Norman in England started in the 13th century. Anglo-Norman became a recognisably regional dialect early on, and gradually acquired a provincial flavour, particularly with the establishment of Parisian French as the language of the French court at the beginning of the 14th century. The loss of Normandy early in the 13th century and subsequent political rivalry between England and France contributed to the growing prestige of English. In the 13th century, French in England continued to be a language of literature, schools, law and government, but it was probably no longer learnt by anyone at birth. Its role as a symbol of belonging to the elite became more prominent as it was more artificially maintained and difficult to acquire. French continued to decline rapidly in the 14th century though it retained its popularity in some fields, such as the law, into the early modern period. John Gower was the last prominent English writer to use Anglo-Norman and Latin in his major works, but he also wrote in English. English came to be seen as a national language in the 15th century, and during the late medieval and early modern periods gradually took over functions earlier reserved for Latin and French.

Middle English literature can be fully appreciated only within the context of Latin and Anglo-Norman literacy (as indeed Old English needs to be compared to Anglo-Latin writing – see Chapter 2(b)). If seen in isolation its history will appear incomplete, lacking consistency and logic in its development. Middle English literary tradition was genuinely multilingual: the boundaries between languages and cultures were transparent and texts were written by multilingual authors for multilingual audiences.

To summarise, we should consider the following key points:

- after the Norman Conquest, Latin and French became the languages of literature, church, government, and administration, while English temporarily assumed a more limited role; most texts written in England in the 12th and 13th centuries were in Latin and French;
- Anglo-Norman was a living language in England in the 12th century but started to decline in the 13th century;
- the Middle English literary tradition was genuinely multilingual; texts were written by multilingual authors for multilingual audiences.

See also   Chapter 1(c), Chapter 2(b) and (d), and Chapter 3(h) and (q).

Further Reading

For surveys of French literature in England, see Calin (1994), Crane (1999), Dean (1999), and Legge (1963). A standard history of post-Conquest Anglo-Latin literature is Rigg (1992); Curtius (1953) is a classic work on Latin literature in the Middle Ages.

(c)   Early Middle English Poetry

Relatively little verse is preserved from the early Middle English period (between the Norman Conquest and the second quarter of the 13th century), and none of the texts we classify as being early Middle English verse can be dated with any precision. The extant texts include:

- the *Orrmulum*, a series of sermons and a synopsis of Gospel history by Orrm, an Augustinian canon who belonged to a monastery in the east Midlands, probably Lincolnshire;
- the anonymous *Poema Morale* ('A Moral Ode'), a homiletic text about sin and Christian life;
- a 'debate' poem called *The Owl and the Nightingale* (possibly by Nicholas of Guildford);
- the *Brut*, by Laȝamon, a chronicle containing the earliest known account of King Arthur in English; and
- the anonymous *Proverbs of Alfred*, a collection of sayings attributed to King Alfred the Great.

Of these the *Brut* and *The Owl and the Nightingale* are preserved in manuscripts from the second half of the 13th century – their dating to an earlier period is debated, and in the case of *The Owl and the Nightingale* hotly disputed. There are also a number of shorter lyrical and didactic poems including the *Canute Song*, St Godric's hymns, *The Grave*, and the Worcester Fragments. The latter, transcribed by the so-called 'Tremulous Hand' of Worcester, include *The First Worcester Fragment* – a poem concerned with Old English learning, literary, and religious heritage; and the *Soul's Address to the Body* – fragmentary passages about the transience of earthly life. In summary then, in comparison with later Middle English verse the surviving collection is small. The main notable features of early Middle English poetry, all briefly discussed below, are:

- the influence of French and Latin literature in the choice of subject matter and literary forms;

- the continuity with Old English poetical tradition;
- the use of both Old English and Continental metres, sometimes in combination; the use of the same prosodic and stylistic devices in both prose and verse;
- its literary character;
- the poor preservation of the material.

Early Middle English poetry was a product of a multilingual society, written by authors familiar with Latin and French literature and interested in the adaptation of its plots, genres, and metrical forms. Thus Laȝamon's *Brut* is a free and considerably expanded adaptation of the French *Roman de Brut*, written by the court poet Wace during the reign of Henry II. Laȝamon's interest in Arthurian material and Celtic and Anglo-Saxon legends and history was inspired by French and Latin works of poets and historians at Henry's court. Arthurian legends became popular in the second half of the 12th century as a way of celebrating a heroic national past and the ideal of kingship, and enjoyed popularity and royal patronage throughout the Middle English period. Similarly *The Owl and the Nightingale* follows a tradition of Latin and French 'debate' poems and is composed in an English version of the French octosyllabic couplet made fashionable by court poets and used by Wace in *Roman de Brut*. Finally, the *Orrmulum* employs a highly regular 15-syllable verse imitating Latin 7-stress metres, whereas the *Poema Morale* has striking resemblances to a late 12th-century Anglo-Norman verse sermon.

Another major influence on early Middle English verse was the Old English literary tradition. A concern with the Old English cultural and political legacy and an interest in Old English poetic technique is strongly present in such poems as *The Grave*, the Worcester Fragments, and Laȝamon's *Brut*. The *First Worcester Fragment*, for example, praises the achievements of the Anglo-Saxon church and the learning of monastic scholars who taught the people in their own language, and mourns their loss. Many poems from the period are written using unrhymed alliterative line, either throughout as in *The Grave*, or in conjunction with rhyming lines (as witnessed in the Worcester Fragments and *Brut*). It is not entirely clear how the early Middle English poets became familiar with alliterative verse, because no manuscripts containing Old English poetry survive from the period. This has given rise to an ongoing discussion among scholars about the nature of continuity between Old and Middle English alliterative poetry and prose: alliterative techniques may have been known to Middle English writers from lost early Middle English manuscripts or from an oral tradition of some kind. Alternatively, Middle English writers could have reconstructed alliterative style from the study of pre-Conquest manuscripts. Several scholars argue that Laȝamon's verse, for example, reads like a learned imitation of Old English alliterative poetry, rather than a product of a contemporary living tradition. Though there is no evidence that Laȝamon read Old English poetry, his imperfect but often impressively detailed knowledge of Old English poetic conventions suggests familiarity with manuscripts of pre-Conquest verse. Daniel Donoghue (1990) argues that such manuscripts were available to Laȝamon; after all he lived only about ten miles away from the monastery at Worcester where the Worcester Fragments were copied, and the library had manuscripts containing Old English poems.

Early Middle English verse presents some notable problems also in terms of its mixing of styles and metres; so much so that it is occasionally difficult to distinguish between prose and poetry. This is not new. In Old English, with the development of the rhythmical prose style, there are also discussions as to whether a particular text is a poem or a piece of prose, as the authors felt free to combine various devices from both modes of writing. The *First Worcester Fragment* is often described as both prose and verse, and the highly ornamental prose of the early 13th-century 'Katherine group' of texts is seen as one of the possible influences on 14th-century Middle English alliterative poetry. The evidence of manuscripts is not always conclusive for distinguishing between different modes of writing. All English poems discussed in this entry (and indeed surviving Old English poems) are 'laid out' as prose in the manuscripts, apart from all but one of the copies of the *Poema Morale* (preserved in seven manuscripts) and both surviving copies of *The Owl and the Nightingale*. It appears that the scribes' choice of layout was at least partly dependent on their perception of poetry as belonging to either a native or a Continental tradition. The *Brut*, with its alliterative verse following Old English tradition, is laid out as prose; whereas poems in syllabic metres, following the Latin and French models, are more commonly laid out as verse.

Most surviving early Middle English poetry, including all longer texts, is literary in character, that is it is not folklore or a product of an oral tradition. Several of the longer texts are by learned self-conscious authors, whose names are either known from their works, as is the case with Laȝamon and Orrm, or at least may be indirectly revealed in the text, as is the case with Nicholas of Guildford, a possible author of *The Owl and the Nightingale*. These poets tell us about themselves in their works and comment directly on events and situations described. This does not happen in surviving Old English poetry. The only poets whose names we know from the Old English period are Cædmon and Cynewulf. We know the name of Cædmon indirectly from Bede's account of his life in *Ecclesiastical History*. The name of Cynewulf is known from his 'signatures', spelt out in runes in a riddle-like manner in his poems, but unlike Laȝamon and Orrm he does not tell about himself and does not discuss his work in his poems; his signatures are part of his requests for prayer.

Finally we should note the preservation of the material. As we declared at the beginning, very little early Middle English verse survives. We tend to divide the small surviving corpus into longer and shorter pieces. The longer pieces, including Laȝamon's *Brut*, *The Owl and the Nightingale*, the *Proverbs of Alfred* and the *Poema Morale*, are all preserved in more then one manuscript copy. The main exception to this is the *Orrmulum*, possibly an unfinished text, which survives as an author's holograph in a single manuscript (Oxford, Bodleian Library MS. Junius 1). Shorter texts are, on the contrary, largely preserved in single copies, e.g. *The Grave*, or the poetry transmitted by the 'Tremulous Hand' of Worcester. An exception to this rule is the shorter texts which are included as part of longer works of prose, such as the hymns of St Godric which appear in his Latin *Life* by Reginald of Durham, in a Latin chronicle by Roger of Wendover, and in other prose works surviving in manuscripts from the end of the 12th century and later. This again has parallels in the transmission of Old English poetry, where texts surviving in multiple copies, such as *Cædmon's Hymn* or *Bede's Death Song*, were short pieces preserved as part of longer prose works. The only established written context of smaller genres of poetry in the 12th and early 13th centuries appears to have been that of a prose work, including chronicles, treatises, and sermons, where verse was used for historical, mnemonic, rhetorical, and other reasons. Otherwise shorter lyrical poetry appears to have existed both literally and figuratively in the margins of the written tradition. Thus the poem entitled 'Ic an witles ful iwis' is pencilled in the top margin of a folio in an early 13th-century manuscript in the British Library, and *The Grave* is added at the bottom of a folio containing the end of an Old English sermon in a manuscript dating from the third quarter of the 12th century, now in the Bodleian Library, Oxford.

To summarise, we should consider the following key points:

- relatively little early Middle English verse survives, but it is diverse, and includes important and original works;

- it was influenced by contemporary French and Latin poetry, but also by the Old English tradition;
- early Middle English poetry is learned and literary, and we know the names of at least some of the authors;
- the transmission, manuscript presentation, and preservation of early Middle English poetry displays some of the same patterns as are found in the transmission of Old English poetry.

See also   Chapter 2(f), Chapter 3(a), (b), (d), (e), and (g), and Chapter 4(d) and (e).

Further Reading

For an account of early Middle English literature see Wilson (1951 and 1970). For discussions of individual works see Allen (1992, especially the verse translation of Laȝamon's *Brut* with its important introduction), Allen, Perry, and Roberts (2002), Donoghue (1990), Franzen (1991), Hill (1977), Le Saux (1989), Morrison (1983), Parkes (1991b), and Stanley (1969).

(d)   Didactic Literature and Saints' Lives

Most of Middle English vernacular religious literature was written for the laity, or for mixed audiences including the laity. Such literature had its opponents and was a subject of intense ideological controversy. Thus, throughout the period there were doubts whether English was sufficiently flexible and developed to be the language of spiritual guidance and theological discourse. Another important concern was whether people without clerical education should have access to theology and doctrine, whether this was safe for them and therefore which texts should be made available in the vernacular.[3] Throughout the period, church authorities attempted to control the content and practice of preaching and translation, and to censor materials addressed to the laity. At the same time the growing emancipation and education of lay believers resulted in a greater number of texts of increasing sophistication and variety which were made available to them.

An important encouragement for providing religious literature for the laity came from the Fourth Lateran Council, convened by Pope Innocent III in 1215. The Council made it mandatory that every

---

[3] Such questions were asked during the Old English period as well. Ælfric, for example, expresses concern in his Preface to his translation of the Book of Genesis that unlearned people may read the Old Testament and emulate some of the practices contained therein, ignorant of how these were changed by the testament of Christ.

member of the church should confess to a priest and receive commu-
nion at least once a year. It emphasised the need to increase the
knowledge and understanding of Christian teaching among the laity.
This coincided with the rise of fraternal orders (notably the
Dominicans and the Franciscans), who engaged in preaching to lay
people. The pastoral reform started by the Fourth Lateran Council
and the activities of the fraternal orders encouraged vernacular
preaching and religious instruction, and resulted in an expansion of
vernacular religious writing. Important religious texts from the
period are discussed below: literature addressed primarily to women,
texts addressed more broadly to lay audiences, saints' lives, and
sermons.

A prominent group of religious texts addressed primarily to
women comes from the west Midlands and includes the *Ancrene
Wisse* ('Guide for Anchoresses') and texts known as the 'Katherine
group' and the 'Wooing group'. These were composed at the beginning of the 13th century and share a manuscript tradition, linguistic
features, and thematic and stylistic parallels. In spite of these important similarities, they have differences in style and approach, and are
believed to have been written by different authors.

What is known as the 'Katherine group' of texts includes the lives
of three virgin martyrs – Sts Juliana, Katherine and Margaret – all
freely translated from Latin. It also contains a treatise on virginity
called *Hali Meiðhad* ('Holy Maidenhood'), and a treatise on the
protection and guardianship of the soul – *Sawles Warde* ('Custody of
the Soul'). The 'Wooing group' includes four meditations on Christ
and the Virgin Mary which are close to the 'Katherine group' in
imagery, language, and themes. The *Ancrene Wisse*, more widely
circulated than the other texts, was a guide or rule for anchoresses –
women who chose to lead a solitary religious life in a cell, often
attached to a church. Its author, possibly a Dominican, says that he is
writing in response to a request from three well-born sisters, who
adopted the life of anchoresses. The guide offers instruction on how
they should regulate their lives. It consists of a preface and eight
parts, covering the 'Outer Rule', concerned with practical matters
and running the household; and the 'Inner Rule', devoted to prayers,
the custody of the senses, temptations, deadly sins, confession,
penance, and the love of God. The author had a good knowledge of
Latin literature, but the *Ancrene Wisse* has no single Latin source. Its
popularity is attested to by its survival in seventeen manuscripts and
its translation into Latin and Anglo-Norman. Though primarily
addressed to anchoresses, it was probably written with a wider lay

audience in mind, and early on it was revised and adapted for different readers, both male and female. On many occasions it uses themes and imagery from secular literature, adapted for a religious context (such as the depiction of Christ as a knight who offers love to his lady the anchoress, or a parable of a king loving a noble poor lady).

Among the most interesting features of these west Midland texts are their style and language. Saints' lives of the 'Katherine group' are in rhythmical prose with heavy alliteration, modelled on the style of Old English writers such as Wulfstan and Ælfric. The *Ancrene Wisse* and *Sawles Warde* display more influence from the style of their Latin sources, but also draw on the prose of English alliterative texts. The *Ancrene Wisse* and texts of the 'Katherine group' survive in two early manuscripts (Cambridge, Corpus Christi College MS 402, and Oxford, Bodleian Library MS Bodl. 34) which share many linguistic features. Scholars call their language the 'AB language' following an influential 1929 article by J. R. R. Tolkien, who drew attention to the similarities in the language of the two manuscripts, which he identified by the sigils A and B. This language shows influence from late Old English spelling conventions and may represent an early post-Conquest local attempt to standardise orthography. Standardised spelling was used by Anglo-Saxon scribes, but did not become established in later English until the early modern period. Early Middle English attempts to regularise orthography witnessed in the AB language are particularly interesting because of their reliance on Old English practice.

Surviving Middle English religious works addressed to the laity use a variety of subject matter and approaches. *Aʒenbite of Inwyt* is a prose translation by Dan Michael of Northgate (a Benedictine) of *La Somme le Roi* (usually referred to as 'The Book of Vices'), an Anglo-Norman treatise on morality. It is preserved in an authorial manuscript dated to 1340. Its title, made famous by James Joyce, who used it in *Ulysses*, can be translated as the 'biting' or 'remorse' of the 'inner knowledge' or 'conscience'. It is a confessional treatise, discussing sins and Christian virtues, partly in allegorical form. Like many other Middle English religious writers, the author explains in the introduction that it is intended for lay readers who do not know French or Latin. *Aʒenbite of Inwyt* can be compared to another contemporary work, Robert Mannyng of Brunne's *Handlyng Synne*, which is also largely a translation, produced between 1303 and 1338, of an Anglo-Norman confessional manual *Le Manuel des Pechiez* (see also Chapter 3(e)). It is intended for a lay audience, though also possibly for preachers. *Handlyng Synne* contains a discussion, illustrated with many stories, of the ten commandments, the seven deadly sins, the seven sacraments, and the confession. The bulk of the narrative is devoted to the deadly sins and the readers are encouraged to make confession to their parish priest. The work, composed in rhyming couplets, was intended to have a popular appeal and includes criticism of sinful priests, dishonest officials, and lords who rob the poor. It contains several stories not found in Mannyng's source, some unique and some contemporary, which presumably would have been more interesting to his readers than some of the better known traditional stories. The author remarks that 'lewed men', for whom the work is written, like to hear 'tales and rimes', and promises to offer a more edifying pastime which will prevent the listeners from committing folly or sin (ll. 43–50).

The most popular Middle English religious work for the laity, judging by the number of surviving manuscripts, is *The Prick of Conscience*, written in the middle of the 14th century, probably in Yorkshire. It is preserved in 115 manuscripts, which is a considerably larger number than *The Canterbury Tales*, or *Piers Plowman*. It is just under 10,000 lines long, and consists of seven parts covering the creation and corruption of mankind, the instability of the world, death, purgatory, Doomsday, the pains of hell, and the joys of paradise. The main aim of the work is comprehensive religious and moral instruction, and it presents man as conducting a constant battle against sin, inspired by the love of God. However, it also provides detailed information on various other subjects, such as the structure of the universe (including a summary of contemporary cosmology in its last, seventh part), biblical history, real and legendary geography, and a wealth of practical information and lore. *The Prick of Conscience* is written in rhyming couplets. Its author is unknown. It used to be ascribed to Richard Rolle (see Chapter 3(j)), but this attribution is no longer supported by scholars.

Nicholas Love (d. 1424) was a monk and a prior of Mount Grace Charterhouse in Yorkshire, a newly founded Carthusian monastery. His *Myrrour of the Blessed Lyf of Jesu Christ* is a series of meditations on the life of Christ, subdivided into seven sections, each representing a day of the week. It is an adaptation of the highly influential Latin *Meditationes vitae Christi* ('Meditations on the life of Christ'), probably composed in Italy by a Franciscan friar, Johannes de Caulibus, about a century earlier. Love's introduction makes it clear that he was writing for a lay audience, but his work supports orthodoxy and is conservative in its respect for ecclesiastical hierarchy, adopting an anti-heretical and anti-Lollard stance, promoting an emphasis on humility, and a belief that the laity is incapable of understanding Scripture without guidance. Love kept the overall structure of his source, but omitted some material which he believed to be more appropriate for the religious, and less interesting for his lay audience. He also added his own didactic passages, and quotations from authorities. A large number of these additions comment directly on Lollard views, particularly on the questions of obedience to ecclesiastical authority, confession, the Eucharist, and church offerings (Lollards believed that tithes should be given directly to the poor). Love's book was presented to Archbishop Thomas Arundel, probably in accordance with Arundel's Lambeth Constitutions of 1409, which required that theological works be examined and licensed for publication.

Saints' lives were an established form of pious reading, circulated in English, Latin, and French. Their appeal was partly due to the fact that they combined the narrative interest of romance with elements of historical and instructional writing. Saints' lives were 'pious romances', providing both entertainment and teaching. Sometimes they were circulated in the same manuscripts as romances, and included similar plot elements, such as temptations, ordeals, and exotic settings. An early example of Middle English hagiography is *The South English Legendary*, a collection of saints' lives in verse. It originated in the west Midlands in the second half of the 13th century, in approximately the same geographical area as the 'Katherine group' of texts, but was more widely circulated and survives in over 50 manuscripts. It is structured around saints' festivals in the Church calendar and feasts relating to the life of Christ. Its earliest late 13th-century manuscript includes around 70 narratives, but more lives were added in the 14th and 15th centuries, so that its fullest surviving manuscript (Oxford, Bodleian Library MS Bodl. 779) comprises around 135 texts. As a narrative genre, saints' lives attracted the attention of many Middle English authors, including Lydgate and Chaucer. Jacobus de Voragine's *Legenda Aurea* ('The Golden Legend'), a tremendously influential Latin collection of saints' lives composed at the end of the 13th century, was translated into Middle English in 1438 by an anonymous author (this version is known as the *Gilte Legende*), and a new translation, known as the *Golden Legende*, was published by Caxton.

Sermons were texts intended for oral delivery and usually addressed to lay or mixed audiences. They were organised around the Church's calendar of saints' days and feasts, and around readings from the Gospels appointed for Sundays, or other occasions. The most comprehensive Middle English cycle of sermons, arranged around Sunday gospel readings, was the Wycliffite Sunday gospel collection. Other important collections were *Mirk's Festival*, compiled in the early 15th century by an Augustinian canon John Mirk, and a 14th-century *Northern Homily Cycle* in verse, possibly also composed by Augustinian canons. Sermon collections were used for both preaching and reading, combined bookish and oral styles, and were usually compilations derived from diverse sources rather than original compositions (see Chapter 2(f) for Old English sermons).

To summarise, we should consider the following key points:

- most of Middle English vernacular religious literature was written for the laity;
- religious texts used a variety of approaches and were addressed to different audiences;
- many, though not all, are adaptations of known French and Latin works.

See also   Chapter 2(f) and Chapter 3(e), (j), (k), and (u).

Further Reading

For accounts of the *Ancrene Wisse* and related texts, see Dahood (1984), Dobson (1976), Millett (1992), Tolkien (1929), and Wada (2003). A very useful annotated bibliography and a historical survey of the research on the *Ancrene Wisse*, the 'Katherine group', and the 'Wooing group' is Millet (1996). For surveys of Middle English religious literature and manuscripts, see Gillespie (1989), Morey (2000), Owst (1961), and Raymo (1986). See also Spencer (1993) and Wenzel (1986).

(e)   Post-Conquest Historical Writing

Historical writing in English flourished during the Anglo-Saxon period, as witnessed in the *Anglo-Saxon Chronicle* and in translations of other major works of European historiography into Old English. After the Norman Conquest, however, and until the late 14th century most historical writing in England was in Latin and French. In spite of this, English vernacular historiography continued to expand throughout the Middle English period. In the 14th and 15th centuries it became sufficiently prominent to challenge the position of Latin as a primary language of historical writing. Middle English authors made the world, national, church, and biblical history available in the vernacular through adaptations and translations of influential historical works, and through new compositions devoted to important historical subjects.

Middle English historical writing existed in a variety of forms, including genealogies (often in the form of rolls,[4] sometimes illustrated, showing the descent of a royal or noble house), different types of chronicles, and various shorter narratives. At the same time the boundaries between literary genres were flexible, and it is not always easy to draw a line between historical and other forms of writing. Interest in the past was shared by several Middle English literary genres, including romances and saints' lives. On the other hand even works primarily concerned with reporting historical events used narrative strategies and approaches borrowed from fiction and could contain clearly fictional elements, such as invented dialogue. On the whole the distinction between history and fiction was not always made in the same way as we expect it to be made today.

Middle English historical writing was didactic and tended to represent the past in the light of contemporary political and ideological concerns. Historians were particularly interested in kingship, government, the qualities of a perfect ruler, biblical history, and the history of the church, and this influenced their choice and treatment of subjects. Whereas at an earlier period history was written largely by clergy, particularly in Benedictine monasteries, in the 14th century it became more secularised and even more politicised. On the other hand, as historical writing developed, authors became more interested in verifying their information and in using documents and written sources. Important Middle English historical narratives, discussed below, include universal histories, the Brut chronicles, and local chronicles.

Universal histories narrate the story of the world from its creation and discuss different countries, peoples, and events. They are large in scope and more religious and moralistic than other types of history: part of their purpose is to uncover the divine plan present in human history in its progress from the Creation towards Judgement Day. Middle English world histories include the *Cursor Mundi* ('The Runner of the World'), probably composed in the north around 1300, and a late 14th-century translation by John of Trevisa of Ranulf Higden's *Polychronicon*.[5] A traditional way of organising world histories was

---

[4] Literally a piece of parchment or paper that was written upon and rolled up, like a scroll.
[5] Several other Middle English translations of the *Polychronicon* survive from the 15th century, including one complete anonymous translation preserved in London (British Library MS Harley, 2261).

to subdivide them into periods corresponding to the ages of the world, reflecting the medieval view that the world was in its last, seventh age (see Chapter 1(f) on the Anglo-Saxon view of the apocalypse). Ages of the world are the organising principle of both the *Cursor Mundi* and the *Polychronicon*. Both works are also often described as encyclopaedic histories, because they provide not only accounts of events from the past, but also diverse materials relating to Christian teaching, theology, geography, and cosmology. The *Cursor Mundi* is about 30,000 lines long and draws on several earlier works including the Bible, *Historia Scholastica* of Peter Comestor, *Legenda Aurea* of Jacobus de Voragine, folklore, and many other sources. According to the author it was addressed to lay people who cannot read Latin or French. The author himself was very knowledgeable in Latin literature, but also familiar with popular romances. In the prologue he tells of his intention to provide a more edifying reading than romances, but they clearly remained one of his most important models in relation to his style. His narrative is lively and entertaining, and he uses romance-like alliterative phraseology. He also addresses the audience as 'louerdinges' in keeping with popular romance tradition.

The main writings of John of Trevisa were translations of important historical, scientific, and political texts. These included an influential universal history, the *Polychronicon* of Ranulf Higden, who was a monk in the Benedictine abbey of St Werburgh in Chester and died in the 1360s. Trevisa was born *c.*1342, almost certainly in Cornwall, and died in 1402. He studied at Oxford, became a priest in 1370, and held various church appointments. Through much of his career he enjoyed the patronage of Thomas IV, Lord Berkeley of Berkeley Castle, in Gloucestershire, a wealthy and powerful nobleman. Through the influence of Thomas Berkeley, Trevisa appears to have received his clerical appointments. Thomas Berkeley was, importantly, the patron of Trevisa's literary works, including the translation of the *Polychronicon* completed in 1387. Through his associations with Oxford, Trevisa was almost certainly aware of the contemporary debates concerning biblical translation. He may even have taken part in the Wycliffite Bible, as William Caxton refers to Trevisa's translation of the Bible in his preface to the printed version of the *Polychronicon*. Whether or not Caxton's remark refers to the Wycliffite Bible, Trevisa was certainly interested in the theoretical aspects of translation. He explained his ideas about translation and its desirability in the prefatory materials to the *Polychronicon*, where among other things he discusses the translation of the Bible into the vernacular. During the 14th century the *Polychronicon* was the most complete world history available, and Trevisa's translation influenced a wide range of other Middle English works. Notably, it was the source of information for Chaucer and Lydgate, and was printed by Caxton in 1482 and by Wynkyn de Worde in 1495.

The so-called Brut chronicles describe the legendary foundation of Britain, beginning with the arrival and conquest of the island by Brutus, great-grandson of Aeneas of Troy. Several of these chronicles survive, composed in prose or verse. Robert of Gloucester's *Metrical Chronicle*, an anonymous *Short Metrical Chronicle*, and Robert Mannyng of Brunne's *The Chronicle of England* were all written between *c.*1300 and 1340. They start with the arrival of Brutus in Britain and end in the first half of the 14th century. What is known as the *Metrical Chronicle* of Robert of Gloucester is actually the work of several compilers. It survives in two versions, which differ in length and in their coverage of events after 1125. It is written in verse and is largely based on Geoffrey of Monmouth's *Historia regum Britanniae*. It is probably a Benedictine production, which started as a compilation of other histories and was extended with original continuations. Robert of Gloucester (*c.*1300), who refers to himself near the end of the longer version, may have been a Benedictine monk in the abbey of Gloucester, responsible for the later parts of the compilation. *The Chronicle of England* by Robert Mannyng of Brunne, written *c.*1338, is a reworking of Wace's verse *Roman de Brut*, an Anglo-Norman work composed during the reign of Henry II, which was widely circulated in England and was also the main source of Laȝamon's *Brut* (see below). It has borrowings from Geoffrey of Monmouth, William of Malmesbury, Bede and several other historians, and Mannyng's account of later English history is indebted to an Anglo-Norman chronicle of Pierre de Langtoft. *The Chronicle of England* is in verse and consists of two parts, the first covering the period from the arrival of Brut in Britain to the Anglo-Saxon invasions, and the second from the invasions to the end of the reign of Edward I. Mannyng discusses his use of English in *The Chronicle*, and justifies it in the same way as in his confessional treatise *Handlyng Synne*, by saying that his aim is to provide instruction for a lay audience.

The Middle English prose *Brut* tells the history of Britain from its foundation to the 15th century. It is a translation from Anglo-Norman which was produced at the beginning of the 15th century and became a highly influential and popular text: it exists in a large number of versions in at least 172 manuscripts. The prose *Brut* was the first English chronicle to be printed, and an edition by William Caxton appeared in 1480.

The earliest and best known of the English Brut chronicles is Laȝamon's *Brut*. It was the first vernacular work to use Arthurian legends. At the beginning of the *Brut* Laȝamon tells that he is a parish priest from Areley (probably Arely Kings, in Worcestershire), and that he decided to write a history of England's noblemen. His most immediate source was Wace's *Roman de Brut*, which he freely adapted. Laȝamon's history is about the rulers of England, who, as he shows, did not represent an unbroken line. It is a story of different peoples, with different interests and qualities, replacing one anther as the rulers of the land. The *Brut* was probably composed in the first half of the 13th century and survives in two versions, London, British Library, Cotton MS. Caligula A. IX; and London, British Library, Cotton MS. Otto C. XIII, both dating from the second half of the 13th century. The Cotton Otto version is abridged and edited, presenting a somewhat modernised text of the *Brut*. Laȝamon's poem was notably written in alliterative verse, imitating the metre, style, and language of Old English poetry. He avoided using words of French origin, even though he was translating from French; and his language and even spelling appear to have an intentionally archaistic feel, designed to give the work a flavour of antiquity (see Stanley, 1969). In the Cotton Otto version the archaistic flavour of the language and orthography was toned down. It appears that its scribe did not share Laȝamon's interest in the language and style of Old English poetry and attempted to modernise the work, bringing it in line with contemporary linguistic usage.

Finally, in addition to world histories and the Brut chronicles we should mention local chronicles as an example of Middle English historical writing. These local compilations and original records produced in monasteries and administrative centres provide an important source of information about the period. Thus London chronicles were year-by-year records which started at the end of the 12th century and continued to be written well into the 16th century. They described London, but also national and European events. The earliest records were in Latin, but the chronicles began to be written in English in the 1430s.

When approaching the post-Conquest historical texts we should consider the following key points:

- after the Norman Conquest, Latin and French became the languages of historical writing, but English vernacular historiography became established in the 14th and 15th centuries;
- interest in history is characteristic of several Middle English literary genres; the boundaries between them were flexible

and the distinction between scholarly historical writing and historical fiction was made differently from how it is made today;
- medieval historical writing was didactic and tended to represent the past in the light of contemporary political and ideological concerns;
- the major types of Middle English historical works are universal histories, the Brut chronicles, and local chronicles.

See also   Chapter 1(f), Chapter 2(d) and (h), and Chapter 3(c), (d), (h), (k), and (m).

Further Reading

For a survey of Middle English historical works and their manuscripts see Kennedy (1989). For comprehensive accounts of early and late Middle English historical writing see Tatlock (1950) and Taylor (1987). For the accounts of individual texts see Allen (1992), Allen, Perry and Roberts (2002), Donoghue (1990), Edwards (2004a), Fowler (1993), Horrall (1985 and 1989), Kennedy (1996), Le Saux (1989), and Stanley (1969).

(f)   Lyrical Poetry

Lyrical expression was central to the Old English elegies. They were often written in the first person singular, and their protagonists were given strong emotions and a compelling lyrical voice. As shown earlier, emotions and mental states which the elegies most commonly portray are loneliness, a longing to be reunited with one's friends, an anxiety about the inevitability of death and decline, and a sad awareness of the transience and instability of the world. All these subjects are common in medieval Christian literature as a whole, but it is impossible to deny that in the Old English elegies they are given individual expression. Elegies were probably a relatively late genre which may have developed in England soon after its Christianization: they have no parallels in other Germanic literatures and their content is partially Christian. Elegies show close thematic and other links with earlier heroic poetry. In spite of its importance, their focus on emotions rather than heroic action seems to have required a justification. That is to say, the protagonists of elegies are usually outcasts who mourn the loss of their past, depicted in very traditional heroic terms: the friendship of their lord, the closeness of friends and kin, being part of the lord's retinue, receiving gifts, feasting, or accompanying the lord into battle.

While Old English elegies had strong ties with heroic poetry, during the Middle English period lyrical poetry becomes more emancipated from other literary genres in terms of style, themes, and approach. Thus it becomes the main literary form for the portrayal of the new subject of romantic love. Romantic love was not depicted in Old English poetry (but see Chapter 2(o) for a discussion of the prose *Apollonius of Tyre*). This does not mean of course that it did not exist in real life, only that literature develops by changing its thematic range to include new subjects, such as romance. At different times, different subjects are seen as more appropriate and interesting for portrayal in literature.

When new subjects become popular following cultural and social changes, writers develop means and techniques for their literary portrayal, and this can be a gradual process. In the 12th century the southern French troubadour poets transformed the concept of feudal service to a lord into a concept of service to a lady, and made idealised romantic love the subject of poetry. Portrayal of love in lyrical poetry can be compared to its portrayal in the narrative genre of romance, which also becomes popular around that time. The 12th century is sometimes described as the age of the 'discovery of the individual'. In literary terms this meant bringing new subjects to do with individual intellectual and emotional life into the sphere of literature. Middle English love poetry is deeply indebted to the French tradition of aristocratic romantic poetry, from its 12th-century beginnings to its later development in the works of such 14th-century poets as Deschamps, Froissart, and Machaut. Much of the surviving Middle English love poetry belongs to the genre known as 'courtly lyric'. It is lyrical verse, aristocratic in inspiration, which typically describes the lover's passion and pleas to his lady, the lady's beauty, and the pain of rejection and separation, and offers instruction in the art of love, and sometimes moral guidance. The audience of such poetry in England probably included not only the royal court, but also gentry, landowners, and their households.

During the Middle English period 'love' became an important subject of devotional poetry as well. Whereas in the Old English poem *The Dream of the Rood*, Christ is described as a victorious hero, in Middle English religious poetry he is often portrayed as a suffering victim, who loves mankind and to whom poets address their love. Middle English devotional poetry was influenced by the tradition of courtly lyric, but it also reflects contemporary devotional practice which is known as 'affective piety'. This dominated religious practice from the 12th century and up to the Reformation. During this time the devout were encouraged to focus their emotions and imagination on their worship and to concentrate on Christ's suffering and humanity. Affective empathy and emotional involvement were believed to make one a participant of Christ's Passion and to facilitate repentance and moral reform. Such piety is reflected in many religious lyrics, particularly those describing the Nativity, the Crucifixion, and other episodes from the lives of Christ and the Virgin Mary. Nativity lyrics commonly explored the pathos of the happiness and tranquillity of Christ's birth and the suffering of his subsequent life. Crucifixion lyrics portrayed Christ's sacrifice using realistic visual imagery and insisted that such an act of love demanded unconditional love in return.[6] The popular lyric *Stond wel, moder, under rode* ('Stand well, mother, under the cross') – surviving in many manuscript copies – depicts a dialogue between Christ on the cross and the Virgin Mary standing at the foot of the cross. Descriptions of Mary's grief alternate with descriptions of Christ's suffering, each heightening each other's pathos and effectiveness. Poems devoted to the Virgin Mary often concentrated on her suffering, but also portrayed her 'joys', such as the Annunciation, the Nativity, Christ's Resurrection, the Assumption, and the Coronation in heaven. They were sometimes modelled on courtly lyrics and proclaimed the poet's devotion to Mary in terms borrowed from romantic poetry.

There was in fact mutual influence between romantic and religious verse. Thomas of Hales's *Love-Ron*, for example, declares that it was written at the request of a young woman dedicated to the service of God. It is modelled on a love poem, but encourages the reader to become aware of the world's transience and presents the love of God as the only secure, enduring and worthy love. Two closely related lyrics – *The Way of Woman's Love* and *The Way of Christ's Love* are preserved in London, British Library MS Harley 2253, a manuscript collection containing some of the best known Middle English lyrical poetry. They are mirror images of one another, however. One describes romantic love, whereas the other describes the love of Christ but in exactly the same terms. Scholarly opinion differs as to which is the original and which is the adaptation.

Closely related to religious lyrics were moral and penitential lyrics, which contained meditations on the inevitability of death and the

---

[6] This was also happening in art at that time, which moved towards realistic depiction of the suffering on the cross.

uncertainty and misery of human life on earth, and expressed a contempt for the joys of the world. The *ubi sunt* motive, common already in Anglo-Saxon poetry (see Chapter 2(i)), is the subject of a lyric entitled *Ubi sount qui ante nos fuerount?* ('Where are those who lived before us?'), in Oxford, Bodleian Library MS Digby 86 – another important manuscript collection containing lyrical poetry. It was circulated as part of a longer poem, *The Sayings of St. Bernard*, but also separately, which attests to the popularity of its subject.

Middle English political verse contained social criticism, satire, and responses to recent political events. Thus Harley 2253 has several lyrics which describe political events from the second half of the 13th to the first quarter of the 14th century, including the defeat of Richard of Cornwall by Simon de Montfort at the Battle of Lewes in 1264, the execution of Simon Fraser in 1306, the Flemish uprising of 1302, and the death of Edward I in 1307. According to Thorlac Turville-Petre these lyrics were still of interest in 1340, at the time when Harley 2253 was produced, because they reflected themes which were still current, such as the baronial struggle against centralised royal power or England's political rivalry with Scotland and France (2005, p. 175). The poetry of social protest focused on the corruption of officials and clergy, poverty, and the effects of excessive taxation.

Middle English lyrical poetry employed a wide range of metrical forms, both rhyme and alliteration, and different, sometimes very complex stanza patterns. Imagery in the descriptions of such traditional subjects as nature, women's beauty, or lovers' feelings, was often conventional and the language contained formulaic expressions and tags such as 'byrde in a bour' or 'beste among the bolde'. Unlike French lyrical poetry the great majority of Middle English lyrics are anonymous. Most early Middle English lyrics are also preserved haphazardly in the margins or unused space in manuscript folios. This seems to have changed during the later Middle English period. Towards the end of the 13th century, lyrics started to be circulated in multilingual anthologies or miscellanies of poetry and prose, such as the two manuscripts mentioned above, the Harley lyrics (copied in the Ludlow area of Shropshire, *c.*1340), and Digby 86 (compiled in the last quarter of the 13th century in Worcestershire). Such anthologies were produced in increasingly large numbers, though thematically organised anthologies of poetry were virtually unknown in Middle English. Verses, mostly religious (but not exclusively so), were also often used in sermons, particularly those associated with the Franciscan order, which emphasised pastoral activities amongst the laity. They were used for various rhetorical and practical purposes, such as to assist memorisation, to stimulate affective piety, and to engage the attention of the audience.

To summarise, we should consider the following key points:

- Old English lyrical poetry, represented primarily by the elegies, has many similarities with heroic poetry in subject matter and approach; in particular the protagonist of the elegies is usually an outcast of the traditional heroic world, and the feelings portrayed are associated with the loss of this world;
- Middle English lyrical poetry is more emancipated from other types of verse and is very diverse in terms of approach and protagonists;
- the development of romantic poetry is paralleled by the development of the narrative genre of romance;
- Middle English religious verse reflected contemporary devotional practice known as 'affective piety', and there were mutual influences between religious and romantic lyrics.

See also Chapter 2(i), (j), and (o).

Further Reading

Essays in Duncan (2005) provide accounts of Middle English lyrical poetry, its metrical forms and manuscript tradition, with the essay by Turville-Petre dealing with reactions to political events. Good introductions to religious lyrics are Gray (1972) and Woolf (1968), and to secular lyrics, Moore (1951). See also D'Arcy (2005), Hill (1964), and Jeffrey (1975).

(g)   Debate Poetry

The genre of debate has its roots in classical tradition and was popular throughout Europe during the Middle Ages. Several poems where participants compete in wisdom and discuss philosophical and theological ideas survive from the Anglo-Saxon period. In later medieval England debate poems were circulated in English, Latin, and French. Debate as a rhetorical exercise, analytical tool, and method of discovering truth, was used in various institutional contexts. Thus disputation was practised in courts of law, appeared in school teaching with its emphasis on rhetoric, and was an established part of teaching and examination in universities. Debates were equally attractive to writers because of their dramatic, descriptive, and analytical possibilities. Middle English poets employed debate as a method of describing objects, personalities, and concepts, and shaping their identity through comparison and contrast. They used the framework of disputation to bring together opposite points of view and to reveal contradictions and differences in their material.

Some surviving Middle English debate poems are serious in the choice of subject matter and approach, such as the religious poem *The Dispute between Mary and the Cross*. In this dialogue the Virgin Mary speaks about her grief and reproaches the Cross for being an instrument of her son's death, to which the Cross responds by describing its role in human salvation. Several other debate poems are humorous, even if their subject matter is ultimately serious and their purpose is to instruct. Such debates tend to emphasise the participants' verbal skills, and delight in rhetoric and the absurd, employing colloquial language and exchanges of insults and threats. The protagonists of Middle English debate poems are often personifications of moral or intellectual categories, or objects and animals representing different ideas, points of view, and types of human behaviour. This allegorical dimension does not prevent the protagonists of debates from having believable personalities which effectively combine the symbolic with the realistic, and human characteristics with animal features. True to their roots in teaching, surviving Middle English debates show a strong interest in morality, conduct, and theology and instruction. They also use proverbs, references to the Bible, and stories and fables to illustrate various points.

The alliterative poem *The Parliament of the Three Ages*, probably composed in the second half of the 14th century, describes the narrator falling asleep and hearing a flyting exchange between the personifications of 'Youthe', 'Medill Elde', and 'Elde' ('Youth', 'Maturity/Middle Age', and 'Old Age'). All three reveal their characteristics and failures, but the dispute remains inconclusive, even though 'old age' seems to have the last word and points out that the wastefulness of youth and the industry of middle age are both futile in the face of death. The poet appears to have been more interested in describing different ages and revealing their moral and spiritual significance, than in resolving their dispute. Another early alliterative poem, *Wynnere and Wastoure* (possibly composed around the middle of the 13th century), is also a dream-vision where the poet describes himself falling asleep and witnessing a debate between the leaders of two hosts, Winner and Waster. Both argue before a king about the proper use of wealth, but the poem is incomplete, the conclusion is missing, and it is not clear who should win the debate. *The Parliament of the Three Ages* and *Wynnere and Wastoure* belong to the same literary tradition and share themes, genre characteristics, part of their manuscript tradition, and the same Midlands dialect, as well as employing a similar metre. Both contain social satire and political allegory and the debate is used to demonstrate the complexity of different concepts and approaches to life, rather than to argue undeniably in favour of a particular point of view.

The Owl and the Nightingale is the best known of Middle English debate poems. It is over 1,700 lines long and its date is uncertain. In lines 1091–2 it refers to 'king Henri' as dead, and some scholars believe that it was written after the death of Henry II in 1189 and probably before the accession of Henry III in 1216. However, it has also been argued that the poem better fits the literary context of the middle of the 13th century, and may have been composed after the death of Henry III in 1272 (see Cartlidge, 1996). It survives in two manuscripts, both from the second half of the 13th century.

In the poem two birds, the Owl and the Nightingale, debate who sings best and who is more useful to mankind. In the course of their debate they discuss marriage, adultery, and various human situations and behaviour. They also touch on various philosophical and theological issues such as permanence and transience, refer to facts and legendary matter about birds, and tell stories to illustrate their views. The Nightingale seems to represent a joyful and light-hearted approach to life, whereas seriousness is advocated by the Owl. The portrayal of the two birds is based on various preconceptions about their nature, though possibly also on observation. The birds' habits are realistically described: the Nightingale sings at night, the Owl is mobbed by other birds and catches mice in churches. At the same time their behaviour receives figurative and moral interpretation, which allows the poet to bring diverse human issues into the discussion. Such an approach ultimately derives from the medieval view that the natural world can be understood in the light of Christian teaching. Medieval bestiaries – books containing short, often illustrated, descriptions of various known and legendary creatures – were religious works which emphasised the moral, symbolic, and theological significance of animals (as did the Old English *Physiologus* – see Chapter 2(l)). *The Owl and the Nightingale* uses a similar approach, but in a light-hearted way. The author gives the disputants a mixture of human and animal features in order to make serious points, but also for comical and satirical effect. The poem is justly celebrated for the lightness of touch with which it approaches a diverse and largely serious subject matter.

At the end of the poem both the Owl and the Nightingale agree that the judge of their debate should be Nicholas of Guildford, who is described as a parish priest living in the village of Portesham in Dorset. He is praised for his wisdom and achievements and represented as a perfect judge of the birds' song. Both birds plead with his superiors for his advancement. Many scholars believe that this may be the author of the poem, though nothing is known about him and there is no other evidence to support this attribution. The poem ends without revealing the judgement of Nicholas of Guildford and the debate remains open-ended. The author's decision to leave it without a solution recalls the inconclusiveness of other Middle English debates whose authors were also more interested in revealing the contradictions and complexities in their subject matter than in judging disputes. Neil Cartlidge (2001) has also suggested that *The Owl and the Nightingale* contains an element of self-parody and self-reflection. The purpose of a debate may be to resolve a conflict and discover truth, but in *The Owl and the Nightingale* rhetoric seems to be more important than finding a solution. The birds' determination to win the debate, and immunity to each other's arguments, cast doubts on the reliability of argumentative discourse.

The Thrush and the Nightingale is another Middle English debate poem where the protagonists are birds. It is preserved in two manuscripts, the earliest from the end of the 13th century. It has a number of similarities with *The Owl and the Nightingale* in terms of approaches and themes, such as its interest in the character and conduct of women. Their nature is in fact the main subject of *The Thrush and the Nightingale*. The Thrush attacks them as false, selfish, and lustful, whereas the Nightingale defends women for being virtuous, chaste, courteous, and meek. Both exchange insults and offer examples from history, literature, and the Bible. At the end, the Nightingale mentions the Virgin Mary and the Thrush immediately admits his error and promises not to speak badly about women. The poem is much shorter, less complex, and less ambitious than *The Owl and the Nightingale*, but it is well structured and has a similar lightness of touch.

In conclusion we should consider the following key points:

- medieval poetic debate had the double aim of teaching and entertaining;
- serious moral, social, and intellectual issues were presented in allegorical form alongside the humorous and the absurd;
- judgement was often withheld or inconclusive, and the main aim was to emphasise the complexity of the debate and offer

an intellectually stimulating and interesting analysis of the subject matter.

See also   Chapter 2(l) and (m), and Chapter 3(r) for debating birds in Chaucer's *The Parliament of Fowls*.

Further Reading

Reed (1990) and Utley (1972) provide general accounts of debate poetry and its manuscripts. The most recent edition of *The Owl and the Nightingale*, with an introduction, translation, and extensive commentary, is Cartlidge (2001). See also Cartlidge (1996) and Hume (1975). *The Dispute between Mary and the Cross* was edited with an introduction by Fein (1998). For alliterative debate poems see Ginsberg's edition, with an introduction and bibliography (1992).

(h)   Romances and Arthurian Literature

Middle English romance is difficult to define as a literary form because of the great variety of themes, approaches, and styles found in works attributed to this genre. Most early romances were in verse, though prose romances also appeared in the 15th century. Perhaps the most important characteristic of a romance is that it is a primarily narrative and recreational genre. Romances always tell a story, which can be simple and tightly structured or a lengthy sequence of episodes with multiple characters, settings, and narrative levels. Romances were written to entertain, even though they could contain moral instruction or historical information, and dealt with serious themes such as kingship, loyalty, fortune, or justice. Romances usually portray an aristocratic feudal world, which provides the setting, characters, and values; and idealise feudal society and its relationships. Common plot elements of romances include courtship, tournaments, mistaken identity, travel to exotic lands, exile, magic and the supernatural, separation and reuniting of lovers, and parents and children.

The growth of romance in Europe began in the 12th century and continued thereafter. This period is sometimes described as the time of the 'discovery of the individual'. If the main interest of earlier epic narratives, as witnessed by the *Chanson de Roland* or ·*Beowulf*, was history, romance displays a much greater interest in the individual. The protagonist of an epic is usually a national hero and events described concern the fate of the whole nation. Romances can also have royal protagonists and depict wars and other events of national significance, but they are chiefly concerned with the characters' private and emotional lives, particularly with their family, love, and marriage. Romances usually have happy endings, whereas epics often end with the hero's death. Though the setting of romances was aristocratic, the audience was not necessarily so. During the Middle English period the audience of romance gradually expanded to include country gentry and the middle class. There is evidence that in England they were the primary audience of vernacular romances, rather than French ones.

The earliest known 'romance' in English is the Old English *Apollonius of Tyre*, which survives in a mid-11th-century manuscript. The earliest post-Conquest romances circulated in England were in French, with the largest number created between 1150 and 1230. The first Middle English romances appeared in the second quarter of the 13th century and were influenced by their French predecessors.

There is a tradition, going back to the Middle Ages, of classifying romances by three 'matters', according to their historical and geographical setting:

- the Matter of France (romances about Charlemagne and his court, poorly represented in English);
- the Matter of Rome (stories about the Trojan War, based on the *Aeneid* and Latin translations of Homer; stories about Thebes, which were known chiefly from the *Thebiad* of Statius; and legendary stories about Alexander the Great); and
- the Matter of Britain (Arthurian romances, which form the largest and best represented group in English).

This classification, though useful, does not do justice to all the variety of romances. There are also romances set in England, and focusing on local legends (as opposed to Arthurian Britain), such as *King Horn*, *Havelock the Dane*, *Bevis of Hampton*, or *Guy of Warwick*, as well as those with an oriental setting, such as *Floris and Blancheflour*. *King Horn* is the earliest surviving Middle English romance, composed *c.*1225. Its hero is a prince who has to leave his homeland invaded by Saracens and take refuge in the kingdom of Westernesse. There he falls in love with Rymenhild, the king's daughter, but is separated from her and banished to Ireland. He proves himself by performing many heroic deeds and eventually wins back his kingdom and marries Rymenhild. *Havelock the Dane*, written *c.*1300, tells the story of a Danish prince who has to live in humble circumstances in exile in England. After many adventures he returns to Denmark, kills a guardian who usurped his throne, becomes king and marries a princess. *Bevis of Hampton* and *Guy of Warwick* were both written in the late 13th century to tell the stories of legendary ancestors of prominent aristocratic families. *Floris and Blancheflour*, written in the first half of the 13th century, is a tale about two lovers, set at the court of the Saracen Emir. A Muslim prince and a daughter of a Christian lady have to overcome many obstacles before they can finally marry.

Another group of romances which clearly stands out is the so-called 'Breton lays'. Original Breton lays appear to have once existed in Brittany but do not survive. They probably were oral narratives performed with musical accompaniment, which were 'discovered' by French writers and reinvented as a literary genre. They became popular after Marie de France (a French poet who probably lived in England and wrote for the royal court) composed, in the late 12th century, a series of French *lais*, short narrative poems which focused on women, love, and magic, rather than on the usual chivalric adventures. The Middle English *Sir Launfal* is a reworking of Marie de France's *Lanval*, for example. Chaucer's Franklin also introduces his tale about love and ordeal as a 'Breton lay', and the Wife of Bath tells a tale set in Brittany involving magic, love, and marriage.

Perhaps the best known of Middle English Breton lays is *Sir Orfeo*, composed in the late 13th or early 14th century in the south Midlands (or possibly London), and celebrated for its outstanding imaginative power. It is based on the classical story of Orpheus and Eurydice, but has a happy ending where Orfeo is reunited with his wife. Like the majority of Middle English romances *Sir Orfeo* may be an adaptation of an earlier lost French romance, but it includes many descriptive and plot elements characteristic of Celtic literature and folklore. It is famous for its portrayal of fairies as mysterious, beautiful, but dangerous beings, whose kingdom is wonderfully rich, but deadly for humans. Episodes involving fairies include such well-known plot elements as the fairy hunt, the fairy dance in the wood, and the abduction of humans by fairies. *Sir Orfeo* also portrays travel to the underworld, which involves entering the fairy kingdom through a rock, an enchanted tree, and a wish granted by the Fairy King. As in many medieval romances the narrative focuses on the love and loyalty between the main characters, Orfeo and Heurodis, and the test of their relationship and values.

The largest group of surviving Middle English romances is based on Arthurian legends. Many of them date from the 14th century. Such romances were influenced by the great tradition of the French Arthurian romance, rather then by the works of native authors such as Geoffrey of Monmouth or Laʒamon, who saw King Arthur as a national hero and the stories about him as part of their national history. By contrast, few European or English romances have Arthur as their main character, though some do, such as the alliterative poem *Morte Arthure* ('The Death of Arthur'), which deals with Modred's betrayal of Arthur and Arthur's death. It is an outstanding work, composed in the North of England before 1400, which focuses on the heroic and tragic, rather than the romantic aspects of the Arthurian legend and in this respect is closer to Laʒamon than to French Arthurian romances. Most romances, however, tell about the adventures of Arthur's knights, such as Gawain, Lancelot, Percevel, and Tristram. Thus, unlike the alliterative *Morte Arthure*, the stanzaic *Morte Arthure* (based on the French prose *Mort Artu* written *c*.1400) focuses on the love affair of Lancelot and Guinevere. Similarly *Ywain and Gawain* is a mid-14th-century abridgement and translation of *Le Chevalier au Lion* by Chrétien de Troyes, which concentrates on the story of Ywain. He is a knight of King Arthur's court, who wins and marries a lady but loses her love because of breaking a vow. He has to perform many deeds, fighting for justice and learning humility until he is redeemed and reconciled with his wife. The Middle English *Ywain and Gawain* focuses on action, omitting many of Chrétien de Troyes's descriptive passages and simplifying characterisation.

On the whole, many Middle English romances are more straightforward and less assured than their French models, though there are important exceptions, such as *Sir Gawain and the Green Knight*, which is both sophisticated and highly original. Unlike French and Anglo-Norman romances Middle English equivalents are also nearly all anonymous. Derek Pearsall observed that Arthurian romance was becoming popular in England at the time when it was going out of fashion in France, and the taste was changing in favour of a different type of narrative, such as the allegorical *Roman de la Rose* (Pearsall, 2003, pp. 60–3). Both Chaucer and Gower were strongly influenced by the *Roman de la Rose*, but make very little use of Arthurian material. In *The Canterbury Tales* Chaucer is condescending in his comments about Arthurian legends, and even includes a direct parody of a romance (*Sir Thopas*). As mentioned already, the audience of English romances was probably provincial gentry and the urban middle class, rather than the royal court and the aristocracy. For such readers vernacular romances provided access to the intellectual and cultural concerns of the social elite.

Most Middle English romances are composed in one of three types of metrical form:

- alliterative verse (particularly associated with the heroic subject matter);
- rhymed couplets;
- tail-rhyme (a stanza containing six, or sometimes twelve lines, rhyming *aabccb*, where lines rhyming in couplets have four stresses and lines rhyming '*b*' are shorter and have three stresses).

The tail-rhyme stanza was particularly associated with romance, as suggested by its use in Chaucer's *Sir Thopas*. Middle English romances share not only metrical form, themes, and elements of plot, but also many features of their style. These include traditional collocations, formulaic tags and expressions, and conventional detail in the descriptions of beautiful women, armour, dress, feasting, and battles. Poets also tend to style themselves as minstrels and oral performers, urging the audience to listen, and insist on the antiquity and truthfulness of their stories.

Middle English prose romances date from the middle of the 15th century. This is much later than in France where Arthurian romances were circulated as large prose cycles from the early 13th century onwards. The best known of the Middle English prose romances and the most influential English Arthurian narrative is *Morte Darthur* by Sir Thomas Malory (*c*.1410–70). Written in the 1460s, it was an attempt to produce a comprehensive account of Arthurian stories drawn from different sources. Much remains unknown about Malory's life and even his identity as the author of *Morte Darthur* is to some extent a matter of conjecture. He was a nobleman involved in various events of the Wars of the Roses, possibly on the Lancastrian side, though it is not entirely clear what his political sympathies were. In his book he refers to himself as 'knight prisoner', and it seems that he spent much of the last 20 years of his life in prison, accused of various crimes. His involvement in politics may have been at least partly responsible for this. It is likely, however, that his confinement was not very strict, and he continued to have access to books. *Morte Darthur* appears to have been written during this time.

Morte Darthur is known from two sources. The first is an edition printed by William Caxton in 1485. It is clear that Caxton edited Malory's text, as he did in several of his other publications, dividing it into books and chapters in order to tighten its structure and make it more accessible to his readers. There is also a manuscript written by two scribes probably after 1470, and discovered in 1934. Though it shows many signs of scribal interference, and is by no means a perfect representation of Malory's work, it became the basis of standard editions and critical discussions.

In the manuscript the work is subdivided into four major parts, which gave rise to debates among scholars whether *Morte Darthur* is a single unified work or a collection of narratives. It starts with an account of Arthur's origin and birth, and ends with his death and its aftermath, and is structured as the history of the rise and fall of the Round Table. Malory's main sources were French prose Arthurian romances, but he also made direct use of the Middle English alliterative and stanzaic *Morte Arthure* (discussed above). The work also has episodes for which there are no known sources.

The first book tells the story of Arthur's election as king, his marriage to Guinevere, and the founding of the Round Table. It has a short conclusion affirming Malory's authorship and asking God to send him 'good recover'. This may mean that originally this was all Malory was going to write, and that his project developed while he was working on it. The narrative continues, however, with a further account of Arthur's career including his imperial coronation by the Pope, and long sections devoted to the adventures of Lancelot, Tristram, Gareth, and other knights, plus the pursuit of the Holy Grail. These sections are based on the alliterative *Morte Arthure* and French prose romances. The final part describes the adulterous love of Lancelot and Guinevere, the decline of Arthur's court, his death, and the death of his queen and Lancelot. It is largely based on the French prose *Mort Artu* and the English stanzaic *Morte Arthure*.

Though the work may appear to be a simple compilation and retelling of earlier narratives, Malory's treatment of the story is significantly different from that of his predecessors in detail and approach. This is particularly evident in his concept of chivalry as a political and moral ideal, his treatment of characters, and his attempts to present the fall of the Round Table as a coherent and intelligible story. In Malory's portrayal the chivalric world is not devoid of conflict, crime, and hate, but nevertheless provides examples of exceptional nobility, love, loyalty, and faith. Malory explicitly compares it with his own world and points out the differences between the age of chivalry and his own age. As a narrator Malory concentrates on relating the events rather than exploring the characters' psychology. However, he does not simplify the individuals, their relationships, or the complex causes of their various actions and the surrounding events. Malory also rarely allows his authorial voice to be heard. He does not moralize or put blame for what happens on any single party, but creates a sense of inevitability around the unfolding tragic events, and of the mutability of the human world. His characters act in accordance with their nature and what they see as their obligations, but are unable to control the outcome in spite of their noble intentions.

Malory used simple diction with few descriptive or analytical passages. His reserved style, devoid of rhetorical flourishes, is seen as eloquent and possessing 'haunting' rhythm and intensity by many readers and critics. His dialogue is particularly expressive, and *Morte Darthur* has many scenes which are memorable because of the striking verbal exchanges between the characters. When descriptions do occur they are vivid and lively. Such a passage describes King Arthur's prophetic dream where he sits at the top of the Wheel of Fortune and sees, beneath, 'hydeous depe blak watir' full of 'all manner of serpentis and wormes and wilde bestis fowle and orryble'. The wheel suddenly turns and the king falls into the water where 'every beste toke hym by a lymme' ('by a limb').

Malory's choice of prose rather than verse for his work is partly due to the popularity of French prose Arthurian cycles and the fact that the style of earlier verse romances seemed dated at that time. Malory probably also thought prose to be more suitable for a serious work which he conceived as a chronicle rather than a romance or fiction. In an introduction to his 1485 publication of *Morte Darthur* Caxton explained that he decided to publish 'the noble histories' of King Arthur out of patriotism (Arthur was considered to be one of the 'Nine Worthies' together with Alexander the Great and Charlemagne), as an example for English nobility, and because of what he claimed to be Arthur's undeniable historicity. *Morte Darthur* also had a profound influence on later English writers from Edmund Spenser in the 16th century to T. H. White in the twentieth.

To summarise, we should consider the following key points:

- the growth of romance in Europe started in the 12th century, but the earliest Middle English romances date from the 13th century;
- Middle English romances are narrative, primarily recreational works, set in an aristocratic feudal world;
- their audience probably included the aristocracy, country gentry, and the middle classes;
- their subject matter is remarkably diverse, but the largest surviving group is based on Arthurian legends;
- romances are primarily concerned with love, family, and individual experience, rather than with history and the fates of the nation, as was characteristic of the earlier epic narratives;

- romances share themes, elements of plot, and many features of style;
- prose romances in English date from the middle of the 15th century, the most notable being Malory's *Morte Darthur*.

See also Chapter 2(o) and Chapter 3(b), (e), (p), and (u).

Further Reading

Standard works on Arthurian romance are Barron (1987 and 2001) and Loomis (1961 and 1963). Mehl provides an account of early Middle English romances (1968), and Keen (1984) has an excellent account of chivalry. See also Cooper (1999), Field (1999), Lucas (2005), Pearsall (2003), Sands (1986), Stevens (1973), and Vinaver (1971). For an account of Middle English prose romances see Cooper (2004). On Malory see Archibald and Edwards (1996), Takamiya and Brewer (1981), Benson (1976), Cowen (1969), Field (1993 and 1971), Lambert (1975), Riddy (1987), and Vinaver (1990).

(i)   Comedy and Satire

Surviving Middle English works which are primarily comic are represented by the beast-fable, fabliaux, and parody. Though all three genres offer moral instruction, they are not essentially didactic in the same way as *exempla*, in which stories serve to illustrate a moral principle. Beast-fables and fabliaux are primarily recreational genres, where comic stories, situations, and characters offer enjoyment rather than direct instruction and are not fully governed by a moral or didactic agenda. All three were used by Chaucer in *The Canterbury Tales*, but here we will concentrate on the best known Middle English examples of these genres before Chaucer.

The Fox and the Wolf is a poem of around 300 lines in rhyming couplets, which survives in a late 13th-century manuscript. It belongs to the genre of animal fable, where the characteristics and behaviour of animals are given a human dimension and used for entertainment, parody, satire, and instruction. It consists of two parts: the tale of the Fox and Chauntecleer, similar to the one told by the Nun's Priest in Chaucer's *The Canterbury Tales*, and the tale of the Fox and the Wolf, where the Fox falls into a well and tricks the Wolf into jumping in to save him. Both stories are ultimately based on the episodes from the French *Roman de Renart*, a cycle of stories put together around 1175–90. These comic stories were linked by the use of the same main characters, particularly a clever, resourceful, and cunning fox called Reynard (Renart) and a fierce but less intelligent wolf called

Isengrim. Like the *Roman de Renart*, *The Fox and the Wolf* exploits comic situations and tricks played upon characters, and uses colloquial language and lively dialogue. Similar to the *Roman de Renart*, it is also satirical and includes, for example, a confession scene where the Fox acts as a confessor and the Wolf as a penitent, and a sermon on the joys of paradise delivered by the Fox. At the end of the poem some friars, who started to establish themselves in England in the 1220s, become part of the comic action: the wolf is beaten by them when they mistake him for a devil. *The Fox and the Wolf* is the only surviving Middle English pre-Chaucerian beast-fable.

Dame Sirith is the earliest English fabliau. Fabliaux were fairly brief comic tales about trickery, often involving money, marriage, and sex, usually in a middle-class setting. They depicted their predominantly stereotypical characters as foolish, deceitful, promiscuous, and egoistic. The genre was popular in France where it developed towards the end of the 12th century and flourished particularly in the 13th century. A number of Anglo-Norman fabliaux also survive. *Dame Sirith* has a traditional middle-class setting and cast of characters: a merchant, his wife, a go-between, and a clerk. The narrative tells how the go-between, Dame Sirith, tricks the wife into surrendering to her admirer, the clerk: Dame Smith pretends that her dog is her daughter transformed by a clerk whose love she refused. The story is known from earlier versions in Latin and French, and may have been oriental in origin. A large part of *Dame Sirith* is dialogue and some scholars believe that this may indicate that it was composed for dramatic performance. Both *The Fox and the Wolf* and *Dame Sirith* survive in single copies in the same manuscript: Oxford, Bodleian Library MS Digby 86, a late 13th-century compilation which preserves many important Middle English literary works.

The audience of fabliaux has been a subject of scholarly debate. According to an earlier view they were written for middle-class audiences, whose life they portrayed and whose values they expressed. A more recent work on fabliaux, however, suggests that such identification of setting with audience is a simplification (Nykrog, 1957). The portrayal of the middle classes in fabliaux is not realistic and is as much a literary invention, governed by the requirements of genre and type of story, as an idealised portrayal of aristocracy in romance. The audience of fabliaux may have been at least partly aristocratic therefore, appreciative of such stories because they offered a parody of attitudes, characters, and situations commonly encountered in romance.

The Land of Cokaygne is a poem in rhyming couplets, probably composed in Ireland in the 13th century. It is a description of an earthly paradise inhabited by monks and nuns. It has parallels in French and Dutch literature, but the Middle English version is not a close translation of any other known text and is independent in much of its detail. It survives in a single manuscript possibly put together by a Franciscan friar, which may explain the satirical portrayal of monks and nuns. It is a parody of the descriptions of heaven, paradise, and the Heavenly Jerusalem, found in many Middle English sermons, in other devotional literature, and in texts such as the Apocalypse or the widely circulated *Visio Pauli* ('The Apocalypse of Paul' – a Latin 5th-century work which describes St Paul seeing the Heavenly Jerusalem). The paradise depicted in *The Land of Cokaygne* is purely material, full of milk, honey, wine, and all kinds of culinary delights. For example, the walls of an abbey are made of pastries and cakes, and roast geese and larks seasoned with spices fly around offering themselves as food. The description of the lives of the monks and nuns has an emphasis on sexual freedom and a comic reversal of all the rules essential for monastic life. In spite of its apparent lack of seriousness the text is moralistic and satirical in its portrayal of the clergy, who are given to gluttony, idleness, and unrestrained sexual desire. However, it treats its subject in a light and amusing way, employing fantasy and the absurd.

To summarise, we should consider the following key points:

- surviving Middle English works which are primarily comic include beast-fables, fabliaux, and parody;
- all these genres were used by Chaucer in *The Canterbury Tales* and by other 14th- and 15th-century writers, but there are also several interesting 13th-century examples;
- fables, fabliaux, and parody were written to entertain, but also to instruct.

Further Reading

Middle English fabliaux are discussed in Busby (1981), Davenport (2004), Furrow (1989), Hines (1993), Lewis (1982), and Nykrog (1957). For individual works see Bercovitch (1966), Busby (1995), Hill (1975), von Kreisler (1970), and Tigges (1995a and b).

(j) Mystics

Discussions of Middle English mysticism usually concentrate on five authors whose work falls within the period of *c.*1330–1440: Richard

Rolle, the anonymous author of *The Cloud of Unknowing*, Walter Hilton, Margery Kempe, and Julian of Norwich. 'Mysticism' is a modern term used to describe a religious movement which became important in Europe in the 13th century. It emphasised the individual's relationship with the divine and saw the direct union of the human soul with God as an ultimate aim. Mysticism attempted to offer guidance on how this aim could be achieved.

There are two traditions of mysticism represented in medieval England: a more austere 'negative' tradition associated with *The Cloud of Unknowing*, which demanded freeing oneself from the distractions of intelligence and the senses as a necessary step towards unity with the divine; and an 'affirmative' tradition which called for contemplation on visual images and involvement of the senses and the imagination. Mystics of both traditions insisted on the importance of meditation. This originated as a monastic exercise, but was adapted and practised more broadly. It involved concentrating on scenes (often from the life of Christ and the Virgin Mary) and subjects that could teach doctrinal and moral concepts, such as the greatness of God, human sinfulness, God's love for mankind, the need of repentance, and so on. One of the most popular guides on meditation was *Meditationes vitae Christi*, a work by an Italian Franciscan written in the 14th century. It was translated into Middle English by Nicholas Love (d. 1424) as *Myrrour of the Blessed Lyf of Jesu Christ*. It describes events in Christ's life, based partly on the Gospels (but supplemented from different sources), emphasising his suffering and humanity. This is accompanied by prayers and meditations, and the reader is encouraged to sympathise and respond to the events described. The works of mystics were often in the form of visions, a genre which reflected personal experience. Mysticism was more closely associated with the laity than other medieval religious movements, and there were several important women writers among English and Continental mystics.

Richard Rolle (*c*.1290–1349) was a hermit, who lived for some of his life and died in Hampole, Yorkshire. He was an author of many theological commentaries, treatises, and instructional works in Latin and English. His English works were written during the final years of his life and include a translation and commentary on the Psalter, composed according to a medieval tradition for the anchoress Margaret Kirkeby. In addition he produced a series of prose epistles, including *Ego dormio*, *The Commandment*, and *The Form of Living*, identified in some manuscripts as also written for Margaret Kirkeby or other religious women. All of Rolle's English works were intended to provide pastoral guidance to his friends and disciples wanting to lead a religious life. They emphasise a rejection of the world, the importance of the contemplative life, and love and meditation as ways of attaining an intimate, personal relationship with God. Rolle's works, lively and approachable, were very popular throughout the 15th and 16th centuries.

The anonymous author of *The Cloud of Unknowing* and the writer Walter Hilton were both working in the east Midlands in the second half of the 14th century. Their texts have similarities in themes and style, and include verbal parallels which suggest that they may have known each other's work. Walter Hilton trained as a lawyer but abandoned law to become a hermit. He died in 1396 in the Augustinian priory of Thurgarton in Nottinghamshire. Most of his works were written in Latin. His English works were composed for lay and religious audiences, particularly women, who could not read Latin. His most famous work, *The Scale of Perfection*, is a book of religious instruction; it begins with directions to a female recluse, but gradually widens and addresses those in 'contemplative life'. It consists of two parts, which have differences in style and subject matter, possibly because of the differences in the times of their composition. Book I is an introduction to the contemplative life and the stages by which an anchoress can progress to the highest degree of contemplation. It discusses devotional reading, prayer, meditation, temptations, and avoidance of sin. Book II describes the reforming of the soul. Hilton distinguishes between the reform that can be achieved by all good Christians and the one that can be achieved only by contemplatives, though full reform is possible only after death. The reform which can be achieved through contemplative life is a long and gradual process in which the soul is transformed and perfected. The final chapters describe the ultimate mystical experience when the soul is purified and connects with God.

The author of *The Cloud of Unknowing*, and of several other theological and instructional English works, may have been a Carthusian monk. He possibly led a solitary contemplative life and could have been a spiritual advisor to other contemplatives, some of whom may be addressed in his works. He makes clear that he directs his teaching only to those with a calling for the life of meditation and is impatient with those without such a vocation. In this respect his position is different from the inclusive and democratising approaches of many vernacular theologians, who addressed their works broadly to lay audiences, and people in need of instruction but without access to theological learning. *The Cloud of Unknowing* consists of a prologue and 75 chapters which gradually instruct readers how to free their mind from false notions that stand in the way of spiritual enlightenment. The author rejects 'sensualised mysticism' and intellect as a way to comprehend God. He argues that the union with God can be reached only by overcoming the interference of reason, imagination, memory, and feeling, which belong to the physical world or are influenced by physical experiences. Everything known must be put aside to achieve the 'cloud of unknowing', which will be the last boundary separating the soul from God, and which God may choose to open.

Margery Kempe (*c.*1373–after 1439) lived in King's Lynn in Norfolk. She came from a wealthy middle-class family, married a wealthy merchant, but started the life of spiritual devotion later on after experiencing a series of religious visions. *The Book of Margery Kempe*, which was written in the 1430s and survives in a unique manuscript, is sometimes claimed to be the first autobiography in English. It is written in the third person singular and describes the author's life and spiritual experiences. It tells about her family, marriage, business ventures, and travels (the latter included visits to the Holy Land, Rome, and Santiago de Compostela). She also details meetings with Julian of Norwich and many major Church figures. The *Book* is valued as a source of detailed knowledge about everyday social and religious life in late medieval England, particularly as experienced by a woman. The focus of the *Book*, however, is on religious experiences, visions, the personal relationship with Christ, and the struggle to live a life of spiritual devotion. It belongs to the tradition of affective piety which emphasised the humanity of Christ, meditation on his life, and emotional participation in his Passion. *The Book of Margery Kempe* mentions several times the *Incendium amoris* ('The Fire of Love'), a highly popular Latin work by Richard Rolle, and shows the influence of his teaching. It also refers to Walter Hilton, the author of the more austere *The Scale of Perfection* and, as mentioned already, describes Margery visiting Julian of Norwich. After the Lollards were condemned, Margery Kempe was suspected of heresy, as a religious lay woman and a travelling teacher, because Lollards encouraged the laity to preach and teach religion. She was arrested several times, interrogated about her beliefs, but always released.

Julian of Norwich (1342–after 1415) is the author of *A Revelation of Love*, an ambitious theological work based on a set of visions experienced at the age of 30. She was an anchoress at St Julian's Church in Norwich, but little else is known about her (unlike Margery Kempe she does not tell us about her life). *A Revelation* exists in two versions: a longer and a shorter one. The shorter version is believed to be earlier, composed fairly soon after the visions occurred. The longer version is probably a reworking of the earlier text after more than fifteen years of contemplation. It is written in the first person, describes the visions, chiefly of Christ's Passion, and offers an interpretation of them, concentrating on discussions of divine love, redemption, the problem of evil, and the nature of humanity's relationship with God. The emphasis is on divine love, presented as the ultimate message of *A Revelation* and key to the interpretation of visions, various theological concepts, history, and human experience as a whole. Unlike many contemporary theologians who emphasised God's anger against sinful humanity, Julian of Norwich insists that only love and not anger is consistent with the nature of God. She rejects the pessimistic view of history as unfolding towards judgement and condemnation, and presents it as a movement towards salvation, affirming with certainty that evil and sin will be defeated. This is summarised in the famous message, repeated in the text several times and presented as coming directly from Christ, that her spiritual experiences teach her that 'all shall be well' in spite of the sins of humanity. God will achieve this in the end by the 'great deed', which will remain unknown and incomprehensible to all creatures until the last day, when it is done.

The works of Middle English women mystics raise important questions concerning the nature of their authorship. The first question is: What was their direct input to the texts that have come down to us, and what was the contribution of their scribes? Margery Kempe is described as illiterate and relying on others to write for her (her book was written by a priest). Julian of Norwich also describes herself as unlettered – she could not read Latin and it is possible that she could not read English either. This corresponds to what we know about Continental female saints such as St Bridget of Sweden or St Catherine of Siena, who also relied on priests or clerks to transmit their revelations. However, the inability to write does not necessarily mean exclusion from literary culture. Margery Kempe describes herself listening to a reader, and tells us that she learned Scripture from sermons and discussions with clerks. Her work and the work of Julian of Norwich show familiarity with a range of Latin theological compositions.

Another question raised in studies surrounding the works of women mystics is: How did the writers' status as women influence their role as authors and spiritual authorities? They lived at a time when the tradition of female authorship was very limited. They clearly felt a responsibility to have their visions written down and made known to the world, but in the case of both Julian of Norwich and Margery Kempe, fifteen or twenty years separate the time of their first revelations from the time when the most complete versions of their books were produced (that survive to us, at least). In spite of the considerable difficulties associated with female authorship, religious teaching, and access to theological learning, the humble standing of women (Julian of Norwich describes herself as 'leued, febille and freyll') seems to have sometimes contributed to their status as visionaries: because they were perceived as weak and unlearned, their work was seen as more likely to be divinely inspired and to demonstrate the power of God.

To summarise, we should consider the following key points:

- 'mysticism' is a modern term which describes a religious movement that became important in England in the late Middle Ages;
- it emphasised the individual's relationship and union with God, and meditation as a way of achieving this aim;
- mysticism was more closely associated with the laity than other medieval religious movements, and there were several important women writers among English and Continental mystics;
- the works of Middle English women mystics raise questions concerning the nature of their authorship, the transmission of their works, and how their status as women influenced their role as authors and spiritual authorities.

See also   Chapter 3(d), (f), (k), and (n).

Further Reading

For accounts of mysticism in medieval England see Glasscoe (1980–2, 1984–92, 2004, and 1993), Hodgson (1967), Knowles (1961), Milosh (1966), Pollard and Boenig (1997), Riehle (1981), and Watson (1991 and 1999). For discussions of works by women mystics see Abbott (1999), Baker (1994), Bynum (1987), Dinshaw and Wallace (2003), Finke (1999), Johnson (1991), Meale (1996), Staley (1994), and Swan (2005).

(k)   John Wyclif and Lollardy

John Wyclif (*c.*1324–84) was a theology master at Oxford University. His views on the government of the Church, the use of the vernacular, the practice of worship, and a number of other important political and theological issues anticipated many ideas of the Reformation. Wyclif argued that clergy should live in simplicity and poverty and should not own property. Disendowment of the Church and 'evangelical poverty' as an ideal for the clergy were argued by earlier writers as well, but much more radically by Wyclif, who believed that it was lawful for kings to deprive monks and clergy of property, which they could not rightfully hold. These views were opposed by the Church authorities and condemned by the Pope, but had significant support among Wyclif's colleagues at Oxford and among the gentry and aristocracy. In fact Wyclif found a powerful ally in the anti-clerical aristocratic party headed by John of Gaunt, Duke of Lancaster (also the patron of Chaucer), who summoned him to London and supported him in his conflict with the Church.

Wyclif's disagreement with the institutional Church involved a number of other important issues. He questioned the authority of the Church as an interpreter of Christian doctrine and considered the Bible to be the most important singular orthodox expression of faith. Wyclif believed that all Christians should have direct access to the Bible in their own language. He emphasised the importance of preaching, the role of lay believers in the Church, and considered the civil state to be the only legitimate source of political authority. In 1380–1 he attacked the doctrine of 'transubstantiation' (the transformation of the consecrated bread and wine into the body and blood of Christ during the Eucharist), but failed to win a following for this view. Some of his former supporters, particularly among the friars, turned away from him, and his teaching on the Eucharist was condemned by an Oxford council of doctors. This coincided with the political reaction that followed the Peasants' Revolt of 1381. Though Wyclif never supported the revolt, his views on Church property were seen as indirectly encouraging a rebellion. Wyclif retired from Oxford in 1378 and lived away from Oxford and the court until his death.

The followers of Wyclif were nicknamed Lollards. This word probably derives from a Dutch word meaning 'to mutter', and was initially used in Middle English with a variety of pejorative meanings. Lollardy was not a centralised movement and covered a range of views, some more widely held than others. Among the most important were anti-clericalism (the belief that the official Church was corrupt), lay priesthood (the denial of the authority of the Church to confer priesthood and a denial of the special authority of priesthood), opposition to clerical celibacy and ownership of property, and opposition to certain religious practices, rituals, and sacraments. These included pilgrimages, the use of images in worship, prayers for the dead, confession, and the Eucharist. Lollards emphasised the importance of preaching and the authority of the Bible, which they believed should be accessible to people in their own language. Precedent for this view can be seen in the Anglo-Saxon period with Alfred's prose translations, and the translations of Ælfric and others.

Lollardy initially appealed to gentry, nobility, the royal court, and intellectuals in Oxford and elsewhere. An important Lollard group were the knights who belonged to the court of Richard II in the late 14th century. They came from the gentry and noble families and served Richard II as councillors and diplomats. 'Lollard knights', such as Lewis Clifford, Richard Stury, John Montagu, and others, are particularly important because of their active role in the court and international literary culture of the time. They are known as owners of books, writers, and patrons of literature; and they were personal acquaintances and friends of Chaucer and major French writers such as Jean Froissart, Eustache Deschamp, and Christine de Pisan. Sympathy with Wyclif's views on the disendowment of the Church and various issues of doctrine at the royal court played an important role in the early development of the movement. However, the association of Lollardy with potential rebellion reduced its support amongst the gentry in the 15th century.

The Lollard movement spread rapidly in the second half of the 14th century in spite of attempts to suppress it during the later years of the reign of Richard II. A major opponent of the Lollards was Thomas Arundel, Archbishop of Canterbury, who influenced royal policy towards heretics. In 1401, two years after the ascension of Henry IV, the anti-heretical statute *De heretico comburendo* ('Regarding the heretic who is to be burnt') was passed, for the first time making relapsed heretics liable for this form of execution in England. Arundel's Lambeth Constitutions of 1407–9 were a set of anti-heretical laws aimed at censoring the content of preaching (making it necessary for preachers to obtain an episcopal licence), theological literature and research, and the teaching of theology at Oxford. Among other things, they forbade any unapproved translations of the Bible or passages from the Bible into English, as well as the making or ownership of English Bibles. During the 15th century the Lollard movement had to go underground but it lasted until the Reformation. The extent of its influence on the Reformation is debated, but several leaders of the Reformation were familiar with Lollard ideas.

John Wyclif produced a large literary output, in both Latin and

English. He started publishing vernacular works in order to make his views more widely known. Perhaps his most important contribution to the development of vernacular literacy was his role in translating the Bible into English. In the early 1380s, on his instigation and under his leadership, two complete translations were produced (though it is unclear how much of the translating he did himself). Anglo-Saxon England had a flourishing tradition of biblical translation as noted earlier, but after the Norman Conquest there was little activity until the late 14th century. Before the Wycliffite Bible there were only summaries, paraphrases, and translations of parts of the Bible into Middle English, such as the *Orrmulum*, the *Cursor Mundi*, or Richard Rolle's *English Psalter*.

Surviving manuscripts of the Wycliffite Bible fall into two textual groups: the early version and the later version. Both are still very close to the Latin Vulgate, even in their word order, but the later version is somewhat more idiomatic. In some manuscripts it has a General Prologue with fifteen chapters, which introduce biblical books and explain the principles of translation.

Lollardy encouraged vernacular writing and Wycliffites produced a large number of works both in Latin and in English, mostly in prose. Apart from the Bible translations, these include commentaries on the Bible, tracts defending the translation of the Bible into the vernacular, instructional and didactic texts, and declarative or polemical lists of conclusions and answers to questions. Sermon literature was particularly important for the Lollard movement. Most surviving Middle English sermons are organised into collections or cycles arranged around the Church calendar. The long Wycliffite sermon cycle, comprising 294 sermons and probably produced in the 1380s–1390s, shows extensive familiarity with Wyclif's works. It was widely circulated and survives in a large number of carefully produced manuscripts. It provides a comprehensive coverage of the church year and may represent an attempt to create and disseminate a uniform body of doctrine and to regulate beliefs among Lollard communities. There is also a group of Lollard texts associated with the Chaucer and Langland traditions, such as *Pierce the Ploughman's Crede* – a poem in alliterative verse probably written about 1394. It is a satire against the friars, who are portrayed as preoccupied with wealth and failing in their pastoral duty towards the laity.

In conclusion, we should consider the following key points:

- the teachings of John Wyclif and his followers anticipated many ideas of the Reformation;

- their views initially had support among the gentry and aristocracy, and intellectuals in Oxford and elsewhere;
- though Wyclif never supported the Peasants' Revolt of 1381, his views on Church property were seen as indirectly encouraging a rebellion;
- Lollardy was not a centralised movement and covered a range of views held by different communities;
- Wycliffites produced a large number of works both in Latin and in English, including a translation of the Bible and the most complete sermon cycles surviving from the Middle English period.

See also   Chapter 2(e) and (f), and Chapter 3(c), (e), (j), and (r).

Further Reading

The following works cover the views, social background, and literary influence of John Wyclif and his followers: Aston and Richmond (1997), Kenny (1986a and 1986b), and Hudson (1985, 1986, and 1988).

(l)   Middle English Theatre

Most surviving medieval drama from England is religious and dates from the end of the 14th century onwards. Poor preservation of earlier texts leaves many questions unanswered about the origin and initial development of dramatic traditions. Thus scholars debate to what extent more 'dramatic' parts of Latin church services can be seen as proto-drama (see Raw, 1991). Already the *Regularis Concordia*[7] describes the *Visitatio Sepulchri*, a ritual performed in churches on Easter morning centred on the visit to the Sepulchre, or burial chamber of Christ. It included a short dialogue between the angel at Christ's empty tomb and the three holy women coming to anoint Christ's body. It was performed by monks, who were instructed how to enact their parts. Similar Latin liturgical pieces performed on feast days are known from the 11th and 12th centuries (and later).

Little is known about medieval English secular drama. There are references to *spectacula* and *ludi* ('spectacles' and 'games'), which

---

[7] A manual of customs and practices to be observed in Benedictine monasteries, drawn on the initiative of St Æthelwold, Bishop of Winchester, *c*.970, a prime mover of the Benedictine Revival.

were part of popular celebrations, but it is not clear whether they were dramatic performances or some other form of entertainment. Drama was performed by professional entertainers, but not much is known about their repertoire and activities until the late Middle Ages. *Dame Sirith*, dating from the late 13th century, is believed by some scholars to be the earliest surviving native secular text intended for dramatic performance. It is a mixture of narrative and dialogue, which may indicate performances by one or more actors.

The native tradition of mystery cycles and other religious plays originated in the second half of the 14th century, though most manuscripts of plays and evidence about their performances date from the middle of the 15th century and later. In the late 14th century, religious plays were part of the Church's effort to educate the laity in their own language. They differ from earlier Latin liturgical drama in being more popular in their appeal and less constrained in their content and techniques. Performances of these plays continued until the last quarter of the 16th century.

Most surviving plays come from two areas: the North of England and East Anglia. The two regions seem to have differed in how plays were performed and financed. In the north, religious drama flourished in large urban centres and was supported by craft guilds. Great cycles of plays survive from York, Chester, and Wakefield, and to a lesser extent from the Midlands (e.g. there are fragments of a Coventry cycle). Cycle plays were performed in East Anglia as well, but there was also an extensive tradition of non-cycle performances supported by local parishes in villages and small towns in rural areas. Processional performances, where plays were staged on pageant wagons which followed a prescribed route through the city, were characteristic of northern towns (though not exclusively), whereas in East Anglia there is evidence for plays being performed in a single location in 'place-and-scaffold' settings (see below).

From the point of view of their content, plays can be subdivided into (1) scriptural plays, (2) morality plays, and (3) hagiographical plays, briefly described below.

(1)   All surviving pageant-wagon cycles have a common basic structure. From the late 14th century they were based on the Old and New Testament stories covering the history of the universe from the Creation to the Fall, the Redemption, and Doomsday. Cycles consisted of individual plays of different length covering such episodes as the Fall of Angels, the Fall of Man, Abraham and Isaac, Moses and Pharaoh, the Annunciation and Visitation,

the Nativity, the Crucifixion, the Resurrection, the Harrowing of Hell, and so on. Their aim was to illustrate the pattern of salvation present in human history.

(2) The struggle of good and evil for the possession of an individual's soul was the main focus of morality plays, of which only five survive. These plays were allegorical and set in abstract rather than historical time. Their protagonists represented the whole of humankind and were given names such as Everyman or Mankind. Other characters were symbolic representations of the forces of good and evil, including supernatural beings such as angels and devils, and personifications of vices, virtues, human qualities, moral states, and similar. The action presented man's life as a journey through temptation, fall, and redemption. For example *The Castle of Perseverance* is a very elaborate, complex, but carefully structured play depicting the life and death of the main character Humankind as a struggle between good and evil until ultimate redemption comes through God's grace. It is the earliest of the surviving morality plays, believed to have been written *c.*1405. A late 15th-century *Everyman*, probably a translation of a Flemish morality play, portrays the main character unexpectedly summoned by death. He has to learn the true value of his earthly friends, such as Beauty, Kindred, Fellowship, and Worldly Goods, who will not go with him. In the end he is assisted by Good Deeds, whom he previously neglected, and who offers to justify him before God.

(3) Finally, hagiographical plays, very few of which survive, depicted lives of saints or episodes from their lives, particularly those involving miracles and conversions. Their purpose was didactic and exemplary, but they extensively used the sensationalism of miracles, torture and executions, and the drama of polarised characters and debates between saints and their opponents, to increase their appeal.

Middle English plays were performed in the open air, or in venues which were not specially designed as theatres, such as churches, or halls of private or civil buildings. Open air productions were either processional performances on pageant wagons or performances in a single location on staging called 'place-and-scaffold'. Cycles of mystery plays were traditionally performed each year on or around the feast of Corpus Christi in late May or June (its date depended on the date of Easter). York had a cycle of over fifty plays, which were probably all performed in one day, whereas in Chester in the 1530s twenty-five plays were performed over three days. The whole cycle was subdivided into episodes or plays (also called 'pageants'), each delegated to a particular guild, or a group of guilds. Sometimes guilds performed plays appropriate for their trade. Thus at York the Fishers and Mariners presented the story of Noah and the flood, while the Bakers presented the Last Supper. Productions were funded by mandatory contributions from all guild members (known in York as 'pageant silver').

Each guild had a 'pageant' – a custom-built mobile stage equipped with stage machinery and decorations. On the day of the performance pageants followed a prescribed route through the city, stopping at pre-arranged 'stations' to enact their part of the cycle. York had between twelve and sixteen stations. When the first episode had been performed at the first station, the wagon moved to the second station where the same episode was performed again. At the same time its place at the first station was taken by the wagon performing the second episode, and so on. Performances started at dawn and probably continued until after midnight. Because of the large number and length of the performances major parts were shared by several players. Women's roles, however, were played by male actors. The style of performance was not realistic – stages were small, texts were in verse, and characters could communicate with the audience and narrate their own stories. In 'place-and-scaffold' productions an open space was surrounded by scaffolds or stages, each representing a particular feature or location required by the play – such as Jerusalem, Heaven, a palace, a house, or a mountain. The action moved from stage to stage, and performances could require numerous scaffolds, dozens of actors, devices for various stage effects, and complex logistics.

The full York cycle comprised over 14,000 lines of verse and included over 300 speaking parts. The surviving script mostly represents the version of the cycle as it existed in the third quarter of the 15th century. This was based on a revision of earlier versions. Parts and individual episodes of the York cycle vary in approach, style, and metre, and are believed to have been composed at different times and by different authors. Plays were probably constantly revised throughout their existence, following changes in religious views, the social structure of communities, and audiences' tastes. One of the surviving manuscripts of the York cycle (now in London, British Library MS Additional 35290) was compiled between 1463 and 1477, probably from scripts of individual pageants held by guilds that were responsible for them. It was an official master-copy of the cycle and was known as the 'Register'. In the 16th century this manuscript was used to check the text as performed by the actors against the official version.

Six pageants from the York cycle are closely related to the parallel pageants in another 15th-century collection of scriptural plays – the Towneley cycle. Its name comes from the family of Towneley, who owned the manuscript in which the plays survive. The Towneley cycle contains 32 short plays, including a group of highly original pageants which have references to places in and around Wakefield. Because of this the anonymous author of this group of plays, who wrote in the 15th century, was nicknamed the 'Wakefield Master'. The association of the cycle with Wakefield is, however, conjectural and its provenance is a matter of scholarly debate. The Wakefield Master is believed to have been an author of five (or possibly six) Towneley pageants and to have contributed to the revision of several others. Characteristic features of his style include the use of a distinctive nine-line stanza with a complex rhyming pattern, masterful command of language, and humour. His characters are vivid and highly individualised, and he was fond of colloquial idiom, play on words, and other experimentations with vocabulary. The best known play by the Wakefield Master is the so-called *Second Shepherds' Play*. It combines a devout portrayal of the Nativity with a funny but not irreverent parody. The two parts are connected by a common theme of forgiveness and redemption.

The content and language of plays reflected their need to attract and keep the attention of a large audience. They included satire, colloquial dialogue, and low comedy. Their performances were spectacles: various stage effects, machinery and pyrotechnics were extensively used. In spite of this the plays were intellectual works, composed by learned authors for popular audiences and primarily concerned with religious instruction. Their carefully planned structure, and thoughtfully chosen characters and episodes, were intended to illustrate and make accessible important theological and ethical concepts.

To summarise, we should consider the following key points:

- most surviving medieval drama from England is religious;
- 'dramatic' parts of the Latin church services that survive are seen by some scholars as proto-drama;
- the native tradition of religious plays originated in the second half of the 14th century, but most manuscripts of plays and

evidence about their performances date from the middle of the 15th century and later;

- most surviving plays come from two areas, the North of England and East Anglia, and there were differences between the two regions in how plays were performed and financed;
- religious plays were part of the Church's effort to educate the laity in their own language; they reflect the need to attract and keep the attention of a large audience, but at the same time they are sophisticated intellectual works, concerned with religious instruction.

See also   Chapter 3(i).

Further Reading

Excellent introductions to medieval English theatre are Beadle (1994) and Dillon (2006). See also Kolve (1966), Tydeman (1986), Walker (2005), and Woolf (1972).

(m)   Science, Information, and Travel

Anglo-Saxon England had an important tradition of vernacular scientific writing, but immediately after the Norman Conquest very few scientific works were written in English. Most texts produced in England in the 12th and 13th centuries were in Anglo-Norman or Latin, whereas most Middle English scientific works date from the late 14th century, but particularly from the 15th century. Texts written in English during the later part of the period are very diverse and include works on medicine, mathematics, astronomy, astrology (such as Chaucer's *Treatise on the Astrolabe*, and the *Equatorie of the Planetis*, possibly also by Chaucer), agriculture, veterinary science, hunting, fishing, cookery, and various collections of recipes for colours, dyes, glue, ink, and similar.

One of the most noticeable characteristics of medieval scientific texts, particularly those associated with university learning, is their reliance on authorities from the past. Western medieval science was influenced by the works of ancient Greek and Arab scientists, known in Latin adaptations, and new generations of writers based their texts on earlier works. Academic medical texts, for example, include numerous references to major *auctores* ('authors') such as Hippocrates, Galen, Avicenna, Rhazes, and others.

Most Middle English scientific works are translations from Latin and French. Some important or popular works such as herbals, surgical treatises, *Mandeville's Travels*, or *Secretum Secretorum* (all discussed below), existed in numerous translations, usually free and reflecting the interests of a translator or a client. Some translations include what may have been original commentary, omissions, and additions from other sources. Different versions of texts were often further adapted, edited, and supplemented by the scribes, again reflecting their interests or those of the intended audience. All this complicates identification of texts and their versions.

Another important feature of scientific works is their reliance on visual materials. Scientific texts are frequently illustrated in manuscripts and include diagrams, maps, marginal drawings, and full-page miniatures, as well as various tables and charts. The illustrations are much more frequent than in literary or any other manuscripts from the period and tend to be sophisticated. Unusually for the book illustration of the period they are also practical rather than decorative in purpose, and are closely related to the text, or sometimes integrated with the text and supplemented with textual commentary. Finally, it is worth remembering that Middle English science was essentially multilingual: English texts often occur in manuscripts side-by-side with texts in Latin and French. They also use Latin rubrics and terminology, or sometimes mix English with another language.

The largest group of Middle English scientific texts are medical works. Linda Voigts (1982) suggested a classification of medical writings into:

- academic treatises (specialised treatises on different areas of medicine, such as blood-letting, urinoscopy, gynaecology, and others);
- surgical texts (surgical and anatomical descriptions); and
- remedy-books (collections of recipes, prognostications and charms).

An example of the first group of texts is the widely circulated treatise *Liber de diversis medicinis* ('The book of different medicines'). This is extant in about 20 manuscripts and contains recommendations for the treatment of different diseases, arranged in a head-to-foot order, a popular structure used in a number of medical works. Similarly organised is the Middle English adaptation of the 13th-century *Compendium medicinae* of Gilbertus Anglicus. It omits gynaecological matter present in the source, but in many manuscripts it is found with a gynaecological treatise *The Sekenesse of Wymmen* ('Diseases of women'), which is an independent adaptation of the chapters on women's diseases found in the *Compendium*. Significant advances were made in surgery in the second half of the 14th century, and several influential surgical works were either translated or composed in English. Important texts include a Middle English translation of *Chirurgia magna* of Guy de Chauliac (d. 1363), probably the most outstanding work on surgery written in Europe during the Middle Ages; and *The Science of Surgery*, a translation of *Chirurgia major* of Lanfranc (d. 1315), a widely circulated standard work on surgery.

Several Middle English herbals (works describing plants and their medicinal uses) are preserved from the late 14th and 15th centuries. Two popular herbals were the *Agnus Castus Herbal*, named after its first entry and derived from a 14th-century Latin original covering 250 herbs, arranged in alphabetical order; and a herbal attributed to Macer Floridus, detailing 89 herbs and derived from an earlier Latin work by a Frenchmen who lived *c*.1070–1112. Both survive in several copies, and were often edited or conflated by scribes. It is also worth mentioning here a unique copy of the Middle English *Bestiary*, a description of real and imaginary animals and their habits, which survives in a manuscript dated to *c*.1275–1300. We should remember, however, that medieval bestiaries were religious works, which offered symbolic and mystical interpretations of the creatures. Their purpose was to inform and entertain, but above all to convey theological ideas in a popular form and to teach a moral lesson. The Middle English *Bestiary* is a verse adaptation of the 11th-century Latin *Physiologus* of Thetbaldus, also in verse. It describes various animals including an eagle, lion, serpent, stag, panther, whale, and others, and supplements each description by a 'significacio' – a passage elucidating their theological and moral significance.[8] The *Physiologus* of Thetbaldus uses five different metres for different parts of the text, and the Middle English *Bestiary* also uses a mixture of alliterative and syllabic verse.

The most influential Middle English encyclopaedic work was Trevisa's translation of *De proprietatibus rerum* ('On the order of things'). John of Trevisa produced translations of several important Latin works, including Ranulf Higden's *Polychronicon*, *De regimine principum* ('On the government of rulers' – a 13th-century book of advice to those in authority) of Aegidius Romanus, and *De proprietatibus rerum* by Bartholomaeus Anglicus, probably the most important

---

[8] In Old English three poems also exist from the *Physiologus*, usually entitled *The Whale*, *The Panther*, and *The Partridge*.

medieval encyclopaedia. The latter was originally compiled by an English Franciscan living in France around 1225. It is an encyclopaedia of different sciences, including theology, philosophy, medicine, astronomy, chronology, zoology, botany, geography, and mineralogy. It was organised into 19 books, each dealing with a different aspect of the universe, and was popular throughout Europe, surviving in a large number of manuscripts and translations across several languages. John of Trevisa completed his translation in 1398 and there is evidence that copies of it were owned by many of his contemporaries. Wynkyn de Worde published its first printed edition *c*.1495, and it remained the most popular work of its kind in England well into the 16th century.

Another popular encyclopaedia was known as the *Secretum Secretorum* ('The secret of secrets'). It is a Middle English adaptation of a widely circulated 12th-century Latin text, itself a translation of a 10th-century Arabic encyclopaedic treatise. It covered good government, ethics, medicine, astronomy, astrology, magic, and other subjects. The text is based around a fictional letter from Alexander the Great to his teacher Aristotle asking for advice on how to govern Persia, which he has recently conquered. Aristotle responds with a letter and various pieces of information needed for a ruler.

The Book of Sir John Mandeville, also known as *Mandeville's Travels*, is the best known of medieval travel narratives. The book's original was written in French around 1360, but the author and the place where it was composed are unknown. Some scholars believe he was a young nobleman, but others, taking into account his biblical knowledge, consider the author to have been a French or Flemish Benedictine monk familiar with travel and other literature. The *Book* quickly became popular and was translated into Latin and several vernacular languages, including five anonymous Middle English versions. It states that it was written from memory in 1356 by John Mandeville of St Albans, a knight, who left England in 1322 spending nearly 34 years travelling in the Near and Far East. Though entirely fictional, it is presented as a first-hand account of a journey around the world. It is organised geographically and describes travel routes from England to India, via Constantinople, Egypt, the Holy Land, and other real and invented lands.

The *Book* combines two traditions of travel writing: a pilgrimage to the Holy Land or Rome, and 'wonders of the East'. It describes different peoples, their history, religion, and customs; as well as natural phenomena with an emphasis on the marvellous and the exotic. Though written from a Christian perspective, it is critical of the arrogance and corruption of Christian nations. It describes differences between Eastern and Western churches and non-Christian religious practices with an open-mined tolerance.

The *Book* is a compilation made from several other works, including Latin encyclopaedias, earlier accounts of travels, and romances with oriental settings. Much of it is fiction and the protagonist is probably fictional as well (there is no evidence for a historical John Mandeville). However, the *Book* is written in lively prose and the protagonist is highly believable, considered by many critics to be one of the most successful medieval fictional characters. John Mandeville is skilfully and realistically presented as a modest and open-mined explorer and a truthful and reliable narrator, concerned with the authenticity of his stories (Davenport, 2004, pp. 183–4). The work was very widely circulated and survives in over 250 manuscripts and a large number of early printed editions in different languages. The French version appears to have been known to the author of *Cleanness*, who used it as a source for the descriptions of the Dead Sea and Belshazzar's feast.

The greatest problem for the study and understanding of Middle English scientific works is that only a very small part of the large extant corpus is available in modern editions. In spite of growing recent interest and considerable scholarly effort, many texts have still never been edited, and remain unstudied.

In conclusion we should consider the following key points:

- most Middle English scientific texts date from the late 14th century, but particularly from the 15th century;
- most are translations from Latin and French, but may include original commentary, additions from various sources, and omissions;
- some important scientific texts exist in multiple versions, as several translations were produced and because works were often edited by scribes to reflect their interests and to suit their intended audience;
- scientific texts are frequently illustrated in manuscripts, and unlike most contemporary book illustration it is practical rather than decorative, closely related to the text and sometimes integrated with it;
- scientific works are diverse but the largest group are medical texts.

See also   Chapter 2(g) for Old English travel works as well as those on science and education, and Chapter 3(e) and (p).

Further Reading

A detailed survey of Middle English scientific works and their manuscripts is found in Keiser (1998). Another important research tool is the catalogue of *incipits* (opening lines of texts) by Voigts and Kurtz (2000). Other useful accounts of scientific texts are Jones (1999), Keiser (2004), Rawcliffe (1995), Taavitsainen and Pahta (2004), and Voigts (1982 and 1989). For *Mandeville's Travels* see Higgins (1997) and Seymour (1993).

(n) Dream-Visions

What we describe here as a 'dream-vision' was one of the most popular medieval literary genres. Most works which belong to this genre are narratives written in the first person singular which present their events as seen in a vision or dream by a narrator. They usually have an introductory scene or a prologue describing the circumstances of the vision, and frequently combine narrative with meditation and an interpretation of the events described. The content of dream-visions is varied and may include religious, philosophical, political, satirical, lyrical, and fictional subject matter.

There are a number of reasons for the exceptional popularity of this genre with medieval writers. First there were the common beliefs about the nature of dreams, and their use in earlier literary and religious traditions. Medieval dream theory postulated that some dreams could be true. Chaucer's description of different types of dreams (for example, *The Parliament of Fowls*, ll. 29–84) follows the account by Macrobius in the commentary on Cicero's *Dream of Scipio*, written *c*.400. This work was well known and often quoted by medieval writers as an authority on the nature of dreams. Macrobius distinguished between five types of dreams. Two of these were false (*insomnium* and *visum*) and three were prophetic and possibly communicating important truths (*somnium* – an allegoric vision of truth; *visio* – a plain view of the future; and *oraculum* – an instruction by an authority). Literary use of dreams was also endorsed by their appearance in the Bible and classical literature, where they are often either prophetic or conveying divine messages. The form of the vision was used in medieval religious literature, as witnessed in the Old English poem *The Dream of the Rood*, and during the later Middle Ages in the works of English and Continental mystics, who used it to describe spiritual experiences and revelations.

There were also other more literary and technical reasons for the popularity of the dream-vision. It was valued by writers because it provided an authoritative framework for fictional narratives.

Medieval writers were not always prepared to admit that they were inventing a story, or writing new fiction. Much more commonly stories were presented as something that was inherited from the past and that described real events. This is to do with literary evolution, shifts in the perception of fiction, and changing views on its ability to reflect reality and act as an adequate vehicle for important ideas. Realistic fiction did not become established until the 19th century, and in the late Middle Ages its potential to represent real human experience (in spite of being an invention) had not yet been tested or fully recognized. Though fiction becomes more established by the end of the period (as can be seen in Chaucer's works), for most medieval writers and readers a story had to be either literally true, or true in a symbolic and allegorical way as an illustration of moral and spiritual realities, in order to be taken seriously.

Dream-visions provided clearly fictional stories with a context which, even if only by way of paying tribute to a convention, presented them as something that could be at least potentially true. It removed the difficulty of explaining and justifying their origin as an invention or new fiction. It also presented them as part of an essentially didactic tradition; that is as narratives that require interpretation and can be understood as a symbolic or allegorical revelation of a moral or spiritual truth. When justifying fiction became less of an issue, for authors such as Chaucer, the dream-vision continued to be valued for its wealth of technical possibilities. It allowed the author to combine narrative with instruction and meditation, realism with allegory, and to bring together multiple stories and episodes as in *Piers Plowman* or *The Legend of Good Women*.

Let us now consider some of the common conventions found in dream-vision narratives. They often describe journeys to the other world as in Dante's *Divine Comedy* or the Middle English *Pearl*. Sometimes it is a journey to an imaginary world inhabited by allegorical characters as in Chaucer's *The House of Fame* and the poems which it influenced, such as *The Kingis Quair*[9] by James I or Lydgate's *The Temple of Glass*. The journey is often inward as in *Pearl*, where the narrator undergoes emotional and mental change, or in *Piers Plowman*, which consists of a series of dreams focused on the narrator's spiritual quest. Many visions are allegorical and represent social, moral, and theological concepts in the form of symbolic characters and events. Some such works were written in the form of a debate between allegorical figures, as seen in the alliterative poems

---

[9] Quair or quire, referring to a short poem or treatise.

The Parliament of the Three Ages and *Winner and Waster*. These poems focus on the failings and advantages of different ages or periods in human life and discuss different ways of using wealth. Dreams often have a guide or teacher as an authoritative figure who helps the narrator to understand their experiences. The narrator can be an active participant in the imaginary events or simply an observer. Chaucer's narrators tend to be spectators, whereas the role of the narrators in *Pearl* and *Piers Plowman* is more active: they take part in the events described and undergo spiritual and moral change.

The content of dream-visions was not always serious, and could include parody and satire. Chaucer preceded the dream in *The House of Fame* with an introduction discussing the truthfulness and origin of dreams. He is quite sceptical and his narrative offers a parody of various conventions of the dream-vision genre. Comic elements are many and include the way the narrator is baffled by his experience, and the setting in which he is being carried by an eagle, a parody of the all-knowing guide who often appears in dream-visions. Chaucer gives similar humorous treatment to dreams in *The Nun's Priest's Tale*, which describes the cock Chauntecleer's dream about an orange-coloured beast, and his debate with his wife Pertelote about the truthfulness of dreams.

The dream-vision as a literary form flourished in the 14th and 15th centuries, but it is found early on in the *Roman de la Rose*, an enormously popular and influential poem. This was composed in France by Guillaume de Lorris, who began writing in the late 1230s, but left the work unfinished at the time of his death around 1278. The poem was completed and greatly expanded some 40 years later by Jean de Meun. It uses many narrative conventions found in the later dream-visions, including an introductory discussion of the truthfulness of dreams, a reference to Macrobius, the first-person narrative, a narrator falling asleep, a May morning setting, allegorical characters, symbolic landscapes, and so on. Another widely read and influential dream-vision was the *Pèlerinage de la vie humaine* ('The pilgrimage of human life'), a religious counterpart of the *Roman de la Rose*, composed by a Cistercian, Guillaume de Deguileville. It was first completed in 1331 and a revised and enlarged version appeared in 1355. It describes an allegorical pilgrimage to the Sacred Jerusalem in which the narrator is guided and assisted by virtues and has to resist vices and mortal sins. The *Pèlerinage* survives in a large number of manuscripts, including some beautifully illustrated ones. It influenced Langland and Chaucer and was translated into Middle English.

Chaucer used the dream-vision form in four of his works: *The*

House of Fame, The Book of the Duchess, The Parliament of Fowls, and *The Legend of Good Women.* The main subject of Chaucer's dream-visions is love, but all include philosophical content and use allegorical narrative for exploration of a wide range of ideas. Chaucer combined literary traditions represented by the *Roman de la Rose* and *The Consolation of Philosophy* by Boethius and created his own interpretation of the dream-vision genre, which had an immediate and lasting popularity.

To summarise we should consider the following key points:

- the dream-vision was one of the most popular medieval literary genres;
- this was partly due to the authoritative tradition of prophetic dreams in the Bible and classical literature;
- the dream-visions also offered excellent possibilities for building a narrative; they gave a didactic framework to fictional stories and allowed authors to combine different approaches and narrative levels in a single work;
- there was an established set of conventions associated with the dream-vision tradition;
- medieval works which helped to establish the dream-vision tradition include *The Consolation of Philosophy, Roman de la Rose,* and *Pèlerinage de la vie humaine.*

See also   Chapter 2(l), Chapter 3(g), (j), (p), (r)–(t), and Chapter 4(e).

Further Reading

An excellent introduction to dream poetry is Spearing (1976). The following works discuss various aspects of dream-visions by Chaucer and other medieval writers: Brown (1999), Edwards (1989), Kruger (1992), Lynch (2000), St John (2000), and Windeatt (1982). See also the useful introductions in Boffey (2003) and Phillips and Havely (1997).

(o)   William Langland, *Piers Plowman*

Historical allusions in the alliterative poem *Piers Plowman* suggest that it was composed *c.*1365–88. Most scholars believe that it is the only known work of a single poet called William Langland, who lived *c.*1325–88. Very little is known about him. The dialect of the poem and notes in its 15th-century manuscripts place him in south-west Worcestershire, though he probably lived part of his life in London.

The poem has numerous references to London and several to Malvern, and it is possible that he was educated at the Great Malvern Priory.

Many critics believe that *Piers Plowman* is the most complex poem in medieval English literature. Scholars repeatedly comment on the difficulty of defining its genre and central theme, or explaining its narrative structure and unity. One of the most difficult aspects of the poem is its text. *Piers Plowman* survives in 56 manuscripts and fragments, which make it by far the most widely circulated alliterative poem in Middle English. It appears to exist in three versions, which modern scholars call A, B, and C. They are usually interpreted as being a result of authorial revision, though this is a hypothesis and there is no evidence that Langland formally released several subsequent versions. Most scholars believe that the A-text was written first, probably around 1370. It is considered to be unfinished and has a prologue and eleven *passus* or chapters. The B-text, most commonly used as the basis of critical discussions, appears to have been produced around 1376–9. It extends and revises the poem, making it more sophisticated and more political, and has a prologue and twenty *passus*. The C-text was produced in the late 1380s and has a prologue and twenty-two *passus*. It is a revision of the B-text, probably in response to a different political situation. Some critics interpret the changes in C as an attempt to distance the work from Lollard views and from the Peasants' Revolt of 1381. Revision undertaken in the C-text may be unfinished, possibly because of Langland's death around 1388. Some scholars believe in the existence of the fourth earliest version, known as Z (surviving in a unique manuscript, in Oxford, Bodleian Library MS Bodley 851), but this view is not accepted by everybody. There is evidence that medieval scribes tried to conflate and edit versions of Langland's text, and Z may represent such an attempt. Some scholars even dispute the hypothesis of the three versions and their chronology all together. Whereas different versions may result from continuous authorial revision, the state of Langland's text is not that different from what is found in other medieval literary works where authorial text can be rarely separated from its history, reception, and transmission. The scribes commonly acted as editors, interpreters, and revisers of the works they copied, and played an active role in the production of texts.

As mentioned already *Piers Plowman* has a complex narrative structure. It is composed as a series of dream-visions experienced by the narrator and is divided into *passus*. In some manuscripts it is also subdivided into *Visio Willelmi de Petrus Plowman* ('William's Vision of

Piers Plowman') and *Vita de Dowel, Dobet et Dobest* ('The Life of Do-Well, Do-Bet and Do-Best'). Many scholars believe that this division may be scribal, but it is not meaningless and reflects the external (the reform of society) and the internal (the reform of an individual) nature of the quest the poem describes. Langland's narrative, its various parts and ending, gave rise to many critical interpretations. His major concerns appear to be an individual's salvation and search for a Christian life, the state of the Church and contemporary society, the necessity of their moral reform, and the spiritual destiny of humanity as a whole. In the first *passus* the dreamer meets an allegorical figure of the Holy Church and his only request to her is to teach him how he might save his soul. The final *passus*, on the other hand, deal with the history of the Church and humanity as a whole and have a tragic, apocalyptic tone and imagery.

As pointed out already, the narrative, structured as a quest, moves from external to internal, and from attempts to reform the community to attempts to reform an individual. The first part (*Visio, passus* I–VII) focuses on the corruption of society and efforts to remedy this corruption, represented as a search for Truth led by Piers Plowman, an idealised Christian. An important theme introduced in the portrayal of different 'estates' of society and the allegorical narrative of the opening *passus*, is the breakdown of the traditional feudal values and social order, and the suffering of the poor – oppressed and unable to control economic forces and social change. These political issues are given a spiritual and moral dimension. The poem introduces the concept of Truth as the opposite of corruption – a principle on which both human society and the heavenly order are based. The Truth underlies the relationship between God and creation and encompasses such principles of conduct as obedience to one's lord (including the Church, king, and social superiors), good works, faith-keeping, justice, and social responsibility. Langland draws attention to the breakdown of these principles in his contemporary world, but his main concern is moral rather than political reform, and he does not call for a simple restoration of the traditional feudal order. Spiritual authority given to Piers the Plowman and his role as a guide in the search for Truth contradicts the position of peasants in a feudal hierarchy. It also elevates the marginalised laity and poor and rural communities, and calls for a re-evaluation of hierarchy and power.

The next *passus* (VII–XVII) are concerned with the inward journey of Will, the dreamer and narrator of the poem, towards an understanding of 'Do-Well', namely the true Christian life which may lead to salvation. He has several visions, and encounters various allegorical figures representing intellectual concepts and values important for 'Do-Well'. He receives partial answers to his questions, experiences doubts and bewilderment, but undergoes spiritual development which prepares him for the final part of the quest, focused on God's grace and redemption – both necessary prerequisites of human salvation. The final *passus* (XVIII–XXII in C-text) are concerned with the history of the Church, in which the triumph of Christ is followed by the struggle between good and evil. An allegorical narrative describes the Passion of Christ, his descent into Hell and victory over Satan. This is followed by the establishment of the Church on earth and finally by an allegorical depiction of its present state as being attacked by sins, temptations, and the forces of the Antichrist. The ending of the poem is inconclusive: the personification of Conscience sets out to wander over the world until he finds Piers the Plowman. This may symbolise the renewal of an individual's search for a Christian life, which remains unfulfilled.

Piers Plowman is often described as an allegorical narrative. Langland uses various forms of personification and symbolism with outstanding skill and originality, creating vivid and multi-dimensional allegorical characters, such as Lady Meed (who represents both reward for truth and greed for profit), Holy Church, Patience, Conscience, and many others. Piers Plowman is probably the most complex character of the poem. At the beginning he represents obedience to God, apostolic poverty and simplicity, truth, and integrity contrasted with egotism and the corruption of the surrounding world. In the course of the poem his image develops into a symbol of Christ's humanity and comes to embody the aspirations of the dreamer in his search for spiritual perfection and salvation. One of the most interesting aspects of the poem is how it combines allegory with realism. Allegorical figures are made more convincing by vivid realistic touches and there are many passages and episodes involving realistic depictions of the life of different social classes. In fact the poem offers an exceptionally rich representation of 14th-century England including its agriculture, trade, social structure, customs and attitudes, domestic life, and material culture.

Many critics have noted similarities between some of Langland's ideas and those of John Wyclif and his followers. Thus Piers the Plowman is closer to God than the clergy described. There is an association of poverty with spiritual authority and Christian life, and there is hostility to the friars and criticism of the institutional Church. The poem is undoubtedly polemical and includes social and ecclesiastical criticism and satire; but there are also significant differences between the views of Langland and of the Lollards. Langland appears to have looked for reform within the Church without any intention of breaking with it. His work was not heretical or politically radical at the time of its writing, though the figure of Piers the Plowman did become associated with religious and social dissent. Thus there are references to *Piers Plowman* in letters claimed to have been written by the leaders of the Peasants' Revolt of 1381, in works associated with the Lollards (such as the alliterative poem *Pierce the Ploughman's Crede* or the rhyming poem known as *The Plowman's Tale*), and later in texts produced during the Reformation. The protagonist of *Pierce the Ploughman's Crede* is trying to get answers about Christian teaching (particularly an important prayer known as *Credo* ('I believe')) from members of several fraternal orders. However, they only ask him for money and make speeches against other religious orders. He finally gets his answers from a peasant, whose poverty and miserable existence are described with striking realism and pathos. *The Plowman's Tale* (also known as *The Complaint of the Plowman*) probably originated at the very end of the 14th century, and was circulated in the 16th century as part of Chaucer's *The Canterbury Tales*. It is an allegorical satire written in the form of a dialogue between a Pelican, who symbolised idealised Christianity, and a Griffon, who represents corruption within the Church.

The study of literary and historical references in *Piers Plowman* suggests that Langland's learning was very broad and complex, including familiarity with political and theological debates, university instruction, and a wide range of literary works. The sources of *Piers Plowman* can by partially identified, but much of it is without precedent. It includes a discussion of subjects which are not found in earlier vernacular texts. Its structure and narrative technique are also highly original. It appears to reject intentionally many conventions of literature, as if declaring that it is not fiction and should be approached with different expectations; possibly even to be read as a sermon or prophesy, rather than poetry.

In conclusion, we should consider the following key points:

- most scholars believe that *Piers Plowman* is the only known work of a single poet called William Langland, who lived c.1325–88;
- one of its most difficult aspects is its text; it appears to survive in three versions (A, B, and C), which most scholars interpret as being the result of authorial revision;

- *Piers Plowman* has a complex narrative form; it is structured as a quest, which moves from external to internal, and from attempts to reform the community to attempts to reform an individual;
- Langland uses various forms of personification, allegory, and symbolism with outstanding skill and originality;
- there are similarities between some of Langland's ideas and those of John Wyclif and his followers, but there are also important differences;
- Langland appears to reject intentionally many conventions of literature, as if declaring that his work should be approached with different expectations.

See also   Chapter 1(e), Chapter 3(k), and Chapter 4(e).

Further Reading

Good introductions to *Piers Plowman* are Alford (1988) and Marshall (2001). A good student edition and modern translations are Schmidt (1992 and 1995) and Goodridge (1959). The studies of literary and historical background include Du Boulay (1991), Coleman (1981), Gradon (1980), and Simpson (1990). See also Aers (1975), Baldwin (1981), Bloomfield (1962), Burrow (1993), Donaldson (1966), Godden (1990), Kane (1965), Middleton (1986), Pearsall (1988 and 1990b), Schmidt (1987) and Stokes (1984). Schmidt (1995–) offers a parallel edition of the four texts of the poem. Brewer (1996) gives an account of the textual transmission and scholarly editing of *Piers Plowman*. Electronic editions of manuscript witnesses to Langland's text are published by *The Piers Plowman Electronic Archive* (http://jefferson.village.virginia.edu/seenet/piers/).

(p)   The *Gawain*-Poet

The famous alliterative poem *Sir Gawain and the Green Knight* is preserved in a single manuscript, in London, British Library, Cotton MS. Nero A. X, written *c*.1400. There it is accompanied by three other poems generally believed to be by the same author, the so-called '*Gawain*-poet' (or '*Pearl*-poet'). These are *Pearl*, *Cleanness* (also known as *Purity*), and *Patience*. The poems, as preserved in the manuscript, share the same north-west Midlands dialect (probably on the border of Cheshire and Staffordshire), as well as many themes and features of style. Nothing is known about the author though scholars have made numerous attempts to identify him. The poems were probably composed in the last quarter of the 14th century, and the poet was clearly educated, with a considerable knowledge of theology and familiarity with aristocratic lifestyle and culture. He may have been a cleric in the service of a nobleman, for whose household some of his poems may have been written.

Three of the poems are on religious themes. *Patience* is based on the Old Testament book of Jonah. The story, with many changes of detail and emphasis, is used to illustrate the Christian virtue of patience as the opposite of anger, arrogance, and disobedience. Jonah is presented as well-meaning but rebellious, and inclined to question the ways of God, which he is unable to understand. The poem has many masterful descriptions and vivid scenes, such as the storm on the sea, Jonah's passage into the whale's stomach, and his prayer to God from the depth of this hell. There is a touch of humour and sympathy in the portrayal of the prophet's human weaknesses, the folly of his anger against God, his futile attempt to escape his mission, and his gradual acceptance of his calling. Whereas *Patience* focuses on the career of a single protagonist, *Cleanness* has a more complex structure. It combines a narrative with meditation on corruption and purity from sin. It illustrates the virtue of purity by telling a series of biblical stories. The narrative sections of *Cleanness* include the Old and New Testament stories of the fall of Lucifer and Adam, Noah and the flood, Abraham, Lot and the destruction of Sodom and Gomorrah, Belshazzar's feast, and Christ's life on earth. The latter is presented as an example of purity and courtesy. Both *Patience* and *Cleanness* share some features with medieval *exempla*, a popular genre where stories were used to illustrate Christian virtues and concepts.

Pearl is a dream-vision, most commonly interpreted as an elegy on the death of the protagonist's infant daughter. A grieving father meets her again in a vision of Paradise and Heavenly Jerusalem. This experience launches a theological debate about salvation by grace, in the course of which the narrator is taught important doctrinal concepts and reassured that his child is saved. Like Jonah he at first questions the ways of God, whose justice and grace appear paradoxical to him, but learns humility and a better understanding of Christian teaching. The poem is influenced by the *Roman de la Rose* and *The Consolation of Philosophy* by Boethius, but does not have any known direct model. It is highly original in its imagery and complex structure; employing elaborate symmetry, and exceptional emotional intensity in both its narrative and the beauty of its descriptions.

Sir Gawain and the Green Knight is the last item in the manuscript and is a romance set at the court of King Arthur. In summary a mysterious Green Knight interrupts the festivities at Camelot, challenging the knights to a beheading game. They are allowed to take a swing at his neck, but if he survives he will return the blow in a year and a day in the Green Chapel. Gawain, a young knight, accepts the challenge but the Green Knight survives through sorcery. The story recounts Gawain's quest to find the Green Knight's chapel to complete the game. Before his final encounter with the Knight he stays in Castle Hautdesert where he is entertained by Sir Bertilak and his wife, and has to undergo a series of temptations. When he eventually arrives at the chapel, the Green Knight is revealed as Sir Bertilak, and the game, as a test set up by Morgan le Fay. Gawain then returns to Camelot.

The plot includes many elements typical for a medieval romance, such as a quest, challenges from supernatural opponents, magic, temptations, courtly celebrations, feasts, and hunts. Some narrative elements, such as the Beheading Game and the Exchange of Winnings, have parallels in folklore and French and Celtic literature. *Sir Gawain* is best appreciated against the background of Arthurian romance: the poet knew its conventions intimately and managed to develop and rework them with great originality and skill. Thus (as many critics have noticed), unusually for a romance *Sir Gawain* combines the romantic with reality. In an account of Gawain's travel, for example, traditional fights with monsters are described in just a few lines, whereas much more space is given to a realistic, highly evocative description of the landscape and winter weather, presented as a greater threat to Gawain than giants and trolls. Gawain's journey starts at King Arthur's court and in the mythical realm of 'Lorges', but very soon the poet describes him riding into North Wales, and uses real place names to trace his route. The emphasis is on the genuine hardship of the winter journey, set in the real world of 14th-century England. Throughout the poem the marvellous coexists with the real, and is made more believable by detailed, colourful, and persuasive descriptions which put flesh and blood on everything the poet portrays. Combining romantic with real occasionally has humorous effect, and the poet's treatment of the main characters is often ironic. Unusually for a romance, comedy and humour are very important, and enrich rather than destroy its conceptual and narrative framework, creating variety and making the main characters more believable. In addition a light-hearted tone is combined with moral seriousness and an interest in psychology.

A focus on moral choice and ethical behaviour is found in all the works in Cotton Nero A. X. In all the poems protagonists learn to abandon pride and egotistic desires. The importance of the same virtues – loyalty, courtesy, patience, purity, and humility – is explored in a variety of contexts and situations, from the exotic, extreme, and pathetic, to the ordinary and humorous. None of the poems, however, are excessively moralistic or didactic. *Sir Gawain* in particular stands out as a narrative where readers are left to make their own moral judgement. In the course of his adventure Gawain discovers that he is capable of feeling fear and cannot forgive himself for failure to achieve perfection and stay true to his very elevated ideals. He is, however, forgiven by his opponent Bertilak and welcomed as a hero by King Arthur's court on his return. Critics have offered numerous interpretations of what constitutes Gawain's fault and of his feelings following the quest. These can be seen as remorse for his *untrawþe* ('disloyalty'), as the pain of humiliation, or as pride and wounded self-esteem. In spite of taking loyalty and honour very seriously, the poet seems to suggest a more light-hearted approach to Gawain's ordeal. He is interested not only in ethics, but also in the problems of conduct, and contradictions in the chivalric code and etiquette. Gawain unknowingly becomes the subject of an experiment, which is not entirely fair to him, because he is faced with conflicting obligations. The final outcome is dependent not only on his virtue, but on his ability to find a middle way between different imperatives, and to resolve opposed requirements of honour and courtesy. At the end the reader is left with many unanswered questions, and many possible solutions to the complex moral puzzle at the heart of the poem.

Complexity and richness also characterise the style and structure of the Cotton Nero poems. All have important, precise, and vivid descriptive passages as witnessed by the heavenly garden in *Pearl*, the seafaring in *Patience*, Belshazzar's feast in *Cleanness*, and many others. Critics have also noticed the poet's interest in elaborate patterning and a complex structural design based on contrasts and symmetries. In *Sir Gawain*, for example, there are a number of parallels and contrasts between the three hunts, the exchanged winnings, and the three encounters between Gawain and the Lady. The circular structure of the quest is emphasised by the change of seasons, and the poet uses contrasts and parallels to portray the main characters, as witnessed by the two *personae* of the Green Knight, or the description of the Lady's beauty contrasted against the ugliness of Morgan le Fay.

Like many medieval writers the poet was interested in number symbolism. *Pearl* has 1,212 lines, 12-line stanzas, and a description of 144,000 virgins of Heavenly Jerusalem. In *Sir Gawain* the number five is used in several elements of its structure and symbolically in the pentangle on Gawain's shield, representing his five virtues. Both *Pearl* and *Sir Gawain* have 101 stanzas, a number symbolising completeness. *Sir Gawain*, *Cleanness*, and *Patience* are written in long alliterative lines, whereas *Pearl* is in syllabic four-stressed lines, also with a frequent use of alliteration. *Patience* and *Cleanness* are in stanzaic units of four lines, whereas *Sir Gawain* is composed in stanzas of different lengths, ending with a five-line 'bob-and-wheel' rhyming *ababa*. Stanzas of *Pearl* have a complex rhyming pattern, and are divided into twenty groups, in which the final line of each stanza has a similar refrain. They are also linked through the repetition of words, with an element of the last line of the previous stanza appearing in the first line of the following stanza. The Cotton Nero poems share language and many features of poetic technique with other Middle English alliterative poems. The *Gawain*-poet used special poetic vocabulary, derived from Anglo-Saxon, French, and Old Norse, and a style associated with Middle English alliterative verse.

To summarise, we should consider the following key points:

- the alliterative poems *Sir Gawain and the Green Knight*, *Pearl*, *Cleanness*, and *Patience* are preserved in a unique manuscript written *c*.1400;
- the poems share themes, imagery, and style and are believed to be the work of a single author (often called the '*Gawain*-poet');
- all poems display an interest in theology, and ethical behaviour, and a familiarity with aristocratic lifestyle;
- *Sir Gawain* is best appreciated against the background of Arthurian romance, but it intentionally opposes many of its conventions;
- all the poems display a complexity and richness of ideas, structure, and style.

See also   Chapter 3(h) and Chapter 4(g).

Further Reading

A well-annotated student edition of the poem is Andrew and Waldron (1987). Excellent introductions to the *Gawain*-poet are Putter (1996) and Brewer and Gibson (1997). See also Barron (1980), Burrow (1965), Davenport (1978), Kean (1967), Lecklider (1997), and Spearing (1970). See annotated bibliographies by Andrew (1979) and Blanch (1983).

(q)   John Gower

John Gower (c.1330–1408), an outstanding poet and an older contemporary of Chaucer, lived most of his life in London. It is not entirely clear what his occupation was, but most likely he had a career in law and was a wealthy gentleman landowner. His situation was not that dissimilar from Chaucer's, apart from his greater independence (he had never been in royal service and was not dependent on royal patronage). His position in London brought him in touch with the same class of people who appear to have been Chaucer's literary community: professionals, civil servants, and knights in royal service. His work offers praise and advice to Richard II in the 1380s, but later he became critical of the king, and switched allegiances to the future Henry IV. A dedication to Richard II in the *Confessio Amantis* ('The Lover's Confession') was replaced by a dedication to Henry IV, and Gower's late works are addressed to Henry after he became king.

John Gower is the author of three major works: the Anglo-Norman *Mirour de l'Omme* ('The mirror of man' – completed in the late 1370s), the Latin *Vox Clamantis* ('The voice of one crying' – produced in the 1380s), and in English the *Confessio Amantis* (first completed in 1390, but later revised in 1392–3). The *Mirour de l'Omme* is a didactic poem of 29,945 lines, rhyming in stanzas of twelve lines. It survives in a single manuscript which lacks the beginning and end. *Mirour de l'Omme* is an ambitious work concerned with the sinful state of humanity and its salvation. It starts with an allegorical narrative describing the fall of Lucifer and the struggle of good and evil for the soul of man. This is followed by a detailed examination of corruption in contemporary society and criticism of the 'three estates' (Church, nobility, and commons). The satire of estates is particularly lively in Gower's criticism of London professional classes, including lawyers, judges, merchants, and retailers. Finally the poem tells the life of the Virgin Mary as an example of purity and compassion.

The *Vox Clamantis* is another poem about society, its estates and government, and consists of over 10,000 lines in unrhymed elegiac couplets. It is subdivided into seven books and includes several dream-visions. The first vision gives an account of the Peasants' Revolt of 1381 in the form of an allegorical narrative, starting with the peasants' march on London and ending with the death of Wat Tyler. At the beginning of the dream the peasants are described as transformed by God's curse into different animals preparing to attack London. Some scholars have suggested that this account may have been added later to an earlier version of six books, because it differs considerably from the rest of the poem. The remaining books are devoted to an estates satire similar to that of the *Miroir*, and deal with the corruption of different classes, the decline of the world, and the seven deadly sins. In some manuscripts the *Vox* appears together with another Latin work, the *Cronica tripartita*, which was written soon after the accession to the throne of Henry IV. It describes the reign of Richard II as disastrous, and ends with his fall from power and the accession of Henry. This early piece of 'Lancastrian propaganda' is particularly striking because Gower was initially a great supporter of Richard II.

The *Confessio Amantis* is Gower's most influential work, partly because it is written in English but also possibly because of its more universal concerns. To it Gower owes his later reputation as a narrative poet and a teller of moralised stories (it contains the tale of Apollonius of Tyre, used in Shakespeare's *Pericles*, where Gower appears as a narrator). The *Confessio Amantis* consists of eight books and more than 33,000 lines. Influenced by the *Roman de la Rose* it is structured as a confession of a lover, Amans, who tells Genius, the priest of Venus, about his unrequited love. Genius is concerned with love but he is also interested in sin as understood in Christian terms. Like Chaucer's *The Canterbury Tales*, the *Confessio Amantis* is a collection of stories. Genius questions Amans first about the sins of Seeing and Hearing and then about each of the Seven Deadly Sins, offering examples from ancient history and legends. As in his other works, Gower's main aim is moral instruction, but moral judgements in the *Confessio Amantis* are less straightforward and more complex than in his earlier works. In an unexpected and highly effective final sequence of the poem Amans gives up his love because the priest reminds him about the love of God, but also because (as we learn) he is an old man. The *Confessio Amantis* survives in 49 manuscripts, which demonstrates its considerable contemporary popularity. The manuscripts attest to three distinct versions, which differ in their dedications, prologues, and various textual detail. This suggests that Gower repeatedly revised the poem, adapting it to changes in the political situation.

Unlike Chaucer, Gower was a very political poet: all his major works are concerned with politics and society. Throughout his career Gower was interested in kingship and good government. These themes are more prominent in his works than in the works of any other 14th-century writer. His position though is largely conservative. He believed in royal power and social hierarchy, in the need for people to be constrained by strong laws, and in the preservation of the established order. He represents the order of the universe as divine, and its support and the acceptance of one's place in society as a moral duty of everyone. This did not exclude criticism across the social hierarchy. Gower's works reflect a belief that the law should apply to all, that good laws are important both for society and for government and should be respected by the monarch, whose power is limited by divine and natural law. In the *Mirour de l'Omme*, following the tradition of the 'mirror for princes' (a book of instruction for rulers), he uses King David as an example of good kingship, and discusses principles of behaviour which all rulers should follow – such as piety, and being shepherds of the people, and role models to others. The question of the good rule is also explored in many of the stories in the *Confessio Amantis*.

Gower's interest in political and social affairs is linked to his understanding of the role of poetry. Inspired by the Latin tradition of political poetry and satire, he took the duties of a poet very seriously. For him a poet is someone who could reform the world and advise princes. In the *Vox Clamantis*, his most political poem, he presents himself as a prophet like those in the Bible, a voice crying in the wilderness and ignored by the world. Such understanding of poetry also accounts for the learned quality and encyclopaedic and moral nature of Gower's works. Like Chaucer he wrote narrative poetry, but unlike Chaucer, his stories are used to illustrate moral and philosophical principles and are presented as historical narratives or visions, rather than fiction. It appears that he wanted his works to be valued for their learning, ethical instruction, and social criticism.

Gower is highly unusual among 14th-century writers in the care he took over the manuscripts of his works. He provided a sophisticated apparatus for *Confessio Amantis*, with summaries, glosses, and notes in Latin. They were set in the margins of the manuscripts of the *Confessio Amantis*, partly in order to give it authority similar to that of Latin books, which were often presented in this way. Such presentation required considerable effort and careful planning and the earliest manuscripts of Gower's works were probably prepared under his supervision. This included making presentation copies of his works for powerful individuals, such as a copy of the *Confessio Amantis* for Henry of Derby (afterwards Henvy IV), or of the *Vox Clamantis* for Thomas Arundel, Archbishop of Canterbury.

John Gower is one of the dedicatees of *Troilus and Criseyde*, and there are other allusions to his works in Chaucer's poetry. A 1378 document survives where Chaucer grants the power of attorney to Gower and another London lawyer before his diplomatic journey to Italy. An earlier version (1390) of the *Confessio Amantis* has a reference to Chaucer near its end; Gower agrees to pass to Chaucer a message from Venus. However, this reference disappears from subsequent recensions of the *Confessio Amantis*. It is not clear why it was removed and critics have speculated about a 'fall out' between Gower and Chaucer, but the reasons for its removal may have been political or simply scribal, and not necessarily personal.

Gower was the last major English poet to write in 'elite' languages: Latin and Anglo-Norman. Scholars observed that features which helped to build his earlier reputation, such as his political and moral stance, learning, and the use of prestigious languages, were received negatively by later critics and readers. A long tradition of comparing Gower with Chaucer often worked against Gower, whose poetry was seen as excessively moralistic, academic, and overloaded with references and borrowings from earlier authors. Recent criticism, however, takes a more historical view. It emphasises Gower's complex use of sources and skill as a narrator, as witnessed, for example, in his effective use of the dialogue framework and multiple narratives in the *Confessio Amantis*. Many readers agree that the *Confessio Amantis* is a highly integrated work where narrative frame and the stories form an effective and original structure. The protagonist, far from being a conventional device for introducing the stories, goes through a process of spiritual growth which culminates in a moving and dramatic final sequence.

To summarise, we should consider the following key points:

- John Gower was a contemporary of Chaucer, whose life in London probably brought him in touch with the same class of people that comprised Chaucer's literary community;
- Gower was the last noteworthy English poet to write major works in Latin and Anglo-Norman;
- his works show an interest in narrative poetry, moral instruction, and in such political subjects as the criticism of society and the problems of good government;
- Gower is highly unusual among 14th-century writers in the care he took over the manuscripts of his works; the earliest manuscripts were probably prepared under his supervision.

See also   Chapter 2(o).

Further Reading

The standard edition of Gower's works is Macaulay (1900–1). Bennett (1968) offers selections from Gower. The following works provide a comprehensive introduction to Gower's poetry: Fisher (1964), Minnis (1983), Nicholson (1991), and Yeager (1990). Nicholson (1989) is a line-by-line commentary which lists references to scholarly works on *Confessio Amantis*.

(r) Geoffrey Chaucer

Geoffrey Chaucer (early 1340s–1400) is probably the best known writer of the Middle English period, and one of the most celebrated of English authors. His poetry continues to delight readers, as witnessed by the number of editions, translations into different languages, and film and theatre adaptations of his works. Modern readers admire his stylistic and thematic range, irony, precise and vivid characterisation, his skill as a storyteller, and his insight as an observer of society and human behaviour.

Many critics believe that Chaucer is the first truly modern author in the English literary tradition. What is meant by this is probably most evident in how he perceived his works and his own role in their making. First, whereas earlier and many contemporary authors preferred to be seen as narrators of history, or as writers of works of instruction, Chaucer is more assured in his role as an author of fiction. In *The Canterbury Tales* he wears (among several others) a traditional authorial mask of a teacher and a writer of didactic treatises, such as *The Tale of Melibee*, and in several of the tales he justifies his fiction by pointing out that it serves as moral instruction and illustrates theological truth. In spite of this, however, Chaucer's understanding of fiction seems to have been much closer to our own than to that of many of his contemporaries. His narrative of the events of the Trojan War in *Troilus and Criseyde*, and the philosophical allegory in *The House of Fame*, emphasise the relativity of our knowledge of history and the deeds of men and women from the past. By pointing this out Chaucer helps to establish the distinction between fiction and historical truth. What is even more important, however, is that even though he recognises that literature, including his own work, is not 'authoritative' in its portrayal of past or present events, this does not make it false or unworthy of his or his readers' attention. He treats it seriously, by showing that invented fictional stories can be a powerful tool for the portrayal of society and human character. In *The Canterbury Tales* he seems to delight in experimentation with a full range of contemporary literary genres and approaches. He juxtaposes different types of narrative, such as romance and fabliaux, with their opposing views of human nature (see below), and reveals their possibilities, weaknesses, and strengths. He invites a conclusion that fictional stories, though not offering historical or literary truth, or direct instruction, nevertheless reflect important aspects of life in different and complementary ways, and thus deserve to be taken seriously.

Secondly, Chaucer more confidently and self-consciously than many of his contemporaries accepts his responsibility and freedom as an author, rather than as a compiler, translator, or narrator of 'real' events or stories from the past. Paying tribute to tradition, in *Troilus and Criseyde* he presents himself as a translator of a book by an invented ancient author called Lollius. One of the traditional masks that he wears in *The Canterbury Tales* is that of a minstrel, a narrator or performer of a popular romance, such as *Sir Thopas*, designed as a collection of clichés which seemingly has little 'authorial' voice. Most of Chaucer's works, however, have a highly individualised fictional narrator, presented as Chaucer himself, and portrayed with humour as a bookish, shy, and impractical person. Such openly playful self-portrayal (found in *The Canterbury Tales* and *The House of Fame*) has little in common with traditional medieval authorial self-representation. In *Troilus and Criseyde* Chaucer creates an illusion of a personal relationship with the readers. He invites their sympathy with the characters, urges them to relate the story to their own experience, and manipulates their response in a confident and sophisticated way. Such a prominent and original authorial persona is not found in earlier or contemporary English works. Normally authors are either anonymous, rarely telling readers about themselves, and disappearing behind the narrative; or are portrayed primarily as teachers, prophets, or seekers for truth, rather than poets and authors of fiction.

In spite of his apparently modest self-portrayal, Chaucer aligns himself, with great confidence, with famous authors from the past already in his early work *The Book of the Duchess*. Helen Cooper pointed out that Chaucer's patron John of Gaunt is personified in the poem as Emperor Octavian, the patron of Virgil and Ovid, thus indirectly inviting a comparison between these poets and Chaucer himself (Cooper, 2005, pp. 268–9). Chaucer presents himself in his works as an author, but not as a medieval 'auctor'. This term was reserved for writers who were seen as particularly authoritative and praiseworthy, usually because they fulfilled the major medieval requirements for literature, which was expected to be historically and theologically true, and morally edifying. In spite of wearing some traditional authorial masks, Chaucer seems to be aware, like modern writers of fiction, that he is not a historian, or a faithful narrator or translator of stories from the past. Instead he sees himself as an author of invented characters and events. At the same time, in *The House of Fame* and *Troilus and Criseyde* (see below) he demonstrates that Virgil, Ovid, and other famous 'auctores', were also authors of fiction.

Finally, unlike the works of many of his contemporaries, Chaucer's poetry is not explicitly didactic. Many critics have observed that we really do not know what his views on society were, for example, or on the position of women, or the contemporary religious and political situation. His works undoubtedly reflect a strong interest in all these subjects, but he chooses to treat them in ways unique to a fictional narrative, letting characters and events in his stories 'speak for themselves'.

Chaucer lived most of his life in London. His father was a prosperous merchant, and Chaucer started his career in royal service in 1357 when he was appointed to the household of Elizabeth, Countess of Ulster, and her husband Prince Lionel (the second son of Edward III). He served in the royal households of Edward III and Richard II and held various administrative appointments under both kings, which included several missions abroad in Spain, Italy, and France. Chaucer had a successful civil career in spite of extremely dangerous times; particularly in the late 1380s, which were marked by the power struggle between Richard II and the aristocratic opposition, when some of his close associates were executed. Most interestingly, literary patronage does not seem to have played an important role in his career, even though several of his works appear to have been written for patrons (see Strohm, 2003). Thus *The Book of the Duchess* was almost certainly intended to console John of Gaunt, the Duke of Lancaster, uncle of Richard II and Chaucer's patron, following the death of his wife Duchess Blanche of Lancaster in 1368. Richard II and Queen Anne may have been partly responsible for the incomplete *The Legend of Good Women*, as the poem portrays the God of Love and Queen Alceste, who set Chaucer the task of telling stories about virtuous women. Both poems, however, can be read and understood without reference to the concerns of their patrons and are steeped in universal ideas of love, death, fortune, virtue, and evil.

We know only approximately when and in what order Chaucer's works were written. They tend to reflect his literary and intellectual interests and have few direct references to contemporary events. His

earlier poems were influenced by his reading of French courtly literature, particularly the *Roman de la Rose* and the works of Machaut,
Deschamps, de Grandson, and Froissart, whereas his later poetry
also reveals deep engagement with the works of Dante, Petrarch, and
Boccaccio.

His earliest datable poem is *The Book of the Duchess*, composed
after 1368 (see earlier). It is a dream-vision where, after an elaborate
symbolic introduction, the narrator speaks to 'a man in blak' (line
445), a knight, who tells the story of his love. It is clear from the
beginning that the knight is oppressed by a great sorrow, but as the
story develops the narrator is seemingly unable to understand what
has happened to the lady whom the knight loved. In a highly dramatic
final sequence the narrator and readers are plainly told the cruel truth
that 'she ys ded' (line 1309). The poem employs many of the conventions of contemporary French love poetry. Its immediate sources
were the *Roman de la Rose*, Froissart's *Paradis d'amour* ('Paradise of
Love' – written *c.*1362), and several works by Machaut, including
Jugement dou roy de Behaingne ('Judgement of the King of Bohemia' –
*c.*1342) and its sequel *Jugement dou roy de Navarre* ('Judgement of the
King of Navarre' – *c.*1341). From these poems Chaucer borrowed
individual passages and lines, as well as many ideas and formal
features. Thus the opening lines of *The Book of the Duchess* are
closely modelled on the opening lines of *Paradis d'amour*.
Furthermore, in Machaut's *Jugement dou roy de Behaingne* the narrator overhears a lady lamenting because her beloved is dead, and a
knight grieving because his beloved was unfaithful. They argue
whose situation is worse. The judgement is eventually made at the
Court of Love of the King of Bohemia, who decides that infidelity is a
greater cause for grief. Chaucer's poem develops this by portraying
fulfilled and loyal love, with its consolatory message (though not
directly expressed) that true happiness and devotion experienced by
the knight have a permanent value which cannot be annihilated by
death. Chaucer's use of didactic and philosophical themes in his
poem about love (such as the knight's complaints against Fortune),
and classical literary and mythological tradition (such as the story of
Ceyx and Alcione, which the narrator is reading when he falls
asleep), were also inspired by the works of his French contemporaries. Their influence is evident in the portrayal of the object of the
knight's love and his service to the lady, and in how the dream and its
characters are introduced and its setting is described.

Formal features borrowed by Chaucer from his French models,
therefore, include a voice overheard by a narrator, a lyric complaint

inserted into the narrative (such as the 'lay' of the Man in Black, ll. 475–86), a melancholy and lovesick authorial persona portrayed with some comic touches, the May morning setting of the dream, and many others. French poetry continued to be an inspiration throughout Chaucer's career, but already in *The Book of the Duchess* his use of its conventions is confident and original. They are fully internalised and integrated into his narrative, and contribute to the striking intensity and compelling realism of his portrayal of love and grief.

Another poem on the theme of love, written probably some time after *The Book of the Duchess*, is *The Parliament of Fowls*. In this poem love is presented in the context of the natural and social order. The narrator is described as searching for answers to his questions about love, portrayed as a powerful and sometimes destructive force. He finds himself reading Cicero's *Somnium Scipionis* ('The Dream of Scipio' – known in the Middle Ages as part of a commentary by Macrobius written *c*.AD400). This is a common theme in Chaucer's works: the narrator of *The Book of the Duchess* has his vision after reading Ovid's *Metamorphosis*. In *The Parliament of Fowls* the book read by the narrator presents humanity and its passions as a small part of the divinely established cosmos. Having finished his reading the narrator falls asleep and has several visions including those of a garden, a temple of Venus, and the assembly presided by Nature, where birds choose their mates on St Valentine's Day (the 'parliament' of the title). The poem portrays different aspects of love, such as its power and danger associated with Venus, and its harmony and fruitfulness associated with Nature. Chaucer relates the experience of love to the divine and universal context of human existence and at the same time highlights its social aspects. The various views of the birds on courtship and love reflect the attitudes of different social classes, and are presented with humour and much unexpectedly revealing detail.

The House of Fame is usually believed to have been written after *The Parliament of Fowls* because it is more indebted to the poets of the Italian Renaissance. As in *The Book of the Duchess*, the narrator (this time called 'Geffrey') falls asleep at the beginning, and finds himself in a glass temple to Venus. There begins a narrative of several episodes from Virgil's *Aeneid*, which presents an intentionally different version of the story told by Virgil. The narrator is then carried away by an eagle to the House of Fame as a reward, granted by Jupiter, for his service to Cupid. The service consists of writing books and songs in worship of love, of which, as we are told very deliberately more than once, he has no direct experience. He does not even receive any 'tidings of Love's folk' or of any other things 'made by God', not only from far countries but even from his immediate neighbours. This is because he lives like a hermit and avoids human society, preferring to read books (ll. 641–60). Chaucer thus emphasises the literary nature of poetic inspiration, which is not always dependent on direct experience. The eagle who carries him to the House of Fame tells him that Jove regards such diligent unrewarded service without personal knowledge of love as 'great humility'. He wants to recompense Chaucer by letting him hear 'more tidings of Love's folk, both truthful sayings and lies' in the House of Fame (ll. 675–6). Thus Chaucer's reward is literary rather than real-life experience and knowledge of different aspects of love (ll. 677–99). In the House of Fame the narrator indeed hears a lot of 'tidings' which he can clearly see have lost every connection with their original source. What seems 'wondermost' to him is that the 'folk' in the House of Fame, having heard a piece of fresh news accompanied by promises that it is true, immediately go and tell it to someone else, but make it somewhat bigger in the telling (ll. 2059–80). What is described seems to emphasise the relativity of any knowledge, particularly historical. Even more importantly, Chaucer's narrative seems to point out that literature is a result of human creativity, even when authors, like the 'folk' in the House of Fame, do not see themselves as creators, but only as faithful narrators of true stories and events.

Indeed, the nature of literature and authorship as the subject of *The House of Fame* is introduced early in the poem. This is at least partly the purpose of telling the story of Dido and Aeneas from an un-Virgilian perspective, and of Chaucer's provocative portrayal of the narrator as a writer who has no experience of his subject. In the House of Fame 'Geffrey' sees great authors from the past, including Homer, Virgil, Ovid, Statius, Josephus, and others. The Goddess Fame who holds her court in the House makes arbitrary judgements about who should have good or bad reputations. True and false 'tidings' grow equally large from being repeated and passed down. They leave her house and go into the world, and the great 'auctores' reside in her palace, bearing on their shoulders the fame of ancient civilisations.

The poem ends abruptly with an announcement of the arrival of a 'man of gret auctorite' (line 2158). Though the poem is almost certainly unfinished, several critics have observed that this is an appropriate ending, because authority is so undermined at this point that there can be no such thing as a 'man of gret auctorite'. The poem seems to tell in allegorical form about literary inspiration, the nature of fiction and its relation to reality, as well as about the nature of authorship and the authority of poets and thinkers from the past.

Troilus and Criseyde is believed to have been written in the early 1380s. It is a narrative set in ancient Troy and written in the tradition of the great classical epics. The history of the Trojan War was known from several accounts in Latin and in European vernaculars, but Chaucer's immediate source was Boccaccio's *Il Filostrato* ('The Love-struck'). *Troilus and Criseyde*, however, represents a new interpretation of the story and its characters.

In summary Troilus, a Trojan prince, becomes the lover of Criseyde, a young widow. Unfortunately, Criseyde is handed over to the Greeks in exchange for a prisoner, at the request of her father Calkas who earlier defected. There she gives up hope of returning to Troy and Troilus, and accepts the love of Diomede. Troilus, on hearing this, is driven to despair. We eventually hear that he has been killed in battle.

One of the most original features of the poem is Chaucer's historicism. He insists on the difference between the world he portrays and his contemporary society, and introduces historical detail through literary references and the description of cultural and religious practices. Unlike many earlier and contemporary writers Chaucer does not claim historical truth for his narrative and instead points out that the real events are unknown to us, and the story almost certainly reached us distorted. He uses this observation to invite readers to be critical of the traditional interpretations of the story and its characters. In particular he refuses to judge Criseyde as an archetypical disloyal lover, and invites the reader to approach her story with compassion and humility, rather than condemnation. Chaucer does not change the outline of events in order to excuse Criseyde, and if anything makes the story even more tragic and cruel. However, he emphasises the complexity of the characters' choices, their competing loyalties and obligations, and the cruelty of Criseyde's experience of a society driven by war, power, and egoistic desires. The characters and their relationship are given seriousness and depth not found in Boccaccio's treatment of the story. Chaucer makes a link between their love and tragedy and the most fundamental questions of human existence, introducing themes inspired by Boethius's *The Consolation of Philosophy*. Contemplating their fate he focuses on the question of predestination and freedom of choice, as well as on the problem of evil, and the contempt for the world experienced by Troilus after his death.

The unfinished *Legend of Good Women* is Chaucer's first collection of stories. It was inspired by Ovid's *Heroides* and Boccaccio's *De mulieribus claris* ('On famous women'), a collection of biographies. The imaginative Prologue recounts the narrator's vision of the God of Love, who reproaches him for speaking unfairly about his 'servants', and for doing injustice to women by writing about Criseyde, but not about faithful and virtuous women. To compensate for this the god sets Chaucer the task of writing stories about loyal women and men who betrayed them. The narratives which follow include the legends of Cleopatra, Dido, Lucretia, Philomela, and several other classical stories, all well known during the Middle Ages. The protagonists are presented as martyrs of faithful love. There is an emphasis on their fidelity and nobility, and their cruel treatment by men. Introduced in the opening lines of the Prologue and present throughout is the theme of fame and the reliability of historical narrative. Chaucer explored it in *The House of Fame* and *Troilus and Criseyde*, but in *The Legend of Good Women* it focuses primarily on women's reputations, misrepresented and defamed by male authors. Several of Chaucer's accounts contradict the traditional treatment of characters and stories, presenting heroines in ways which disagree with their accepted reputations.

The Canterbury Tales was left unfinished at the time of Chaucer's death. As can be seen from the above, this is true of several of his major works. The introduction known as the 'General Prologue' describes pilgrims who gathered at the Tabard Inn in Southwark, a borough south of London, on their way to Canterbury. It also recounts their agreement to tell two stories on the way to Canterbury and two on the way back. The Host of the Inn, Harry Bailly, is appointed to judge the competition and to choose the best story. In what survives, however, most pilgrims (apart from the narrator) tell only one tale, and some are not given any stories at all. It is not clear whether Chaucer had a definite plan for the collection and what its final form was intended to be. In the surviving manuscripts the order of tales varies, though the stories seem to have been transmitted as part of 'fragments', many of which contained more than one tale, linked together by dialogue and interactions between the pilgrims. The stories form complex relationships which highlight similarities and contrasts in their themes and narrative form. The narrator is represented as Chaucer himself, who does not interfere in the pilgrims' exchanges, but observes and presents complex, often ironic or satirical portraits of men and women from a wide range of occupations and ways of life. The portraits are highly individualised but roughly follow the model of the 'three estates' and include representatives of the nobility, clergy, and peasantry. Most stories have recognisable sources but nearly all offer an unexpected treatment of traditional narratives and invite discussion rather than offering a definitive view of their subject matter.

Chaucer produced several translations, including *The Consolation of Philosophy* by Boethius, and probably part of the Middle English *Roman de la Rose*, which survives as a series of fragments. Chaucer's translation of Boethius shows that he used a 13th-century French version by Jean de Meun and a Latin commentary by the English Dominican Nicholas Trevet written late in the 13th century. *The Consolation of Philosophy* was a major influence on several of his works. *The Knight's Tale* and *Troilus and Criseyde* include passages closely based on the treatise (a speech by Duke Theseus, ll. 2987–3016 and 1034–40; and by Troilus, book 4, ll. 953–1085), containing a contemplation of predestination and free will. Troilus explicitly points out the lack of a solution to this crucial question, debated by 'grete clerces' some of whom believe in 'destyne' while others, in 'fre chois'. In *The Knight's Tale* this paradox determines the structure of the narrative. The elaborate setting of the tournament between two knights competing for the love of Princess Emelye, and its date and outcome, are all related to planetary influences and suggest that the fate of the three protagonists is dictated by the stars. The ending, however, implies that the characters get what they earlier prayed for, and what they freely chose for themselves (see Tasioulas, in Ellis, 2005, pp. 179–81). The change of fortune and predestination are also treated in *The Monk's Tale* and in humorous form in *The Nun's Priest's Tale*.

In the middle of the 1380s Chaucer developed an interest in astronomy which led to the composition of the *Treatise on the Astrolabe* and possibly another treatise, *Equatorie of the Planetis* (though the authorship of the latter is disputed). As mentioned already, Chaucer's interest in astronomy is reflected in his poems, where references to time are often in the form of astronomical allusions, with descriptions of the position and movements of the planets. Such references appear to point to contemporary astronomical events and indicate a sense of observation and calculation.

Chaucer's works share a number of common themes, techniques, and literary approaches. Four of his poems – *The Book of the Duchess*, *The House of Fame*, *The Parliament of Fowls*, and *The Legend of Good Women* – use the framework of a dream-vision. Two major works – *The Canterbury Tales* and *The Legend of Good Women* – are collections of stories. Literary collections assembled for different purposes, such as selections of *exempla* (short stories illustrating doctrinal or moral statements, e.g. *The Monk's Tale*) or saints' lives, were common in medieval Europe. Some collections had elaborate narrative frames, as for example Boccaccio's *Decameron*, Chaucer's works, or John Gower's *Confessio Amantis*. Chaucer's achievement and major innovation in *The Canterbury Tales* was the stylistic and formal variety of the stories, not limited by any didactic or narrative agenda.

The role played by the story-tellers is also highly effective. They are given individual voices and emotions, personal histories, different social backgrounds, and the freedom to interact and shape the narrative. The story-tellers in the *Decameron* are less individualised and all aristocratic, whereas in *The Legend of Good Women* the stories about suffering virtuous women have similar protagonists and interpretation. In *The Canterbury Tales* dramatic tensions between characters and the competition between different types of stories become the driving force in the development of the narrative. High and low, comic and tragic, serious and playful, prose and differing verse forms are all brought together, and compared, tested, and used to generate new ideas.

Thus at the beginning of *The Canterbury Tales* different views of reality, characteristic of the romance and fabliaux and represented by *The Knight's Tale* and *The Miller's Tale*, are brought into contact. Middle English romances were stories about love and heroic adventure in an aristocratic setting, which presented an idealised view of human behaviour as driven by noble and unselfish motives; whereas fabliaux, comic tales about trickery, marriage and sex, usually in a bourgeois setting, depicted characters egotistically pursuing their desires in a harsh world of greed, folly, and deceit. The opposition of the two literary forms within the frame of *The Canterbury Tales* highlights their individual features, and emphasises their contrasting yet complementary approach. In fact *The Canterbury Tales* includes several romances (*The Knight's Tale*, *The Wife of Bath's Tale*, *The Tale of Sir Thopas*, *The Squire's Tale*, and *The Franklin's Tale*) and several fabliaux (*The Miller's Tale*, *The Reeve's Tale*, *The Shipman's Tale*, and *The Merchant's Tale*), which allows Chaucer to explore more fully their potential. Other genres are also brought together with their opposites: stories about Christian miracles and saints (*The Prioress's Tale*, *The Second Nun's Tale*) are counterbalanced by satire against the corruption in the Church (*The Friar's Tale* and *The Summoner's Tale*); whereas a light-hearted beast-fable (*The Nun's Priest's Tale*) follows a series of 'tragedies', i.e. stories about a change of fortune and a fall from high estate to misery (as in *The Monk's Tale*).

One of the most important themes in Chaucer's works is the role of women: in love, in marriage, and more generally in society. At the heart of several of his poems is a debate focusing on the contradicting requirements of courtly love and Christian marriage: a knight was expected to serve his lady, but a wife had to be obedient to her husband. At the same time, on many occasions Chaucer asserts that love should be based on mutual respect and is possible only among equals. These themes are prominent in many of his poems. Troilus sees himself as Criseyde's 'knight' and 'servant' in love, in spite of his superior social rank. *The Wife of Bath's Prologue* and *Tale* deal with the problem of 'sovereignty' in marriage. This theme is also prominent in *The Franklin's Tale* and its portrayal of the relationship between Dorigen and her husband Arveragus. In both *The Wife of Bath's Tale* and *The Franklin's Tale* the conflict is resolved and harmony achieved through the generosity of both parties and mutual 'releases', where one party adopts a self-sacrificing behaviour and the other rejects this sacrifice. The requirement of obedience in its extreme form is explored in *The Clerk's Tale*, in which a peasant's daughter gives a promise of complete obedience to a marquis, who marries her and tests her vow. Though partly religious in its message and symbolic of the obedience which the devout owe to God, the story presents obedience and patience as an ideal, but warns against a literal reading of what is described, or taking it as a model for imitation. Many of Chaucer's poems are concerned with the nature and experience of love. The loss of love is explored in *The Book of the Duchess*, its power and potential for both destruction and renewal, in *The Parliament of Fowls*, whereas its origin and psychological effects, as well as the loyalty expected in love and society, are the focus of *Troilus and Criseyde*.

Chaucer's poems are not as directly political as the works of Gower and Langland. Social issues are nevertheless commented upon in a variety of ways. Pilgrims in *The Canterbury Tales* represent a cross-section of society, and the birds who gather on St Valentine's Day in *The Parliament of Fowls* are portrayed as members of various classes of feudal society. Several stories in *The Canterbury Tales* contain direct political commentary. *The Monk's Tale*, *The Physician's Tale*, *The Knight's Tale*, and several others criticise tyranny or give examples of abuses of power and its consequences, but also of good kingship. *The Parson's Tale*, which completes *The Canterbury Tales*, comments directly on the structure of society and social order, presenting the orthodox conservative view that society and its hierarchy are divinely ordained. Men in 'lower degree' should accept the authority of those in 'higher degree', and wives should be obedient to their husbands. However, this does not seem to be the only view expressed in *The Canterbury Tales*. Many critics believe that the poem presents a polyphony of different voices, without excluding those who, like the Wife of Bath, question the roles traditionally assigned to them within society and family. The ideas of social responsibility, order, moderation, control of individual desires, and the love of 'commune profyt' are also explored in *The Parliament of Fowls*.

Like many Middle English authors Chaucer was self-conscious about language and interested in its implications for political and cultural identity. His choice of English for his works partly reflects his desire to test its adequacy and potential as a medium for different kinds of texts, from courtly poetry to scientific and philosophical writing. *Troilus and Criseyde*, as a large-scale narrative set in the classical world, reflects his ambition to create a vernacular poem that could stand equal to major European contemporary works and past literary achievements. *Troilus and Criseyde* has many epic features as well as a masterful portrayal of individual emotional life, and at its end Chaucer aligns himself with the great European poets, bidding his 'litel book' to 'kis the steppes' of Virgil, Ovid, Homer, Lucan, and Statius.

No manuscripts of Chaucer's poetry survive from his lifetime. Even the earliest copies of his works vary in textual detail and contain evidence of scribal error and editing. Attempts to reconstruct Chaucer's originals and to understand what kind of texts served as exemplars for the earliest manuscripts have achieved only partial success.

To summarise, we should consider the following key points:

- many critics believe that Chaucer is the first truly modern author in the English literary tradition;
- Chaucer was a successful civil servant, but literary patronage did not seem to have played an important role in his career;
- Chaucer's works reflect his intellectual and literary interests; they are not directly political or didactic but nevertheless comment on a wide range of social issues;
- Chaucer experimented with a full range of contemporary literary genres and developed them in highly original ways;
- one of the most important themes in his works is the role of women in love and in society;
- the chronology of Chaucer's works is known only approximately, the attribution of some works is disputed, and even the

earliest copies of his poems vary in textual detail and contain evidence of scribal error and editing.

See also   Chapter 1(f), Chapter 2(e), Chapter 3(n), and Chapter 4(e).

Further Reading

The standard edition of Chaucer's works is Benson (1987). Excellent introductions to Chaucer are the Oxford Guides to Chaucer, including Windeatt (1992), Minnis, Scattergood, and Smith (1995), Cooper (1996), and Ellis (2005). Other useful introductory collections of essays are Brewer (1966 and 1974), Boitani and Mann (2003), Burrow (1971), Donaldson (1970), Mehl (2001), and Rowland (1979). See also Boitani (1983, 1984), Brewer (1984), Havely (1980), Lawton (1985), Mann (1973 and 1991), Mehl (1986), Minnis (1982), Muscatine (1957), Patterson (1991), Pearsall (1992), Percival (1998), Strohm (1989), and Wimsatt (1991). Important collections of source texts and analogies are Correale and Hamel (2002–5) and Bryan and Dempster (1941). Records relating to Chaucer's life were published by Crow and Olson (1966). Scholarly literature on Chaucer is enormous. The *Chaucer Metapage* (www.unc.edu/depts/chaucer/index.html) provides links to online bibliographies, online texts of Chaucer's works, and information about relevant periodicals and websites.

(s)   Thomas Hoccleve and John Lydgate

There are a number of similarities in the careers of the two contemporary authors Thomas Hoccleve and John Lydgate. Both poets' connections with the Lancastrian court are well documented, though their works were addressed to a variety of patrons: royal, aristocratic, institutional, and middle class. Lydgate in particular performed the role of a semi-official poet-laureate of the Lancastrian court, advancing the prospects of Henry V, first as a prince and then as king, and later the prospects of his son. He received numerous royal commissions, and was rewarded for his role as a 'Lancastrian propagandist'. Hoccleve too was a much more political poet than Chaucer (for example) ever was. Several of his works are either addressed directly to Henry V or praise him, affirming the legitimacy of the Lancastrian dynasty at the time when the deposition of Richard II, and the House of York, was still remembered. Hoccleve's works also include anti-Lollard material that would have appealed to the Lancastrian government.

There are several reasons for the royal and aristocratic patronage of the late 14th-century/early 15th-century poets. Henry V's policy and ambitions focused on consolidating his power as the King of England and unifying the crowns of England and France after decades of war. His literary patronage suggests that he recognised the potential of vernacular poets in promoting his interests. Raising the profile of the English language as a way of building national unity and identity appears to have been part of his deliberate policy (see Fisher, 1992). His efforts to suppress the Lollard movement, as a threat to his ambition to rule a unified nation, may have also been a factor in his literary patronage. It has been suggested that he saw Lydgate's religious poetry as providing an orthodox alternative to the Lollards' use of English as a language of religion (Pearsall, 1997, p. 17). Henry V's patronage of Lydgate served the purposes of promoting his own interests and providing a body of orthodox religious texts. At the same time the composition of authoritative epics and historical works in English helped to build up national prestige.

Thomas Hoccleve (c.1367–1426) was a clerk and scribe in the office of the Privy Seal, were he would have written documents and correspondences for the king, his council, and others. In his poems he often complains about the hardship of his work and his lack of money. His first datable work, written in 1402, is *The Letter of Cupid*, an adaptation of Christine de Pisan's 1399 *Epistre au Dieu d'Amours* ('Letter to the God of Love'). Presumably he wrote poetry before this date but his earlier verse does not survive. Hoccleve's major works are poems on political themes addressed to Henry V, first as the Prince of Wales and later as King, during the years c.1409–15. The best known and the longest is *The Regement of Princes*, written in 1410–11 during Henry's ascendancy. It is a didactic poem about the qualities and obligations of a good ruler. It includes a discussion of truth, justice, observing the law, mercy, patience, generosity, prudence, and other virtues and vices, illustrated throughout by numerous moral *exempla*. It belongs to the tradition of books of instruction for princes and presents legitimacy and orthodoxy as an ideal for a ruler. All these themes are prominent in most of Hoccleve's works.

Another feature which *The Regement of Princes* shares with most of Hoccleve's works is its autobiographical content. It has an unusually lengthy prologue, comprising more than a third of its length, written in the form of a dialogue with an old beggar whom the poet meets when he wanders the streets at night, unable to sleep. In this prologue Hoccleve describes London life, his own work, and that of other scribes in the office of the Privy Seal. He complains about his financial situation, his poor health, and the instability of his life, and praises Chaucer as his master. Most interestingly, Hoccleve writes that he has included Chaucer's portrait to remind the readers of him.

One of the early manuscripts of *The Regement* does indeed have a portrait of Chaucer in its margins.

Developed autobiographical content is perhaps the most interesting and innovative feature of Hoccleve's poetry. Like many others, this convention originated with Chaucer, whose works have a prominent, believable, and down-to-earth authorial persona with many realistic touches. In *The House of Fame*, for example, Chaucer mentions his occupation as a poet and his 'rekynynges' (line 654), probably referring to his work as a Controller of Customs between 1374 and 1386. Hoccleve developed this convention much further, and is probably the first English poet to use events from his life as the subject of poetry. Several of his works are moralising complaints or begging poems. These were established literary genres, used by poets for practical purposes of bringing one to the attention of one's superiors. Such literary forms agreed well with Hoccleve's interest in autobiographical writing. In 1406 he composed *La Male Regle* ('The bad rule'), a complaint about his poverty and poor health, which he attributes to his earlier excessive drinking, eating, and spending (which he vividly describes).

Hoccleve's other major work is what is known as the *Series*, written around 1420. It includes five linked poems: *Complaint*, *Dialogue with a Friend*, *Tale of Jereslaus's Wife*, *Learn to Die*, and *Tale of Jonathas*. The *Tale of Jereslaus's Wife* and *Tale of Jonathas* are based on the *Gesta Romanorum* ('Deeds of the Romans'), a popular collection of moralised stories in Latin, written in the late 13th or early 14th century. They are about women, one faithful, another treacherous. Both the *Complaint* and the *Dialogue* are autobiographical and describe a severe mental breakdown which Hoccleve experienced in the years 1415–20, and how it affected his present life. The *Complaint* describes the poet unable to sleep on a November night, and gives an account of his illness, during which he lost contact with the outside world. He explains that his former acquaintances continue to avoid him and do not believe in his recovery. In the *Dialogue* he is visited by a fictitious friend who encourages the poet to regain hope and self-confidence, and discusses other poems from the *Series*, suggesting changes and additions. The friend is based on a literary convention which probably goes back to *The Consolation of Philosophy* by Boethius, a work whose influence on Hoccleve was profound. However, the poet's exchange with the friend is far from being conventional. Its unusually personal and intimate tone has no precedent in medieval English literature. *Learn to Die* is a free translation of a part of *Horologium sapientiae* by Heinrich Suso ('The

computer/clock of wisdom' – 1334). It contains a fictional mono-
logue of a dying man, who complains about his misspent life. It
describes the pains of hell and joys of heaven and encourages readers to be prepared for the end.

Three manuscripts of Hoccleve's poetry survive in his own hand.
This is not surprising considering his occupations as a scribe (his
hand has been also identified in a manuscript of Gower's *Confessio
Amantis*), but very unusual for medieval literature. Hoccleve's holographs provide invaluable evidence for the study of the metre and
language of Middle English verse, and of authors' treatment of their
works. Among other things, they show that Hoccleve used strict
metre and consistent orthography, which were altered by his scribes
(see Jefferson, 1987, and Burrow, 1999). This sheds new light on other
Middle English poetry, such as Chaucer's, for which we do not have
surviving authorial manuscripts. At the very least it raises the question of how faithfully authorial language and metre are reflected in
surviving manuscripts, and whether editors of Middle English texts
are justified in trying to recover authorial practice and changing the
language of manuscripts in accordance with it.

John Lydgate (*c*.1371–1449) was a monk at the Benedictine
monastery of St Edmund at Bury. He was ordained priest in 1397 and
studied at Oxford for several years at the beginning of the 15th
century. He was appointed a prior at Hatfield Broadoak in Essex and
lived there some of the time in the 1420s and 1430s. Lydgate is
responsible for an enormous literary output. Already by the time he
was at Oxford, the Prince of Wales and future Henry V became his
patron. Lydgate's earliest major poem is the *Troy Book*, a 30,000-line
free translation of the *Historia destructionis Troiae* by Guido delle
Colonna ('The history of the destruction of Troy'), started in 1412 and
finished in 1420. As Lydgate states in his Prologue, it was commissioned by Prince Henry who wanted to make the great story of
chivalry available in English. Almost immediately after completing
the *Troy Book* (around 1421), Lydgate started to work on *The Siege of
Thebes*, which during the Middle Ages was often associated with the
story of Troy as part of the history of the ancient world (see the
'Matter of Rome' in Chapter 3(h)). The work may have been also
undertaken for Henry V. It is framed as one of the Canterbury Tales
and has a prologue where Lydgate the monk meets Chaucer's
pilgrims as they leave Canterbury, and tells his tale.

Lydgate started work on his longest poem, *The Fall of Princes*,
around 1431 and finished it around 1438. It is a translation and
augmentation of a French version by Laurent de Premierfait of

Boccaccio's *De casibus virorum illustrium* ('Examples of famous men'). It was supported by the patronage of Humphrey of Gloucester, brother of Henry V, and is a collection of framed moralised narratives, accompanied by didactic envoys and united by the main theme of the mutability of fortune. Lydgate's longest work apart from *The Fall of Princes* was *The Life of Our Lady*. Its date is disputed, but it was written sometime during the reign of Henry V and possibly for him. Lydgate's other major religious work *The Lives of St Edmund and St Fremund* was written for his own house at Bury on the request of Abbot William Curteys to commemorate a royal visit to Bury in 1344. Lydgate also produced pageants and mummings for important royal events, plus many other works including instructional poems, hymns and prayers, various lyrics, fables, and debates. His influential *The Temple of Glass* is a dream-vision set in a palace designed to recall Chaucer's *The House of Fame*. In this poem two lovers, an unhappily married lady and a knight she loves, make pleas at the court of Venus.

Both Hoccleve and Lydgate are major representatives of the Chaucerian poetic tradition in the 15th century. They both refer to Chaucer as their master and teacher and proclaim their admiration for his poetry. They actively engage with his legacy in their works, and develop his poetic and narrative techniques in a variety of ways. It is not clear whether Hoccleve knew Chaucer personally. His poetry implies that he did, but many critics believe that his praise of Chaucer is somewhat conventional. Lydgate also refers to Chaucer as his 'master' but it is very unlikely that he knew him. Like Gower, both Lydgate and Hoccleve are often unfavourably compared with Chaucer. Many features of their style and approach are seen as the opposite of what is admired in Chaucer by modern readers. It is useful to remember, however, that the poets' rhetorical ornamentation, displays of learning, and moralisation were greatly appreciated by their contemporaries. Lydgate's ornate diction, his use of elaborate vocabulary and complex syntax (often called the 'aureate style'), and his classical and biblical erudition were admired by readers and imitated in the 15th and 16th centuries. In view of this it is important to understand exactly how Lydgate and Hoccleve developed the Chaucerian legacy, and what this can teach us about the literary evolution and reception of literature in the 15th century.

Derek Pearsall (1997) suggested that such features of Lydgate's verse as the looseness of syntax, the use of irregular forms of iambic pentameter, rhetoric and ornamentation in language, the choice of great epic stories from antiquity, and amplification of the length of narratives, all represent a conscious attempt to adopt systematically Chaucer's poetic techniques and innovations, and adapt them to the tastes of a 15th-century audience. This includes features which were practised by Chaucer only occasionally.

Like Gower's poetry, Lydgate's verse was valued by his contemporaries for its moral seriousness and the instruction that it offered. The same feature, however, is often judged negatively by modern readers. This highlights again a very important difference between Chaucer and many of his contemporaries and successors. Chaucer appears to have appreciated fiction as a literary form, and valued it for its ability to reflect life in its own unique way, without being literally true, and in spite of being human invention. This view is shared by many modern readers. However, most 15th-century and earlier writers and audiences valued narratives for being historically true, or for their ability to serve as illustrations of moral principles. Such an understanding of literature is implicit in the treatment of stories by narrative poets such as Lydgate (see Pearsall, 1997). It is also evident, for example, in the views on literature expressed by Caxton, who is sometimes seen as the first literary critic in English, notably in the prologues to his publications. It is very significant that what Caxton praises in literary works and what he clearly believes would appeal to his readers are the qualities of being truthful and morally edifying.

When evaluating the significance of the 15th-century poets we should remember that it was Lydgate who, through his influence and appeal to 15th-century readers, was primarily responsible for establishing Chaucer's literary reputation amongst his contemporaries (see Pearsall, 1997). Both Lydgate and Hoccleve successfully continued establishing English as the language of serious poetry, venturing into many new areas such as autobiographical writing. Lydgate's poetry was admired not only by his contemporaries but for at least a century afterwards. Together with Chaucer and Gower, Lydgate was seen as a founder of new English poetry and a symbol of literary excellence. Hoccleve, however, did not achieve the same reputation at the time and much of the interest in his poetry begins in the 20th century.

To summarise, we should consider the following key points:

- many of Thomas Hoccleve's and John Lydgate's works are addressed to Lancastrian monarchs and promote their interests;
- patronage of vernacular poets may have been part of Henry V's deliberate policy;

- perhaps the most innovative feature of Hoccleve's poetry is its developed autobiographical content;
- both poets are major representatives of the Chaucerian tradition in the 15th century, who developed Chaucer's literary legacy and helped to establish his reputation amongst their contemporary readers.

See also   Chapter 3(h), (q), (r), and (u), and Chapter 4(e).

Further Reading

Excellent introductions to Hoccleve and Lydgate are Burrow (1994) and Pearsall (1970). See also Burrow (1982a and 1990), Ebin (1985), Edwards (1984a), Fisher (1992), Green (1980), Jefferson (1987), Mitchell (1968), Pearsall (1990a and 1997), Renoir (1967), and introductions in Seymour (1981) and Burrow (1999).

(t)   Medieval Scottish Literature

Scotland was an independent kingdom throughout the medieval period. As with England, its culture was essentially multilingual and literature in English, Latin, French, and Gaelic was composed during the Middle Ages. Scottish poets were influenced by English writers, particularly Chaucer and Lydgate, but strong political ties with France and a widely spread knowledge of Latin and French encouraged literary influences from the Continent. Scottish poets of the 15th and early 16th centuries produced some of the most original and powerful poetry surviving from the period.

The earliest Scottish Gaelic manuscript is *The Book of Deer*, an incomplete 9th-century Latin Gospel, which contains 12th-century *notitiae* (official notes or lists) in Gaelic. These were written by the monks of Deer, a 6th-century foundation at Old Deer in Aberdeenshire. They appear in blank spaces and margins in the book, and record details of grants of land to the Monastery of Deer and detail its foundation legend. The Gaelic *Duan Albanach* ('The Song of the Scots'), a verse compilation about the early history of Scotland, was written possibly by an Irish writer during the reign of Malcolm III (1058–93), but is preserved in later manuscripts.

From the 13th to the 17th century the Gaelic poetry of the bards also survives. They were responsible for composing genealogies, panegyrics, and satires for Gaelic chieftains. The oldest collection of Gaelic poetry extant from Scotland is the *Book of the Dean of Lismore*, a miscellany of Scottish and Irish poetry compiled between

1512 and 1526, chiefly by Sir James MacGregor (a notary public and the Dean of Lismore in Argyll). It contains religious, heroic, satirical, and love poetry written in phonetic spelling based on Middle Scots orthography.

Medieval Scots was a language closely related to Middle English which existed from *c*.1350 to *c*.1700. It descended from the Northumbrian dialect of Old English and spread in Gaelic-speaking areas of Scotland in the 12th and 13th centuries, with the establishment of trade and a centralisation of royal power. Its history is subdivided into two periods: 'Older Scots' covers the period up to the middle of the 15th century, when it became clearly differentiated from northern English; 'Middle Scots' runs from the middle of the 15th century until the removal of the court of James VI to England when he became king following the death of Queen Elizabeth I.

Medieval Scots is a separate language, however, rather than a dialect of Middle English, even though they share many linguistic features. The terms 'language' and 'dialect' refer to social and functional aspects of language use. Unlike dialects, Medieval Scots was used across all registers and was the language of a written literary tradition. Interestingly, medieval Scottish writers refer to their language as 'English', and the term 'Scots' was not used as the name for the language until the very end of the 15th century. In a poem, *The Goldyn Targe*, William Dunbar refers to his language as 'oure Inglysch', expresses his admiration for Chaucer, Gower, and Lydgate, and praises their literary achievements in the language of 'Britane', which he shares with them.

Scots written literary tradition began in the 14th century: the earliest surviving document entirely in Scots dates from 1379. Scots flourished particularly in the 15th century, a time of relative political stability, which encouraged the development of literature. The surviving corpus of Medieval Scottish literature is smaller than what survives from England in the same period, but it is diverse and includes chronicles, romances, dream-visions, fabliaux, religious, didactic, and lyrical poetry.

Of all the events which influenced the political and literary history of Scotland during the period, the Wars of Independence in the 13th and 14th centuries were probably the most important. They followed a succession crisis after the death of Alexander III of Scotland in 1286. Edward I of England used this as an opportunity to claim rule over Scotland, and subsequently invaded. This started a series of military campaigns which continued until the middle of the 14th century. It is not surprising therefore, that national identity and

independence are important concerns of medieval Scottish literature. Such ideas are apparent in Scottish Latin historiography also.
For example, John of Fordun, probably a chantry priest at Aberdeen,
wrote the *Chronica gentis Scotorum* ('Chronicle of the Scottish
nation'), which was the first detailed history of Scotland. It was
composed between *c.*1363 and 1385 but left unfinished at his death.
Among other things it counteracted propaganda, which originated at
the time of Edward I, that the legend of the foundation of Britain by
Brutus supported the English claim to Scotland. Instead, the *Chronica*
told the Scottish foundation myth of a Greek prince, Gathelos, and
Egyptian princess, Scota, whose descendants were all Scottish kings.
The most important and widely read Scottish medieval Latin chronicle is the *Scotichronicon* by Walter Bower (1385?–1449), Abbot of
Inchcolm in West Fife from 1418. It also asserts the antiquity of
Scottish sovereignty using the myth of Gathelos and Scota, and
demonstrates that Scottish kings form an unbroken line. It ends with
contemporary events and the death of James I in 1437.

Political concerns raised by the Wars for Independence were also
responsible for the emergence of literary texts in Scots. John Barbour
(*c.*1320–95) was the Archdeacon of Aberdeen (*c.*1356–94) but also a
diplomat and administrator. His *Bruce* (1376) is the earliest substantial Scots literary work. It was written for Robert II, the first monarch
of the Stuart dynasty, to glorify his ancestry and affirm the legitimacy
of his rule. It covers the years 1286 to 1332, describing the first War of
Independence (1296–1314), fought by Robert I and his supporters. It
focuses on the events from the time of Edward I's invasion until the
English army was defeated at the Battle of Bannockburn under
Edward II (1314). It is written from a nationalist perspective and glorifies the events of the war. The Scottish leaders Robert Bruce and
William Wallace were seen as national heroes, and Robert Bruce is
presented as a model military leader, king, and protector of freedom
and independence. William Wallace was the hero of another epic
poem – *The Wallace*, by Blind Hary (also known as Henry the Minstrel)
– which dates from 1476–8. Very little is known about the poet but he
was educated, with a knowledge of Latin and vernacular histories
and romances. His poem displays an anti-English sentiment plus a
sense of patriotism, and, like the *Bruce*, glorifies a heroic national
past.

A group of important 15th-century Scottish poets, some
connected with the royal court, is known as the Scottish Chaucerians
(though most scholars now disagree with this title because it does
not do justice to the independence of their work). They include

Robert Henryson, William Dunbar, Gavin Douglas, and King James I. These poets share a number of interests, attitudes, literary techniques, and themes with Chaucer, but their poetry is original and Chaucer's influence is only one among many. Features shared with Chaucer include, for example, the use of the dream-vision framework, the importance of love, an interest in philosophical and allegorical narrative, digressions and self-mocking authorial persona, and the use of rhyme royal and other Continental metrical forms. Barbour's *Bruce*, written in octosyllabic couplets, marks the beginning of the adaptation of Continental verse forms, which eventually replaced earlier unrhymed alliterative verse. However, the 14th- and 15th-century poets continued to use alliterative verse in some of their works and it survived longer in Scotland than in England.

The Kingis Quair ('The King's Book') survives in a single manuscript (Oxford, Bodleian Library MS Arch. Selden B.24). The manuscript is an anthology of love poetry produced in Scotland around 1488 for Henry, Lord Sinclair, the third Earl of Orkney. *The Kingis Quair* was almost certainly written by King James I of Scotland (1394–1437), to whom it is attributed in the manuscript. It is a philosophical poem about love, happiness, and changes in fortune, composed in rhyme-royal stanzas and showing familiarity with the poetry of Chaucer and Lydgate. It is a dream-vision in which the author recollects the final stages of his imprisonment and release. It starts with the narrator recalling reading *The Consolation of Philosophy* by Boethius. This is followed by a scene, reminiscent of Chaucer's *The Knight's Tale*, in which the narrator sees a beautiful woman out of his prison window. This leads to a dream in which Venus, Minerva, and Fortune appear to him, and promise happiness and help with his sincere and devoted love. The allusion to imprisonment is autobiographical and refers to James I's imprisonment in England. In 1406 his father Robert III had attempted to send him, at the age of 11, secretly to France to escape the political turmoil in Scotland, but on the way to France he was captured at sea by the English and imprisoned in the Tower of London. He remained in England until 1424.

Robert Henryson was the most important vernacular poet of the reign of James III. However, virtually nothing is known about his life. He may have been a public notary and a schoolmaster in the 1470s in Dunfermline. This was an important royal burgh with a wealthy Benedictine abbey. Henryson is the author of three narrative poems or collections and a number of shorter works. His poetry shows a good knowledge of Chaucer's and to some extent Lydgate's verse and a wide familiarity with Latin devotional, literary, and scientific works. *Orpheus and Euridice* is a symbolic interpretation of the classical story, based on *The Consolation of Philosophy* by Boethius. *The Moral Fabillis* is a collection of thirteen Aesopic fables, based on earlier Latin fables and stories about Reynard the Fox, which were circulated in various forms including the French cycle *Roman de Renart*. The fables, probably addressed to an educated aristocratic and clerical audience, are witty and playful, but also learned and have allusions to classical literature, theology, philosophy, canon and civil law, and science. Some fables have political references and are concerned with the duties of a good ruler. They may have been addressed to the royal court and possibly the king. Each fable tells a story with animal protagonists, which is followed by a moral explication. The poems are lively and combine colourful realistic descriptions, humour, sophisticated rhetoric, and moral seriousness. *The Testament of Cresseid* is a continuation and a critical response to Chaucer's *Troilus and Criseyde*. In this work Henryson questions the truthfulness of Chaucer's version of the story and the credibility of poets in general. In *The Testament* Troilus meets Cresseid for one last time when she is an outcast of society, ill with leprosy. Abandoned by Diomede and punished by gods she acknowledges her guilt, and pities Troilus, whose love she feels she betrayed. This work was often interpreted as anti-feminist, but many critics acknowledge its complexity and believe that Henryson places emphasis on grief rather than vengeance, and is sincerely sympathetic with the heroine. The poem was well known, as is demonstrated by the 16th-century tradition of including it in editions of Chaucer.

William Dunbar (*c.*1460–*c.*1520) wrote for the court of James IV and is celebrated for his enormous literary range and technical excellence. Though he repeatedly refers to himself in his works, little is known about his life. He was a priest and may have served as a diplomat, a chaplain, or in some other capacity for King James IV. He is an author of a very diverse corpus of poetry. This included religious and moral lyrics, comic verse, satire on the life of the court, visions, allegorical poems, and many others. Dunbar's three best known poems are his longer works. *The Thrissill and the Rois* ('The Thistle and the Rose') is an allegoric dream-vision, influenced by Chaucer's *The Parliament of Fowls*, which celebrated the marriage of James IV and Margaret Tudor (1503). *The Tretis of the Twa Mariit Wemen and the Wedo* ('The treatise of the two married women and the widow') is an anti-feminist satire written in unrhymed alliterative verse. In this poem, set on Midsummer's Eve, three women, portrayed as hedonistic and promiscuous, tell about their marriages and confess to cheating and exploiting their husbands. Both the characters and the stories of the women are influenced by *The Wife of Bath's Prologue* and *The Merchant's Tale*. *The Goldyn Targe* ('The golden shield') is a dream-vision influenced by the *Roman de la Rose*. It has a famous envoy praising Chaucer, Gower, and Lydgate.

Gavin Douglas (*c.*1476–1522) was provost of St Giles in Edinburgh by 1503 and Bishop of Dunkeld in 1516. Coming from a prominent aristocratic family, he was involved in a power struggle and feuds among the aristocracy which resulted in his downfall, and he died in exile in London. His allegorical dream-vision *The Palice of Honoure* is influenced by Chaucer's *The House of Fame* and dedicated to James IV. His other important work, *Eneados*, is a translation of the entire *Aeneid* and its 15th-century continuation by Maphaeus Vegius in decasyllabic couplets. Douglas wrote a prologue to each of the thirteen books and an extended farewell. The prologues provide a commentary and moral or Christian interpretations of the classical work. The prologue to the first book discusses earlier attempts to translate Virgil into English, and includes a famous 'flyting' with Willam Caxton. Douglas points out that Caxton's translation, based on a free French adaptation of Virgil, has little resemblance to the original, and explains his own approach of being faithful to the original text. He also accuses Chaucer of misrepresenting Virgil in his treatment of the story of Dido and Aeneas. Douglas's work displays a strong sense of identity as a Scottish poet writing for a Scottish audience, and a belief in the importance of Scotland's role in European culture.

In conclusion we should consider the following key points:

- Scottish culture was multilingual and literature in English, Latin, French, and Gaelic was written during the Middle Ages;
- Medieval Scots was closely related to Middle English, but it was a separate language rather than a dialect of Middle English;
- the Scots written literary tradition began in the 14th century and flourished particularly in the 15th century owing to relative political stability;
- the Scottish Wars of Independence in the 13th and 14th centuries had a profound effect on the literary culture;
- the earliest substantial literary work in Scots is *Bruce* (1376), by John Barbour, which describes the first War of Independence (1296–1314);

- Scottish 15th-century poets were familiar with the poetry of Chaucer and Lydgate and used some of the Chaucerian themes and literary forms.

See also   Chapter 4(k) – the section on 'Postcolonialism'.

Further Reading

A comprehensive history of Scottish literature is Jack (1988). A detailed account of primary sources and scholarship on Middle Scots writers is Ridley (1973). Useful shorter overviews include Goldstein (1999) and Royan (2005). Important studies of the 15th-century literature include Bawcutt (1976 and 1992), Burrow (1984), Gray (1979), Kratzmann (1980), Lyall (1976), and Mapstone (1991).

(u)   Willam Caxton

William Caxton was born between *c*.1415 and 1420 in Kent. In 1438 he was an apprentice to the Mercers' Company, one of the most powerful guilds in the City of London. He finished his apprenticeship and took the livery of the Mercers' Company around 1452. In the 1460s he moved between England and Flanders and by 1463 became the Governor of the English merchants in Bruges, which was the largest settlement of English merchants on the Continent. This was an important position with responsibilities for overseeing the activities of English merchants in the Low Countries and conducting negotiations with the authorities in Flanders and elsewhere.

Bruges was part of the Duchy of Burgundy, and as the Governor, Caxton was involved in diplomatic relations between England and Burgundy, which was (together with France) England's most important trading partner at that time. Caxton was an influential and wealthy merchant and a trusted diplomat who was called upon to conduct negotiations on behalf of the Mercers' Company and the King of England. In the early 1470s he travelled to Cologne, apparently to learn the art of printing and acquire a printing press. Printing with movable type was introduced in Europe at Mainz in the first half of the 15th century and spread to Cologne in the 1460s. Caxton appears to have recognised the financial possibilities of printing and the fact that by publishing in English he would establish a monopoly and avoid competition from Continental printers.

Caxton's subsequent career is that of a printer, publisher, and bookseller; though he continued to be a merchant and an important member of the Mercers' Company, occasionally employed on diplomatic missions on behalf of Edward IV. He set up his own press in Bruges in 1473. The first book he printed there was his own translation of the French *Le recuyell des histoires de Troie* ('The collection of Trojan histories'), adapted from a Latin version in 1446 by Raoul Le Fèvre, chaplain to the Burgundian prince Phillip the Good. This was followed by the publication of an edition of *The Game of Chess*, a popular didactic work by Jacobus de Cessolis where chess pieces and their moves were interpreted to comment on the estates of society. It was originally written in Latin, but Caxton used a French version for his translation. These two English books were followed by four French works.

Caxton returned to England in 1476 and set up a shop near Westminster Abbey with a printing press. Over the next fifteen years he published editions of all the major works of Middle English prose and poetry. Among the first English books he printed were the works of Lydgate and Chaucer, popular among both gentry and middle classes as products of new English poetry endorsed by royal and aristocratic patronage. These included *The Parliament of Fowls*, *Anelida and Arcite*, *The Canterbury Tales*, and *The Temple of Glass*. Caxton also published a number of religious and didactic works, including the English poem *Book of Curtesye* (a translation of the *Distichs of Cato* by Benedict Burgh), and a poetic translation by Earl Rivers of Christine de Pisan's *Moral Proverbs*. Caxton's choice of books reflects the interests of 15th-century gentry and bourgeois readers, who appreciated didactic and 'courtly' works aimed at social, moral, and religious education. Caxton's later publications are of a similar kind, but more ambitious, and throughout his career as a printer his strategy was to publish works which were likely to be in demand and appeal to the tastes of his readers.

In the early 1480s Caxton continued to print authoritative vernacular works by canonical English authors, including Chaucer, Gower, and Lydgate, who in the 15th century had become synonymous with literary excellence. However, he chose more lengthy and serious books, demonstrating an interest in philosophy, history, and religion. Caxton appears to have been particularly attracted to works which he saw as *compendia*, bringing together diverse literary forms, doctrine, and learning (Lerer, 1999b, p. 728). In the early 1480s he published Chaucer's *Troilus and Criseyde*, *The House of Fame*, a second edition of *The Canterbury Tales*, Lydgate's *Life of Our Lady*, as well as the English poem *The Court of Sapience* and a Middle English translation of Guillaume de Deguileville's *Pèlerinage de la vie humaine*. He also published Gower's *Confessio Amantis* and Malory's *Morte Darthur*.

Caxton's role in the production of texts was by no means passive. He was a publisher who traded in books, but also a translator, and a self-conscious editor and textual critic. He acted as 'ordinator of received texts' (Lerer, 1999b, p. 730), dividing works into books and chapters to give them structure. If needed he provided missing closures, tables of contents, a commentary, and interpretations for the readers' convenience. He produced many translations, mostly from French but also from Latin and Dutch, to which he added his own passages. His translation of *The Golden Legend* was a new compilation based on three texts: a Latin version original written by Jacobus de Varagine, a French version, and an earlier Middle English adaptation known as the *Gilte Legende*. Therefore he did not follow an easy route of simply printing the *Gilte Legende*.

As noted above, Caxton also produced two editions of Chaucer's *The Canterbury Tales*, the first appearing in 1476, and the second in 1482. In the prologue to the second edition he explained in detail his reasons for producing a new version and how he had got hold of a superior text of the poem. Caxton's second edition of *The Canterbury Tales* is corrected from an important (now lost) manuscript which appears to have been close to the archetype of the whole tradition. Equally typical of his editorial style is his prologue to the *Confessio Amantis*, where Caxton expressed the view that this was a demanding work containing a diverse range of stories, and explained that he had included in his edition an index of stories by book and page. In 1482 he published a revised text of Trevisa's 1385 translation of Higden's *Polychronicon*. This time his criticisms are reserved for the epilogue, where he comments that he found its language old-fashioned and had attempted to modernise it.

It is generally agreed that the purpose of the prefaces and epilogues which accompany Caxton's publications was to promote his editions and advertise books to potential customers. In his prologues and epilogues he mentions aristocratic patrons whose involvement gives authority to his productions. He also discusses his editorial and publishing projects, and comments on the virtues of texts and authors, acting as a literary critic. His views on literature are fairly conservative. He draws attention to the moral and didactic values of works and presents secular narratives and romances as illustrating virtues and points of conduct. He accepts the contemporary view of Chaucer, Gower, and Lydgate, as the founders of a new, sophisticated form of English literature based on French models. On several occasions he writes about the contemporary state of the

English language, describing it as 'rude', and discusses the need to improve it. Such improvement, in agreement with contemporary tastes, is seen by him as rhetorical embellishment and ornamentation. His interest in language is evident in the 1490 prologue to *Eneydos*, a translation of the French version of the *Aeneid*. There he discusses the variability of English, regional differences in speech, and tells an amusing story about London mercers who tried to buy eggs in Kent but were not understood by an innkeeper.

Caxton was a very successful businessman. Many printing businesses failed in the 15th century, mainly because print publication required a considerable investment, and printers were faced with competition for a limited market. Caxton's press existed for nearly 20 years and published over 100 books. His decision to publish mostly in English for lay audiences meant that he avoided competition from publishers on the Continent, who produced books mainly in Latin for clerical and university markets.

Caxton's books preserve close ties with the earlier manuscript tradition. Their types imitate Flemish book-hands of the late 15th century and many were printed with space left for illuminated initials and borders. Capital letters, illumination, paragraph marks, and in some cases rubrics were added by hand by rubricators and artists. Some works were illustrated with woodcuts imitating manuscript illumination. Like earlier manuscripts Caxton's publications were sold unbound as booklets and fascicles, and bound together with other texts into anthologies by their owners. We should remember that when printing was introduced it did not immediately replace manuscript culture but existed within its context and was influenced by it. The mass production of books for commercial purposes developed later on when printers, including Richard Pynson and Wynkyn de Worde (Caxton's assistant and successor, who took over the press in Westminster after Caxton's death), greatly expanded the number and variety of printed books. In many histories of the English language and literature, including this book, Caxton's activities as a printer are used as a conventional borderline between the Middle English and early modern periods. This reflects a recognition of the fact that printing had a major impact on various aspects of literary culture, including the standardisation of English, dissemination of national norms, transmission and availability of texts, and literary authorship.

In conclusion we should consider the following key points:

- William Caxton was an important and wealthy merchant overseeing the activities of English merchants in the Low Countries and conducting negotiations with the authorities in Flanders and elsewhere;

- he appears to have recognised the financial possibilities of printing and the fact that by publishing in English he would establish a monopoly and avoid competition from Continental printers;

- throughout his career as a printer his strategy was to publish works which were likely to be in demand and appeal to the tastes of his readers, mainly among the gentry and middle class;

- he focused on authoritative vernacular works by canonical English authors, including Chaucer, Gower, and Lydgate, and on books which offered religious and social education;

- his role in the production of books was not passive; he acted as a publisher, translator, editor and textual and literary critic.

See also Chapter 3(e).

Further Reading

Important works on Caxton include Blake (1969, 1976, and 1991), Lerer (1999b), Rutter (1987), and Sands (1957).

4 Approaches, Theory, and Practice

(a) Old English Language

Students of medieval literature will have to encounter the texts in their original language at some point in their career. For the most part this will be in textbooks or editions, and the texts will be surrounded by critical apparatus to help the students read and translate the original. However, although there are many books which take one through the first steps of approaching the language it is worthwhile at this point presenting some basic information about the two periods of English covered in this book: Old English and Middle English.

In the 'family tree' of languages Old English is said to be a Germanic language, and in particular a West Germanic language. In Figure 1 we can see this more clearly. This presents the Indo-European languages (so-called because it is assumed they all originate from a common language conventionally referred to as 'Indo-European'). As we can see there are several main branches beneath the main heading; however, in this case we have only illustrated the Germanic family. This is split into three 'geographical' regions, and the important route to follow is the West Germanic branch. Following this we can see Old English and then Middle English. A diagram like this, then, shows not only the accepted development route of English, but also how it relates to other languages. However, this tree is very simplistic. It does not attempt to show the influences on languages from other languages and language groups. For example, in Old English we can discern words borrowed from Latin (a member of the Italic subgroup within the Indo-European family) before the migration period (e.g. 5th century), and later as a result of Christianisation and cultural contacts with other European countries (6th century onwards). English also came under the influence of the North Germanic languages as a result of the Viking invasions (8th century onwards), and in the latter stages, and especially following the Norman Conquest, under the influence of Norman French (a member of the

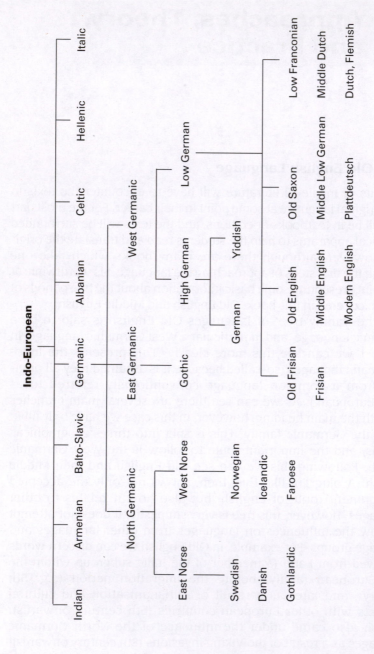

Figure 1 Indo-European family of languages

Italic subgroup again). For further information on the history of English see Algeo and Pyles (2005), and Freeborn (1998).

Yet this simple illustration does answer immediately a common observation of many students when they first encounter Old English – namely that it does not 'feel' like English, but more like German or Dutch. As we can see, the distinction is misguided as all three languages have a common source, and what we are witnessing with Old English is an early stage when: (a) its vocabulary was almost purely Germanic; and (b) it was still an inflected language. The other Germanic languages could be termed 'cognate languages' and can also assist us in finding out more about Old English (see Robinson, 1992).

Looking at Old English itself as presented in modern scholarly editions, the main problems students will encounter are:

(1) the characters/letters;
(2) pronunciation;
(3) vocabulary;
(4) inflections;
(5) syntax.

Taking these in order, in Old English editions most of the characters one will encounter are from the familiar Roman alphabet (but missing a few letters). Difficulties will occasionally arise when a rune appears. Runes were the earliest form of writing in the Germanic world, consisting of angular characters (each of which had its own name, which in turn was a word in ordinary vocabulary), used for predominantly short epigraphic inscriptions. The Anglo-Saxon runic alphabet is often referred to as *futhorc*, named after the sound values of the first six runes. It is a version of the Common Germanic runes (called *futhark*), which was gradually abandoned and replaced by the Roman alphabet with the coming of Christianity. However, runic characters continued to be occasionally employed in manuscripts as abbreviations for words (as in the *The Rune Poem*, or Cynewulf's signature).

The Anglo-Saxon version of the Roman alphabet used by the scribes had several characters which will look very unfamiliar to a student but once learnt are not too problematic. They represent the sounds of the Old English language for which the Roman alphabet did not have obvious equivalents, and are by origin ligatures and modifications of Latin letters or runic characters. The ones commonly retained in modern editions are:

Æ æ   called 'ash' and pronounced like the 'a' in 'cat';

Þ þ   called 'thorn' and pronounced 'th';

Ð ð   called 'eth' and also pronounced 'th'.[1]

So the Old English word *þæt* may at first seem strange, but when we pronounce it using the above guide it comes out as 'that', and not surprisingly it means just 'that'.

Considering pronunciation there are also a few other tips to remember:

'cg' is pronounced 'dg', so *ecg* is 'edge';

'sc' is pronounced 'sh', so *scip* is 'ship';

'c' and 'g' can be either hard ('k' and 'g') or soft ('tch' and 'y'), so *cyning* is pronounced *kining*, which is 'king', whilst *cilde* is pronounced *childe*, or 'child'; similarly *god* is 'God' whilst *gear* is 'year'.[2]

Knowing how to pronounce words may also make them more recognisable (as in the example of *scip*), but undeniably the vocabulary of Old English is challenging. Although many words from Old English have survived to the present day (e.g. he, his, it, am, son, daughter, father, stone, bone, home, etc.), many words did not. For this then, dictionaries and glossaries will be required.

Common questions which many students raise are 'What was the Old English word for . . .?' or 'How do I find out what the Anglo-Saxons thought of . . .?' Both indicate a need for a thesaurus of Old English, and thankfully there is one available. In 1995 Jane Roberts, Christian Kay, and Lynne Grundy produced *A Thesaurus of Old English* (which is now also available online at: http://libra.englang.arts.gla. ac.uk/oethesaurus/). Using this, one can quickly see if the Anglo-Saxons' term for something is known to us from the surviving texts, and also whether the word appears only in poetry. Taking this information one could then go to the searchable Corpus of Old English[3]

---

[1] Thorn and eth were both used to represent voiced 'th' as in 'clothes' and voiceless 'th' as in 'thorn'. The rules explaining when to pronounce it voiced and when to pronounce it voiceless can be found in guides to pronunciation in Old English textbooks.

[2] Occasionally textbooks will attempt to indicate hard and soft consonants, often by placing a small dot above a soft 'c' or 'g'.

[3] Available online via subscription only, but also can be ordered from the Oxford Text Archive (http://ota.ahds.ac.uk/).

and look up occurrences of that word. Not only will this lead you to texts, it will also show you how the word was used.

For example, in the poem *The Battle of Maldon*, one of the criticisms levelled at the leader of the English, Byrhtnoth, is that he allowed the Vikings too much ground to fight a pitched battle. To justify this argument scholars point to the comment by the poet that Byrhtnoth did this *for his ofermōde* (line 89b). This is usually translated as 'because of his pride'. If we look at the *Thesaurus* by Roberts, Kay, and Grundy then, in Volume II we are given the entry:

ofermōd 07.06.01   Pride arrogance; 07.06.01.01   Proud arrogant[4]

– plus a series of derivations of the word, all implying the same meaning. If we turn to the Old English Corpus and search for *ofermōd* we see the word occurs 360 times in the surviving texts, used in both prose and poetry. In the majority of occasions it clearly seems to be a critical reference to someone's pride. Therefore, we could argue that the evidence supports the idea that the poet of *Maldon* was being critical of Byrhtnoth.

The most problematic issue for many newcomers, however, is the fact that Old English, like modern-day German, is an inflected language. In short, it means a word may change its form according to what part it plays in the sentence. We still retain inflections in Modern English (e.g. the plural of 'cat' is 'cats', with the inflection 's' indicating the number) but to a far lesser extent than in Old English. Moreover, the latter part of the Anglo-Saxon period indicates a breaking down of inflections, when some of the original distinctions disappear or change their meaning, and this is the period from which most written material survives.

With nouns, pronouns, and adjectives, inflections will relate to gender (Old English has masculine, feminine, and neuter); cases (nominative, accusative, genitive, dative, and instrumental); and number (singular or plural). Standard textbooks will present paradigms illustrating these inflections. With verbs one will encounter tense (past or present[5]), person and number (e.g. 'third person

---

[4] '07.06.01' etc. refers to the section in the first volume, in this case on p. 416 where we get all of the words associated with pride and arrogance.

[5] There is no grammatical future tense in Old English. Instead it is constructed by using the present tense and various references to the future, such as adverbs of time (for example, 'tomorrow', 'later', and so on), or the broader context, which usually makes clear that the statement refers to the future.

singular'), and mood (indicative, imperative, or subjunctive); again these will be detailed in textbooks. In Chapter 4(c) we give some suggestions as to how one might approach these issues when it comes to translating from the original texts to Modern English. This may seem extremely daunting at first but actually the Old English that survives to us is very uniform in terms of its spelling and grammar, and mainly represents the Late West Saxon dialect (mid- to late 10th century onwards).

Finally, the syntax (i.e. the order and functions of words in a sentence) of Old English, especially in verse, may seem problematic. Even with Old English prose, where the word order is more familiar, students attempting to read the original will encounter strange sentence structures and must be prepared to tackle these and reconstruct the meaning.

See also Chapter 2(j) and Chapter 4(j).

Further Reading

As mentioned throughout, the easiest way to start learning Old English is via a textbook. These are generally used at universities across the world as course books, so will be available in good bookshops or online. For books which deal primarily with how the language works and attempt to guide students through the grammar, see Hasenfratz and Jambeck's step-by-step course (2005), Stephen Pollington's excellent and very approachable contributions (2003), and any of the following: Hogg (2002); McCully and Hilles (2005), Smith (1999); and Stevick (2003). In the past, favoured books included those by the Victorian scholar Henry Sweet (notably his *Anglo-Saxon Reader* and *Anglo-Saxon Primer*) but although these can still be found they are generally not used now by teachers. For detailed studies of Old English grammar and Old English syntax see Campbell (1962) and Mitchell (1985) respectively. For runes and epigraphic inscriptions, see Looijenga (2003) and Page (1999).

One of the most heavily used textbooks containing original pieces and critical apparatus is Mitchell and Robinson (2001) which is now in its 7th edition. This presents a collection of texts, a fairly thorough introduction to the grammar, and a glossary. Mitchell also produced *An Invitation to Old English and Anglo-Saxon England* (1995), a much lighter introduction, but alas more difficult to get hold of. Recent publications which contain texts and translations or critical apparatus are Richard Marsden's *The Cambridge Old English Reader* (2004), Elaine Treharne's *Old and Middle English c.890–c.1400: An Anthology* (2004), and Peter Baker's *Introduction to Old English* (2003), supported by an excellent website at www.engl.virginia.edu/OE/, which includes exercises in Old English. The best approachable and affordable dictionary is probably J. R. Clark Hall's *A Concise Anglo-Saxon Dictionary* (4th edn 1960; the 2nd edition is available online for free at: www.ling.upenn.edu/~kurisuto/germanic/oe_clarkhall_about.html), but there is also Joseph Bosworth, T. Northcote Toller, and

Alistair Campbell's *An Anglo-Saxon Dictionary*, 3 vols (1882–98, 1908–21, 1972; available online for free at: www.ling.upenn.edu/~kurisuto/germanic/oe_bosworthtoller_about.html), and the long-running Dictionary of Old English Project (www.doe.utoronto.ca/) at the University of Toronto.

Studying Old English
There is no substitute for being taught Old English. This generally happens at university level, and Old English is mainly taught as part of the English Literature degree. A preliminary list of courses is available from the Teachers of Old English in Britain and Ireland (TOEBI) website (www.toebi.org.uk) or one can send a note to the Anglo-Saxonists' email discussion list (ansax-l@listserv.wvu.edu). There may also be options with evening classes at a local Adult Learning centre. The TOEBI site also contains a web gateway for numerous online resources of interest to Anglo-Saxonists.

(b)   Middle English Language

The term 'Middle English' describes the period in the history of English from the Norman Conquest to the 1470s when William Caxton established a printing press in London. Like Old English, or any living language, Middle English was not uniform and had regional varieties or dialects, which differed in pronunciation, grammar, and vocabulary. However, unlike later Old English, where West Saxon dominated, Middle English did not have a standard written form. Middle English writers and scribes wrote and copied their works in their regional forms of language without trying to adhere to a national norm of any kind. Because of this we are much more familiar with Middle English dialects than we are with Old English. This also means that there is a lot more variation in the language of surviving Middle English texts. Thus the language of the West Midland *Sir Gawain and the Green Knight* and *Pearl* (probably dating from the late 14th century) is more difficult for a modern reader than the contemporary language of Chaucer. This is because Chaucer's London dialect is historically much closer to the variety of English which developed into the modern literary standard.

There is also more variation in the spelling of Middle English texts, again because of the absence of a written norm. A beginner may have to read introductions to editions of individual texts in order to understand their spelling, though many conventions were shared and can be recognised without much difficulty. Many features which make Middle English orthography different from Old English were adopted from the spelling used in Latin and French manuscripts, including the distinction between *c*, *ch*, and *k*, as well as spellings such as *–ou-*, *-ie-*, *-qu-*, and others. Middle English scribes continued to employ þ 'thorn' and ӡ 'yogh', a letter form used by Old English scribes to represent 'g'. In Middle English yogh can correspond to Modern English 'y' as in ӡet ('yet'), but also to Modern English 'gh' as in liӡt ('light'). In this latter case yogh was pronounced as the 'ch' in Modern German 'ich' or 'ch' in Scots 'loch' depending on the phonetic context.

Middle English had a much simpler system of inflections than Old English, and was much closer to Modern English in this respect. Simplification and loss of inflections was happening already in Old English and this was due to several reasons. First there was 'reduction', which was the phonetic levelling of inflectional endings experienced by languages with a certain type of accent, described by linguists as 'dynamic'. Another reason was the mutual influences between English and the languages of the Scandinavian settlers in England: the loss of inflections was happening much faster in the North and East (the old Danelaw), whereas the dialects of the South were more conservative, and preserved Old English linguistic features for longer. Inflections which did survive into Middle English often had different forms in different dialects. Again, the introductions to editions of Middle English texts often have a discussion of those features of the grammar that may be difficult for a modern reader. Here we offer only some general observations.

In 14th-century texts (such as Chaucer's works, *Sir Gawain*, or *Pearl*), very little remains from the Old English system of gender and cases. The relationships between words in a sentence are expressed, as in Modern English, largely through word order and function words, such as prepositions. The endings most commonly encountered in nouns are *–(e)s* for possessive case, as in Modern English *brother's*; *-(e)s* for plural, as in Modern English *brothers*; and *–(e)n* for plural, as in Modern English *brethren*. In Old English an adjective agreed with a noun in gender, number, and case, but Middle English adjectives, particularly in texts from the North, do not change their form consistently.

On the other hand in Middle English, as in Old English, the verb had only two tense forms: past and present. Future was expressed by using the context and references to time, such as 'tomorrow' or 'soon'. Verbs 'shall' and 'will' were widely used but preserved much of their original lexical meaning of obligation and willingness. Similar to Modern English (MnE), the majority of Middle English verbs formed their past tense by adding 'a dental suffix', usually spelled *–d*, *-ed*, or *-t*. Some verbs changed a root vowel, as in Modern English *write – wrote*. The ending of the third person singular in the present tense (MnE *he/she/it goes*) is usually *–es* in the North and *–eth* in the South. The ending of the third person plural in the present tense (MnE *they go*) is *–eth*, *-en*, or *–es* depending on the dialect. The ending of the present participle or verbal noun (MnE *going*) is either *–ing* or *-ande/-inde/-ende*, again depending on the dialect. Both þou 'thou' and ȝe 'you' were used as forms of address, and ȝe was used as both plural and polite forms.

Many Middle English words are likely to be familiar to a modern reader, though some regional words, for example part of the *Gawain*-poet's vocabulary, did not survive and their understanding will require the help of glossaries and translations. The important difference between Old and Middle English is the mixed character of Middle English vocabulary. While Old English vocabulary was mostly Germanic, Middle English had a large number of words borrowed not only from Latin, but also from French and the language of the Scandinavians who settled in the North and East of England during the Viking Age. A particularly large number of French words were borrowed during the 14th and 15th centuries, a time when French was dying out in England, and English was taking over areas earlier dominated by French and Latin (such as scientific or historical writing).

Middle English was a period of great linguistic diversity, partly accessible to us through the surviving texts. One of the most important developments at the end of the period, in the 15th century, however, was the emergence of the written standard, which eventually developed into Modern Standard English. Its ancestor was the 'Chancery Standard' employed by scribes who worked in government offices in Westminster. The advent of printing helped to establish and disseminate the national written norm.

Further Reading

Middle English is described in histories of the English Language, including Baugh and Cable (2002), Blake (1992), Fennell (2001), Görlach (1997), and Smith (1999). See also *An Introduction to Middle English* by Simon Horobin and Jeremy Smith (2002), and Burnley (1989) for an account of Chaucer's language and style. The *Middle English Dictionary*, editor-in-chief Robert E. Lewis (2001), is now also available as part of the *Middle English Compendium* (http://ets.umdl.umich.edu/m/mec/), where it is combined with a HyperBibliography of Middle English Prose and Verse, and a Corpus of Middle English Prose and Verse. The standard work on Middle English dialectology is A. McIntosh, M. L. Samuels, and M. Benskin (eds), *A Linguistic Atlas of Late Medieval English*, 4 vols (Aberdeen: Aberdeen University Press, 1986), abbreviated LALME; in particular see the General Introduction to vol. I.

Studying Middle English

Students are sometimes introduced to Middle English literature at school, when they read extracts from Chaucer's works. A popular choice of textbook in introductory university courses is J. A. Burrow and Thorlac Turville-Petre, *A Book of Middle English* (2004). It has a selection of texts, a glossary, and a detailed introduction to the Middle English language. Another useful publication is Elaine Treharne's *Old and Middle English c.890–c.1400: An Anthology* (2004), where editions of Middle English texts are accompanied by introductions, and marginal translations of words and phrases likely to be unfamiliar to a modern reader. Editions of Middle English texts are all widely available. These include selections by author (e.g. Chaucer, or the *Gawain*-poet), or by genre, such as Middle English lyrics, drama, and romances.

(c) Translating and Commentary

A student of medieval literature is often set three key tasks. These are:

- translating from the original English into Modern English;
- commenting on a medieval text;
- writing an essay on a specific theme, text, or author.

In this section we will deal with the first two of these tasks, as they can require specific technical skills that are often unfamiliar to students of English. Essay writing is a generic skill which we do not have the space to deal with.

Translation

One of the most common tasks set for students is to present a translation of a medieval text in Modern English. For students of English Literature whose previous experience of assessments has been based around presenting a standard essay, the first time they are asked to provide a translation can be a daunting experience. Outside of exam conditions this will usually be a set number of lines from a particular text, which the students will be asked to translate and present at the next opportunity. Within an exam, beginning students will often face a 'seen' translation exercise, that is they will be asked to translate from a text they have worked on prior to the exam. At a more advanced level students are often asked to work on an 'unseen' exercise, i.e. translate from a text they have not been exposed to before.

Regardless of the conditions, it is an undeniable truth that translating will require at the very least a basic knowledge of Old or Middle

English. One will need to know roughly how the language works, especially with the heavily inflected Old English, and some key signals. The second undeniable truth is that in the early stages of one's translation career it is a very slow process. Do not be surprised if the first line of Old English you attempt to translate takes over half an hour, and leave yourself enough time to allow for this. At the beginning you will be constantly 'looking words up' in the glossary of the textbook you are using, and then attempting to make sense of the various abbreviations used.

First steps

In Bruce Mitchell's *An Invitation to Old English and Anglo-Saxon England* (1995), the author presented an entire section under the heading 'No paradigms, please!' (p. 38). A paradigm is a set of rules presented to the student of grammar, usually in tabular form. Many textbooks include pages of these along the lines of Figure 2. But Professor Mitchell, co-author of the widely used *A Guide to Old English*, chose not to include many of these in his *Invitation*. This was a welcome change. Although paradigms do still proliferate they can seem daunting to students of literature, especially those who are not familiar with grammatical terminology and/or learning a foreign language.

This is not to say that paradigms are not crucial but they should only be approached when needed, as a reference tool, and the concept of learning paradigms by rote is now viewed as outdated. It is much more important to understand the abbreviations, and meaning of the abbreviations, that one will commonly encounter in glossaries.

	Singular	**Plural**
Nominative	*word*	*word*
Accusative	*word*	*word*
Genitive	*wordes*	*worda*
Dative	*worde*	*wordum*

Figure 2   Paradigm for *word* 'word' in Old English

Yet the paradigm in Figure 2 does point to something extremely valuable to students, namely common patterns (in this case inflections) which are evident in many Old English texts. As one becomes more and more familiar with these, the speed of translating will increase. For example, the ending –*es* often indicates a genitive singular, and the ending –*um* a dative plural. However, such are the variations in inflections associated with different types of nouns that such rules are not hard and fast. Moreover the paradigm indicates the problems of the language, namely that endings (or lack of them) are often insufficient. Again in the above example, *word* could be nominative singular, nominative plural, accusative singular, and accusative plural.

Aside from the glossary then, the two key tools students often use to supplement the above information is the surrounding context of the term and the punctuation found in modern editions. For example, if presented with *word* in the Old English, in the context of 'he wrote down several *word*' we could establish that it is plural. Moreover, we can extend this to the idea of association, namely if the associated adjective is clearly in the plural then so will be the noun.

Editorial interventions in the form of punctuation can also prove extremely helpful. In the hypothetical sentence below, there are several signals we can immediately use:

Se cyning Cnut sæde: 'Hwær is se bisceop?'

There is a surprising amount of information inherent in this. The capital 'C' in *Cnut* implies this is a proper noun as it is mid-way through a clause; the inverted commas tells us we have direct speech, so before the colon we would expect a verb that implies talking (in this case *sæde* 'said'). In turn we can see that the direct speech is a question by the appearance of the '?' at the end. This means that we may need to look for an interrogative such as 'who', 'what', 'where'. Finally, if we attempt to read this out we will see some familiar sounding words – *cyning* 'king', *hwær* 'where', *is* 'is', *bisceop* 'bishop', and so on.

This is, of course, a simple example but it does show how much information one can draw from punctuation signals.

Presenting your work
Once one gets familiar with the mechanics of the languages, the glossaries, and the abbreviations in glossaries and editions, the next issue is how does one present a translation. In particular:

- How close should one keep to the original text?
- How does one present the final piece?

The first is the most problematic. Many students find the balance between presenting a verbatim translation (keeping to the word order of the original) and one more in keeping with the syntax of Modern English a real concern. Sometimes they will stray too far either way, presenting a stilted translation or a far too colloquial one. The general rule is to keep as close to the original as possible, but if you have to stray from this make it clear that you are aware you are doing so.

Let us use the first three lines of the Old English poem *The Dream of the Rood* as an example:

> Hwæt, ic swefna cyst   secgan wylle,
> hwæt mē gemætte   tōmidre nihte,
> syðþan reordberend   reste wunedon.

A word for word translation would be as follows:

> Lo, I of dreams the best   to tell I wish,
> what to me it dreamed   in the middle night,
> when the speech-bearers   at rest they dwelt.

Strictly speaking this is correct but it is hardly readable. We wish to alter the word order to approach Modern English but are we allowed to? The general answer is yes, but if we move beyond simply reordering the words to keep with expected syntax we should indicate this. So, for example, a more common presentation might be:

> Lo, I wish to tell of the best of dreams,
> that (lit. 'what') came to me (lit. 'it dreamed to me') in the middle
>   (of) the night,
> when the speech-bearers dwelt at rest.

Here we are adopting modern syntax, but where we have made changes beyond that we are indicating this by the abbreviation 'lit.' or 'literally', to show we know what the original Old English states, or, with '(of)', we are inserting something to help convey the meaning.

This is one way of presenting the translation. Another common format is to adopt an interlinear approach. Here we could, for example, present our translation as:

Hwæt, ic swefna cyst   secgan wylle,
Lo, I of dreams the best   to tell I wish,
Lo, I wish to tell of the best of dreams,

hwæt mē gemætte   tō midre nihte,
what to me it dreamed   in the middle night,
that came to me in the middle (of) the night,

syðþan reordberend   reste wunedon.
when the speech-bearers   at rest they dwelt.
when the speech-bearers dwelt at rest.

Here we present each line of the Old English separately, followed by the word-for-word literal translation and then the Modern English version. Again we are demonstrating a knowledge of the original, but also presenting a more approachable version.

These are just possible examples and ultimately it will depend on one's own preferences, and more importantly, on the expectations of your teacher or examiner.

Presenting a Commentary

Increasingly students are asked to comment on particular texts as opposed to simply translating them. This is perhaps due to the widening of medieval literature studies, in which there is a desire to engage with the text more in terms of its context, and not simply in terms of the language. Students are required to demonstrate an awareness of the language to a certain degree, but moreover, the contextual and analogous material that might relate to the passage being examined.

To comment on a text you will need to know it well. Specifically you should understand and comment on what is happening in the text, its context, the type of text (e.g. genre), the ideas presented and language used, images used, anything that is particularly characteristic of the author (if known), and so on. In particular, you may be asked to demonstrate a specific knowledge of the changing use of language in the medieval period and how one word could have several different meanings.

For a simple example, let us look at these few lines from King Alfred's *Preface to the Pastoral Care* (ll. 14–18):

Swǣclǣne hīo wæs oðfeallenu on Angelcynne ðæt swīðe fēawa
wǣron behionan Humbre ðe hīora ðeninga cūðen understondan

on Englisc oððe furðum ān ǣrendgewrit of Lǣdene on Englisc
āreccean; ond ic wēne ðætte nōht monige begiondan Humbre
nǣren.

What is one expected to comment on here? First one could begin with
a literal analysis. Here an understanding of what the text is saying is
key. A word-for-word translation would be:

> So utterly it was fallen away in the English people that very few
> were on this side of the Humber who their divine services might
>   know how to understand
> in English or even one letter from Latin to English
> translate; and I believe that not many beyond the Humber
> were not.

In terms of our literal analysis then, we could remark:

(1) This is part of the King's preface to his translation of Gregory
     the Great's *Pastoral Care*.
(2) Here the King is pointing out that 'it', i.e. learning and educa-
     tion, had fallen so low in England that many were unable to
     understand (and presumably read) the divine services in
     English, let alone translate from Latin to English.
(3) The demise seems widespread on both sides of the Humber
     river (the border with Northumbria).

We may then wish to move to some remarks on the language:

(1) The whole extract is one sentence in the modern edition but
     displays a sophisticated use of prose in terms of clause struc-
     ture and subjunctives (*cūðen*, l. 15).
(2) The text contains some unfamiliar spellings such as *hīo*,
     hīora, etc., where one would expect *hēo*, or *hēora*. The former
     are indications of Early West Saxon (expected from the
     period of King Alfred) as opposed to the more customary
     Later West Saxon spelling.

Finally we may wish to make some contextual remarks:

(1) The King deliberately refers to his nation as *Angelcynne*, 'the
     English people', and to the language as English. This is in
     keeping with his attempts at nation building in the face of the
     Viking onslaught.

(2)   He recognises the lack of literacy and this provides evidence to support his educational programme outlined later in the *Preface*.

(3)   In particular we can detect the emphasis on English, which was to be a lasting monument of his reign, i.e. the elevation of English as the language of the state, the Church, education, and literature.

This simple example illustrates a few of the features one might wish to identify in this short extract for further commentary.

See also   Chapter 4(a), (b), and (j).

(d)   Manuscripts

Medieval literature survives to us predominantly in two forms:

- manuscripts – hand-written documents from the period, or later transcriptions from original (now lost) sources;
- editions – later works by scholars (editors) who bring together the various surviving copies of a text and produce a scholarly edition.

The defining characteristic of a manuscript is that it is written by hand, as opposed to being printed. William Caxton is credited with establishing the first printing press in England but that was not until the 1470s, and thus the overwhelming majority of medieval texts survive to us (described as being 'extant') in these handwritten collections. It is important that every student of medieval literature has at least some understanding of the basic terminology surrounding manuscripts, but also of how features of the manuscripts and practices of the scribes who created them can have an impact on one's approach to the literature.

Ker, in his seminal catalogue (1990), lists over 400 items that contain Old English, but when one leaves aside fragments or material not from the period the number is greatly reduced. Even so, the surviving corpus of manuscripts containing vernacular material from the Anglo-Saxon period is impressive (though we must always remember that literacy was rare and the majority of information was communicated orally). Many more manuscripts survive from the Middle English period, though again we should keep in mind that many of these were written in Latin and French. The information about manuscripts of Middle English texts can be found in a number of indexes and catalogues. Good starting points are the following general reference works:

The Index of Middle English Verse (Brown and Robbins, 1943–5; Robbins and Cutler, 1965; and Boffey and Edwards, 2005) and The Index of Middle English Prose (Edwards (gen. ed.), 1984–), which both list Middle English texts and their surviving copies.

A Manual of the Writings in Middle English, 1050–1500 (Severs and Hartung, 1967–). Its eleven volumes cover literary prose, poetry, drama, religious, historical, scientific, philosophical, and instructional writings, recipes, proverbs, and letters, and provide information on manuscript and early printed sources of texts.

There are also catalogues of manuscripts organised by library, period, author, and type of text. Editions of texts often also provide information about manuscripts the texts survive in.

Construction

Most medieval manuscripts were constructed in the form of a codex (still used in the modern book) where leaves were gathered in booklets and bound together with a cover. The usual writing material was parchment, though paper also became common in Europe at the end of the 14th century. Parchment was animal skin (strictly speaking from a goat or sheep; 'vellum' is a term reserved for calf skin) that was de-fleshed in alum and lime, stretched, scraped, treated with a whitener, and cut into sheets. When working with manuscripts written on parchment one can still see that one side of the leaf is coarse (the 'hair' side, or the external part of the skin) and the other is smooth (the 'flesh' side, or the internal side of the skin).[6] The whole process is described in the Old English 'book' riddle (number 26) from the Exeter Book:

An enemy *ended my life*, deprived me
of my physical strength; then *he dipped me
in water* and drew me out again,
and put me in the sun where *I soon shed
all my hair*. After that, *the knife's sharp edge
bit into me and all my blemishes were scraped away*;

[6] Often abbreviated H and F.

fingers folded me and the bird's feather
often moved over my brown surface,
sprinkling meaningful marks . . .

(Crossley–Holland, 2002, p. 241)

Parchment sheets were pricked using an awl or point to give equal distances for the lines, then ruled (sometimes by a pencil, but usually by just a hard point), and then they would have been ready to be used. After scribes and artists had finished writing the text and painting initials, miniatures and any other decoration, the sheets were sewn into gatherings or quires, and these in turn were stitched together to form a codex. Some form of binding and cover would then have been used (board covered by leather, for example). Many medieval manuscripts are also termed 'composite' volumes. They are formed of booklets, consisting of one or more quires, produced at different times and by different scribes. These were bound under a single cover by their owners, and may reflect the owners' interests. Such collections could include literary and non-literary texts, both poetry and prose, in different languages (Latin and English, and later also French).

The leaves of manuscripts are usually 'numbered' but in most cases this is modern. When we refer to manuscripts and the texts within them we need to recognise this numbering, but also to distinguish between the system of foliation and pagination. The latter is akin to the way modern books are numbered where each side of each page gets paginated (page 1, page 2, etc.). Under the folio system each leaf is given a single number and then the two sides of that leaf are referred to as the recto (the right-hand side when a manuscript is opened) and the verso (the left). Very often therefore, medieval texts are listed according to the folios they survive on in manuscripts, such as f. 2r or f. 10v ('folio 2 recto' and 'folio 10 verso' respectively).

Analysis of the above information is what we term 'codicology'. Codicological and scribal practices can be key when attempting to date the manuscript and identify its provenance. Different scriptoria ('writing offices') in monasteries where manuscripts were constructed and copied, and later Middle English scribal workshops, had different practices over different periods, and thus by assembling the above information one can give rough estimates (usually to around 25 years) of the date of the manuscript (when combined with other information outlined below).

What the above tells us also is that manuscript construction was an expensive and time-consuming process. Therefore Fulk is quite correct to state that:

every Old English manuscript, unlike a printed book, is unique . . . that the sheer fact of a text's preservation in a manuscript attests to its usefulness . . . given that manuscript space was too precious to be squandered on texts of no practical use. (Fulk and Cain, 2003, pp. 46–7)

Scribal practices

Before the 13th century, manuscripts were produced predominantly in the monasteries, where there were trained scribes based in the scriptorium who would copy manuscripts from master versions. Towards the end of the 12th century monasteries lost their near-monopoly on the production of books. The economic conditions in the 13th century, such as the rise of guilds, the growth of trade and of the middle class, the growth of literacy and the expanding market for books, made it possible for secular scribes to set up their own workshops and not rely on the resources of an institution such as a monastery. The 13th century, in effect, marks the start of commercial book production in England.

Whatever the circumstances of their production it is important to realise that medieval texts continuously changed in the course of their written transmission. This is due partly to copying errors, but also to the widespread practice of scribal editing of texts. Scribes played an active role in their production, modernising and adapting their presentation, spelling, style and content for their intended audiences. As Treharne notes:

Not only, therefore, are surviving manuscripts of texts often one remove or more away from the author's original, but also each individual copy of a text is a unique witness to the way that the text was received and transmitted at its moment of writing. (2005, p. 8)

It is not surprising then that when a work survives in more than one copy, we are presented with several versions of the same text, each with notable differences.

Scribes tended to conform to standard practices, most notably in terms of the style of handwriting they adopted (i.e. the script), though they all had their idiosyncrasies. The study of this area comes under the term 'palaeography'; i.e. a focus on the handwriting used in the manuscript, the number of scribes and the changes in scribe, the writing implements, abbreviations, glosses, corrections, marginalia, layout, and so on. Palaeographers can also present considerable evidence when it comes to dating manuscripts. This is facilitated by the fact that over the medieval period the script, i.e. the handwriting itself, had noticeable set styles in set periods. For example, in Old English in the later period vernacular material was written in 'Anglo-Saxon minuscule' (a modern name for the script), which can be segmented into 'pointed minuscule' (9th century), 'square minuscule' (early 10th century), and 'round minuscule' (early 11th century). The scripts which were used in England from the end of the 12th and into the 16th century are known as 'Gothic'. These can be broadly subdivided into 'formal' and 'cursive'. Cursive scripts were initially reserved for documents, but started to be used for books from the end of the 13th century. Scripts differed in their formal features, like fonts used by modern publishers, but were more closely related to the type of text than modern fonts. Scripts formed a hierarchy suitable for use with a well perceived hierarchy of texts from *de luxe* liturgical manuscripts to university textbooks and documents (see Brown, 1990, p. 80). If we add this palaeographical evidence to the information provided to us by codicology, any linguistic evidence from the text itself, and any other historical information, we can soon assemble a weight of evidence that points towards the dating of the manuscript and possibly its provenance (i.e. where it was written, or at least where it was held).

Occasionally manuscripts would have been illuminated. This ranges from simple daubs on letters, to decorative motifs, to full-page designs (an elaborate early example being the Lindisfarne Gospels). Illustrations were also used in combination with the text, for example, the Harley Psalter from the Anglo-Saxon period contains a series of drawings bringing the Psalms to life. Beautifully illustrated liturgical manuscripts, including Psalters, survive from the Middle English period as well. Throughout the period we also find examples of important illuminated literary and historical manuscripts, such as the works of Matthew Paris, or the poetry of Chaucer and Gower. Of particular interest is Old and Middle English scientific illustration found in herbals, bestiaries, and medical and astronomical manuscripts.

Manuscript contents

There is evidence that a considerable amount of editorial work went into selecting texts for inclusion in manuscripts. The need to point this out may seem strange, especially when we are surrounded by anthologies and a tradition of scholarly editions where the selection and editorial work is clear. However, in many instances when dealing with medieval manuscripts it may appear that texts were almost randomly put together with little or no cohesion. Yet on closer investigation this is not necessarily so.

If we take the Old English Junius manuscript, for example, clearly all the poems share a biblical theme, perhaps linked specifically by the readings in Lent (Raw, 1991, p. 231). Similarly Zimmerman (1995) presents a historicist study of the contents of the Old English poetical manuscripts beginning with an analysis of the religious and political order in late Anglo-Saxon England (the period of manuscript composition), followed by a study of the manuscripts in terms of their historical and social context. Of the four surviving codices of Old English poetry, the Junius manuscript is seen in the context of late Anglo-Saxon politics; the Exeter Book is looked at with the focus on the individual; the Vercelli manuscript is related to the impact of Christianity; and the *Beowulf* manuscript is placed alongside discussions of national identity.

The content of Middle English manuscripts often responds to a similar kind of analysis. Thus the codex containing the Harley lyrics, copied c.1340, is best described as a multilingual miscellany of poetry and prose. However, it also shows clear anthologising tendencies for parts of its contents, where texts are arranged by topic, genre, language, metre, and so on (see Fein, 2000, pp. 1–15). Another famous example is the manuscripts of Chaucer's *The Canterbury Tales*. There is evidence that the early scribes were involved in developing an authoritative and coherent form of Chaucer's fragmentary poem, supplying missing passages, editing text, and using different aspects of manuscript presentation to obscure the work's unfinished state (see Cooper, 1995, pp. 245–61; Hanna, 1996, pp. 140–55; Scott, 1995, pp. 89–95).

Working with manuscripts

Although one may never get access to an actual manuscript, facsimiles, microfilms, and digital images abound allowing many people to see these original artefacts. A good starting handbook is Jane Roberts's *Guide to Scripts Used in English Writings up to 1500* (British Library, London, 2005). In this, Roberts includes a range of facsimiles illustrating all the major scripts used during the period with covering notes and transcriptions.

The fullest collection, however, is the Early English Manuscripts in Facsimile series (often abbreviated to 'EEMF *volume number*', e.g.

EEMF XXV) published by Rosenkilde and Bagger. Facsimiles are also available as part of the Early English Text Society (EETS) series, including, for example, manuscripts Harley 2253 and Digby 86, which contain many of best known Middle English poems, the Winchester manuscript of Malory's *Morte Darthur*, and manuscripts of *The Owl and the Nightingale*, *Pearl*, *Cleanness*, *Patience*, and *Sir Gawain and the Green Knight*. Facsimiles are produced by many major publishers who print medieval texts, and are now also increasingly available on CD-ROM and online (see, for example, an online facsimile of the Auchinleck manuscript, which contains an important collection of Middle English poetry, particularly romances, at www.nls.uk/auchinleck/index.html). Editions of texts, critical works, and bibliographies often provide information about published print and digital facsimiles.

One of the first things you need to do is identify the surviving or extant manuscripts containing the work you are interested in (occasionally called 'witnesses'). Good editions of medieval texts will list the manuscripts the text survives in, but for the most part one will use a catalogue of some description. These have been noted above, covering Old and Middle English, but let us use Neil Ker's *Catalogue* by way of example. Ker's numbering is now standard, and his descriptions of the manuscripts are still widely used (especially his dating). With the latter one would need to become familiar with the abbreviations used by Ker. For example, the *Beowulf* manuscript is noted as 'S. X/XI', which roughly means 'late 10th or early 11th century'. Looking through Ker one would also immediately be able to identify that the main collections of Old English material are held in the British Library, Oxford University's Bodleian Library, and Corpus Christi College at Cambridge University. Manuscripts are sometimes referred to by their common titles – such as 'the *Beowulf* manuscript' – but formally we would use the library shelfmark. Again, by way of example, the poem *Beowulf* appears on ff. 132r–201v in the following manuscript:

London, British Library, Cotton MS. Vitellius A. XV

Here, the first part tells us that the holding library is the British Library. 'MS' is the simple abbreviation for 'manuscript' and the rest is the reference to a particular collection within the library. In this case the shelfmark tells us that the book was originally held in the collection of Sir Robert Cotton (a major collector of Old English manuscripts, whose library at Ashburnham House was badly damaged in a fire in 1731), and that it may have been placed in the bookcase that had a bust of the Roman Emperor Vitellius on top of it, and then on shelf A, fifteen books along. Although this is a unique example, familiarity with the concept of shelfmarks is important.

Once the manuscripts have been located the scholar will work through them, attempting to read the original, possibly transcribing from it, but looking at codicological and palaeographical details. The main problems that one encounters when dealing with manuscripts are:

- the physical state of the codex, which may be damaged by water, fire, rips, etc.;
- different scripts – throughout the medieval period different scripts were adopted, and some were more approachable than others;
- abbreviations which were used for common words or their endings to conserve space;
- word division and punctuation – medieval punctuation was very different from modern practices and word division in handwritten documents was often inconsistent;
- additions, deletions and corrections by contemporary and later readers.

See also   Chapter 3(b), (f), (m), (r), and (u), and Chapter 4(j) and (k).

Further Reading

As well as the catalogues and studies mentioned above for general introductions to the main codicological and palaeorgaphical features of Anglo-Saxon manuscripts and the terminology used in codicology and palaeography see Brown (1990, 1994, and 1998), and Rumble (2001). For more specific studies on manuscripts and scribal practices see Dumville (2001), Parkes (1979, 1991a and 1992), Wright (1960), and the series Beal and Griffiths (eds), *English Manuscript Studies, 1100–1700* (1989–97). For information on the holdings of Anglo-Saxon libraries, see Dumville (2001); Gneuss (2001); Lapidge and Gneuss (1985); and Ogilvy (1967). For general studies related to specific periods see Backhouse et al. (1984), Brown (1991), Hanna (1996), Richards (2001), Webster and Backhouse (1991), and Wilcox (2001). Many medieval manuscripts are now available in digital form. See www.hcu.ox.ac.uk/toebi/man.html for a list of Anglo-Saxon examples, and for Middle English examples see the list at http://ets.umdl.umich.edu/m/mec/digitMSS.html.

(e)   Authorship, Dating, and Transmission of Texts

Authorship

We know very little about most Old English writers, but in the Middle English period, though there are still many gaps in our knowledge, the situation is somewhat better. There are two major differences between the periods:

(1)   Though there are notable exceptions, much of Old English poetry and prose is anonymous. Such anonymity is common in the Middle English period as well, but nevertheless we know much more about the identity of certain authors.

(2)   Middle English writers are more willing to tell the reader about themselves, outlining their attitudes and commenting on what they describe in their works. For example, already early in the 13th century, Laȝamon at the beginning of his *Brut* tells us that he is a priest living at Areley. He also gives us the name of his father, tells us that he loved the place where he lived, that he decided to write a history of England's noblemen, what his sources were, and so on. Similar and more extensive comments and declarations are found in the works of many later Middle English poets as well, such as Chaucer, Langland, and Hoccleve.

Anonymity of Old and Middle English literature is often interpreted as an accident of its textual transmission. But is this really so? When we know the names of Old English writers it is mostly in one of two ways:

(1)   We know the names of authors of short poems transmitted as part of important works of prose by learned writers who describe the circumstances in which the poems were composed (such is *Cædmon's Hymn* recorded in the margins of Bede's *Ecclesiastical History*, and possibly also *Bede's Death Song*, which was circulated as part of Cuthbert's letter describing the death of Bede).[7]

(2)   We know the names of highly learned authors of prose, such as Ælfric, Wulfstan, Alfred, and the Anglo-Latin writers, whose

---

[7] The evidence for Bede's authorship is uncertain, because only a small number of manuscripts attribute the composition of the poem to Bede himself.

work was influenced by the tradition of Latin literacy. We should perhaps add to this category the poet Cynewulf, whose runic signatures testify to the learned literary context of his work and form part of his requests for readers to pray for him.

This situation persists to some extent into the early Middle English period. In both periods anonymity seems to be connected with the genre and the type of text. That is to say, the more learned writers, influenced by the tradition of Latin literacy, were more likely to be self-conscious authors than the writers of the English vernacular poetry and romances.[8]

Anonymous authorship is related to the development of authorial function and represents a stage in this process. We have to accept that authorial mentality was not always the same as it is today. Most obviously in the Middle Ages there were not the same concepts of publication, copyright, and authorial will as we find in modern times, but there were also several other important differences. Below we discuss three such major areas of difference between medieval and modern literary culture: authorial presence, understanding of fiction, and the authors' perception of their roles and works.

Authorial presence

This has already been discussed at the start of this chapter. In medieval Europe self-conscious authorship was more established in the Latin literary tradition because of its classical heritage, and only gradually began to develop in vernacular traditions. In classical literature we see a similar development, from anonymous epics, which raise many of the same problems of authorship and shared 'formulaic' style as early medieval epics, towards highly self-conscious authors of late antiquity. Medieval vernacular genres most influenced by classical and Christian literature were generally more likely to have a strong authorial presence. Modern critical approaches to authorship differ, and in the 19th and early 20th centuries scholars put considerable effort into the identification of anonymous Old and Middle English writers. Nowadays this task is often seen as unachievable, and sometimes also irrelevant for critical analysis. In any case it is important to realise that the anonymity of much of Old and Middle English literature is not an accident which can be remedied through scholarly effort, but a part of the literary-historical process: the

---

[8] Anonymity is often associated with several other genres including sermons, glosses, commentaries, and translations.

degree of authorial presence in texts differs according to period, but also according to the genre and the type of text.

Fiction

Medieval authors were not always happy to admit that they were writing new fiction. In fact this is virtually unknown. Medieval fiction presents itself either as true accounts of real events or as *exampla*, illustrating ethical and theological truths and serving the purpose of moral instruction. This can be seen in the writers' use of 'framed narratives' such as the dream-visions, and in the 'fictionalisation' of sources, such as the authors' claims that they had used ancient historical texts when their sources were modern and literary. It can be seen in writers' frequent insistence that their stories are true, or morally edifying, and also in their treatment of the narratives. Describing Lydgate's poetry, Derek Pearsall observes that his prime interest in stories is in 'destroying them as imagined realities so as to reveal more clearly the hidden truth that is the justification for their existence' (1990a, p. 48). According to Pearsall, Lydgate 'empties the story of everything but *sentence* and in so doing restores it to that world of stable truths which fiction always threatens to subvert' (1990a, p. 47). Pearsall emphasises the differences between Lydgate and Chaucer in their treatment of narratives, and undeniably Chaucer is probably the most modern Middle English author in terms of his understanding and use of fiction. The distrust of fiction evident in medieval literature is linked to changing views on its ability to portray reality and to act as a vehicle for important ideas. Realistic fiction became established properly and proved itself in the 19th century, and so it is seen by modern audiences as a powerful tool for the portrayal of the human mind and the world. However, even modern audiences can be suspicious of non-realistic fiction, such as science-fiction and 'fantasy', which are sometimes marginalised in university studies and elsewhere.[9]

Authors' attitudes to their works

Medieval writers sometimes act or style themselves as craftsmen, historians, compilers or translators, rather than creators of their works.[10] If the content of their works is 'true' or inherited from the past (rather than created), they may see their role as limited to the

---

[9] To give an example from a different but related area, Peter Jackson's *The Lord of the Rings* appears to be the first 'fantasy' film ever to receive an Oscar.

[10] Medieval views on authorial roles are analysed in Minnis (1988).

faithful reproduction and skilful delivery of this content. The following observations made by Pearsall in his analysis of Lydgate's poetry (1970, pp. 1–18) may illustrate this point. They concentrate on the problems of self-expression, and the choice and treatment of the subject matter:

- Lydgate's works include little of what would now be expressed in poetic form – they are different only in style but not in kind from other forms of discourse;
- Lydgate acts like a highly professional and skilful craftsman capable of treating any subject;
- all his poetry is occasional, and 'determined by outer needs and pressures, not by inner ones';
- in his works we can see the development of his style but not of his personality;
- his personality is irrelevant for understanding his poetry, and 'every mask he puts on is a well-worn medieval one'.

Authors' perception of themselves as craftsmen, responsible for the delivery as opposed to the creation of the content of their works, does not reflect of course what really happens in the writing of literature. Lydgate is clearly the author of all aspects of the *Troy Book*, even though it is a free translation of the *Historia destructionis Troiae* of Guido delle Colonna. However, such authorial self-perception reduced the distance between creation and delivery, and between authors and scribes, and is almost certainly at least partly responsible for the widespread scribal editing of medieval texts. Another consequence of such perceptions was 'amplification', or the use of ornate and elaborate style, of embellishment, of rhetoric, and of intricate descriptive detail. Pearsall characterised 'amplification' as 'the governing principle in medieval stylistics' (1970) and extensively demonstrated it in his analysis of Lydgate's poetry (1970 and 1990a). Such exaggeration of form was an obvious way in which writers/craftsmen could demonstrate their skills.[11]

All the features described above are associated with earlier stages in the development of authorial function. They are more characteristic of earlier and vernacular texts, than of texts that are later, learned, and influenced by classical and Christian traditions.

---

[11] Pearsall, however, explains 'amplification' as a feature of verse composed for oral delivery and persisting as a stylistic tradition in verse composed for reading (1970, p. 9).

Transmission

Before the Anglo-Saxons started to write using the Latin alphabet (sometime during the 7th century) texts were composed and transmitted orally. In an oral culture texts were inevitably fluid, not so much because it is impossible to memorise and repeatedly perform a poem exactly, but because change was necessary for their continued existence and preservation. Texts had to develop in order to meet the needs and expectations of their audience, and changes introduced into them as they were passed from generation to generation must have reflected developments in language, tastes, ideas, and the cultural situation.

It is easy to understand why texts were fluid in an oral culture, but what is often overlooked is that the situation did not change drastically or immediately after the transition of literature to parchment (which was itself a gradual process). The evidence from works surviving in multiple copies shows that literacy in the Middle Ages did not ensure the stability of individual texts. Apart from simply making errors, scribes changed the spelling of their exemplars, substituted their own dialect forms, and introduced various interpretative changes. For example, they attempted to modernise texts, tried to resolve errors made by previous copyists, and adapted texts for their audiences in various ways.

This is sometimes interpreted by scholars as a mechanical process of deterioration of 'authorial originals'. However, this was not a result of ignorance, carelessness, or lack of respect, and should not be seen as simple corruption. The reasons for such textual fluidity in written transmission are basically the same as in an oral culture: texts changed not so much because of the scribes' inability to copy exactly, but because they were understood differently by different generations of readers and because they needed to remain current. As in oral transmission, the distinctions between an author and a performer or a copyist, as well as between an act of composition and an act of performance or of recording a text, were not as clear cut as they are today (see the discussion of authorship above). In this situation we can expect a continual reinterpretation of texts, but it is unlikely that the resulting development was always simple corruption. Integrity was vital for texts' continuous appeal and survival, and they would not have reached us if their transmission was inevitably linked to its loss.

Such 'participatory' transmission undoubtedly affected earlier vernacular texts more than the later ones, and probably vernacular verse more than prose, because of the use of a formulaic style in poetry, shared by poets and scribes. There is evidence from such writers as Ælfric, that learned Anglo-Saxons did have a sense of authorial integrity, drawing a clear distinction between their role as authors and the role of scribes as mere copyists, and issuing pleas to scribes not to make emendations to their texts. Nevertheless, surviving works of Ælfric present a picture of extensive scribal editing.

These problems of transmission bring us back to the question of the authorship of medieval texts. Textual fluidity enormously complicates the notion of a single author. It is particularly important to understand that it affected not only textual detail but also almost certainly the content and the 'message' of texts. Though it is entirely legitimate to discuss authorial intention in early medieval texts, and such intention may even be recoverable (depending on one's views on the subject), we should not dismiss the possibility of its transformation as part of the texts' subsequent histories. Again this does not have to lead to the loss of unity and integrity, but may result in multiple layers of meaning in texts (see 'Christian elements' in Chapter 2(n)).

Dating

The above discussion is also relevant to the problem of dating anonymous early medieval texts. We usually do not know the dates when anonymous Old English works were composed, even very approximately. Such a famous and much studied poem as *Beowulf* has been assigned various dates by scholars, ranging from the 7th to the early 11th centuries. Our inability to date Old English poems using linguistic, metrical and stylistic analysis, the study of manuscripts, or historical evidence and literary parallels is not so much a result of our ignorance about the Old English language and the literary history of the period, but is at least partly due to the nature of their authorship and transmission. Traditional dating to an exact time is appropriate for manuscripts but often not for the texts themselves, as such dating ignores many issues to do with their composition and subsequent history (see 'Authorship' and 'Transmission' above). It is likely that a text such as *Beowulf* existed in some form long before its only surviving early 11th-century manuscript, but it is also very likely that it was considerably different from the poem as we have it today.

To summarise, we should consider the following key points:

- authorship is a historical category and authorial self-perception was different in the Middle Ages from what it is today;

- this difference affects the authorial presence in texts, the treatment of subject matter, the style, and the transmission of texts;
- both oral and written transmission resulted in changes to texts which complicate the notions of a single author, or of identifying the provenance and dates of texts.

For a discussion of how these features of medieval literature may affect the theoretical approach one can adopt, see Chapter 4(k).

See also Chapter 2(f) and (n), Chapter 3(c), (n), and (r), and Chapter 4(f), (g), and (k).

Further Reading

For discussions of medieval authorship, fiction, and textual transmission, see Auerbach (1953), Burrow (1982a and 1982b), Carruthers (1990), Davenport (1978), Justice and Kerby-Fulton (1997), Middleton (1978), Millett (1985), Minnis (1988), O'Brien O'Keeffe (1990), Pearsall (1970 and 1990a), Spearing (2003), and Watson (1991).

(f) Source Studies

In the section on literary theories (Chapter 4(k)), we note that medieval scholarship has often adopted a 'text-centred' approach. One aspect of this is 'source studies', namely identifying the source material that the medieval author may have had access to directly, or indirectly through an intermediary, and how they used it. This can tell us several things:

(1) by observing changes to the original source we may be able to identify issues of importance to the author and, by extension, their audience, and reveal insights into their style;

(2) by listing together the possible source material we can begin to build up a picture of scholarship and access to scholarly and literary material in the Middle Ages (e.g. see Ogilvy, 1967 and 1984–5; and Gneuss, 2001);

(3) this in turn demonstrates the place of Old and Middle English in the context of classical, patristic, and contemporary literature, and shows a continuity of thought;

(4) finally, we can identify trends in the use of sources in terms of what texts and which authors had particular influence at particular times.

To begin with we must distinguish between a source and an analogy. The latter is where two or more texts have similarities, but this can be due to a common (possibly lost) original, the shared interests of authors and audiences, or simply a coincidence. For example, Beowulf's fight with Grendel is similar to the fight between the hero and a ghost in the Old Norse *Grettis saga*, possibly due to common folk-tale sources. It is an analogy, and we cannot state that the author of either was aware of the other story. A source, however, is a text that directly influences another text. This could be that the source text is translated or paraphrased in parts, or that it influenced the interpretation presented in the later text. Scragg (1997) further refines the definition by distinguishing immediate sources (i.e. the text, but not necessarily the manuscript, an author used), and antecedent sources (a text that may have been the background to the immediate source).

How does one identify possible sources of a text? In some cases authors may simply declare their sources (often in order to give the work authority). Obviously this helps, but if this is not the case then scholars have to identify similarities across a range of texts, and then decide whether they are seeing an analogy or a source. One should also remember that attributions found in medieval texts are not always reliable for a variety of reasons. Thus in *Troilus and Criseyde* Chaucer presents his work as a translation of a text by a fictional author Lollius, repeatedly refers to 'olde bokes' and 'myn auctour', and acts as if he is translating from Latin. In fact he makes use of a variety of earlier texts, particularly *Il Filostrato* by Boccaccio, which he never mentions and to which the poem owes its plot and much of its detail. There is evidence that Chaucer and his contemporaries may have believed in the existence of an ancient author Lollius, an authority on the Trojan War; and thus by using his name Chaucer may be paying tribute to a tradition well attested in medieval and later literature. Boccaccio does something similar in the proem to *Il Filostrato*, presenting his work as the result of his study of ancient legends and making no mention of his real more modern French and Italian sources. Such 'fictionalisation' of sources is found in the literature of different periods when authors claim to have used lost and rediscovered manuscripts, chronicles, eye-witness accounts, or invented literary works. This can have a variety of functions, such as lending the work authority and authenticity; providing links with a particular historical period or literary tradition; or on the contrary, distancing the work from undesirable associations. One of the most common reasons for 'fictionalisation' of sources is the authors' wish to comment on the work's relationship to history, reality, and literary and interpretative tradition; thus masking (or emphasising) it's nature as fiction.

A variety of online and printed collections are used by scholars to help with identifying sources. Students of Old English may wish to start with the highly approachable books by Allen and Calder (1976), Calder et al. (1983), Davidson (1980), and Garmonsway and Simpson (1980). In addition two large-scale research projects should be consulted. The first is the *Fontes Anglo-Saxonici* project (http://fontes.english.ox.ac.uk). This online database allows one to look at an Old English text and to see what source texts were used in its compilation. The second is the *Sources of Anglo-Saxon Literary Culture* (SASLC – www.wmich.edu/medieval/research/saslc) and its printed publications. When wishing to access the original source texts themselves (as opposed to simply identifying them) the standard series of books for classical, patristic, and hagiographic texts are the *Patrologia Latina*, the *Corpus Christianorum*, and the *Acta Sanctorum*.

There is also a large literature on the sources and literary background of specific Old and Middle English texts. Such works include discussions of analogies and authors' use of earlier texts, but also collections of source material and analogies for individual works. There is, for example, an impressive body of research dedicated to the identification and study of sources and analogies of Chaucer's works. The key publication is *Sources and Analogies of the 'Canterbury Tales'* by Robert M. Correale and Mary Hamel (2002–5), which is an update of an earlier collection of source texts and analogies by Bryan and Dempster (1941). It has chapters dedicated to individual tales and links, and provides facing-page translations of texts in foreign languages. Havely (1980) illustrates Chaucer's use of Boccaccio's works in *The Canterbury Tales* and *Troilus and Criseyde*, while Windeatt (1982) offers modern English translations of the sources and analogies of Chaucer's dream poetry. The Chaucer Library (gen. ed. Robert E. Lewis) publishes scholarly editions with facing-page translations of works which were used by Chaucer. Seven volumes have been published so far (mostly by University of Georgia Press, Athens).

Once a source is identified, what should one look for? The key things are:

- How directly does the medieval author follow the source – is it a close translation or a paraphrase?

- Does the author use a variety of sources and do they identify these?
- Is there any possibility that the author was using an intermediate source?
- If the medieval writer makes any changes (e.g. alters, omits, or expands), can this tell us anything about the purpose and cultural context of the later text?

All of these can present us with useful insights into the author's style and intention.

See also   Chapter 3(r), and Chapter 4(k).

Further Reading

For introductions to source studies as a subject see Scragg (1997). In addition to the resources mentioned above, see Lees (1991). See Brewer (1997) and Newhauser (1997) for a representative approach (this time applied to *Sir Gawain*) to analysing common narrative structures, familiar type-scenes (e.g. the 'beheading game'), common images, and similarities in language and descriptions.

(g)   Metre and Language of Poetry

In Chapters 2 and 3 we discussed major works of Old and Middle English poetry, and in Chapter 2(h) we outlined some of the key features of Old English poetry. Now we will look in more depth at the language, metre, and style of verse surviving from both periods, and attempt to point out some important similarities and differences.

Old English verse

One of the most striking features of Old English poetry is the almost ubiquitous use of alliteration. This is the repetition of initial sounds of words for emphasis or aesthetic and metrical reasons, which was common in the poetry of different Germanic nations. Apart from Old English, alliterative poems survive in Old Norse, Old Saxon, and Old High German. Alliterative verse in Old English is known from the 8th century onwards and was used until the end of the Old English period. Though pre-Christian and pre-literary in origin, at the end of the Old English period alliterative verse flourished within the literary Christian tradition.

Old English poets used five basic metrical patterns (and their variants) when composing alliterative verse. They are known as Sievers's types, because they were first systematically described by the German scholar Eduard Sievers. The first three of these patterns (called A, B, and C) have two metrically stressed and two metrically unstressed positions in different combinations ('/' represents metrically stressed positions, and 'X' metrically unstressed positions):[12]

A /X/X *gomban gyldan* (*Beowulf*, l. 11a)

B X/X/ *þǣr ȳt hǣðe stōd* (*Beowulf*, l. 32a)

C X//X *þēah hē him lēof wǣre* (*Beowulf*, l. 203b).

Two more metrical types (D and E) have a secondary stress (marked '\'), necessary to differentiate between the two unstressed positions and prevent them from falling together into a single metrical dip. Type D has two variants, depending on the position of the secondary stress: // \X – *lēof lēodcyning* (*Beowulf*, l. 54a) and //X\ – *hār hilderinc*, (*Beowulf*, l. 1307a). Type E also has two variants, depending on the position of the secondary stress: / \X/ – *murnende mōd* (*Beowulf*, l. 50a) and /X\/ – *morþorbed strēd* (*Beowulf*, l. 2436b). The second variant of E was rare, because two metrical stresses were avoided at the end of a verse. For the same reason type XX// was not used in alliterative verse, but otherwise Sievers's five types cover between them all possible combinations of two stressed and two unstressed positions. Verses E and D can often be recognised by the use of compound words: the second part of such words provided the required secondary stress, as in the examples above.

When studying Old English metre it is important to remember that a metrical position (marked above as X, /, or \) is not the same as a syllable: a stressed position could correspond to either one long or two short syllables, following the rules of resolution. Thus *swutol* in line 90 from *Beowulf* (*swutol sang scopes*) corresponds to a single metrically stressed position. The number of unstressed syllables in metrically weak positions also varied but usually within strictly defined limits. The gap between stresses was normally no longer than two syllables, though more unstressed syllables were allowed before the first stress.

Metrical patterns described by Sievers correspond to the half-lines of Old English verse. Pairs of these formed four-stressed long lines, bound together by alliteration. Alliteration always fell on metrically

---

[12] Stress is occasionally referred to as 'accent', e.g. accented = stressed.

stressed words, and its position was subject to several rules. The third metrical stress always alliterated, whereas the fourth never did. The first half-line allowed three possible patterns of alliteration: alliteration on both metrical stresses, only on the first, or only on the second (alliterating sounds in the following examples are highlighted in bold):

aa/aX (three stresses alliterate): **m**onegum **m**ǣgþum **m**eodosetla oftēah   (Beowulf, l. 5)

aX/aX (two stresses alliterate): **l**ange hwīle; him þæs **L**īffrēa (Beowulf, l. 16)

Xa/aX (two stresses alliterate): Gewāt ðā **n**ēosian, syþðan **n**iht becōm (Beowulf, l. 115)

In Old English verse each consonant alliterated with itself, as in the examples above, apart from the clusters sc, sp, st, which always alliterated as a group. Thus, in the line:

Oft Scyld Scēfing sceaþena þrēatum   (Beowulf, l. 4)

the group sc alliterates with sc. In contrast, all vowels alliterated between themselves, indiscriminately; for example, in line 3 from Beowulf, æ in æþelingas alliterates with e in ellen:

hū ðā æþelingas ellen fremedon

Metrical stresses in alliterative verse coincided with major linguistic stresses. Words carrying metrical accent and alliteration were usually lexical words that normally carry stress in a sentence, such as nouns, adjectives, adverbs, and verbs, rather than unstressed function words such as prepositions or pronouns. Metrical prominence of lexical words depended on their part of speech: nouns appeared in stressed positions and alliterated more often than verbs; adjectives alliterated more often than nouns, though half-lines containing both adjectives and nouns frequently had double alliteration. This traditional hierarchy of the parts of speech was little affected by the context or emphasis, and was observed within individual lines as a system of rank and subordination: verbs could alliterate, but usually only if nouns and adjectives alliterated as well, or if other positions were filled with words of even lower ranks. Thus in wēox under wolcnum (Beowulf, l. 8), 'grew under the skies', both the verb (wēox) and the noun (*wolcnum*) alliterate, whereas in *ofer hronrāde hȳran scolde* (*Beowulf*, l. 10) '[each of the neighbours] across the sea must obey', the notional verb *hȳran* ('to listen, to obey') alliterates, whereas the modal verb *scolde* ('must') does not.

Old English poetry differed from prose in its syntax, grammar, vocabulary, and idiom. Among the most prominent features of the style of poetry are the use of compound words and synonyms. Compound words, that is words consisting of two parts, were common in the Old English language, but were particularly frequent in poetry. Their number was not fixed, and they were probably coined by poets freely to suit their needs. Some compound words appear only once in the surviving corpus of Old English poetry; others, such as *gūðcyning*, a combination of Old English *gūð* 'war, battle' and *cyning* 'king', or *medobenc*, a combination of Old English *medo* 'mead' and *benc* 'bench', are frequent. In some cases the meaning of a compound word is a reasonably straightforward combination of the meanings of its parts, for example *iren-heard* (*iren* 'iron' and *heard* 'hard') – 'iron hard', or *niht-long* (*niht* 'night' and *long* 'long') – 'lasting a night'. In other cases the whole word is a metaphor: *sǣ-hengest* – 'sea-stallion' ('ship'). Such metaphors are known as 'kennings'.

Some compound words may appear redundant or stating the obvious: *heaðo-rinc* ('battle-warrior'), *here-rinc* ('army-warrior'), *beado-mece* ('battle-sword'). The first elements of such words are sometimes interpreted as line-fillers mechanically used to supply alliteration. What probably happens in such cases is that the first element is used figuratively, as a poetic epithet. For example, *Gār-Dene* 'spear Danes' does not necessarily mean 'Danes fighting with spears', but 'war-like Danes', whereas *heaðo-fȳr* 'battle-fire' when used to describe the fire coming from a dragon, rather than from a battle, probably means 'deadly, frightening fire' (Steblin-Kamensky, 1978, pp. 4–39). Translation of such compound words can present considerable difficulties, not only because of the absence of similar formations in Modern English, but because of the difficulty of understanding the exact meaning of an epithet.

Old English poetry also had a large number of synonyms for important notions of the heroic world, such as 'king', 'sea', 'ship', 'warrior', 'battle', and so on. Many of the synonyms were used only in poetry. The differences between synonyms were not necessarily referential, for example *scip* ('ship'), *cēol* ('ship, keel'), *fær* ('ship, vessel'), and *hringed-stefna* ('ring-prowed ship') are all used at the beginning of *Beowulf* to describe the same ship in which the body of

Scyld Scefing, the founder of the Danish dynasty, is set adrift at sea. Words of different etymology, and various descriptive or metaphoric compounds, highlighted different features of an object. Thus, the sea could have been described from the point of view of its movement (*flōd-weg, strēamas, ȳþ, ȳþ-gewinn*), from the point of view of human efforts to cross it (*sund, wad, seglrād*), or as a home of birds and beasts (*hron-rād, seolh-pæþ, fisces eþel*). In spite of a widely held opinion, synonyms were not fully interchangeable formal elements fitted in a line 'according to the demands of alliteration'. Apart from differences described above, their use in verse points to a system of metrical rank, or a tendency to use some synonyms in alliteration and others without alliteration, and in predictable positions within a line of verse. Synonyms were not equal, and had different aesthetic values, which reflected their traditional use in poetry.

Finally a reader of Old English poetry can hardly fail to notice that lines of verse are sometimes reproduced exactly, or with some variation within a single poem, or have exact and close parallels in other poems in Old English. In the following passage from *Beowulf*, underlined groups of words appear elsewhere in Old English poetry, unchanged or virtually unchanged (Magoun, 1953, pp. 446-67):

> HWÆT, WĒ GĀR-DEna in gēardagum,
> þēodcyninga þrym gefrūnon,
> hū ðā æþelingas ellen fremedon!
> Oft Scyld Scēfing sceaþena þrēatum,
> monegum mægþum meodosetla oftēah,
>
> (*Beowulf*, ll. 1–5)

According to F. P. Magoun (1953, pp. 449–50) about 70% of the text in the first 25 lines from the beginning of *Beowulf* appears elsewhere in Old English verse, even though the surviving corpus of poetry is quite small (around 30,000 lines). Reproducible lexical and syntactic units, such as the ones underlined in this passage, are known as 'formulas'. Various stable expressions are actually found in the poetry of any period or literary movement: poets tend to develop their own metrical and linguistic style where the same words may appear in rhyme, and the same phrases may be used with a predictable rhythm in predictable places in lines of verse. In modern poetry, however, this is a marginal phenomenon, rarely noticed by readers, and judged negatively, as with the use of clichés if sufficiently prominent. Formulaic style on the scale found in Old English is an archaic feature of poetry, shared by traditional epic verse and to some extent by folklore.

Formulaic style was first extensively researched and described by Milman Parry (1971) and Albert Lord (1960), who studied Homeric epic poetry and twentieth-century folk poetry in Yugoslavia. They demonstrated that the use of formulas was linked to how the verse was composed in pre-literary societies, such as existed in early Anglo-Saxon England. Parry and Lord showed that oral poets did not learn a fixed text, even when they believed they were reproducing exactly an already existing poem, but improvised, or composed their verse using a stock of metrically organised phrases or formulas. Performance of such poetry was inseparable from its re-creation, even though the poets did not consider themselves to be its authors. Such transmission of poetry ensured the preservation of traditional plots, ideas, style and language, but also their constant renewal following changing needs of audiences and society. This constant development and creative effort aimed at the individual situation of a particular performance must have protected the formulaic poetry from stagnation, or from becoming repetitive or clichéd.

According to Parry a formula is 'a group of words which is regularly employed under the same metrical conditions to express a given essential idea' (1971, p. 80). In traditional poetry metrically organised formulas and their systems matched conventional subjects or narrative themes, such as the descriptions of battles, feasts, and so on. In Old English the use of formulas which originated in heroic pre-literary verse was extended to Christian subjects. Formulas persisted therefore as a feature of the poetic language after the poetry became literary and learned, towards the end of the Old English period.

Middle English alliterative verse

The earliest known examples of Old English verse are essentially in the same style and language as the poetry (written in the traditional manner) which survives from the end of the Old English period. Because of this, the style and metre can tell us little about when, where, or by whom the poems were composed. However, from the end of the Old English period we also have examples of poetry that is metrically free and has lost many traditional features. Verse in classic alliterative metre disappeared from written records in the second half of the 11th century, though alliteration continued to be used in poetry after the Norman Conquest. Cultural changes played a major part in its decay: its vocabulary, phraseology, and ultimately metre were designed to express the traditional subject matter and depended on its continuity and stability.

Middle English alliterative poetry flourished particularly in the 14th and 15th centuries. This period is often described as the 'Alliterative Revival'. It covers poems produced mostly between 1350 and 1415, though the dating is often problematic. In origin this was a regional poetry of the North and West (the early evidence is overwhelmingly from the old diocese of Worcester, York City, and the area immediately to the north (Hanna, 1999, p. 509)). However, it spread and became a national form in both England and Scotland. Thus the manuscripts and transmission of alliterative verse were not limited to the North and West; and books containing alliterative poetry, including *Piers Plowman* and *The Siege of Jerusalem*, were produced in London (Hanna, 1999, pp. 509–11).

The range of the subject matter of alliterative poetry was very broad, and included learned, historical, and theological content (as in *Pearl*, *Cleanness*, and *Patience*, for example). However, as Hanna observed:

> Virtually all extensive alliterative poems concern themselves with *gesta*, 'public deeds'. . . . the tradition focuses upon historical narrative, in which the past provides a model for the present. (Hanna, 1999, p. 504)

The poetry of the 'Alliterative Revival' is largely anonymous. Its authors commonly use oral rhetoric, even in spite of the poems' learned content, and affirm that they are following a tradition (as witnessed by the common formula '*as the boke tellis*').

Some scholars object to the term 'Revival' because the relationship between the 14th-century and earlier alliterative poetry is by no means clear. We do not know which models were used by Middle English poets, and in what form the alliterative tradition was known to them. As pointed out by Pearsall (1981), La3amon's *Brut* and the late 13th-century *Bestiary* appear to be the last examples of unrhymed alliterative line for over a hundred years. Though alliteration continued to be used in rhymed poetry, between the second recension of *Brut* in Cotton Otho C. XIII and the earliest poems of the 'Revival' (1275–1350) there are now extant a mere 28 lines of unrhymed alliterative poetry. In spite of this some details of the metrical practice and style of Old English alliterative verse and the verse of the 'Revival' are strikingly similar. Like their Anglo-Saxon predecessors Middle English alliterative poets used special poetic vocabulary. In Middle English this vocabulary was mixed and included words derived from Anglo-Saxon, French, and Old Norse.

Middle English poets also employed synonyms for important concepts such as 'knight, hero', and distinguished between synonyms of different metrical rank. Some of the synonyms were Old English in origin and used only in verse already in Old English. Poets of the 'Revival' also employed a form of formulaic style, which included shared alliterative collocations and recurring phrases. However, such phraseology had a number of important differences from Old English formulas. Thus, several scholars have drawn attention to the broad syntactic and rhythmical variability of the Middle English 'formula' (Lawrence, 1970). Because of this, following Thorlac Turville-Petre, many prefer to call such phraseology a 'shared style' rather than formulas (1977, pp. 89–92).

Middle English alliterative poetry was composed using a literary language. It had a North-West Midland dialect base, but included forms from other dialects, and vocabulary which was not likely to be present in any local speech (Duggan, 1997). It had considerably more words of Germanic origin than Chaucer's language or, generally, Middle English of that time. This language may seem difficult and provincial today because it is further removed from the Modern Standard English than the London dialect of Chaucer, but in the 14th century, before the Standard English became established, this was not so.

There is extensive literature describing the metrical rules used by Middle English alliterative poets. Some aspects of their usage are not fully understood or are debatable because of the diversity and complexity of surviving evidence, and it is only recently that scholars have started to build a comprehensive theory of Middle English alliterative metre. Important studies include Borroff (1962), Cable (1991), Duggan (1976, 1986a, 1986b, 1988, and 1990), Lawton (1982), McCully and Anderson (1996), and Oakden (1930–5).

We should note the following similarities between Old English poetry and the poetry of the 'Alliterative Revival':

- common features of metre and style;
- largely historical subject matter (including Bible stories);
- anonymity and the use of formulaic phraseology and a 'shared style' (see the discussion of authorship in Chapter 4(e));
- the use of literary language, rather than dialect.

This set of shared features shows that in both cases sophistication and the literary character of poetry (which used a literary language rather than dialect and was a national rather than regional form) can be combined with anonymity and formulaic style.

Other Middle English poetry

The disappearance of the 'classical' alliterative verse at the end of Old English period was followed by the establishment in the 12th century of an international literary culture with an interest in experiment and a lively exchange of ideas and literary forms between languages and countries. Already early Middle English poets used different forms of syllabic verse, mostly inspired by Continental models. Syllabic verse tends to have a fixed number of syllables per line and the rhythm is created by the alternation of stressed and unstressed syllables. Thus the *Orrmulum* is written in regular 15-syllable lines imitating seven-stress metres, which were commonly used in medieval Latin religious poetry.

Much of the Middle English verse, however, is not, or at least does not appear to be, metrically as regular as the *Orrmulum*. Most surviving texts employ rather free versions of different syllabic metres. By this we mean the presence of such irregularities as, for example, omitted unstressed syllables, or on the contrary, more than one unstressed syllable between the stresses. Thus Chaucer's *The Canterbury Tales* is written in iambic pentameter. The basic form of this metrical pattern requires five stressed and five unstressed positions (X for unstressed and / for stressed):

X / X / X / X / X / (X)

Many of Chaucer's lines conform to this model, for example:

A Knight ther was, and that a worthy man.　(l. 43)

However, Chaucer also has less regular lines, supported by surviving manuscripts and accepted as authentic by most editors, for example:

Hath in the Ram his half cours yronne.　(l. 8)

And by his syde a swerd and a bokeler.　(l. 112)

In the first of these lines there seems to be a missing unstressed syllable after the third metrical beat ('half'), while in the second line there are two, rather than one, unstressed syllables after the third metrical beat ('swerd'). Such freedom may have been the poets' preference, and indeed some of Chaucer's metrical 'irregularities' seem to have a stylistic or compositional function in his verse. However, it may be also partly due to the fact that very few manuscripts in the authors' own hand survive from the period. Some metrical irregularity may simply be a result of scribal changes. Thus surviving holographs of Hoccleve's verse present his metrical practice as much more regular than it appears to be in scribal copies. We also cannot always be sure as to how words were pronounced in Middle English. Unstressed final –*e* (such as at the end of the word 'yronne' in l. 8 above) was still pronounced in some Middle English dialects. Obviously its presence or absence makes a difference for metre by creating or dropping an extra syllable. Moreover, there is evidence that many words had pronunciation variants (for example, with or without the final –*e*), and that poets used such variants in order to achieve regular metre (a practice which was almost certainly obscured by scribal copying).

One of the most interesting developments in Middle English verse was the introduction of iambic pentameter, illustrated above. Chaucer seems to have been the first poet to use it. This flexible and versatile metrical form became popular with the 15th-century poets and later continued to be one of the most widely used metres in English (it was employed by Shakespeare in his plays and sonnets, for example). Much of the early Middle English syllabic verse is either in four-stressed lines or in longer, seven- or eight-stressed lines. These longer lines were broken into halves by a metrical pause (i.e. the caesura, which we also find in alliterative Old and Middle English verse), and as a result also followed the basic four- or three-stressed pattern noted earlier. Even though the iambic pentameter line is only slightly longer, its uninterrupted rhythmical movement made an enormous difference for syllabic verse. It helped Chaucer to achieve a greater and much needed rhythmical variety (lacking in the *Orrmulum*, for example) and to demonstrate the potential of syllabic verse in English. This, and his prosodically varied vocabulary (which included a large number of French- and Latin-derived words), allowed Chaucer to move further away from the earlier poetic tradition and to create what sounded to his contemporaries like a new English poetry. Chaucer also introduced 'rhyme royal', a stanza of seven lines rhyming *ababbcc* (used in *Troilus and Criseyde*, for example). Complex rhyming patterns were used by other Middle English poets as well – such are some of the patterns found in the Harley Lyrics (see Chapter 3(f)) or the stanza used by the *Gawain*-poet in *Pearl*, but the most common Middle English rhyming pattern was a couplet. It is found in a wide range of verse across the period, particularly in longer narrative works such as chronicles and romances. Rhyme royal, however, became very popular with 15th-century authors, for whom it was one of the trademarks of the Chaucerian tradition.

See also   Chapter 2(h), Chapter 3(a), (c), (e), (f), (p), and (s), and Chapter 4(e).

Further Reading

For the accounts of alliterative verse see Bliss (1962), Borroff (1962), Brodeur (1959), Cable (1991), Lester (1996), Pearsall (1977 and 1981), Robinson (1985), Shippey (1972), and Turville-Petre (1977). The following accounts of Chaucer's prosody illustrate different approaches to the study of metre, and include a discussion of textual problems and the use of manuscript evidence: Minkova (2005), Mustanoja (1979) and Pearsall (1991).

(h)   Genres of Old and Middle English Literature

Genre Studies asks such questions as whether a work can be described as a chronicle, novel, romance, lay, and so on. It places texts within the context of similar works and helps to see their relationship with earlier and later traditions. Many critics believe that ideas about a text's generic identity and the expectations it gives rise to are crucial for an audience's understanding and reception of the work (Strohm, 1980). Genres provide a set of rules and preconceptions with which readers approach a literary work and which help them to interpret and appreciate the text. Understanding the generic expectations of audiences is therefore important for the study of a work's contemporary reception. This, however, can be a difficult task, and in many cases we do not have enough evidence to recover fully the generic expectations of medieval audiences. This is particularly true of the Old English period, where the corpus of surviving texts is relatively small. As Donoghue remarks:

> We do not know for example, whether they [the Anglo-Saxons] distinguished a long poem like *Beowulf* as an 'epic' as opposed to a shorter 'lyric', however familiar these genres seem to us. Even categories as broad as 'fiction' and 'non-fiction' would probably seem strange.   (Donoghue, 2004b, p. xii)

The first point we need to make is that literary genres should be studied in their historical context. Genres develop, change, and influence each other. There is no absolute definition one can give, for example, of lyrical poetry or historical writing which would be true for all times. One always has to look at the full range of texts which existed during a particular period, and how they performed and shared different functions. In medieval England, for example, the relationship between fiction and history was different from what it is today: historical texts such as Bede's *Ecclesiastical History* could contain fictional elements, such as invented dialogue, whereas what we now see as literary works, such as the Old English poem *Widsith*, could contain genealogies. Middle English 'world histories' related historical events, but also included a wealth of theological and scientific information. Because of this the present book uses a broad view of what constitutes 'literature', 'poetry', 'history', and so on, and includes a discussion of a wide range of texts in both Old and Middle English.

The most basic distinction we need to make for the Old English period is between prose and poetry. Old English alliterative verse goes back to a common Germanic tradition which must have existed already during the pre-literary period. The surviving Old English prose is much later in its origin: originating chiefly with King Alfred's educational programme started in the second half of the 9th century, and developing in the 10th and 11th centuries. The different origin and early history of prose and verse influenced their subsequent development; for example, Old English prose was the main medium during the later part of the period for the transmission of Christian learning, of factual information, and so on. It is therefore perhaps not surprising that it is better preserved than poetry, that its written presentation was more sophisticated, and that it was copied well after the Conquest. Verse constitutes a much smaller part of the surviving Old English literature (Robinson, 2004, p. 215). It was composed using a special literary language which was quite archaic and developed to express traditional heroic and Christian subject matter. Some scholars believe that poetry may have achieved the highest point of its development in pre-Viking Age Northumbria, though this is disputed by others. As a literary form Old English verse is more ancient than Old English prose, but the surviving manuscripts of verse are few and all date from the very end of the Old English period (*c*.975–*c*.1025). This highlights problems which the study of verse has to face, but also the fact that the evidence from the written tradition should be supplemented by other evidence, such as the study of genres. The written tradition is not a straightforward reflection of the literary-historical process, and can even disguise some aspects of its development (for example, which literary forms are earlier and which are later).

Major genres and types of Old and Middle English texts are described earlier in Chapters 2 and 3. Some genres are fairly coherent and bring together texts which display many similarities of content and form, such as the Old English Riddles, for example. Others include very different texts, so that scholars may even doubt the value of describing them using common terms, notably the Old English Elegies and to some extent medieval romances. We should note that literary works often combine features of more than one genre: most obviously Chaucer's *The Canterbury Tales* is a collection of stories of different kinds, whereas *Troilus and Criseyde* can be described as epic, romance, history, tragedy, and so on (see Windeatt 1992, pp. 138–79). Authors sometimes tried to challenge and redefine the generic expectations of their audiences, and this is particularly characteristic of Chaucer, whose works combine and transform different earlier traditions.

In this connection a good example to focus on is the development and transformation of one specific literary genre, namely that of 'epic poetry' and how it applies to Old English literature. Poetry such as *Beowulf* and *The Fight at Finnsburg* (see Chapter 2(g)) is often described as heroic or epic; yet there are many different interpretations of what is epic literature. M. M. Bakhtin, for example, believed that epic literature, as witnessed in such works as the Greek *Odyssey* and *Iliad*, is characterised by the following features:

(1) its subject is a national heroic past;
(2) its source is a national tradition, rather than personal experience;
(3) the world it describes is separated from the present by an 'absolute epic distance' (Bakhtin, 1981, p. 13).

This last statement means that the epic world is idealised, and described not as a real historical period, but as a remote time of 'beginnings' and 'peaks' of national history. These are incomparably greater than contemporary reality, and inhabited by heroes who cannot be matched by anyone living. Such an approach to representing the past is of course totally different from what is found in modern historical novels. 'Epic past' according to Bakhtin is not just a period of time, but a category within a system of traditional values: it is not devoid of evil and struggle, but it is devoid of uncertainty and contradictions. It is revered as a time when heroic ideals were a reality. Whereas the past in epics is idealised, the present is never portrayed, and the future is often associated with catastrophes, death, and decline.

Bakhtin believed that an epic generally predetermined not only the choice of events and characters it described, but also their evaluation, and that this evaluation was built into its language. He wrote that epic language was inseparable from its subject. Epic poets described events from the heroic past, using language where important words such as 'king', 'family', or 'fate' had predetermined connotations and associations. Epic poets could be said to have used an 'absolute language' which expressed and supported a system of values developed within the tradition. Bakhtin's description of this language agrees with what we know of how epic poetry was composed. Its narrative usually falls into traditional themes, such as 'battle', 'travel across the sea', 'feasting', 'the giving of gifts', and so on. Such themes were then used as building blocks of stories and were associated with their own traditional vocabulary and phraseology.

Bahktin also believed that the epic represents a historical stage in the development of literature which preceded the emergence of the modern novel. He observed that epic literature reached us as a very 'old' genre, with a long history. The implication of this is that the surviving examples may not be epics in 'pure' form, but may have been influenced by later developments in literature. This is certainly true of the Old English *Beowulf*. Though it has many characteristics which conform to Bakhtin's description of the epic, it also has features which firmly place it very late in the epic tradition.

When scholars try to classify epic poetry they often follow Heusler, who believed that there are two major types: 'classical' epics such as the *Niebelungenlied* and *Beowulf*, and shorter epic poems (e.g. *The Fight at Finnsburg*, or the heroic songs of the *Poetic Edda*) (1920, 1921, 1943). Shorter lays are characterised by dynamic action, and the speeches of characters, if present, tend to be quite succinct. There are also few descriptions, and usually no digressions. Longer epics have slow-developing action, digressions, lengthy monologues, and elaborate descriptions of weapons, ships, and so on. Heusler believed that shorter heroic lays are more ancient and that their size makes them more suitable for an oral performance. He regarded longer epics as a later development which had probably happened already in literate cultures. *Beowulf* conforms to this observation. Moreover it also shares features with another relatively late genre – the Old English elegies. Elegies may have originated early in Christian Anglo-Saxon England (they have no parallels in other Germanic cultures), and generally their content is at least partially Christian and shows influences from Latin literature. The second part of *Beowulf* in particular has a number of similarities with such poems, and even includes a passage, sometimes entitled 'The Lay of the Last Survivor', which is close to the Old English elegies in both content and form. These features of *Beowulf* cannot be explained as later additions or reworkings because they are well integrated into its generally very consistent structure. *Beowulf* thus is another example of a work which combines features from different genres and can be understood only with reference to a range of other Old English texts. By comparing it with other works we can perceive generic influences, and can even start building up a picture of the transformation that epic undergoes in Old English literary culture.

Finally there is the need to re-emphasise the continuity between the Old and Middle English periods in terms of the development of genres. Among the innovations we can see in the Middle English period are the popularity of romance, and dream-visions, and the flourishing of lyrical poetry. However, all these genres have roots in Old English Literature. All three have Old English predecessors but develop into distinct traditions during the Middle English period.

To summarise, we should consider the following key points:

- literary genres provide sets of rules and expectations with which a reader approaches a literary work;
- genres change, develop, and disappear; and it is impossible to give a definition of a genre, such as romance or lyrical poetry, which will be true for all historical periods;
- works often display features of more than one genre.

See also   Chapter 2(c), (e)–(g), (i), (k), (l), and (o); and Chapter 3(a), (f), (h), and (n).

Further Reading

Dubrow (1982) and Fowler (1982) provide a good introduction to genre studies. Important studies and overviews of Old and Middle English genres include Amsler (1980), Boitani (1982), Davenport (2004), Fulk and Cain (2003), Greenfield and Calder (1986), and Strohm (1980).

(i)   Placing Literature in Context

In Chapter 4(k) we note the predominance of the New Historicist approach to Medieval Literary Studies. Here scholars attempt to place the text in its historical, social, artistic, and archaeological context as well as identifying intertextual links with other works of literature. Although the certainty of the New Historicist approach may not always be applicable (such as in the early medieval period where the amount of unknowns can negate any attempt to define a time and place of composition), a general contextualising approach is the norm. As Hines argues, there is always a 'close and deep affinity between material artifacts and literature as products of human cultural activity' (Hines, 2004, p. 26). Therefore students of medieval literature need to have some basic knowledge of the history, social culture, art, architecture, and archaeology of the period (a stance that is adopted in this book). Moreover they should not be surprised if they are exposed to evidence from these disciplines either in their courses or in textbooks.

Three short examples can be presented as illustrating the interdisciplinary nature of the subject.

Beowulf *and Sutton Hoo*

The discovery of the Anglo-Saxon ship-burial at Sutton Hoo presented literary scholars with a glimpse into burial practices which illuminated customs described in *Beowulf*, and more importantly with a wealth of artefacts that reflected and brought to life some of the details in the poem. In a reverse twist of fate, *Beowulf* was actually cited at the inquiry that was launched after the discovery of Sutton Hoo, to decide whether the treasure was the property of the Crown or property of the landowner. For key studies of the relationship between the poem and archaeological finds see Cramp (1968), Davidson (1980), and Hills (1996).

The Benedictine Revival and Carolingian art

The explosion of literary activity in the mid-10th century as a result of the Benedictine Revival is one of the notable milestones of Old English literature. The chief protagonists in this were St Dunstan, St Æthelwold, and St Oswald. Faced with the rebuilding of the Benedictine monastic order after the wars with the Vikings they looked abroad to the monasteries of mainland Europe, notably those of the Carolingian Empire. As well as influencing the focus and practices of religious prose, the Benedictine Revival had a considerable impact on the art of the period. The so-called Winchester School of art, which emerged at the time, copies many motifs and ideas from Carolingian art, which in turn had been influenced by Byzantine art. Not only does this illuminate the artistic practices, it also provides evidence for the religious and literary direction of the period (in such writers as Ælfric), and the renewed political and social ties with mainland Europe.

Social and political context of 14th-century poetry

Many 14th-century poets, notably Langland and Gower, describe and comment on their society in their works, criticising its flaws and looking for ways of reforming it. Their poems include references, commentary, and direct or allegorical descriptions of such things as the Peasants' Revolt of 1381, the Wycliffite movement, social changes caused by the Black Death, increased social mobility, and the rise of the professional and middle classes. They actively engage in contemporary debates about kingship and government, the role of the Church, and the responsibilities of different social classes.

Even the less political poetry of Chaucer is steeped in the social and political thought of its time. The traditional model of society as consisting of three estates, including those who work, those who fight, and those who pray (e.g. the Knight, the Parson, the Ploughman), is used in the description of the pilgrims in *The Canterbury Tales*. It offers idealised and satirical portraits of the representatives of the traditional three estates, yet at the same time presents a disorganised (or at least more complicated) society via the range of pilgrims, an example being the depiction of the Church through the characters of the Parson, the Summoner, the Pardoner, and the Friar. They all reveal the various attitudes (both positive and negative) to the Church and the roles that it attracted, which in turn reflect the unparalleled (to that point) questioning and criticism of its practices that had emerged throughout the 14th century. Similarly Chaucer's *The Parliament of Fowls* is ostensibly about love and attitudes to love and sexuality, but it is also about plurality, the stratification of society, and the views and customs of different classes. The themes of love and nature progressively widen as Chaucer introduces the ideas of social harmony, responsibility, and the love of 'comune profyt'; and represents social order as part of the natural order.

See also   Chapter 1(f) for the use of the estates model in Old English.

Further Reading

For introductory works on medieval art see Alexander (1975), Backhouse et al. (1984), Camille (1992 and 1996), Marks and Morgan (1981), Webster and Backhouse (1991), Wilson (1984), and Zarnecki et al. (1984). For material relating specifically to archaeology see Hines (2004), which outlines links across chronological periods, but also Cramp (1968), Davidson (1980), Hills (1996), Karkov (1995), and Wilson 1981) for Anglo-Saxon archaeology; and Aston (1993), Clarke (1984), Greene (1992), Grenville (1997), Kenyon (1990), Platt (1994), Rodwell (1989), and Schofield and Vince (1994) for late medieval archaeology. On Anglo-Saxon architecture see Taylor and Taylor (1965–78), and on late medieval architecture see Johnson (1990) and Webb (1956). Important works on late medieval culture and society include Horrox (1994), Huizinga (1955), Keen (1984), Medcalf (1981), Myers (1952), Scattergood and Sherborne (1983), Southern (1953), and Swanson (2000).

(j) Editorial Practices

Students of medieval literature will be exposed to the texts of the period mainly through modern scholarly editions. These may appear in anthologies and coursebooks, or in printed and (increasingly) web-based publications which focus on a single text. It is important therefore that one becomes familiar with the types of editions that are generally available and how to interact with them.

There are several different types of editions that one will encounter. The first, and simplest to understand, is the 'facsimile edition', which presents you with photographs (paper-based or digital) of the manuscript containing the selected text. Although these may have some preliminary explanatory material, a bibliography, and in a digital edition multiple sets of images and special tools for their study, predominantly they simply offer a substitute for accessing the manuscript or manuscripts in real life. In other words there has been little or no editorial intervention. Good examples of this appear in the series entitled *Early English Manuscripts in Facsimile* and as part of the Early English Text Society's publications.

Editorial intervention is much more obvious in the 'diplomatic edition'. This usually focuses on a single manuscript but this time presents a transcript of its contents (i.e. not in photograph format). It may seem to be a straightforward record of what appears in the manuscript because editors of diplomatic texts try to preserve as much of the original as possible. Thus a diplomatic edition may retain not only manuscript orthography but also punctuation, capitalisation, features of the layout and sometimes abbreviations and variant letter forms. One should remember, however, that even when editors simply try to copy what they see in a manuscript, making as few changes as possible, such transcription and subsequent presentation of the text may require making numerous decisions and interpretations. Identifying letter forms in manuscripts, deciding which marks on the page are meaningful, which features of presentation are 'part of the text' and which are decorative or accidental, can result in a highly interpretative outcome. To give just a few examples, the spacing between words in manuscripts is often uneven and it may not be clear whether the spelling is as one word or two, or even something else. Similarly, capital letters are not always clearly distinguished from lower case and there may be a hierarchy of capitals used for different divisions within the text. Finally, the scribal styles of writing were much more intimately connected with the type of text than modern-day fonts are, and could convey important contextual information. Representing such features in a diplomatic edition may present considerable difficulties, and these difficulties are largely conceptual rather than technical. Many meaningful characteristics of writing and textual presentation were used inconsistently or had multiple functions in handwritten documents. An editor may have to make an interpretative decision in all such cases in order to provide modern typographical equivalents.

It has to be said that facsimiles and diplomatic editions are rare in the books most students will encounter. Predominantly one is exposed to a text where there has been considerable editorial intervention at all levels, and which is surrounded by 'critical apparatus' (the record of textual variants), as well as glossaries, footnotes, end notes, and so on. The important thing to recognise here, from the outset, is that any edition of this kind involves numerous decisions made by the editors concerning what to keep in, what to leave out, what to change, and so on. Thus, if two editors edit the same text they may differ in their decisions and the text presented may itself vary.

As noted in Chapter 4(d), medieval works survive to us in manuscripts, or handwritten documents. Usually the first task of the editors is to locate all the surviving manuscripts that contain the text or part of the text. They will then transcribe these and attempt to collate them. At this point ideologies and methodologies differ. For example, in terms of editorial beliefs, Scragg and Szarmach note that there are:

> Those who believe that they can ascertain and fix a text once and for all and those who believe that such certitude is neither possible nor desirable.   (Scragg and Szarmach, 1994, p. 2)

Szarmach (1997) suggests that in practice, opinion is divided between the 'optimist' and 'recensionist' traditions. The former would consider all the manuscript versions, select one of these as the 'best' text, and produce an edition of that single witness.[13] The recensionist tradition, on the other hand, would bring all the copies of a text together and collate readings from all of them, describing their relationship to one another. By extension, recensionists can even attempt to re-create a non-existent master from which the surviving witnesses presumably originated.

What do editors make decisions about? First there is the need to decide about which manuscript reading to follow, if two or more of them differ. What usually happens is that the editor will tend to stick consistently to one witness (his or her base manuscript) and only vary if they consider it to be clearly wrong (or where the 'text breaks down', Szarmach, 1997, p. 127; see also Hill, 1994). However, what is common is for the editor to note these changes, and to record readings from other manuscripts (termed 'variants'), usually at the bottom of the page or as end notes. Szarmach suggests that changing the text of the best or the only manuscript witness is probably the most contentious area of editing, and 'to intervene or not to intervene is still the practical question for an editor . . . when the text fails' (1997, p. 132).

The editor will then need to make decisions about punctuation. Medieval manuscripts often have little punctuation, and when it is used it is very different from modern practices and may indicate, for example, the metrical structure of verse but not its division into sentences, phrases, and so on. Editorial punctuation will reflect the editor's understanding and interpretation of the text and thus different editions could well vary in their use of punctuation.

The editor will also need to make a decision as to the layout of the text. This will range from lineation decisions, page layout (see below), and even whether to present a text as verse or not (in the case of Ælfric and his rhythmical prose, and some early Middle English poetry and rhythmical prose). When the text is in verse an editor may have to make further decisions to do with its layout. This may involve answering such questions as what constitutes a metrical line and should therefore start on a new line on the page; whether to emphasise the caesura (mid-line metrical pause) with a break, whether to capitalise initial letters of metrical lines, and so on. Such decisions will depend on the editor's understanding of the text's metrical form, but also partly on previous editorial tradition. One of the key decisions in terms of page layout, however, is how to present the Modern English equivalent (if indeed one decides to). In this case there are four standard practices:

---

[13] It should be noted that in the case of Old English poetry there often is only one manuscript copy and thus the choice is already made.

(1) Present only the Modern English translation, i.e. do not present the original text. See, for example, Crossley-Holland (2002), Spearing (1998), and Moseley (1983).

(2) Present a facing translation (i.e. the Modern English sits opposite the original text). See, for example, Cartlidge (2001), Treharne (2004) and Lee and Solopova (2005).

(3) Present only the original text but with a 'running gloss'. Here the key words that may cause difficulties are glossed at the end of each line. See, for example, Sands (1986) and Marsden (2004).

(4) Present a stand-alone original text but with a glossary at the end of the book. See for example, Mitchell and Robinson (2001) and Benson (1987).

Translations can offer students a quick and easy access to the text but can also create difficulties. Translators always have to face choices over which Modern English words they will use, and can never really present the full range of possibilities found in the original. Moreover they are usually attempting to offer a translation that can be 'read' by an average reader and thus may use modern syntax, and possibly simplified vocabulary and style. Translators also need to decide whether they render poetry as prose, and if attempting to maintain verse structure, whether they try to retain alliteration, rhyme, and other metrical features. In general the translation tends to be more readable than the original, but often as a result of sacrificing its complexity and uniqueness. Because of this, students who slavishly follow a modern translation without consulting the original will face problems.

Glossaries can be extremely useful, of course, but also require some understanding. The standard format is to present the original word as a lemma, using nominative singular forms for nouns and adjectives, and infinitives for verbs. Bearing in mind that words may appear in a number of different spellings and grammatical forms, especially in the heavily inflected language of Old English, students will often be relying on cross-referencing. Key tips that should be used to assist in navigating glossaries are:

- Always familiarise yourself with the abbreviations used. Standards are: n = nominative; a = accusative; g = genitive; d = dative; i = instrumental; m = masculine; f = feminine; n = neuter; s = singular; p = plural; pres. ptc. = present participle; pptc. = past participle; pres. = present; prêt. = preterite (the past tense); 1 = first person; 2 = second person; 3 = third person. Glossaries may also have ways of referencing particular words from particular texts, e.g. in Mitchell and Robinson (2001), '3/14' would mean the word occurs in text '3' on line 14.

- For Old English, familiarise yourself with the order of the alphabet. In particular, words beginning with þ or ð will all be listed under the former after entries for 'T'. Words beginning with æ will be listed after 'A'. Words beginning with the *ge-* prefix can often cause problems as they are frequently listed under the third letter in the case of verbs (e.g. *gebindan* would be under 'B'). Finally, proper nouns often have their own separate glossary.

Further Reading

For good introductions to editing, and the problems that beset editors, see Edwards (1996), Hill (1994), McCarren and Moffat (1998), McKenzie (1999), Minnis and Brewer (1992), Moorman (1975), Rigg (1977), Scragg and Szarmach (1994), Szarmach (1997), and Tanselle (1983).

(k)   Theoretical Approaches

It is reasonably true to say that the 'formal' application of literary theory to the study of medieval literature came late in the day. Courses in universities and colleges tended to follow a traditional route of translating key texts, writing essays on key themes, and occasionally looking at the historical or artistic context of the piece. This certainly is the perceived wisdom and has done nothing to dissuade people from the view that medieval literature is an antiquarian subject surrounded by outdated and culturally irrelevant texts and practices. Yet this somewhat disguises the truth. Although it is only over the last fifteen to twenty years that medieval scholars have engaged fully with the terminology of literary theorists, there is no doubt that in the past they have adopted many of their practices and stances. Even the briefest of surveys reveals a willingness by scholars of the past to consider such things as:

- the historical and social context of the text and author;
- how the text can further our understanding of the society of the time, and the place in society of the men and women portrayed;

- the nature of the intended audience for the texts and the delivery of the text;
- the nature of the dissemination of the text, and textual authority;
- the links between medieval literature, history, art, religious practices, and architecture;
- the links to practices, beliefs, and the literature of other contemporary cultures;
- the place of medieval English literature in the context of medieval European literature.

This demonstrates the wide range of approaches medieval scholars have adopted in the past. Moreover, the traditional approaches, such as close analysis and explanation of the text and the search for sources and analogues, which at first appear to adopt a purely text-centred approach, could be argued as going hand in hand with 'historicism', 'interdisciplinarity', and 'intertextuality'.

The 'text-centred' approach

Considering the history of medieval literary studies, the dominant theoretical approach has undoubtedly been a 'text-centred' one. Philology was the driving force of many early studies (going back to the 16th and 17th centuries) as scholars attempted to understand the language better, and to place it in its context among other ancient and modern European languages. Unsurprisingly then, the new criticism approach was a natural extension of this in that it advocated a close reading of the text, focusing directly on syntax, vocabulary, themes, metaphors, etc., and rejecting extra-textual material such as biographies (see below).[14]

The 'text-centred' approach, however, extends beyond simple close reading. It covers research into stylistic influences, such as the use of classical rhetorical devices by medieval authors, and source studies. More importantly, it widens the field to look at comparative literature, especially in terms of intertextuality; for example, asking how one text relates to another. This can include comparing the text with other surviving pieces in the same language, but also with texts in other languages (especially Old Irish, Old Welsh, and Old Norse for Old English, and French and Italian for Middle English) to see if any commonalities can be discerned. Lapidge (1997) provides a good

---

[14] For a brief introduction to structuralist and post-structuralist approaches to Old English literature see Pasternack (1997).

example of the 'comparative approach' wherein he uses the headings: 'literary movements and trends', 'motifs, types, and themes', and 'genres and forms'. Undoubtedly this type of study has been eased by the advent of new technologies that allow scholars access to complete corpora of texts for searching and analysing. The hypertext medium of the Web can also help to clearly demonstrate associations between different texts.

Yet the domination of the text-centred school has been diminishing for some time to be replaced by other approaches to the literature (Frantzen, 1990, p. 20). In particular there is growing interest in studying 'the relation of texts to other material forms of society and culture' (Lees, 1999, p. 13). Yet in so doing, scholars find that the peculiar aspects of medieval literature throw up some fascinating questions. In particular the uncertainties over who the author was, and the text's unity, intention, and date. These are often inherent in much of early medieval literature and offer the critic considerable challenges.

What follows then is a look at some of the other main approaches and theories which are applied to medieval literary studies. This cannot be an exhaustive study but it attempts to bring together some of the main discussions that medievalists have concentrated on.

New Historicism

The New Historicist approach, emerging in the 1980s, views a literary work as a product of its time. It looks at the text in context by considering historical documents and cultural artefacts, whilst at the same time it uses the literature to further understand the period in question. Key steps involve looking at the other texts that the author and his or her audience would have had access to in order to establish a context for a literary work.

This more or less has been the dominant approach of most medieval scholars. Indeed, as one scholar suggests, 'all works on Old English language and literature are historical in method and intent' (Howe, 1997, p. 79), or as Swanson (2000, p. 397) argues:

> To understand him [Chaucer] properly requires an appreciation of the world in and for which he produced his works, which in turn necessitates some consideration of social structures.

Making such links and attempting to relate the text to its surrounding historical, social, and cultural context seems natural to many (see, for example, Greenfield and Calder, 1986). The list at the beginning of this section indicates the importance of this model – we can see attempts by scholars to place key texts alongside historical events, analogous material in other contemporary literature, artistic movements, changes in religious practices, and so on. However, a few examples drawn from both Old English and Middle English will serve to illustrate this further.

In Old English, a straightforward example would be Conner (2005), who attempts to link the contents of the Exeter Book to the emergence of city guilds in the later Anglo-Saxon period – providing a direct link between the literature and a change in social structure. In Middle English there are similar examples. The relationship of Chaucer to his political and social surroundings, for example, has often led to scholarly investigations. Can we discern Chaucer's views on his contemporary society, and by extrapolation, his audience's views? If we can, does this affect our interpretation of the text? Strohm (1989), by way of example, argued that the social contacts of Chaucer, and by extension his intended audience, could lead us to a changed perception of his major works. His *Book of the Duchess* and *Trolius and Criseyde* were written during the time when he had direct contact with the nobility, and reflect the need to address that specific audience; whereas *The Canterbury Tales* emerged during his estrangement from court and have a wider base. Chaucer's language in the *Tales* also implies to Strohm (p. 65) that he was envisaging 'an audience of distant and future readers' with which the author would have little to no contact.

One of the major writers in this area is Aers (e.g. Aers, 1986), whose underlying principle, clearly a New Historicist one, is that both the author and the reader are shaped by their social and historical context, and we must understand these to fully interpret the text. Aers suggests with Chaucer, for example, that such an understanding can reveal to us that not only was the writer reflecting his society and contemporary attitudes, but he was also openly dissecting them for analysis and criticism.

Another good example of placing Middle English literature in its context can be seen in Brewer and Gibson's *Companion* to the writings of the *Gawain*-poet (Brewer and Gibson, 1997). Here, as well as the expected essays on the poems, there are also essays on the historical background to the texts, the geography of England, castles, feasts, hunts, jewellery, armour, and so on.

Gender Studies (including Queer Studies)

Gender Studies focuses on the issues surrounding sex, sexuality, and the roles and attitudes of different genders (i.e. male and female). In medieval scholarship there is an established tradition of Gender Studies, and it is now complemented by the emerging theoretical field of Queer Studies.

Scholars pursuing the former are interested in the roles of the different genders, and depictions of femininity and masculinity (see Chapter 2(j), for example, for a discussion of 'heroism'). Undoubtedly, when concentrating on attitudes to women and their depiction in the text, more work is evident in the Middle English arena. This is due naturally in part to the much larger corpus, but also to the fact that there we can find not only more female characters but also female authors. That is not to say that Women's Studies does not have a strong foothold in Old English – Olsen (1997), Lees (1997), Damico and Hennessey (1990), and the more specialised studies of Horner (2001), or Lees and Overing (2001), prove otherwise – but the major studies have been in the later period.

In Middle English scholarship we see research focusing on the inherent messages within texts aimed at women, the writings by or about women, depictions of women, and anti-feminism. Equally prominent are studies concerned with the status and role of women in contemporary society, and subsequent interpretations and appropriations of female characters. For discussions of all of these see Blamires (1997), Evans and Johnson (1994), Fenster (1996), Hallett (2000), Meale (1996), and Millett and Wogan-Browne (1990).

For illustration we can look at three examples. Hansen (1992), in her work on Chaucer's *The Legend of Good Women*, studied the way attitudes to women are transposed to the male characters ('feminisation'). She argues that Chaucer is ostensibly trying to illustrate the demasculisation of men brought about by love, and is not concentrating on the role of women at all. Hansen claims that Chaucer's work reinforces male positions in spite of its apparent focus on women, and objects to a notion of Chaucer as a feminist writer, proposed by some earlier critics (see, for example, Dinshaw, 1989). Moreover, in her analysis of the portrayal of the Wife of Bath, Hansen argues that Chaucer is adopting a misogynist view of Alison, turning her into a character that endorses rather than challenges anti-feminist attitudes.

Dinshaw and Wallace (2003) present us with the expected essays on the major female writers of the period (Margery Kempe, Julian of

Norwich, etc.), but we can also see interesting explorations of the various 'estates' of women (childhood, celibacy, marriage, widow-hood), and how they influence women's roles as authors and audience of literary works. In a similar vein, Erler (2002) investigates the literacy of women, including the scope of their reading and their access to books. In all these studies the discussions move beyond simple literary analysis to historical investigation of women's experience of life in medieval society.

An interesting study by Lochrie (2003) brings us to Queer Studies. This approach, in its widest interpretation, looks at any form of sexual orientation or gender-bending that would be considered different from the 'norm' in terms of the culture which produced the text. In Medieval Studies this tends to concentrate on same-sex relationships and the associated imagery (e.g. homoeroticism). Lochrie, for example, explores the relationships between women in medieval literature. She notes a misogynist attitude towards the simple verbal exchanges between women (which rapidly become characterised as 'gossip') and to the notion of lesbian relationships (as alluded to, for example, in the *Ancrene Wisse*). She perceives from this that many contemporary writers and commentators saw same-sex relationships between women as being 'more frequent than those of men' (p. 80), but also recognises that Gower, in his *Confessio Amantis* for example, takes a much more lenient view in the story of Iphis and Ianthe (p. 81).

Queer Studies is a growing field of scholarship, especially in Middle English (though notably Frantzen, 1998, begins his exploration in Old English). Many studies (e.g. Klosowska, 2005) seem to draw heavily on the works of the French theorist Jacques Lacan, and look to such motifs as cross-dressing, same-sex relationships (friendships and sexual), and homoerotic imagery. Immediately they often raise the question of what would have seemed queer to a Middle English audience (i.e. different from the norm). Zeikowitz (2003), for example, looks at the homoerotic imagery that emerges from the close male relationships within the chivalric world, as depicted in *Troilus and Criseyde* or *Sir Gawain and the Green Knight*. Yet the study conjectures that such acts as men kissing, expressing adoration for each other, forming lifelong bonds, or eulogising over fellow knights, would not have seemed unsettling to the medieval audience at all and therefore could be argued as being 'not-queer'. Once we acknowledge this we can see that the medieval audience was able to recognise the possibility of male–male relationships at a deeper level of sophistication and understanding than more recent generations can.

Where 'queer' is used by an author it can be presented as a means of challenging the audience. Gilbert (1997), for example, analyses the depiction of gender and sexual transgression in the works of the *Gawain*-poet. She concludes that all poems affirm proper conduct, but all have elements of sexual transgression in them (e.g. Gawain kissing Bertilak while attempting to conceal the Lady's gift of a girdle) which would have been of concern to the characters and author. She concludes that *Sir Gawain* is the most complicated of the three texts (compared with *Cleanness* and *Pearl*), and that the sexuality of the characters is its over-riding theme, stemming chiefly from the protagonist's paranoia over his celibacy. But why should this be? Pugh (2004) presents a possible answer, seeing the use of 'queer' (as in – 'against the norm') within the texts as a form of characterisation empowering or disabling the characters, but outside of the text as a means of shocking the audience into adopting a more pure and Christian lifestyle.

Postcolonialism

It may seem strange to include postcolonialism in this survey, as it tends to be associated with the writings of people in countries previously colonised in the 18th and 19th centuries. If, however, we adopt the wider definition of 'the literature of people suppressed' we can see that it does have application in the Middle Ages. If we consider the minority and subjugated voices of medieval England, outside of the imbalance between genders, this primarily focuses on the indigenous population. In the Old English period we have the conquest of the British by the Anglo-Saxons, and the few glimpses found in writers such as Gildas of the attitudes of the conquered. After 1066 it was the Anglo-Saxons who were to feel the heel of oppression under the Normans, and then the Irish, the Scots, and the Welsh following the subsequent invasions. In the collection edited by Cohen (2000), we can see analyses of all of these, plus a study of attitudes towards Orientalism, Jews, and Saracens. The editor argues that by adopting a postcolonial approach to medieval literature we begin to break certain strangleholds and in so doing decentre Europe and displace Christianity, replacing both with a promotion of the marginalised.

Postcolonial Studies would also be interested in the growth of Empire. In the Old English period this would tie in with attempts to develop a national identity by Alfred and the Kings of Wessex, and after the Conquest with the attempts to argue for the continued links with the French mainland by the Plantagenets. We would also be interested in seeing how the effects of Empire can alter the interpretation of a specific writer. An example of such investigation is Bowers (2000), who looks at how Chaucer's writings were re-used after his death by the expansionist Lancastrians.

Psychoanalytic literary theory

This approach, based originally on the work of Sigmund Freud, seeks to analyse the text as a means of ascertaining more about the author, or a character, and their way of thinking. In particular psychoanalytic criticism attempts to go beyond analysis which entirely relies on claims made by authors explicitly in their texts. Psychoanalytic critics use the study of language, contradictions, silences, and ambiguities in the text as a means of looking beyond what texts explicitly proclaim. A psychoanalytical approach can be seen in Staley (2000) for example. She explores Chaucer's ideas of personal identity, looking in particular at his characterisations. She demonstrates how Chaucer uses language, actions, dress, emblems, and so on to reveal the subconscious attitudes of his pilgrims and their individual attempts to express their unique identity.

The author, the reader, and literacy

Critical studies centred on the author and the reader (in particular reader-response theory) throw up some interesting issues with medieval literature, especially in the earlier period. These also by and large affect many of the above theoretical approaches. Principally this settles on the issue of how much we know about the date, authorship, and provenance of the text. Until we are certain about these it is very difficult to elaborate on discussions of the author or the reader, or the historical context. Yet at the same time that does not preclude such discussions. As we noted in the section on *Beowulf* (Chapter 2(n)), the uncertainties about when it was written, who it was written by, and for what audience or purpose, have engendered lively debates which have led to wider discussions about Anglo-Saxon society. This issue tends to dissipate somewhat when we move to the Middle English period, but even then we are still presented with a series of unknowns.

To begin with, let us consider an 'author-centred' approach, i.e. discussions concerning the author, authorship, and by consequence the authority of a text. Medieval literature, especially Old English, enforces a new attitude to this as most of the material is anonymous.

Swan (2001, p. 73) notes that 'we cannot "construct" an individual author . . . and therefore cannot use what we define as significant about the author's personality to interpret the text'. She argues that this has led to the side-lining of Old English by critics intent on the pursuit of the author, but concludes that:

> The fact that it is possible for people to write texts and *not* put their names to them has profound implications for the nature of Anglo-Saxon textual culture and for the applicability of our concepts of authorship, textuality, creativity and originality.   (Swan, 2001, p. 73; our emphasis).

In addition, when we consider the texts that survive in manuscripts does the notion of an author really exist? In the case of writers like Ælfric or Wulfstan the answer may be 'yes', as they state their authorship, but even then challenges arise. First, as source studies demonstrate, writers such as Ælfric were drawing on previous texts; indeed he often cited these to give 'authority' to his arguments. Could he then be considered the author if he is presenting a close translation or paraphrase? Moreover, because of the lack of textual 'fixity' in the medieval period, even Ælfrician texts that survive to us do so in different versions, with interventions by later anonymous scribes. As Pasternack observes, 'manuscript texts, like oral productions, could be remade and recontextualized with any new production' (Pasternack, 1995, p. 200). Scribes often altered and reinterpreted a text, and this was perfectly acceptable practice. Who then is the author? Moreover, is there a single author? The issue becomes even more complicated with anonymous verse, which may have had a lengthy and complex textual transmission. The questions of whether one can or should attempt to identify 'a' poet, and how we should understand the unity of the text, have appeared in key studies such as those by the early 'liedertheorists', and researches into the oral-formulaic style and composition (see Chapter 2(h)).

Similar challenges arise in applying reader-response studies. This concentrates on the experience of the reader or audience of the text, in terms of who they were, how they encountered the text, and how they interpreted it. Questions along the lines of 'Who was the intended audience of *Beowulf*?' or 'What would a monk have made of the message in *The Battle of Maldon*?' appear regularly in scholarly articles and point again to a lack of certainty. In some cases the audience of a text is defined: thus in Ælfric's homily on the Old Testament Book of Judith the epilogue is clearly aimed at nuns. However, this may not always have been the case. The epilogue could easily have been added at a later stage to form an exegesis of the text specifically aimed at nuns, with the main story being targeted at a wider audience. Such adaptation of texts for different audiences is well attested in the Middle English period, particularly in the case of popular religious works. Thus the author of the *Ancrene Wisse* says that he is writing in response to a request from three well-born sisters, who adopted the life of anchoresses. There is evidence, however, that the work was written with a wider audience in mind, and early in its history it was revised and adapted for different audiences, and also translated into Latin and Anglo-Norman.

In Middle English we often have more certainties about the text and the author, and its historical context, than in Old English. We have noted above Strohm's (1989) study into Chaucer's intended audience, and Clopper (1991) demonstrates how clues within the morality play *Mankind* can provide evidence of its staging and audience. He deduces, for example, from evidence within the text, that it would have been staged indoors for a learned aristocratic audience.

Clopper is illustrative of another concept we must be aware of when approaching medieval literature, namely 'performance'. With modern literature we can be fairly certain of the interaction the audience/reader has with the text – a play is seen communally in a theatre, a novel is read by an individual, poetry may be read or recited, and so on. We can also be fairly certain of the levels of literacy. Such certainties may not exist in the earlier period.

For example, what did 'reading' mean in the medieval period? We assume that this was generally aloud, either in solitude or to a public audience. We also deduce that many poems and sermons may have been intended solely for oral delivery in the Anglo-Saxon period, but later on this may have changed (see Howe, 2002; or Magennis, 2001). The oral culture and the nature of restricted literacy (which existed throughout the Middle Ages, see below) allowed the non-literate to be exposed to literature via the notion of 'textual communities', where the audience had access to scholars who could read for them and/or interpret the meaning for them.[15] The study of such communities is particularly important for understanding female authors and audiences, who in many cases did not have access to literacy in English or Latin (see Chapter 3(j) and below).

Many scholars have tried to identify formal features in surviving

---

[15] Ælfric's exegeses of homilies, for example, provided the monastic houses with such a 'community'.

texts that could point to an oral origin, transmission, or reception. For example, does *Hwæt* ('Lo!') at the opening of an Old English poem indicate it was only ever intended to be performed, not read? Does the oral rhetoric in Middle English romances and Chaucer's poetry mean that these works were written for public rather than private reading? Does the runic signature of Cynewulf indicate that his text was intended to be read from the page, as this is the only way one could have understood the puzzle? Does the *Her* ('here, at this point') opening of many of the annals in the *Anglo-Saxon Chronicle* show that the intended audience was a reader, as it refers to the specific date on the page? Similarly an early 15th-century manuscript of Chaucer's *Troilus and Criseyde* (Cambridge, Corpus Christi College, MS. 61) has a miniature which shows Chaucer reading to a courtly audience. Is this reliable evidence as to how his works reached their public, or is it a traditional portrait of an idealised author, one of many conventional 'author portraits' found in manuscripts at the beginnings of texts? The appearance of illuminations on the manuscript page makes the discussions even more complicated. Clearly this is decorative art that was intended to be viewed, but does this also indicate that the text was intended to be read?

The transition from an oral culture to a literate one is also a topic for analysis filled with uncertainties; namely, when the written word came to be viewed as the main means of communication (O'Brien O'Keeffe, 1990; and Wilcox, 2001). Howe (2002, p. 18), for example, argues that the repeated opposition between an oral culture and a literate culture is in fact facile and there is no clear point of transition between illiteracy and literacy. Indeed, is there any point in even attempting to answer the question? As is clear, the majority of the population remained illiterate and would stay so until the educational initiatives of the Victorian age, so it was never a fully 'literate' culture. Moreover, how do we define 'literacy'? Throughout the medieval period it appears that there were different levels of 'literacy'. The Middle English women mystics, for example, refer to themselves as illiterate, but demonstrate familiarity with a wide range of texts. Such knowledge could result, of course, from listening to sermons and books being read out loud, and taking part in theological discussions. On the other hand, a person might be able to read, but not necessarily write; or one could read and write, but not master the art of interpretation. To add to the complexity there is the difference between clerical and lay literacy, and the levels of literacy in Latin, English, and in the Middle English period, French.

Medieval literary theory

We also should not overlook research into medieval literary theory and the theory of language. A major step in this area was the publication of A. J. Minnis's *Medieval Theory of Authorship* in 1984. This and subsequent studies (particularly Minnis and Scott, 1988, and Wogan-Browne et al., 1999) demonstrated the sophistication and variety of medieval views on authorship, historiography, translation, language, genre, and much else. Scholars started to use medieval theoretical discussions in their interpretations of medieval texts and in research into their production, reception, and transmission. A major area of interest is the influence of Latin literacy on vernacular writing, including its style, its influences on approaches to authorship, and how it can assist in the understanding of various aspects of literary works. Contemporary theoretical discussions of literature and language are often found in prologues and epilogues to Old and Middle English Latin and vernacular texts. Medieval prologues and epilogues represent a literary convention which performed some of the functions reserved in modern literature for title pages and introductions. Prologues and epilogues were used by writers to declare their names, and to discuss their intentions, and the audience and the circumstances of their work. They were also used to set up a context for the works through references to other texts, to influence readers' responses, and to discuss various controversial and theoretical issues (such as the methods and appropriateness of biblical translation). Medieval literary theory is a new area of research in the field which is proving to be exceptionally promising and illuminating.

What is 'medieval' in any case?

Finally, the very definition of 'medieval', Old English, and the transition to Middle English is also now open to much discussion. Frantzen (1990, p. 19) argued, for example, that we needed to break down the barriers between Old English and early Middle English to avoid artificial separation and demonstrate continuity. It has been clear to linguists for a long time that the linguistic boundary between Old and Middle English is not very well marked, and that it is difficult to answer the question 'When did Middle English begin?' Many linguistic developments which we find in early Middle English are present already in late Old English (see, for example, McCully and Hilles, 2005, pp. 241–4, who use the interlinear gloss to the Lindisfarne Gospels to demonstrate linguistic changes, such as inflectional loss, in late 10th-century Old English). In a similar vein then, we would look at the work being undertaken by Mary Swan and Elaine Treharne (2000) on the survival of Old English into the 12th and 13th centuries, which challenges the concepts of a clear barrier between the periods.

In addition, increasingly the context of medieval studies has also become more modern. There is a growing interest in showing how the literature of the period can have applicability to modern-day culture. Again Frantzen (1990, p. 17), for example, concentrates on Thomas Jefferson's interest in Old English to show to students how the literature of a 1,000 years ago could have a direct impact on the education and political thought of early American society. Included in this has been the emerging discussions surrounding the rise of 'medievalism', and appropriations and distortions of Old and Middle English literature and culture by later generations. This perhaps should not come as any surprise when one considers that the first printed edition of an Old English text appeared in the 16th-century, having been commissioned by Archbishop Matthew Parker to demonstrate its applicability to the arguments at the time between Catholics and Protestants.

See also   Chapter 2(d), (h), and (j), Chapter 3(d), (e), (j), and (t), and Chapter 4(d)–(f) and (i).

Further Reading

Studies covering this area are numerous. As well as the ones mentioned above, students who want a general introduction to literary theory could try Barry (1995) and Klarer (1999) amongst many others. For a handy reference book of historical (textual and visual) material analogous to Middle English literature see Goldie (2003). For a brief introductory study of how some of the major literary theories have been applied to Chaucer, see Ellis (2005) and Knapp (2006). For wider studies on the application of literary theory to medieval studies see Auerbach (1953), Copeland (1991), Dalrymple (2004), Ellis (1989), Frantzen (1990, 1991, and 1996), Frantzen and Niles (1997), Howe (1997 and 2002), Magennis (2001), Mahan (1991), Mann (1991 and 2002), Millett (1985), Minnis (1988), Minnis and Scott (1988), O'Brien O'Keeffe (1990 and 1997), Pasternack (1995), Patterson (1989), Simons (1993), Swan (2001), Wilcox (2001), Wogan-Browne (2002), and Wogan-Browne et al. (1999). On women writers see also *Feminae* (www.haverford.edu/library/reference/mschaus/mfi/mfi.html), Medieval Women Writers (http://go.owu.edu/~o5medww/), and Other Women's Voices (http://home.infionline.net/~ddisse/index.html). For comparisons with texts in other languages, see for example, Boitani (1983), Calin (1994), Muscatine (1957), Pulsiano and Treharne (2001, pp. 325–400), and Wallace (1985). For an overview of discussions of literary and language in prologues and epilogues, see Galloway (2005).

For the relevance of medieval studies to more modern education and political thought, see also the collection of essays under the title 'Dragons in the Sky' (Lee and Conner, 2001). On the use of Old and Middle English literature and culture associated with the rise of medievalism: for Old English see Frantzen and Niles (1997); Pulsiano and Treharne (2001, pp. 401–505); and Scragg and Weinberg (2000). For Middle English see Ellis (2005), especially part IV for the reception of Chaucer from the 15th to 21st centuries, Chaucer in performance, and translations of his works; see also Pearsall (2003) for the account of the Arthurian tradition in early modern and modern culture.

Chronology

Key events	General remarks
360s Scots, Picts, and Saxons lead renewed attacks on Roman Britain	
406 Rhine freezes over and the western border of the Roman Empire is breeched.	Collapse of Roman rule in Britain.
410 Rome is sacked by the Goths. Roman troops pulled back from Britain for good.	
449 'Adventus Saxonum' – the arrival of the Anglo-Saxons in Britain (according to Bede).	Migration period.
477 Establishment of Sussex (traditional date).	
495 Establishment of Wessex (traditional date).	Early Anglo-Saxon kingdoms established – British pushed westwards.
***c*.500** Battle of Mons Badonicus – British resistance in the West to Saxon expansion.	
***c*.521/2** The death of Chlochilaichus (in *Historia Francorum* – 'History of the Franks' – by Gregory of Tours) during a raid on Frisian territory.	He is identified with Hygelac, Beowulf's king and uncle, and this is central for dating the events in *Beowulf*.

Key events	**General remarks**

***c.*525**
Composition of *De consolatione philosophiae* ('The Consolation of Philosophy') and the death of Boethius.

***c.*540**
Gildas produces *De excidio Britanniae* ('On the Ruin of Britain').

Arrival of Irish missionaries in Britain.

547
Ida founds the kingdom of Bernicia.

563
St Colomba founds missionary on Iona.

590
Gregory the Great becomes Pope.

597
St Augustine arrives in England, beginning the conversion of the Anglo-Saxons to Christianity

Reappearance of Roman Christianity.

***c.*602**
Possible date of Æthelberht's Law Codes, the first in English.

***c.*624**
Death of Rædwald of East Anglia, thus possible date of Sutton Hoo ship burials.

635
Lindisfarne founded.

Dominance of Northumbria.

664
Synod of Whitby.

660–70
Possible date of *Cædmon's Hymn*.

Aldhelm writing (born *c.*639, d. 709).

681
Jarrow founded.

***c.*720**
Possible date for the Lindisfarne Gospels.

Key events	General remarks
731 Bede's *Historia ecclesiastica gentis Anglorum* ('Ecclesiastical History of the English Nation').	Dominance of Kingdom of Mercia. Alcuin writing (born *c*.735, d.804).
793 Lindisfarne sacked by Vikings.	First Viking wars.
806 Iona sacked by Vikings.	
865 Great Danish Army Lands.	
867 Northumbria submits to Danish rule.	
869 East Anglia falls to the Danes, death of King Edmund.	
871 Alfred becomes king of Wessex.	King Alfred leads English resistance and begins educational programme which leads to the rise of learning, prose, and English as the language of state and church.
874 Mercia falls to the Danes.	
878 Battle of Edington – truce with Vikings declared, Danelaw established.	
937 Battle of Brunanburgh – Athelstan completes reconquest of England started by Alfred.	England a united nation.
940 St Dunstan refounds Glastonbury – beginning of the Benedictine Revival.	Benedictine Revival beings under Sts Dunstan, Æthelwold, and Oswald.

Key events	**General remarks**

990s
Ælfric begins his major series of *Catholic Homilies*.

991
Battle of Maldon, Essex; treaty between Æthelred, King of England, and Normandy.

Second Viking wars.
Composition of four great Old English poetical manuscripts (late tenth, early eleventh centuries).

1014
Wulfstan's *Sermo Lupi ad Anglos* ('Sermon of the Wolf to the English').

1016
Cnut becomes King of England.

1066
Battle of Hastings – rule of England passes to Norman hands on 25 December with the coronation of William the Conqueror.

Anselm (1033–1109).
Norman rule begins. End of Anglo-Saxon England.

1085–7
Domesday Book.

The copying of Old English verse appears to have stopped, but the copying of prose continues into the 13th century.

1100–35
Reign of Henry I.

1135–54
Reign of Stephen of Blois.

***c*.1138**
Geoffrey of Monmouth's *Historia regum Britanniae* ('History of the Kings of Britain').

1154
Last entries in *The Peterborough Chronicle*.

Most Anglo-Norman romances created between 1150 and 1230.

1154–89
Reign of Henry II.

Key events	General remarks
1155 Wace, *Roman de Brut* ('The Romance of Brut').	
***c.*1170s** *Orrmulum*.	
1170–80 *Lais* ('Lays') of Marie de France.	
1189–99 Regin of Richard I.	The establishment of universities in England and Europe (12th and 13th centuries).
1199–1216 Reign of King John.	
***c.*1200** 'Worcester Fragments'.	
1204 King John loses Normandy to Philip II of France.	Deterioration of relations between England and France.
1215 *Magna Carta* and Fourth Lateran Council.	
1216–72 Reign of Henry III.	
***c.*1220** Laȝamon's *Brut*.	
1221–4 The arrival of the Dominican and Franciscan friars in England.	
***c.*1225** *Ancrene Wisse* ('Guide for Anchoresses'), the 'Katherine group', the 'Wooing group', *King Horn*.	
1272–1307 Reign of Edward I.	The establishment of commercial book production (13th century and later).

Key events

c.1275
Guillaume de Lorris, *Roman de Rose* ('The Romance of the Rose').

c.1280s
The surviving manuscripts of *The Owl and the Nightingale*.

1296–1328
First Scottish War of Independence.

c.1290–1349
Richard Rolle.

c.1300
Cursor Mundi ('The Runner of the World'), Robert of Gloucester, *Metrical Chronicle*.

1303–38
Robert Mannyng of Brunne, *Handlyng Sinne* ('Manual of Sins'); *The Chronicle of England*.

1307–27
Reign of Edward II.

c.1324–1384
John Wyclif.

c.1325–1388
William Langland.

1327–77
Reign of Edward III.

c.1330–1408
John Gower.

1337–1453
The Hundred Years War.

General remarks

The South English Legendary originated in the west Midlands (second half of the 13th century).

*c.*1330–*c.*1440 works of Middle English 'mystics' (Richard Rolle, the anonymous author of *The Cloud of Unknowing*, Walter Hilton, Margery Kempe, and Julian of Norwich).

Key events	General remarks

1340
Dan Michel of Northgate,
Aӡenbite of Inwit ('The Biting
of Conscience').

*c.*1340–*c.*1400
Geoffrey Chaucer.

*c.*1340–*c.*1402
John of Trevisa.

1342–1416?
Julian of Norwich.

1348–51
The Black Death

The beginning of the 'Alliterative
Revival'.

1351
The Statute of Labourers.

*c.*1352
Wynnere and Wastoure
('Winner and Waster').

The beginning of the native
tradition of mystery cycles and
other religious plays (second
half of the 14th century).

1355
Guillaume de Deguilville,
Pèlerinage de la vie humaine
('The Pilgrimage of the Life of
Man').

*c.*1360
The Prick of Conscience,
French original of *Mandeville's
Travels*.

Rising demand for and
production of vernacular scientific
and practical works (most date
from the second half of the 14th
century and from the 15th
century).

*c.*1367–1426
Thomas Hoccleve.

1371–1449
John Lydgate.

*c.*1373–after 1439
Margery Kempe.

Key events	General remarks

c.1375
Northern Homily Cycle.

1376
Earliest record of York *Corpus Christi* plays; John Barbour, *The Bruce*.

1377–99
Reign of Richard II.

c.1377
Langland, *Piers Plowman* (B text).

1380s
The Cloud of Unknowing, Chaucer, *Troilus and Criseyde*; the Wycliffite Bible.

1381
The Peasants' Revolt.

1387
John of Trevisa's translation of the *Polychronicon* of Ranulf Higden.

1390
Gower, *Confessio Amantis* ('The Lover's Confession').

1390s
Chaucer, *The Canterbury Tales*.

c.1396
Walter Hilton, *The Scale of Perfection*.

Attempts to suppress the Lollard movement (*De heretico comburendo*, 'Concerning Heretic who should be Burned', of 1401, and Arundel's Constitutions, of 1407–9).

1399–1413
Reign of Henry IV.
*c.*1400
Alliterative and stanzaic *Morte Arthure* ('The Death of Arthur'); Manuscript of *Sir Gawain*, *Pearl*, *Cleanness* and *Patience*.

Key events	General remarks

1411–12
Hoccleve, *The Regiment of Princes*.

1413–22
Reign of Henry V.

*c.*1420
The Book of Margery Kempe.

1422
Accession of Henry VI.

1424
Death of Nicholas Love.

1431–8
Lydgate, *The Fall of Princes*.

*c.*1435
James I, *The Kingis Quair*
('King's Book').

1438
Gilte Legende ('The Golden
Legend').

1455
First battle in the Wars of the
Roses.

*c.*1460–*c.*1520
William Dunbar.

1461
Deposition of Henry VI; accession
of Edward IV.

*c.*1470
Morality plays *Wisdom*, *Mankind*.

1470–1
Restoration and murder of Henry VI;
Edward IV regains throne.

1470s
Robert Henryson, *Morall Fabillis*
('Moral Fables'), *Testament of
Cresseid*, *Orpheus and Eurydice*.

Key events	General remarks

1473–4
Caxton, *Le recuyell des histoires de Troie* ('The collection of Trojan histories'), the first book printed in English.

1476
Caxton returns to England and sets up a shop near Westminster Abbey with a small printing press.

1476–1522
Gavin Douglas.

1477
Blind Hary, *The Wallace*.

References

Abbott, Christopher (1999) *Julian of Norwich: Autobiography and Theology* (Cambridge: D. S. Brewer).

Acker, P. (1998) *Revising Oral Theory: Formulaic Composition in Old English and Old Icelandic Verse* (London: Garland).

Aers, David (1986) *Chaucer*, (Brighton: Harvester Press).

—— (1975) *Piers Plowman and Christian Allegory*, (London: Edward Arnold).

Aertsen, H. and Bremmer, R. H. (eds) (1994) *A Companion to Old English Poetry* (Amsterdam: University Press).

Alexander, J. J. (1975) 'The Middle Ages' in David Piper (ed.), *The Genius of British Painting* (London: Weidenfeld and Nicolson).

Alexander, M. (trans.) (1966) *The Earliest English Poems* (London: Penguin).

Alford, John A. (ed.) (1988) *A Companion to Piers Plowman* (Berkeley and Los Angeles: University of California Press).

Algeo, J. and Pyles, T. (2005) *The Origins and Development of the English Language*, 5th edn (Boston, MA: Thomson Wadsworth).

Allen, M. J. B. and Calder, D. G. (trans.) (1976) *Sources and Analogues of Old English Poetry: The Major Latin Texts in Translation* (Cambridge: D. S. Brewer).

Allen, Rosamund (trans.) (1992) *Brut* (New York: St Martin's Press).

Allen, Rosamund, Perry, Lucy and Roberts, Jane Annette (eds) (2002) *Laʒamon: Contexts, Language, and Interpretation*, King's College London Medieval Studies no. 19 (London: King's College, London, Centre for Late Antique and Medieval Studies).

Allott, S. (ed.) (1974) *Alcuin of York, c.AD 732 to 804: His Life and Letters* (York: William Sessions).

Amsler, Mark E. (1980) 'Literary Theory and the Genres of Middle English Literature', *Genre* 13, pp. 389–96.

Anderson, E. R. (2002) 'Social Idealism in Ælfric's Colloquy', in R. M. Liuzza (ed.) (2002), pp. 204–14.

Anderson, R. S. (2005) 'Saints' Legends', in Fulk and Cain (eds) (2005), pp. 87–105.

Andrew, Malcolm (1979) *The Gawain-poet: An Annotated Bibliography*, 1839–1977, (New York: Garland).

Andrew, Malcolm and Waldron, Ronald (eds) (1987) *The Poems of the Pearl Manuscript: Pearl, Cleanness, Patience, Sir Gawain and the Green Knight*, rev. edn (Exeter: University of Exeter Press).

Archibald, Elizabeth and Edwards, A. S. G. (eds) (1996) *A Companion to Malory* (Cambridge: D. S. Brewer).

Ashton, G. (1998) *Chaucer: The Canterbury Tales* (Basingstoke: Macmillan).

Aston, M.(1993) *Monasteries* (London: Batsford).

Aston, M. and Richmond, C. (eds) (1997) *Lollardy and the Gentry in the Later Middle Ages* (New York: St Martin's Press).

Auerbach, E. (1953) *Mimesis: The Representation of Reality in Western Literature*, trans. W. R. Trask (Princeton, NJ: Princeton University Press).

Backhouse, J., Turner, D. H., and Webster, L. (1984) *The Golden Age of Anglo-Saxon Art, 966–1066*, (London: British Museum Publications).

Baker, Denise Nowakowski (1994), *Julian of Norwich's Showings: From Vision to Book* (Princeton, NJ: Princeton University Press).

Baker, P. S. (2003), *Introduction to Old English* (Oxford: Blackwell).

Baker, P. S. (ed.) (2000) *The Beowulf Reader*, Basic Readings in Anglo-Saxon England (New York: Garland).

Bakhtin, M. M. (1981) *The Dialogic Imagination: Four Essays*, ed. Michael Holquist, trans. Caryl Emerson and Michael Holquist (Austin, Tx: University of Texas Press) .

Baldwin, Anna P. (1981) *The Theme of Government in Piers Plowman* (Cambridge: D. S. Brewer).

Ball, C. N. (1995) *Apollonius of Tyre: A Hypertext Edition* (www.georgetown.edu/faculty/ballc/apt/apt_oe.html, accessed January 2006, based on Thorpe's 1834 edition).

Barr, Helen (2001) *Socioliterary Practice in Late Medieval England* (Oxford: Oxford University Press).

Barron, W. R. J. (1987) *English Medieval Romance* (London: Longman).

—— (1980) *Trawthe and Treason: The Sin of Gawain Reconsidered* (Manchester: Manchester University Press).

Barron, W. R. J. (ed.) (2001) *The Arthur of the English: The Arthurian Legend in Medieval English Life and Literature*, rev. edn (Cardiff: University of Wales Press).

Barry, P. (1995) *Beginning Theory: An Introduction to Literary and Cultural Theory* (Manchester: Manchester University Press).

Bately, J. (1991) 'The Nature of Old English Prose', in Godden and Lapidge (eds), pp. 71–87.

Baugh, Albert C. and Cable, Thomas (2002) *A History of the English Language*, 5th edn (London: Routledge).

Bawcutt, Priscilla (1992) *Dunbar the Makar* (Oxford: Clarendon Press).

—— (1976) *Gavin Douglas: A Critical Study* (Edinburgh: Edinburgh University Press).

Beadle, Richard (1994) *The Cambridge Companion to Medieval English Theatre* (Cambridge: Cambridge University Press).

Beal, Peter and Griffiths, Jeremy (eds) (1989–97) *English Manuscript Studies, 1100–1700*, 6 vols (Oxford: Blackwell).

Bennett, J. A. W. (1968) *Selections from John Gower* (Oxford: Clarendon Press).

Benson, Larry D. (1976) *Malory's Morte Darthur* (Cambridge, Mass.: Harvard University Press).

Benson, Larry D. (gen. ed.) (1987) *The Riverside Chaucer, based on The Works of Geoffrey Chaucer edited by F. N. Robinson*, 3rd edn (Oxford: Oxford University Press).

Bercovitch, Sacvan (1966) 'Clerical Satire in *The Fox and the Wolf*', *JEGP* 65, pp. 287–94.

Bethurum, D. (ed.) (1971) *The Homilies of Wulfstan* (Oxford: Clarendon Press).

Bjork, R. E. (1985) *The Old English Verse Saints' Lives: A Study in Direct Discourse and the Iconography of Style* (Toronto: University of Toronto Press).

Bjork, R. E. (ed.) (2001) *The Cynewulf Reader* (London: Routledge).

Bjork, R. E. and Niles, J. D. (eds) (1997) *A Beowulf Handbook* (Exeter: University of Exeter Press).

Blair, J. (2005) *The Church in Anglo-Saxon Society* (Oxford: Oxford University Press).

—— (2000) *The Anglo-Saxon Age: A Very Short Introduction* (Oxford: Oxford University Press).

Blake, N. F. (1991) *William Caxton and English Literary Culture* (London: Hambledon).

—— (1976) *Caxton: England's First Publisher* (London: Osprey Publishing).

—— (1969) *Caxton and his World* (London: André Deutsch).

Blake, N. F. (ed.) (1992) *The Cambridge History of the English Language:* vol. 2: *1066–1476* (Cambridge: Cambridge University Press).

Blamires, A. (1997) *The Case for Women in Medieval Culture* (Oxford: Clarendon Press).

Blanch, Robert J. (1983) *Sir Gawain and the Green Knight: A Reference Guide* (Troy, NY: Whitston).

Bliss, Alan (1962) *An Introduction to Old English Metre* (Oxford: Blackwell).

Bloch, Marc (1961) *Feudal Society*, trans. L. A. Manyon (London: Routledge & Kegan Paul).

Bloomfield, Morton W. (1962) *Piers Plowman as a Fourteenth-century Apocalypse* (New Brunswick, NJ: Rutgers University Press).

Boffey, Julia (2003) *Fifteenth-century English Dream Visions: An Anthology* (Oxford: Oxford University Press).

Boffey, J. and Edwards, A. S. G. (2005) *A New Index of Middle English Verse* (London: British Library).

Boitani, Piero (1984) *Chaucer and the Imaginary World of Fame* (Cambridge: D. S. Brewer; Totowa, NJ: Barnes & Noble).

—— (1982) *English Medieval Narrative in the Thirteenth and Fourteenth Centuries*, trans. Joan Krakover Hall (Cambridge: Cambridge University Press).

Boitani, Piero (ed.) (1983) *Chaucer and the Italian Trecento* (Cambridge: Cambridge University Press).

Boitani, Piero and Mann, Jill (eds) (2003) *The Cambridge Companion to Chaucer*, 2nd edn (Cambridge: Cambridge Univeristy Press; rev. edn of 1986 *The Cambridge Chaucer Companion*, ed. Piero Boitani and Jill Mann).

Bolton, W. F. (1986) 'How Boethian is Alfred's Boethius?' in Szarmach (ed.) (1986), pp. 153–68.

Borroff, Marie (1962) *Sir Gawain and the Green Knight: A Stylistic and Metrical Study* (New Haven and London: Yale University Press).

Bowers, J. M. (2000) 'Chaucer after Smithfield: from Postcolonial Writer to Imperialist Author', in Cohen (ed.) (2000), pp. 53–66.

Bradley, S. A. J. (trans.) (1982) *Anglo-Saxon Poetry* (London: Everyman).

Bredehoft, T. A. (2005) 'History and Memory in the *Anglo-Saxon Chronicle*', in Johnson and Treharne (eds), pp. 109–121.

Bremmer, R. H. 2005, 'Old English Heroic Literature' in Johnson & Treharne (eds) (2005), pp. 75–90.

Brewer, Charlotte (1996) *Editing Piers Plowman: The Evolution of the Text* (Cambridge: Cambridge University Press).

Brewer, Derek (1984) *Chaucer: The Poet as Storyteller* (London: Macmillan).

Brewer, Derek (ed.) (1974), *Geoffrey Chaucer*, Writers and their Background (London: Bell).

—— (ed.) (1966) *Chaucer and Chaucerians: Critical Studies in Middle English Literature* (London: Nelson).

Brewer, Derek and Gibson, J. (eds) (1997) *A Companion to the Gawain-Poet* (Cambridge: D. S. Brewer).

Brewer, E. (1997) 'Sources I: The Sources of *Sir Gawain and the Green Knight*', in Brewer and Gibson (eds) (1997), pp. 243–55.

Brodeur, Arthur Gilchrist (1959) *The Art of Beowulf* (Berkeley: University of California Press; repr. 1969).

Brooke, R. B. (1975) *The Coming of the Friars* (London: George Allen & Unwin; and New York: Barnes & Noble).

Brown, C. and Robbins, R. H. (1943–5) *The Index of Middle English Verse* (New York: Columbia University Press).

Brown, M. P. (1998) *The British Library Guide to Writing and Scripts: History and Technique* (London: British Library).

—— (1994) *Understanding Illuminated Manuscripts* (London: British Library).

—— (1991) *Anglo-Saxon Manuscripts* (London: British Library).

—— (1990) *A Guide to Western Historical Scripts from Antiquity to 1600* (London: British Library).

Brown, P. (ed.) (2000) *A Companion to Chaucer* (Oxford: Blackwell).

—— (ed.) (1999) *Reading Dreams: The Interpretation of Dreams from Chaucer to Shakespeare* (Oxford: Oxford Univeristy Press).

Bryan, W. F. and Dempster, Germaine (eds) (1941) *Sources and Analogues of Chaucer's Canterbury Tales* (Chicago: University of Chicago Press).

Burnley, David (1989) *The Language of Chaucer* (Basingstoke: Macmillan).

Burrow, J. A. (1994) *Thomas Hoccleve* (Aldershot: Variorum).

—— (1993) *Langland's Fictions* (Oxford: Clarendon Press).

—— (1990) 'Hoccleve and Chaucer', in Morse and Windeatt (eds) (1990), pp. 54–61.

—— (1984) 'Dunbar, Henryson and other Makars', *Review* 4, pp. 113–27.

Burrow, J. A. (1982a) 'Autobiographical Poetry in the Middle Ages: the Case of Thomas Hoccleve', *Proceedings of the British Academy* 68, pp. 389–412.

—— (1982b) *Medieval Writers and their Work: Middle English Literature and its Background, 1100–1500* (Oxford: Oxford University Press).

—— (1981) 'The Poet as Petitioner', *SAC* 3, pp. 61–75; rpt. in J. A. Burrow, (1984) *Essays on Medieval Literature* (Oxford: Clarendon Press), pp. 161–76.

—— (1971) *Ricardian Poetry: Chaucer, Gower, Langland and the Gawain Poet* (London: Routledge & Kegan Paul).

—— (1965) *A Reading of Sir Gawain and the Green Knight* (London: Routledge & Kegan Paul).

Burrow, J. A. (ed.) (1999) *Thomas Hoccleve's Complaint and Dialogue*, EETS o.s. 313 (Cambridge: Boydell and Brewer).

Burrow, J. A. and Turville-Petre, Thorlac (2004) *A Book of Middle English*, 3rd edn (Oxford: Blackwell).

Burton, Janet E. (1994) *The Monastic and Religious Orders in Britain, 1000–1300*, Cambridge Medieval Textbooks (Cambridge: Cambridge University Press).

Busby, Keith (1995) '*Dame Sirith* and *De Clerico et Puella*', in Veldhoen and Aertsen (eds) (1995), pp. 69–81.

—— (1981) 'Conspicuous by its Absence: the English Fabliau', *Dutch Quarterly Review of Anglo-American Letters* 12, pp. 30–41.

Bynum, Caroline Walker (1987) *Holy Feast and Holy Fast* (Berkeley: University of California Press).

Cable, Thomas (1991) *The English Alliterative Tradition* (Philadelphia: University of Pennsylvania Press).

Calder, D. G. (1981) *Cynewulf*, Twayne's English Authors Series 327 (Boston: G. K. Hall).

—— (1979) 'The Study of Style in Old English Poetry: a Historical Introduction', in D. G. Calder (ed.), *Old English Poetry: Essays on Style* (London: University of California Press), pp. 1–66.

Calder, D. G. et al. (trans.) (1983) *Sources and Analogues of Old English Poetry II: The Major Germanic and Celtic Texts in Translation* (Cambridge: D. S. Brewer).

Calin, William (1994) *The French Tradition and the Literature of Medieval England* (Toronto: University of Toronto Press).

Camille, M. (1996) *Gothic Art: Glorious Visions* (New York: Harry N. Abrams).

—— (1992) *Image on the Edge: The Margins of Medieval Art* (London: Reaktion Books).

Campbell, A. (1962) *Old English Grammar* (Oxford: Oxford Univeristy Press).

Campbell, J. (ed.) (1991) *The Anglo-Saxons* (Harmondsworth: Penguin).

Campbell, J., John, E., and Wormald, P. (eds) (1991) *The Anglo-Saxons* (London: Penguin).

Cannon, Christopher (1999) 'Monastic Productions', in Wallace (ed.) (1999), pp. 316–48.

Carruthers, Mary J. (1990) *The Book of Memory: A Study of Memory in Medieval Culture* (Cambridge: Cambridge University Press).

Cartlidge, Neil (1996) 'The Date of *The Owl and the Nightingale*', *MA* 65, pp. 230–47.

Cartlidge, Neil (ed.) (2001) *The Owl and the Nightingale: Text and Translation*, Exeter Medieval English Texts and Studies (Exeter: University of Exeter Press).

Chance, J. (1986) *Woman as Hero in Old English Literature* (New York: Syracuse University Press).

Chaney, W. A. (1970) *The Cult of Kingship in Anglo-Saxon England* (Manchester: Manchester University Press).

Charles-Edwards, T. (ed.) (2003) *After Rome*, Short Oxford History of the British Isles (Oxford: Oxford University Press).

Chibnall, Marjorie (1987) *Anglo-Norman England, 1066–1166* (Oxford: Blackwell).

Clanchy, M. T. (1998) *England and Its Rulers, 1066–1272*, 2nd edn (Oxford: Blackwell).

—— (1993) *From Memory to Written Record, England, 1066–1307* (Oxford: Blackwell).

Clarke, H. (1984) *The Archaeology of Medieval England* (London: British Museum Publications).

Clark Hall, J. R. (1960) *A Concise Anglo-Saxon Dictionary* (Cambridge: Cambridge University Press).

—— (1950) *Beowulf and the Finnesburg Fragment: A Translation in Modern English Prose*, rev. edn, with Notes and Introduction by C. L. Wrenn and Prefatory Remarks by J. R. R. Tolkien (London: Allen & Unwin).

Clemoes, P. (1966) 'Ælfric', in Stanley (ed.), pp. 176–209.

Clopper, L. M. (1991) 'Mankind and its Audience', in Davidson and Stroupe (eds) (1991), pp. 240–8.

Cohen, J. J. (ed.) (2000) *The Postcolonial Middle Ages* (Basingstoke: Macmillan).

Coleman, Janet (1981) *Piers Plowman and the Moderni* (Rome: Edizioni di storia e letteratura).

Colgrave, B. and Mynors, R. A. B. (eds) (1969) *Bede's Ecclesiastical History of the English People* (Oxford: Oxford Univeristy Press).

Conner, P. W. (2005) 'The Old English Elegy: a Historicization', in Johnson and Treharne (eds) (2005), pp. 30–45.

—— (2001) 'Religious Poetry', in Pulsiano and Treharne (eds) (2001), pp. 250–67.

Cooper, Helen (2005) 'The Classical Background', in Ellis (ed.) (2005).

—— (2004) 'Prose Romances', in Edwards (ed.) (2004), pp. 215–29.

—— (1999) 'Romance after 1400', in Wallace (ed.) (1999), pp. 690–719.

—— (1996) *The Canterbury Tales*, Oxford Guides to Chaucer, 2nd edn (Oxford: Oxford University Press).

—— (1995) 'The Order of the Tales in the Ellesmere Manuscript', in Stevens and Woodward (eds) (1995), pp. 245–61.

Copeland, R. (2006) 'Chaucer and Rhetoric', in Lerer (ed.) (2006), pp. 122–43.

—— (1991) *Rhetoric, Hermeneutics and Translation in the Middle Ages: Academic Traditions and Vernacular Texts* (Cambridge: Cambridge University Press).

Correale, Robert M. and Hamel, Mary (gen. eds) (2002–5) *Sources and Analogies of the 'Canterbury Tales'*, 2 vols (Cambridge: D. S. Brewer).

Cowen Janet (ed.) (1969) *Le Morte d'Arthur*, 2 vols (Harmondsworth: Penguin).

Cramp, R. (1968) '*Beowulf* and Archaeology', in Fry (ed.) (1968), pp. 114–40; originally published in *Medieval Archaeology* I (1957), pp. 57–77.

Crane, Susan (1999) 'Anglo-Norman Cultures in England, 1066–1460', in Wallace (ed.) (1999), pp. 35–60.

Crossley-Holland, K. (trans.) (2002) *The Anglo-Saxon World* (Woodbridge: Boydell).

—— (trans.) (1978) *The Exeter Book Riddles* (Harmondsworth: Penguin).

Crow, Martin M. and Olson, Clair C. (eds) (1966), *Chaucer Life-records from Materials Compiled by John M. Manly and Edith Rickert* (Oxford: Clarendon Press).

Crystal, D. (2003) *The Cambridge Encyclopaedia of the English Language*, 2nd edn (Cambridge: Cambridge University Press).

Curtius, Ernst Robert (1953) *European Literature and the Latin Middle Ages*, trans. Willard R. Trask (London: Routledge & Kegan Paul).

Dahood, Roger (1984) '*Ancrene Wisse*, the Katherine Group, and the *Wohunge* Group', in Edwards (ed.) (1984), pp. 1–33.

Dalrymple, R. (ed.) (2004) *Middle English Literature: A Guide to Criticism*, Blackwell Guides to Criticism (Oxford: Blackwell)

Damico, H. and Hennessey, A. (eds) (1990) *New Readings on Women in Old English Literature* (Bloomington: Indiana University Press).

Damon, J. E. (2003) *Soldier Saints and Holy Warriors: Warfare and Sanctity in the Literature of Early England* (Aldershot: Ashgate).

D'Arcy, Anne Marie (2005) 'The Middle English Lyrics', in Johnson and Treharne (ed.) (Oxford: Oxford University Press), pp. 306–22.

Davenport, Tony (2004) *Medieval Narrative: An Introduction* (Oxford: Oxford University Press).

—— (1978) *The Art of the Gawain-poet* (London: Athlone Press).

Davidson, C. and Stroupe, J. H. (1991) *Drama in the Middle Ages: Comparative and Critical Essays* (New York: AMS Press).

Davidson, H. E. (1980) 'Archaeology and *Beowulf*', in Garmonsway and Simpson (eds) (1980), pp. 351–64.

Davies, W. (ed.) (2003) *From the Vikings to the Normans*, Short Oxford History of the British Isles (Oxford: Oxford University Press).

Dean, Ruth J., with Boulton, Maureen B. M. (1999) *Anglo-Norman Literature: A Guide to Texts and Manuscripts* (London: Anglo-Norman Text Society).

Dillon, Janette (2006) *The Cambridge Introduction to Early English Theatre*, Cambridge Introductions to Literature (Cambridge: Cambridge Univeristy Press).

Dinshaw, Carolyn (1989) *Chaucer's Sexual Poetics* (Madison: University of Wisconsin Press).

Dinshaw, Carolyn and Wallace, David (eds) (2003) *The Cambridge Companion to Medieval Women's Writing* (Cambridge: Cambridge University Press).

Discenza, N. G. (2005) 'The Persuasive Power of Alfredian Prose', in Johnson and Treharne (eds) (2005), pp. 122–35.

Dobson, Eric J. (1976) *The Origins of Ancrene Wisse* (Oxford: Oxford University Press).

Donaldson, E. Talbot (1970) *Speaking of Chaucer* (London: Athlone Press).

—— (1966) *Piers Plowman: The C-text and its Poet*, Yale Studies in English 113 (Hamden, Conn.: Archon Books; first published in 1949).

Donoghue, D. (2004a) 'The Vow', in Donoghue (2004b), pp. 1–28.

—— (2004b) *Old English Literature: A Short Introduction* (Oxford: Blackwell).

—— (1990) 'Laȝamon's Ambivalence', *Speculum* 65, pp. 537–63.

Du Boulay, F. R. H. (1991) *The England of Piers Plowman: William Langland and his Vision of the Fourteenth Century* (Cambridge: D. S. Brewer).

Dubrow, Heather (1982) *Genre* (London: Methuen).

Duggan, H. N. (1997) 'Meter, Stanza, Vocabulary, Dialect', in Brewer and Gibson (ed.) (1997), pp. 221–42.

—— (1990) 'Stress Assignment in Middle English Alliterative Poetry', *JEGP* 89, pp. 309–29.

—— (1988) 'Final –e and the Rhythmic Structure of the b-verse in Middle English Alliterative Poetry', *Modern Philology* 86, pp. 119–45.

—— (1986a) 'Alliterative Patterning as a Basis for Emendation in Middle English Alliterative Poetry', *Studies in the Age of Chaucer* 8, pp. 73–105.

—— (1986b) 'The Shape of the b-verse in Middle English Alliterative Poetry', *Speculum* 61, pp. 564–92.

—— (1976) 'The Role of Formulas in the Dissemination of a Middle English Alliterative Romance', *Studies in Bibliography* 29, pp. 265–88.

Dumville, D. N. (2001) 'English Libraries Before 1066: Use and Abuse of the Manuscript Evidence', in Richards (ed.) (2001), pp. 169–220; originally published in M. W. Herren (ed.) (1981) *Insular Latin Studies: Papers on Latin Texts and Manuscripts of the British Isles: 550–1066* (Toronto: Pontifical Institute of Mediaeval Studies).

Duncan, T. G. (ed.) (2005) *A Companion to the Middle English Lyric* (Cambridge: D. S. Brewer).

Ebin, Lois (1985) *John Lydgate* (Twayne: Boston).

Edwards, A. S. G. (2004a) 'John Trevisa', in Edwards (ed.) (2004b), pp. 117–26.

—— (1996) 'Middle English Literature' in D. C. Greetham (ed.), *Scholarly Editing: A Guide to Research* (New York: MLA Publications).

Edwards, A. S. G. (ed.) (2004b) *A Companion to Middle English Prose* (Cambridge: D. S. Brewer).

—— (1984a) 'Lydgate Scholarship: Progress and Prospects', in Yeager (ed.) (1984), pp. 29–47.

—— (ed.) (1984b) *Middle English Prose: A Critical Guide to Major Authors and Genres* (New Brunswick, NJ: Rutgers University Press).

—— (gen. ed.) (1984–) *The Index of Middle English Prose* (Cambridge: D. S. Brewer).

Edwards, Robert R. (1989) *The Dream of Chaucer* (Durham, NC: Duke University Press).

Ellis, Roger (ed.) (1989) *The Medieval Translator: The Theory and Practice of Translation in the Middle Ages* (Cambridge: D. S. Brewer)

Ellis, Steve (ed.) (2005) *Chaucer: An Oxford Guide* (Oxford: Oxford Univeristy Press).

Erler, M. C. (2002) *Women, Reading, and Piety in Late Medieval England* (Cambridge: Cambridge University Press).

Evans, R. and Johnson, L. (eds) (1994) *Feminist Readings in Middle English Literature: The Wife of Bath and all her Set* (London: Routledge).

Fein, Susanna (ed.) (2000) *Studies in the Harley Manuscript: The Scribes, Contents, and Social Contexts of British Library MS Harley 2253*, published for TEAMS (The Consortium for the Teaching of the Middle Ages) in association with the University of Rochester (Kalamazoo, Mich.: Medieval Institute Publications, Western Michigan University).

—— (ed.) (1998) *The Dispute between Mary and the Cross* in *Moral Love Songs and Laments* (Kalamazoo, Mich.: Medieval Institute Publications).

Fell, C. E. (1991) 'Perceptions of Transience', in Godden and Lapidge (eds) (1994), pp. 172–89.

—— (1984) *Women in Anglo-Saxon England* (London: British Museum Publications).

Fennell, Barbara A. (2001) *A History of English: A Sociolinguistic Approach* (Oxford: Blackwell).

Fenster, T. S. (ed.) (1996) *Arthurian Women* (London: Routledge).

Field, P. J. C. (1993) *The Life and Times of Sir Thomas Malory* (Cambridge: D. S. Brewer).

—— (1971) *Romance and Chronicle: A Study of Malory's Prose Style* (London: Barrie & Jenkins).

Field, Rosalind (1999) 'Romance in England, 1066–1400', in Wallace (ed.) (1999), pp. 152–76.

Finke, Laurie A. (1999) *Women's Writing in English: Medieval England* (Longman: London).

Fischer, O., Kemanade, A. V., Koopman, W., and van der Wurff, W. (2000) *The Syntax of Early English* (Cambridge: Cambridge Univeristy Press).

Fisher, John H. (1992) 'A Language Policy for Lancastrian England', *PMLA* 107, pp. 1168–80.

—— (1964) *John Gower: Moral Philosopher and Friend of Chaucer* (New York: Methuen).

Fletcher, R. A. (2003) *Bloodfeud: Murder and Revenge in Anglo-Saxon England* (London: Penguin Books).

Fowler, Alastair (1982) *Kinds of Literature: An Introduction to the Theory of Genres and Modes* (Oxford: Oxford University Press).

Fowler, David C. (1993) *John Trevisa*, Authors of the Middle Ages, English writers of the Late Middle Ages (Aldershot: Variorum).

Frank, R. (1991) 'Germanic Legend in Old English Literature', in Godden and Lapidge (1991), pp. 88–106.

—— (1990) 'The Ideal of Men Dying with their Lord in *The Battle of Maldon*: Anachronism of Nouvelle Vague', in I. Wood and N. Lund (eds), *People and*

Places in Northern Europe, 500–1600: Essays in Honour of Peter Hayes Sawyer (Woodbridge: D. S. Brewer).

Frantzen, A. J. (1998) *Before the Closet: Same-Sex Love from Beowulf to Angles in America* (Chicago: University of Chicago Press).

—— (1996) 'The Fragmentation of Cultural Studies and the Fragments of Anglo-Saxon England', *Anglia* 114, pp. 310–39.

—— (1990) *Desire for Origins: New Language, Old English, and Teaching the Tradition* (London: Rutgers University Press).

Frantzen, A. J. (ed.) (1991) *Speaking Two Languages: Traditional Disciplines and Contemporary Theory in Medieval Studies* (New York: State University of New York Press).

Frantzen, A. J. and Niles, J. D. (eds) (1997) *Anglo-Saxonism and the Construction of Social Identity* (Gainsville: University of Florida Press).

Franzen, Christine (1991) *The Tremulous Hand of Worcester. A Study of Old English in the Thirteenth Century* (Oxford: Oxford University Press).

Freeborn, D. (1998) *From Old English to Standard English*, 2nd edn (Basingstoke: Macmillan).

Fry, D. K. (ed.) (1968) *The Beowulf Poet* (Englewood Cliffs, NJ: , Prentice-Hall).

Fulk, R. D. (ed.) (1991) *Interpretations of Beowulf* (Indiana: Indiana University of Press).

Fulk, R. D. and Cain, C. M. (2003) *A History of Old English Literature* (Oxford: Blackwell).

Furrow, Melissa (1989) 'Middle English Fabliaux and Modern Myth', *English Literary History* 56, pp. 1–18.

Galloway, Andrew (2005) 'Middle English Prologues', in Johnson and Treharne (eds) (2005), pp. 288–305.

Garmonsway, G. N. (trans.) (1972) *The Anglo-Saxon Chronicle* (London: Dent).

Garmonsway, G. N. and Simpson, J. (eds) (1980) *Beowulf and its Analogues* (London: Everyman).

Gaskoin, C. J. B. (1966) *Alcuin: His Life and his Work* (New York: Russell & Russell).

Gatch, M. McC (1991) 'Perceptions of Eternity', in Godden and Lapidge (eds) (1991), pp. 190–205.

—— (1985) 'The Office in Late Anglo-Saxon Monasticism', in Lapidge and Gneuss (eds) (1985), pp. 341–62.

—— (1977) *Preaching and Theology in Anglo-Saxon England: Ælfric and Wulfstan* (Toronto: University of Toronto Press).

Gilbert, J. (1997) 'Gender and Sexual Transgression', in Brewer and Gibson (eds) (1997), pp. 53–69.

Gillespie, V. A. (1989) 'Vernacular Books of Religion', in Griffiths and Pearsall (eds) (1998), pp. 317–44.

Gillingham, J. and Griffiths, R. A. (2000) *Medieval Britain: A Very Short Introduction* (Oxford: Oxford University Press).

Ginsberg, Warren (ed.) (1992) *Wynnere and Wastoure and The Parlement of the Three Ages* (Kalamazoo, Mich.: Medieval Institute Publications).

Given-Wilson, C. (1987) *The English Nobility in the Late Middle Ages: The Fourteenth-century Political Community* (London: Routledge & Kegan Paul).

Glasscoe, Marion (1993) *English Medieval Mystics: Games of Faith* (Longman: London).

Glasscoe, Marion (ed.) (1980–2, 1984–92, 2004), *The Medieval Mystical Tradition in England: Proceedings of the Exeter Symposium*, 7 vols (vols I–II, Exeter: Exeter University Press; vols III–VII; Cambridge: D. S. Brewer).

Gneuss, H. (2001) *Handlist of Anglo-Saxon Manuscripts: A List of Manuscripts and Manuscript Fragments Written or Owned in England up to 1100* (Tempe, AZ: Arizona Center for Medieval and Renaissance Studies).

Godden, M. (2000) *Ælfric's Catholic Homilies: Introduction, Commentary and Glossary*, EETS s.s. 18 (Oxford: Oxford Univeristy Press).

—— (1991) 'Biblical Literature: the Old Testament', in Godden and Lapidge (eds) (1991), pp. 206–26.

—— (1990) *The Making of Piers Plowman* (London: Longman).

—— (1979) *Ælfric's Catholic Homilies: The Second Series: Text*, EETS s.s. 5 (Oxford: Oxford University Press).

Godden, M. and Lapidge, M. (eds) (1991) *The Cambridge Companion to Old English Literature* (Cambridge: Cambridge University Press).

Godman, P. (ed.) (1982) *Alcuin's 'The Bishops, Kings, and Saints of York'* (Oxford: Oxford University Press).

Goldberg, P. J. P. (2004) *Medieval England: A Social History, 1250–1550* (London: Edward Arnold).

Goldie, M. B. (2003) *Middle English Literature: A Historical Sourcebook* (Oxford: Blackwell).

Goldstein, R. James (1999) 'Writing in Scotland', in Wallace (ed.) (1999), pp. 229–54.

Goodridge, J. F. (trans.) (1959) *Piers the Ploughman* (Harmondsworth: Penguin Book).

Goolden, P. (ed.) (1958) *The Old English Apollonius of Tyre* (Oxford: Oxford University Press).

Görlach, M. (1997) *The Linguistic History of English* (Basingstoke: Macmillan).

Gracia, J. J. E. (2003) 'Philosophy in the Middle Ages: an Introduction', in Gracia and Noone (eds) (2003), pp. 1–11.

Gracia, J. J. E. and Noone, T. B. (eds) (2003) *A Campanion to Philosophy in the Middle Ages* (Oxford: Blackwell).

Gradon, Pamela (1980) 'Langland and the Ideology of Dissent', *Proceedings of the British Academy* 66, pp. 179–205.

Gray, Douglas (1979) *Robert Henryson*, Medieval and Renaissance Authors (Leiden: Brill).

—— (1972) *Themes and Images in the Medieval English Religious Lyric* (London: Routledge and Kegan Paul).

Green, M. (ed.) (1983) *The Old English Elegies: New Essays in Criticism and Research* (Rutherford: Fairleigh Dickinson University Press).

Green, Richard Firth (1980) *Poets and Princepleasers: Literature and the English Court in the Late Middle Ages* (Toronto: University of Toronto Press).

Greene, J. P. (1992) *Medieval Monasteries* (Leicester: Leicester University Press; also published 2005, London: Continuum).

Greenfield, S. B. (1972) *The Interpretation of Old English Poems* (London: Routledge).

Greenfield, S. B. and Calder, D. G. (1986) *A New Critical History of Old English Literature* (New York and London: New York University Press).

Greenfield, S. B. and Robinson, F. C. (1980) *A Bibliography of Publications on Old English Literature to the End of 1972* (Manchester: Manchester University Press).

Grenville, J. (1997) *Medieval Housing* (Leicester: Leicester University Press).

Griffiths, B. (1996) *Aspects of Anglo-Saxon Magic* (Hockwold-cum-Wilton: Anglo-Saxon Books).

—— (1995) *An Introduction to Early English Law* (Hockwold-cum-Wilton: Anglo-Saxon Books).

Griffiths, Jeremy and Pearsall, Derek (eds) (1989) *Book Production and Publishing in Britain, 1375–1475* (Cambridge: Cambridge University Press).

Hall, T. N. (2005) 'Old English Religious Prose: Rhetorics of Salvation and Damnation', in Johnson and Treharne (eds) (2005), pp. 136–48.

Hallett, N. (2000) 'Women', in Brown (ed.) (2000), pp. 480–94.

Hamer, R. (2006) *A Choice of Anglo-Saxon Verse* (London: Faber and Faber).

Hanna, R. (1999) 'Alliterative Poetry', in Wallace (ed.) (1999), pp. 488–512.

—— (1996) *Pursuing History: Middle English Manuscripts and their Texts* (Stanford: Stanford University Press).

Hansen, E. T. (1992) *Chaucer and the Fictions of Gender* (Berkeley: University of California Press).

Harrington, David V. (1986) 'Indeterminacy in *Winner and Waster* and *The Parliament of the Three Ages*', *Chaucer Review* 20, pp. 246–57.

Hasenfratz, R. and Jambeck, T. (2005) *Reading Old English* (Morgantown: West Virginia University Press).

Havely, N. R. (1980) *Chaucer's Boccaccio: Sources for Troilus and the Knight's and Franklin's Tales: Translations from the Filostrato, Teseida and Filocolo* (Cambridge: D. S. Brewer; paperback reprint, 1992).

Heaney, S. (1999) *Beowulf* (London: Faber and Faber).

Hellinga, Lotte and Trapp, J. B. (eds) (1999) '1400–1557', in *The Cambridge History of the Book in Britain*, vol. III, gen. eds D. F. McKenzie, David McKitterick, and I. R. Wilson (Cambridge: Cambridge University Press).

Heusler, A. (1943) *Die altgermanische Dichtung*, 2nd edn (Potsdam: Akademische Verlagsgellschaft Athenaion).

—— (1921), *Nibelungensage und Nibelungenlied: die Stoffgeschichte des deutschen Heldenepos* (Dortmund: Ruhfus).

—— (1920), 'Heliand, Liedstil und Epenstil', *Zeitschrift für deutsches Altertum und deutsche Literatur* 57, pp. 1–48.

Hieatt, Constance (1966) '*Wynnere and Wastoure* and *The Parlement of the Thre Ages*', *American Notes and Queries* 4, pp. 100–4.

Higgins, Iain Macleod (1997) *Writing East: The 'Travels' of Sir John Mandeville* (Philadelphia: University of Pennsylvania Press).

Hill, B. (1977) 'The Twelfth-century *Conduct of Life*, formerly the *Poema Morale* or *A Moral Ode*', *Leeds Studies in English* 9, pp. 79–144.

Hill, B. (1964) 'The "Luue-Ron" and Thomas de Hales', *Modern Language Review* 59, pp. 321–30.

Hill, D. (1981) *An Atlas of Anglo-Saxon England* (Oxford: Blackwell).

Hill, John (2000) 'Shaping Anglo-Saxon Lordship in the Heroic Literature of the Tenth and Eleventh Centuries', *The Heroic Age* 3, www.mun.ca/mst/heroicage/issues/3/hill.html.

Hill, Joyce (2001) 'The Benedictine Reform and Beyond', in Pulsiano and Treharne (eds) (2001), pp. 151–69.

—— (1994) 'Ælfric, Authorial Identity and the Changing Text', in Scragg and Szarmach (eds), pp. 177–89.

Hill, T. D. (2005) 'Wise Words: Old English Sapiential Poetry', in Johnson and Treharne (eds) (2005), pp. 166–82.

—— (1975) 'Parody and Theme in the Middle English *Land of Cockayne*', *Notes and Queries* 28, pp. 55–9.

Hills, C. M. (1996) '*Beowulf* and Archaeology', in Bjork and Niles (eds), pp. 291–310.

Hines, John (2004) *Voices in the Past: English Literature and Archaeology* (London: D. S. Brewer), especially pp. 37–70.

—— (1993) *The Fabliau in English* (London: Longman).

Hodgson, Phylis (1967) *Three 14th-century English Mystics*, rev. edn (London: Longman).

Hogg, R. (2002) *An Introduction to Old English* (Edinburgh: Edinburgh University Press).

Hollis, S. (2001) 'Scientific and Medical Writings', in Pulsiano and Treharne (eds) (2001), pp. 188–208.

Hollis, S. and Wright, M. (1992) *Old English Prose of Secular Learning*, Annotated Bibliographies of Old and Middle English Literature 4 (Cambridge: D. S. Brewer).

Holmes, G. (ed.) (1988) *The Oxford Illustrated History of Medieval Europe* (Oxford: Oxford University Press).

Horner, S. (2001) *The Discourse of Enclosure: Representing Women in Old English Literature* (New York: State University of New York Press).

Horobin, Simon and Smith, Jeremy (2002) *An Introduction to Middle English* (Edinburgh: Edinburgh University Press).

Horrall, Sarah M. (1989) ' "For the commun at understand": *Cursor Mundi* and its Background', in Sergeant (ed.) (1989), pp. 97–107.

—— (1985) '*Cleanness* and *Cursor Mundi*', *ELN* 22, pp. 6–11.

Horrox, Rosemary (ed.) (1994) *Fifteenth-century Attitudes: Perceptions of Society in Late Medieval England* (Cambridge: Cambridge University Press).

Hough, C. (2001) 'Legal and Documentary Writings', in Pulsiano and Treharne (eds) (2001), pp. 170–87.

Howe, N. (2002) 'The Cultural Construction of Reading in Anglo-Saxon England', in Liuzza (ed.) (2002), pp. 1–22.

—— (1997) 'Historicist Approaches', in O'Brien O'Keeffe (ed.) (1997), pp. 79–100.

—— (1985) *The Old English Catalogue Poems*, Anglistica XXIII (Copenhagen: Rosenkilde and Bagger).

Hudson, Anne (1988) *The Premature Reformation: Wycliffite Texts and Lollard History* (Oxford: Clarendon Press).

—— (1986) 'Wyclif and the English Language', in Kenny (ed.) (1986), pp. 85–103.

—— (1985) *Lollards and their Books* (London: Hambledon Press).

Huizinga, J. (1955) *The Waning of the Middle Ages* (London: Penguin).

Hume, Kathryn (1975) *The Owl and the Nightingale: The Poem and its Critics* (Toronto: Toronto University Press).

Hunter Blair, P. (1990) *The World of Bede* (Cambridge: Cambridge University Press).

Hurt, J. (1972) *Ælfric* (New York: Twayne).

Jack, G. (ed.) (1994) *Beowulf: A Student Edition* (Oxford: Clarendon Press).

Jack, R. D. S. (ed.) (1988) 'Origins to 1660', in *The History of Scottish Literature*, vol. 1, gen. ed. Cairns Craig (Aberdeen: Aberdeen University Press).

Jacobs, Nicolas (1985) 'The Typology of Debate and the Interpretation of *Wynnere and Wastoure*', *Review of English Studies* 36, pp. 481–500.

Jefferson, Judith A. (1987) 'The Hoccleve Holographs and Hoccleve's Metrical Practice', in Pearsall (ed.) (1987), pp. 95–109.

Jeffrey, David L. (1975) *The Early English Lyric and Franciscan Spirituality* (Lincoln: University of Nebraska Press).

John, E. (1996) *Reassessing Anglo-Saxon England* (Manchester: Manchester University Press).

Johnson, D. and Treharne, E. (eds) (2005) *Readings in Medieval Texts* (Oxford: Oxford University Press).

Johnson, Lynn Staley (1991) 'The Trope of the Scribe and the Question of Literary Authority in the Works of Julian of Norwich and Margery Kempe', *Speculum* 66, pp. 820–38.

Johnson, Paul (1990) *Cathedrals of England, Scotland, and Wales* (London: Weidenfeld & Nicolson).

Jones, E. A. (ed.) (2004) *The Medieval Mystical Tradition in England: Proceedings of the Exeter Symposium*, vol. VII (Cambridge, D. S. Brewer).

Jones, Peter Murray (1999) 'Medicine and Science', in Hellinga and Trapp (eds) (1999), pp. 433–48.

Jost, K. (ed.) (1959) *Die Institutes of Polity, Civil and Ecclesiastical: Ein Werk Erzbischof Wulfstans von York* (Bern: Francke).

Justice, Steven and Kerby-Fulton, Katherine (eds) (1997) *Written Work: Langland, Labor, and Authorship* (Philadelphia: University of Pennsylvania Press).

Kane, George (1965) *Piers Plowman: The Evidence for Authorship* (London: University of London, Athlone Press).

Karkov, C. E. (1995) *The Archaeology of Anglo-Saxon England*, Basic Readings in Anglo-Saxon England (New York: Garland).

Kaske, R. E. (1958) '*Sapientia et Fortitudo* as the Controlling Theme of *Beowulf*', *SP* 55, pp. 423–56; also in Nicholson (ed.) (1963), pp. 269–310.

Kean P. M. (1967) *The Pearl: An Interpretation* (London: Routledge & Kegan Paul).

Keats-Rohan, K. S. B. (ed.) (2002) *Domesday Descendants: A Prosopography of Persons Occurring in English Documents, 1066–1166,* vol. II: *Pipe Rolls to `Cartae Baronum'* (Woodbridge: Boydell Press).

—— (ed.) (1999–2002) *Domesday People: A Prosopography of Persons Occurring in English Documents, 1066–1166,* 2 vols (Woodbridge: Boydell Press)

—— (ed.) (1997) *Family Trees and the Roots of Politics: The Prosopography of Britain and France from the Tenth to the Twelfth Century* (Woodbridge: Boydell Press).

Keefer, S. L. (2005) 'Old English Religious Poetry', in Johnson and Treharne (eds) (2005), pp. 15–29.

Keen, M. (1984) *Chivalry* (London: New Haven Yale University Press).

—— (1973) *England in the Later Middle Ages: A Political History* (Methuen: London).

Keiser, George R. (2004) 'Scientific, Medical and Utilitarian Prose', in Edwards (ed.) (2004), pp. 231–47.

—— (1998) *Works of Science and Information. A Manual of the Writings in Middle English, 1050–1500,* vol. 10, ed. J. B. Severs and A. E. Hartung, (New Haven: Connecticut Academy of Arts and Sciences).

Kelly, S. (1990) 'Anglo-Saxon Lay Society and the Written Word', in R. McKitterick (ed.), *The Uses of Literacy in Early Medieval Europe* (Cambridge: Cambridge University Press), pp. 36–62.

Kennedy, Edward Donald. (1989) *Chronicles and Other Historical Writing: A Manual of the Writings in Middle English, 1050–1500,* vol. 8, ed. J. B. Severs and A. E. Hartung (Hamden: Connecticut Academy of Arts and Sciences).

Kennedy, Edward Donald (ed.) (1996) *King Arthur: A Casebook* (New York: Garland).

Kennedy, Edward Donald, Waldron, Ronald, and Wittig, Joseph S. (eds) (1988) *Medieval English Studies Presented to George Kane* (Woodbridge: D. S. Brewer).

Kenny, Anthony (ed.) (1986a) *Wyclif in his Times* (Oxford: Clarendon Press).

Kenny, Anthony (1986b) *Wyclif* (Oxford: Oxford University Press).

Kenyon, J. R. (1990) *Medieval Fortifications* (Leicester: Leicester University Press; also published 2005, London: Continuum).

Ker, N. R. (1990) *Catalogue of Manuscripts Containing Anglo-Saxon,* 2nd edn with supplement (Oxford: Oxford University Press).

Keynes, S. and Lapidge, M. (trans.) (1983) *Alfred the Great: Asser's Life of King Alfred and Other Contemporary Sources* (Harmondsworth: Penguin).

King, P. (2003) 'Philosophy in the Latin Christian West: 750–1050', in Gracia and Noone (eds) (2003), pp. 32–5.

Klaeber, F. (1950) *Beowulf and the Fight at Finnsburgh,* 3rd edn (Boston, MA: D.C. Heath).

Klarer, M. (1999) *An Introduction to Literary Studies* (London: Routledge).

Klinck, A. L. (ed.) (1992) *The Old English Elegies: A Critical Edition and Genre Study* (Montreal: McGill-Queen's University Press).

Klosowska, A. (2005) *Queer Love in the Middle Ages* (Basingstoke: Palgrave Macmillan).

Knapp, E. (2006) 'Chaucer Criticism and Its Legacies', in Lerer (ed.) (2006), pp. 324–56.

Knowles, David (1969) *Christian Monasticism* (London: Weidenfeld and Nicolson).

—— (1963) *The Monastic Order in England: A History of its Development from the Times of St Dunstan to the Fourth Lateran Council, 940–1216* (Cambridge: Cambridge University Press).

—— (1961) *The English Mystical Tradition* (London: Burns & Oates).

—— (1948–59) *The Religious Orders in England*, 3 vols (Cambridge: Cambridge University Press).

Kolve, V. A. (1966) *The Play Called Corpus Christi* (Stanford, Cal.: Stanford University Press).

Krapp, G. P. and Dobie, E. V. K. (eds) (1931–53) *The Anglo-Saxon Poetic Records: A Collective Edition* (London and New York: Columbia University Press).

Kratzmann, Gregory (1980) *Anglo-Scottish Literary Relations, 1430–1550* (Cambridge: Cambridge University Press).

Krueger, R. L. (ed.) (2000) *The Cambridge Companion to Medieval Romance* (Cambridge: Cambridge University Press).

Kruger, Stephen F. (1992) *Dreaming in the Middle Ages* (Cambridge: Cambridge University Press).

Lacey, R. and Danziger, D. (1999) *The Year 1000: What Life was Like at the Turn of the First Millennium?* (London: Little, Brown and Company).

Lambdin, L. C. and Lambdin, R. T. (eds) (2002) *A Companion to Old and Middle English Literature* (London: Greenwood Press).

Lambert, Mark (1975) *Malory: Style and Vision in Le Morte Darthur* (New Haven, Conn.: Yale University Press).

Lapidge, M. (1997) 'The Comparative Approach', in O'Brien O'Keeffe (ed.) (1997), pp. 20–38.

—— (1996) *Anglo-Latin Literature, 600–899* (London: Hambledon Press).

—— (1993) *Anglo-Latin Literature, 900–1066* (London: Hambledon Press).

—— (1991) 'The Saintly Life in Anglo-Saxon England', in Godden and Lapidge (eds) (1991), pp. 243–63.

—— (1986) 'The Anglo-Latin Background', in Greenfield and Calder (eds) (1986), pp. 5–37.

—— (1985) 'Surviving Booklists from Anglo-Saxon England', in Lapidge and Gneuss (eds) (1985), pp. 33–90.

Lapidge, M. and Gneuss, H. (eds) (1985) *Learning and Literature in Anglo-Saxon England : Studies Presented to Peter Clemoes on the Occasion of his Sixty-fifth Birthday* (Cambridge: Cambridge University Press).

Lapidge, M. and Herren, M. (eds) (1979) *Aldhelm: the Prose Works* (Cambridge: D. S. Brewer).

Lapidge, M. and Rosier, J. L. (eds) (1984) *Aldhelm: The Poetic Works* (D. S. Brewer: Cambridge).

Lapidge, M. et al. (eds) (1999) *The Blackwell Encyclopaedia of Anglo-Saxon England* (Oxford: Blackwell).

Larrington, C. (1983) *A Store of Common Sense: Gnomic Theme and Style in Old Icelandic and Old English Wisdom Poetry* (Oxford: Oxford University Press).

Lawrence, C. H. (2003) *Medieval Monasticism: Forms of Religious Life in Western Europe in the Middle Ages*, 3rd edn (Harlow: Longman).

—— (1994) *The Friars: The Impact of the Early Mendicant Movement on Western Society* (London: Longman).

Lawrence, R. F. (1970) 'Formula and Rhythm in *The Wars of Alexander*', *ES* 51, pp. 97–112.

Lawton, David (1985) *Chaucer's Narrators* (Cambridge: D. S. Brewer).

—— (1982) *Middle English Alliterative Poetry and its Literary Background: Seven Essays* (Woodbridge, Suffolk and Totowa, NJ: D. S. Brewer).

Lecklider, Jane K. (1997) *Cleanness: Structure and Meaning* (Woodbridge: D. S. Brewer).

Leclercq, Jean (1982) *The Love of Learning and the Desire for God: A Study of Monastic Culture*, trans. Catharine Misrahi, 3rd edn (New York: Fordham University Press); first published 1961.

Lee, S. D. and Conner, P. W. (eds) (2001) *Dragons in the Sky* – http://users.ox.ac.uk/~stuart/dits/.

Lee, S. D. and Solopova, E. (2005) *The Keys of Middle-earth* (Basingstoke: Palgrave Macmillan).

Lees, C. A. (1999) *Tradition and Belief: Religious Writing in Late Anglo-Saxon England*, Medieval Cultures 19 (London: University of Minnesota Press).

—— (1997) 'At a Crossroads: Old English and Feminist Criticism' in O'Brien O'Keeffe (ed.) (1997), pp. 146–69.

—— (1991) 'Working with Patristic Sources: Language and Context in Old English Homilies', in Frantzen (ed.) (1991), pp. 157–80.

Lees, C. A. and Overing, G. R. (eds) (2001) *Double Agents: Women and Clerical Culture in Anglo-Saxon England* (Philadelphia: University of Pennsylvania Press).

Legge, M. Dominica (1963) *Anglo-Norman Literature and its Background* (Oxford: Oxford University Press).

Lendinara, P. (1991) 'The World of Anglo-Saxon Learning' in Godden and Lapidge (eds) (1991), pp. 264–81.

Lerer, S. (1999a) 'Old English and its Afterlife', in Wallace (ed.) (1991), pp. 7–34.

—— (1999b) 'William Caxton' in Wallace (ed.) (1999), pp. 720–38.

Lerer, S. (ed.) (2006) *The Yale Companion to Chaucer* (London: Yale University Press).

Le Saux, Françoise (1989) *Laȝamon's Brut: The Poem and its Sources* (Cambridge: D. S. Brewer).

Lester, G. A. (1996) *The Language of Old and Middle English Poetry* (Basingstoke: Macmillan).

Lewis, Robert E. (1982) 'The English Fabliau Tradition and Chaucer's "Miller's Tale" ', *Modern Philology* 79, pp. 241–55.

Lewis, Robert E. (editor-in-chief) (2001) *Middle English Dictionary* (Ann Arbor: University of Michigan Press).

Liuzza, R. M. (2005) '*Beowulf*: Monuments, Memory, History', in Johnson and Treharne (eds) (2005), pp. 91–108.

—— (2001) 'Religious Prose' in Pulsiano and Treharne (eds) (2001), pp. 233–50.

—— (2000) *Beowulf: A New Verse Translation* (Peterborough, Ontario: Broadview Press).

Liuzza, R. M. (ed.) (2002) *Old English Literature* (London: Yale University Press).

Livingstone, E. A. (ed.) (2005) *The Oxford Dictionary of the Christian Church*, ed. F. L. Cross, 3rd rev. edn (Oxford: Oxford University Press).

Lochrie, K. (2003) 'Between Women', in Dinshaw and Wallace (eds) (2003), pp. 70–88.

Looijenga, T. (2003) *Texts and Contexts of the Oldest Runic Inscriptions* (Brill: Leiden).

Loomis, Roger Sherman (1963) *The Development of Arthurian Romance* (New York: Harper and Row).

Loomis, Roger Sherman (ed.) (1961) *Arthurian Literature in the Middle Ages: A Collaborative History*, 2nd edn (Oxford: Clarendon Press).

Lord, A. (1960) *The Singer of Tales* (London: Oxford University Press).

Loyn, H. R. (1991) *The Making of the English Nation: From the Anglo-Saxons to Edward I* (London: Thames and Hudson).

Lucas, Peter J. (2005) 'Earlier Verse Romance', in Johnson and Treharne (eds) (2005), pp. 229–40.

Lutz, C. E. (1977) *Schoolmasters in the Tenth Century* (Hamden, CT: Archon Books).

Lyall, R. J. (1976) 'Politics and Poetry in Fifteenth and Sixteenth Century Scotland', *Scottish Literary Journal* 3, pp. 5–29.

Lynch, Joseph H. (1992) *The Medieval Church: A Brief History* (London: Longman).

Lynch, Kathryn L. (2000) *Chaucer's Philosophical Visions* (Cambridge: D. S. Brewer).

Macaulay, G. C. (1900–1), *The English Works of John Gower, Edited from the Manuscripts, with Introduction, Notes, and Glossary*, EETS e.s. 81–2, K. Paul, Trench (London: Trübner).

Machan, Tim William (1994) *Textual Criticism and Middle English Texts* (Charlottesville: University of Virginia Press).

Machan, Tim William (ed.) (1991) *Medieval Literature: Texts and Interpretation* Medieval and Renaissance Texts and Studies (Binghamton, NY: Center for Medieval and Early Rennaissance Studies).

Magennis, H. (2001) 'Audience(s), Reception, Literacy', in Pulsiano and Treharne (eds) (2001), pp. 84–101.

Magoun, F. P. Jnr (1953) 'The Oral-Formulaic Character of Anglo-Saxon Narrative Poetry', *Speculum* 28, pp. 446–67.

Mahan, T. W. (ed.) (1991) *Medieval Literature: Texts and Interpretation* (Binghamton, NY: Center for Medieval and Early Renaissance Studies).

Mann, Jill (2002) *Feminizing Chaucer* (Woodbridge, UK and Rochester, NY: D. S. Brewer).

—— (1991) *Geoffrey Chaucer*, Feminist Readings (New York and London: Harvester Wheatsheaf).

—— (1973) *Chaucer and Medieval Estates Satire: The Literature of Social Classes and the General Prologue to the Canterbury Tales* (Cambridge: Cambridge University Press).

Mapstone, S. L. (1991) 'Was there a Court Literature in Fifteenth-century Scotland?', *Studies in Scottish Literature* 26, pp. 410–22.

Marks, Richard and Morgan, Nigel (1981) *The Golden Age of English Manuscript Painting, 1200–1500* (London: Chatto & Windus).

Marsden, J. (ed.) (1989) *The Illustrated Bede* (London: Macmillan).

Marsden, R. (ed.) (2004) *The Cambridge Old English Reader* (Cambridge: Cambridge University Press).

Marshall, Clare (2001) *William Langland, Piers Plowman*, Writers and their Work (Tavistock: Northcote House).

Mattingly, H. (trans.) (1970) *Tacitus: The Agricola and the Germania*, Penguin. Classics, revised S. A. Handford (London: Penguin).

McCarren, V. and Moffat, D. (eds) (1998) *A Guide to Editing Middle English* (Ann Arbor: University of Michigan Press).

McCully, C. B. and Anderson, J. J. (eds) (1996) *English Historical Metrics* (Cambridge: Cambridge University Press).

McCully, C. B. and Hilles, S. (2005) *The Earliest English: An Introduction to Old English Language* (Harlow: Pearson Education).

McFarlane, K. B. (1973) *The Nobility of Later Medieval England* (Oxford: Clarendon Press).

—— (1972) *Lancastrian Kings and Lollard Knights* (Oxford: Clarendon Press).

McGowan, J. P. (2001) 'An Introduction to the Corpus of Anglo-Latin Literature' in Pulsiano and Treharne (eds) (2001), pp. 11–49.

McGrade, A. S. (ed.) (2003) *The Cambridge Companion to Medieval Philosophy* (Cambridge: Cambridge University Press).

McIntosh, A., Samuels, M. L., and Benskin, M. (eds) (1986) *A Linguistic Atlas of Late Medieval English*, 4 vols (Aberdeen: Aberdeen University Press).

McKenzie, D. F. (1999) *Bibliography and the Sociology of Texts*, 2nd edn (Cambridge: Cambridge University Press).

McKisack, May (1959) *The Fourteenth Century, 1307–1399* (rpt. 1991, Oxford: Clarendon Press).

McTurk, R. (ed.) (2005) *A Companion to Old Norse-Icelandic Literature and Culture* (Oxford: Blackwell).

Meale, Carol M. (ed.) (1996) *Women and Literature in Britain, 1150–1500*, 2nd edn (Cambridge: Cambridge University Press).

Medcalf, Stephen (ed.) (1981) *The Later Middle Ages* (London: Methuen).

Mehl, Dieter (2001) *English Literature in the Age of Chaucer*, Longman literature in English series (Harlow: Longman).

—— (1986) Geoffrey Chaucer: An Introduction to his Narrative Poetry (Cambridge: Cambridge University Press).

—— (1968) *The Middle English Romances of the Thirteenth and Fourteenth Centuries* (London: Routledge).

Middleton, Anne (1990) 'William Langland's "Kynde Name": Authorial Signature and Social Identity in Late Fourteenth-century England', in Patterson (ed.) (1990), pp. 15–81.

—— (1986) 'Piers Plowman', in *A Manual of the Writings in Middle English, 1050–1500*, vol. 7, ed. J. B. Severs and A. E. Hartung (New Haven: Connecticut Academy of Arts and Sciences), pp. 2211–34 and 2417–43.

—— (1978) 'The Idea of Public Poetry in the Reign of Richard II', *Speculum* 53, pp. 94–114.

Miller, T. (ed.) (1997) *The Old English Version of Bede's Ecclesiastical History of the English People*, EETS o.s. 95, 96, 110, 111 (Oxford: Oxford University Press).

Millett, B. (1992) 'The Origins of *Ancrene Wisse*: New Answers, New Questions', *MA* 61, pp. 206–28.

—— (1985) 'Chaucer, Lollius, and the Medieval Theory of Authorship', in P. Strohm and T. J. Hefferman (eds), *Reconstructing Chaucer: Selected Essays from the 1984 New Chaucer Society Congress* (Knoxville, Tenn.: New Chaucer Society).

Millett, B., with the assistance of George B. Jack and Yoko Wada (1996) *Ancrene Wisse, the Katherine Group, and the Wooing Group*, Annotated Bibliographies of Old and Middle English Literature no. 2 (Woodbridge: D. S. Brewer).

Millett, B. and Wogan-Browne, J. (eds) (1990) *Medieval Prose for Women: Selections from the Katherine Group and the Ancrene Wisse* (Oxford: Clarendon Press).

Milosh, Joseph E. (1966) *The Scale of Perfection and the English Mystical Tradition* (Madison: University of Wisconsin Press).

Minkova, Donka (2005) 'Chaucer's Language: Pronunciation, Morphology, Metre', in Steve Ellis (ed.) (2005), pp. 130–57.

Minnis, A. J. (1988) *Medieval Theory of Authorship*, 2nd edn (Aldershot: Wildwood House; first published London: Scolar Press, 1984).

—— (1982) *Chaucer and Pagan Antiquity* (Cambridge: D. S. Brewer; Totowa, NJ: Rowman & Littlefield).

Minnis, A. J. (ed.) (1983) *Gower's Confessio Amantis: Responses and Reassessments* (Cambridge: D. S. Brewer).

Minnis, A. J., and Brewer, C. (eds) (1992) *Crux and Controversy in Middle English Textual Criticism* (Cambridge: D. S. Brewer).

Minnis, A. J. with Scattergood, V. J. and Smith, J. J. (1995) *The Shorter Poems*, Oxford Guides to Chaucer (Oxford: Clarendon Press).

Minnis, A. J., and Scott, A. B. (eds) (1988) *Medieval Literary Theory and Criticism c.1100–c.1375: The Commentary-Tradition* (Oxford: Clarendon Press; revised edn, Oxford: Clarendon Press, 1991).

Mitchell, B. (1995) *An Invitation to Old English and Anglo-Saxon England* (Oxford: Blackwell).

—— (1985) *Old English Syntax* (Oxford: Oxford University Press).

Mitchell, B. and Robinson, F. C. (eds) (2001) *A Guide to Old English*, 6th edn (Oxford: Blackwell).

—— (eds) (1998) *Beowulf: An Edition* (Oxford: Blackwell).

Mitchell, Jerome (1968) *Thomas Hoccleve: A Study in Early Fifteenth-century English Poetic* (Urbana: University of Illinois Press).

Moore, A. K. (1951) *The Secular Lyric in Middle English* (Lexington: University of Kentucky Press).

Moorman, C. (1975) *Editing the Middle English Manuscript* (Jackson: University Press of Mississippi).

Morey, James H. (2000) *Book and Verse: A Guide to Middle English Biblical Literature* (Urbana: University of Illinois Press).

Morris, C. (1972) *The Discovery of the Individual, 1050–1200* (London: S.P.C.K. for the Church Historical Society).

Morrison, S. (1983) 'Sources for the *Orrmulum*', *Neuphilologische Mitteilungen* 84, pp. 410–36.

Morse, Ruth and Windeatt, Barry (1990) *Chaucer Traditions. Studies in Honour of Derek Brewer* (Cambridge: Cambridge University Press).

Moseley, C. W. R. D. (trans.) (1983) *The Travels of Sir John Mandeville* (Harmondsworth: Penguin Books).

Muir, B. J. (ed.) (2000) *The Exeter Anthology of Old English Poetry: An Edition of Exeter Dean and Chapter MS 3501*, 2nd edn (Exeter: University of Exeter Press).

Murfin, R. C. and Ray, S. M. (2003) *The Bedford Glossary of Critical and Literary Terms* (Boston, MA: Bedford Falls).

Muscatine, Charles (1957) *Chaucer and the French Tradition: A Study in Style and Meaning* (Berkeley: University of California Press).

Mustanoja, I. J. (1979) 'Chaucer's Prosody', in Rowland (ed.) (1979), pp. 65–94.

Myers, A. R. (1952) *England in the Late Middle Ages* (London: Penguin).

Newhauser, R. (1997) 'Sources II: Scriptural and Devotional Sources', in Brewer and Gibson (eds) (1997), pp. 257–75.

Nicholson, L. E. (ed.) (1963) *An Anthology of Beowulf Criticism* (Notre Dame: University of Notre Dame Press).

Nicholson, Peter (1989) *An Annotated Index to the Commentary on Gower's Confessio Amantis*, Medieval and Renaissance Texts & Studies no. 62 (Binghamton, NY: Center for Medieval and Early Renaissance Studies).

Nicholson, Peter (ed.) (1991) *Gower's Confessio Amantis: A Critical Anthology* (Cambridge: D. S. Brewer).

Niles, J. D. (1991) 'Pagan Survivals and Popular Belief' in Godden and Lapidge (eds) (1991), pp. 126–41.

North, R. (1997) *Heathen Gods in Old English Literature*, Cambridge Studies in Anglo-Saxon England 22 (Cambridge: Cambridge University Press).

Nykrog, P. (1957) *Les Fabliaux* (Copenhagen: Ejner Munksgaard).

O'Brien O'Keeffe, K. (1997a) 'Introduction', in O'Brien O'Keeffe (ed.) (1997b), pp. 1–19.

O'Brien O'Keeffe, K. (ed.) (1997b) *Reading Old English Texts* (Cambridge: Cambridge University Press).

—— (1991) 'Heroic Values and Christian ethics', in Godden and Lapidge (eds) (1991), pp. 107–25.

—— (1990) *Visible Song: Transitional Literacy in Old English Verse*, Cambridge Studies in Anglo-Saxon England 4 (Cambridge: Cambridge University Press).

—— (ed.) (1994) *Old English Shorter Poems*, Basic Readings in Anglo-Saxon England (New York: Garland).

Oakden, J. P. (1930–5) *Alliterative Poetry in Middle English* (Manchester: Manchester University Press).

Oakley, Francis (1979) *The Western Church in the Later Middle Ages* (Ithaca, NY: Cornell University Press).

O'Donnell, D. (2005) *Cædmon's Hymn: A Multi-media Study, Edition, and Archive* (Cambridge: D. S. Brewer).

O'Donnell, J. J., *Augustine of Hippo* (http://ccat.sas.upenn.edu/jod/augustine.html – referenced December 2005).

O'Donoghue, H. (2004) *Old Norse-Icelandic Literature: A Short Introduction* (Oxford: Blackwell).

Ogilvy, J. D. A. (1984–5) *Books Known to the English 597–1066: Addenda et Corrigenda*, Old English Newsletter Subsidia 11 (New York: Center for Medieval and Early Renaissance Studies).

—— 1967, *Books Known to the English, 597–1066* (Cambridge, MA: Medieval Academy of America).

Olsen, A. H. (1997) 'Gender Roles', in Bjork and Niles (eds) (1997), pp. 311–24.

—— 1988, 'Oral-Formulaic Research in Old English Studies, I and II', *Oral Tradition* 3, pp. 138–90.

Orchard, A. (2003a) 'Latin and the Vernacular Languages' in T. Charles-Edwards (ed.), *After Rome* (Oxford: Oxford University Press), pp. 191–219.

—— (2003b) *A Critical Companion to Beowulf* (Cambridge: D. S. Brewer).

—— (1997) 'Oral Tradition', in O'Brien O'Keeffe (ed.) (1997), pp. 101–23.

—— (1994) *The Poetic Art of Aldhelm* (Cambridge: Cambridge University Press).

Owst, G. R. (1961) *Literature and Pulpit in Medieval England: A Neglected Chapter in the History of English Letters and of the English People*, 2nd rev. edn (Oxford: Blackwell).

Page, R. I. (1999) *An Introduction to English Runes*, 2nd edn (Woodbridge: Boydell Press).

—— (1970) *Life in Anglo-Saxon England* (London: Batsford).

Pantin, W. A. (1955) *The English Church in the Fourteenth Century* (Cambridge: Cambridge University Press).

Parkes, M. B. (1992) *Pause and Effect: Punctuation in the West* (Aldershot: Scolar Press).

—— (1991a) *Scribes, Scripts and Readers: Studies in the Communication, Presentation and Dissemination of Medieval Texts* (London: Hambledon Press).

—— (1991b) 'On the Presumed Date and Possible Origins of the *Orrmulum*: Oxford, Bodleian Library, MS Junius 1', in M. B. Parkes, *Scribes, Scripts and Readers: Studies in the Communication, Presentation and Dissemination of Medieval Texts* (London: Hambledon Press), pp. 187–200.

Parkes, M. B. (1979) *English Cursive Book Hands, 1250–1500* (London: Scholar Press, also published in 1980 by University of California Press, Berkeley; first published by Oxford University Press in 1969).

Parry, M. (1971) *The Making of Homeric Verse: The Collected Papers of Milman Parry* (Oxford: Clarendon Press).

Pasternack, C. B. (1997) 'Post-structuralist Theories: the Subject and the Text', in O'Brien O'Keeffe (ed.) (1997), pp. 170–91.

—— (1995) *The Textuality of Old English Poetry*, Cambridge Studies in Anglo-Saxon England 13 (Cambridge: Cambridge University Press).

Patterson, L. (1991) *Chaucer and the Subject of History* (London: Routledge).

—— (1989) *Negotiating the Past: The Historical Understanding of Medieval Literature* (Madison: University of Wisconsin Press).

Petterson, L. (ed.) (1990) *Literary Practice and Social Change in Britain, 1380–1530* (Berkeley, CA: University of California Press).

Pearsall, Derek (2003) *Arthurian Romance: A Short Introduction* (Oxford: Blackwell).

—— (1997) *John Lydgate (1371–1449): A Bio-bibliography*, English Literary Studies 71 (Victoria: University of Victoria Press).

—— (1992) *The Life of Geoffrey Chaucer: A Critical Biography* (Oxford: Blackwell).

—— (1991) 'Chaucer's Metre: the Evidence of the Manuscripts', in Machan (ed.) (1991), pp. 41–57.

—— (1990a) 'Chaucer and Lydgate', in Morse and Windeatt (eds) (1990), pp. 39–53.

—— (1990b) *An Annotated Critical Bibliography of Langland* (New York and London: Harvester Wheatsheaf).

—— (1988) 'Poverty and Poor People in *Piers Plowman*', in Kennedy, Waldron and Wittig (eds) (1988), pp. 167–85.

—— (1985) *The Canterbury Tales* (London: Allen & Unwin).

—— (1981) 'The Origins of the Alliterative Revival', in *The Alliterative Tradition in the Fourteenth Century*, ed. Bernard S. Levy and Paul Szarmach (Kent, Ohio: Kent State University Press), pp. 1–24.

—— (1977) *Old English and Middle English Poetry* (London: Routledge).

—— (1970) *John Lydgate* (London: Routledge and Kegan Paul).

Pearsall, Derek (ed.) (1987) *Manuscripts and Texts: Editorial Problems in Later Middle English Literature* (Cambridge: D. S. Brewer), pp. 95–109.

Pelteret, D. A. E. (ed.) (2000) *Anglo-Saxon History: Basic Readings* (London: Routledge).

Percival, Florence (1998) *Chaucer's Legendary Good Women* (Cambridge: Cambridge University Press).

Phillips, Helen and Havely, Nick (eds) (1997) *Chaucer's Dream Poetry* (London and New York: Longman).

Platt, C. (1994) *Medieval England: A Social History and Archaeology from the Conquest to AD 1600* (London: Routledge, originally published 1978).

Pollard, William F. and Boenig, Robert (eds) (1997) *Mysticism and Spirituality in Medieval England* (Cambridge: D. S. Brewer).

Pollington, S. (2003) *The Mead-Hall: Feasting in Anglo-Saxon England* (Norfolk: Anglo-Saxon Books).

—— (1994) *An Introduction to the Old English Language and its Literature* (Norfolk: Anglo-Saxon Books).

Poole, Austin Lane (1955) *From Domesday Book to Magna Carta, 1087–1216*, 2nd edn (Oxford: Clarendon Press).

Poole, R. G. (1998) *Old English Wisdom Poetry*, Annotated Bibliographies of Old and Middle English Literature, no. 5 (Cambridge: D. S. Brewer).

Pope, J. C. (ed.) (1967–8) *Homilies of Ælfric: A Supplementary Collection*, EETS o.s. 259 and 260 (London: Oxford University Press).

Powicke, F. M. (1962) *The Thirteenth Century, 1216–1307*, 2nd edn (Oxford: Clarendon Press).

Pugh, T. (2004) *Queering Medieval Genres* (Basingstoke: Palgrave Macmillan).

Pulsiano, P. and Treharne, E. (eds) (2001) *A Companion to Anglo-Saxon Literature* (Oxford: Blackwell).

Putter, Ad (1996) *An Introduction to the Gawain-Poet* (London and New York: Longman).

Raw, B. (1991) 'Biblical Literature: the New Testament', in Godden and Lapidge (eds) (1991), pp. 227–42.

Rawcliffe, Carole (1995) *Medicine and Society in Later Medieval England* (Stroud: Alan Sutton).

Raymo, Robert R. (1986) 'Works of Religious and Philosophical Instruction', in *A Manual of the Writings in Middle English, 1050–1500*, vol. 7, ed. J. B. Severs and A. E. Hartung (New Haven: Connecticut Academy of Arts and Sciences), pp. 2255–378 and 2467–582.

Reed, Thomas L., Jr (1990) *Middle English Debate Poetry and the Aesthetics of Irresolution* (Columbia and London: University of Missouri Press).

Renoir, A. (1967) *The Poetry of John Lydgate* (London: Routledge & Kegan Paul).

Richards, M. P. (ed.) (2001) *Anglo-Saxon Manuscripts: Basic Readings* (London: Routledge).

Riddy, Felicity (1987) *Sir Thomas Malory*, Medieval and Renaissance Authors, 9 (Leiden: Brill).

Ridley, Florence H. (1973) 'Middle Scots Writers', in *A Manual of the Writings in Middle English, 1050–1500*, vol. 6, ed. J. B. Severs and A. E. Hartung (New Haven: Connecticut Academy of Arts and Sciences), pp. 961–1060 and 1123–284.

Riehle, Wolfgang (1981) *The Middle English Mystics*, trans. Bernard Strandring (London: Routledge & Kegan Paul).

Rigg, A. G. (1992) *A History of Anglo-Latin Literature, 1066–1422* (Cambridge: Cambridge University Press).

—— (ed.) (1977) *Editing Medieval Texts* (New York: Garland).

Robbins, R. H. and Cutler, J. L. (1965) *Supplement to the Index of Middle English Verse* (Lexington: University of Kentucky Press).

Roberts, J., Kay, C., and Grundy, L. (1995) *A Thesaurus of Old English*, 2 vols, King's College London Medieval Studies (Exeter: Short Run Press).

Robinson, F. C. (2004) 'Old English', in Brian Murdoch and Malcolm Read (eds), *Early Germanic Literature and Culture*, The Camden House History of German Literature, vol. 1 (Rochester, NY: Camden House), pp. 205–33.

—— (2001) 'Secular Poetry', in Pulsiano and Treharne (eds) (2001), pp. 281–95.

—— (1991) *'Beowulf'*, in Godden and Lapidge (eds) (1991), pp. 142–59.

—— (1985) *Beowulf and the Appositive Style* (Knoxville: University of Tennessee Press).

Robinson, O. W. (1992) *Old English and its Closest Relatives* (Stanford: Stanford University Press).

Rodrigues, L. J. (ed. and trans.) (1995) *Anglo-Saxon Didactic Verse* (Felinfach: Llanerch Publishers).

Rodwell, W. (1989) *Book of Church Archaeology*, 2nd edn (London: Batsford and English Heritage).

Rowland, Beryl (ed.) (1979) *Companion to Chaucer Studies*, rev. edn (Oxford and New York: Oxford University Press).

Royan, Nicola (2005) 'Scottish Literature', in Johnson and Treharne (eds) (2005), pp. 354–69.

Rumble, A. R. (2001) 'Using Anglo-Saxon Manuscripts', in Richards (ed.) (2001), pp. 3–24.

Rutter, R. (1987) 'William Caxton and Literary Patronage', *SP* 84, pp. 440–70.

Salter, Elizabeth (1988) *English and International: Studies in the Literature, Art and Patronage of Medieval England*, ed. Derek Pearsall and Nicolette Zeeman (Cambridge: Cambridge University Press).

Sands, D. B. (1957) 'Caxton as a Literary Critic', Publications of the Bibliographical Society of America, 51, pp. 312–18.

Sands, D. B. (ed.) (1986) *Middle English Verse Romances* (Exeter: University of Exeter Press).

Sawyer, P. H. (1968) *Anglo-Saxon Charters: An Annotated List and Bibliography* (London: Royal Historical Society).

Scattergood, V. J. and Sherborne, J. M. (eds) (1983) *English Court Culture in the Later Middle Ages* (London: Duckworth).

Schmidt, A. V. C. (1987) *The Clerkly Maker: Langland's Poetic Art* (Cambridge: D. S. Brewer).

Schmidt, A. V. C. (ed.) (1995–) *Piers Plowman: A Parallel-text Edition of the A, B, C and Z Versions* (London: Longman).

—— (ed.) (1995) *The Vision of Piers Plowman: A Critical Edition of the B-text Based on Trinity College Cambridge MS B.15.17*, 2nd edn (London: Dent).

—— (trans.) (1992) *Piers Plowman: A New Translation of the B-text*, World's Classics (Oxford: Oxford University Press).

Schofield, J. and Vince, A. (1994) *Medieval Towns* (London:Leicester University Press).

Science, M. (ed.) (1999) *Boethius: De Consolatione Philosophiae translated by John Walton*, EETS o.s. 170 (Oxford: Oxford University Press).

Scott, Kathleen L. (1995) 'An Hours and Psalter by Two Ellesmere Illuminators', in Stevens and Woodward (eds) (1995), pp. 87–119.

Scragg, D. G. (2001) 'Secular Prose', in Pulsiano and Treharne (eds) (2001), pp. 268–80.

—— (1997) 'Source Study', in O'Brien O'Keeffe (ed.) (1997b), pp. 39–58.

—— (1991) 'The Nature of Old English Verse', in Godden and Lapidge (eds) (1991), pp. 55–70.

Scragg, D. G. and Szarmach, P. E. (1994) *The Editing of Old English* (Cambridge: D. S. Brewer).

Scragg, D. G. and Weinberg, C. (eds) (2000) *Literary Appropriations of the Anglo-Saxons from the Thirteenth to the Twentieth Century* (Cambridge: Cambridge University Press).

Sergeant, M. G. (ed.) (1989) *De Cella in Seculum: Religious and Secular Life and Devotion in Late Medieval England* (Cambridge: D. S. Brewer).

Severs, J. B. and Hartung, A. E. (eds) (1967–) *A Manual of the Writings in Middle English, 1050–1500* (New Haven: Connecticut Academy of Arts and Sciences).

Seymour, M. C. (1993) *Sir John Mandeville*, Authors of the Middle Ages, English writers of the Late Middle Ages (Aldershot: Variorum).

Seymour, M. C. (ed.) (1981) *Selections from Hoccleve* (Oxford: Clarendon Press).

Sherley-Price, L. (trans.) (1968) *Bede: A History of the English Church and People*, Penguin Classics (Harmondsworth: Penguin).

Shippey, T. A. (1976) *Poems of Wisdom and Learning in Old English* (Cambridge: D. S. Brewer).

—— (1972) *Old English Verse* (London: Hutchinson).

Simons, J. (ed.) (1993) *From Medieval to Medievalism* (London: Longman).

Simpson, James (1990) *Piers Plowman: An Introduction to the B-Text* (London: Longman).

Skeat, W. W. (ed.) (1966) *Ælfric's Lives of Saints*, EETS o.s. 76, 82, 94, 114 (Oxford: Oxford University Press).

Smith, J. J. (1999) *Essentials of Early English* (London: Routledge).

Solopova, E. (2006) 'English Poetry of the Reign of Henry II', in *Writings of the Reign of Henry II: Twelve Essays*, ed. Ruth Kennedy and Simon Meecham-Jones (Basingstoke: Palgrave Macmillan), pp. 187–204.

Southern, R. W. (1953) *The Making of the Middle Ages*, Hutchinson's University Library (London: Hutchinson).

Spearing, A. C. (2003) 'The Canterbury Tales IV: Exemplum and Fable', in Boitani and Mann (eds) (2003), pp. 159–77.

—— (1976) *Medieval Dream-Poetry* (Cambridge: Cambridge University Press).

—— (1970) *The 'Gawain' Poet: A Critical Study* (Cambridge: Cambridge University Press).

Spearing, E. (trans.) (1998) *Julian of Norwich, Revelations of Divine Love (Short Text and Long Text* (London: Penguin).

Spencer, H. Leith. (1993) *English Preaching in the Late Middle Ages* (Oxford: Clarendon Press).

St John, Michael (2000) *Chaucer's Dream Visions: Courtliness and Individual Identity* (Aldershot: Ashgate).

Staley, L. (2000) 'Personal Identity', in Brown (ed.) (2000), pp. 360–77.

—— (1994) *Margery Kempe's Dissenting Fictions* (University Park, PA: Pennsylvania State University Press).

Stanley, E. G. (2000) *Imagining the Anglo-Saxon Past: 'The Search for Anglo-Saxon Paganism' and 'Anglo-Saxon Trial by Jury'* (Cambridge: D. S. Brewer).

—— (1969) 'Laȝamon's Antiquarian Sentiments', *MA* 38, pp. 23–37.

—— (ed.) (1966) *Continuations and Beginnings: Studies in Old English Literature* (London: Nelson).

Steblin-Kamensky, M. I. (1978) *Istoricheskaia poetika* [Historical poetics] (Leningrad: Izdatelstvo Leningradskogo Universiteta).

Stenton, F. M. (1971) *Anglo-Saxon England*, 3rd edn (Oxford: Oxford University Press).

—— (1961) *The First Century of English Feudalism*, 2nd edn (Oxford: Oxford University Press).

Stevens, John (1973) *Medieval Romance: Themes and Approaches* (London: Hutchinson).

Stevens, Martin and Woodward, Daniel (eds) (1995) *The Ellesmere Chaucer: Essays in Interpretation* (San Marino, Ca.: Huntington Library; and Tokio: Yushodo).

Stevick, R. D. (2003) *A Firstbook of Old English* (Oregon: Wipf and Stock).

Stokes, Myra (1984) *Justice and Mercy in Piers Plowman: A Reading of the B Text Visio* (London: Croom Helm).

Storms, G. (1948) *Anglo-Saxon Magic* (The Hague: Martinus Nijhoff).

Strohm P. (2003) 'The Social and Literary Scene in England', in Boitani and Mann (eds) (2003), pp. 1–18.

—— (2000) *Theory and the Premodern Text* (Minneapolis: University of Minnesota Press).

—— (1989) *Social Chaucer* (Cambridge, MA: Harvard University Press).

—— (1980) 'Middle English Narrative Genres', *Genre* 13, pp. 379–88.

Sumption, Jonathan (2002) *Pilgrimage: An Image of Mediaeval Religion* (London: Faber; originally published 1975).

Swan, M. (2005) 'Religious Writing by Women', in Johnson and Treharne (eds) (2005), pp. 257–72.

—— (2001) 'Authorship and Anonymity', in Pulsiano and Treharne (eds) (2001), pp. 71–83.

Swan, M. and Treharne, E. M. (2000) *Rewriting Old English in the Twelfth Century*, Cambridge Studies in Anglo-Saxon England no. 30 (Cambridge: Cambridge University Press).

Swanson, R. (2000) 'Social Structures', in Brown (ed.) (2000), pp. 397–413.

Swanton, M. (trans.) (1996) *The Anglo-Saxon Chronicle* (London: Dent).

—— (trans.) (1993) *Anglo-Saxon Prose*, 2nd edn (London: Dent).

Sweet, H. (ed.) (1975) *Sweet's Anglo-Saxon Reader in Prose and Verse*, 15th edn, revised by D. Whitelock (Oxford: Oxford University Press).

—— (ed.) (1965) *Anglo-Saxon Primer*, 9th edn, revised by N. Davis (Oxford: Oxford University Press).

Szarmach, P. E. (1997) 'The Recovery of Texts', in O'Brien O'Keeffe (ed.) (1997), pp. 124–45.

Szarmach, P. E. (ed.) (2000) *Old English Prose*, Basic Readings in Anglo-Saxon England (New York: Garland).

—— (ed.) (1986) *Studies in Earlier Old English Prose* (New York: State University of New York Press).

Taavitsainen, Irma and Pahta, Päivi (eds) (2004) *Medical and Scientific Writing in Late Medieval English* (Cambridge: Cambridge University Press).

Takamiya, Toshiyuki and Brewer, Derek (eds) (1981) *Aspects of Malory* (Cambridge: D. S. Brewer).

Tanselle, G. T. (1983) 'Classical, Biblical, and Medieval Textual Criticism and Modern Editing', *Studies in Bibliography* 36, pp. 21–68.

Tatlock, John S. P. (1950) *The Legendary History of Britain: Geoffrey of Monmouth's Historia Regum Britanniae and its Early Vernacular Versions* (Berkeley: University of California Press).

Taylor, H. M. and Taylor, J. (1965–78) *Anglo-Saxon Architecture*, 3 vols (Cambridge: Cambridge University Press).

Taylor, John (1987) *English Historical Literature in the Fourteenth Century* (Oxford: Oxford University Press).

Teachers of Old English in Britain and Ireland: Manuscript Studies (www.hcu.ox.ac.uk/toebi/man.html, consulted February 2006).

Thrupp, S. L. (1948) *The Merchant Class of Medieval London, 1300–1500* (Ann Arbor: University of Michigan Press).

Tigges, W. (1995a) '*The Fox and the Wolf*: A Study in Medieval Irony', in Veldhoen and Aertsen (eds) (1995), pp. 79–91.

—— (1995b) '*The Land of Cockayne*: Sophisticated Myth', in Veldhoen and Aertsen (eds) (1995), pp. 93–101.

—— (1994) 'Snakes and Ladders: Ambiguity and Coherence in the Exeter Book Riddles and Maxims', in Aertsen and Bremmer (eds) (1994), pp. 95–118.

Tolkien, J. R. R. (1997) *The Monsters and the Critics, and Other Essays*, ed. Christopher Tolkien (London: HarperCollins).

—— (1929) 'Ancrene Wisse and *Hali Meiðhad*', *Essays and Studies* 14, pp. 104–26.

Toswell, M. J. (1996) 'Tacitus, Old English Heroic Poetry, and Ethnographic Preconceptions', in M. J. Toswell and E. M. Tyler (eds), *Studies in English Language and Literature: 'Doubt Wisely': Papers in Honour of E. G. Stanley* (London: Routledge), pp. 493–507.

Trahern, J. B. Jnr (1991) 'Fatalism and the Millennium', in Godden and Lapidge (eds) (1991), pp. 160–71.

Treharne, E. (2005) 'The Context of Medieval Literature', in Johnson and Treharne (eds) (2005), pp. 7–14.

—— (2001) 'English in the Post-Conquest Period', in Pulsiano and Treharne (eds) (2001), pp. 403–14.

Treharne, E. (ed.) (2004) *Old and Middle English c.890–c.1400: An Anthology* (Oxford: Blackwell).

Treharne, E. and Pulsiano, P. (2001) 'An Introduction to the Corpus of Anglo-Saxon Literature', in Pulsiano & Treharne (eds) (2001), pp. 3–10.

Trigg, S. (2006) 'Chaucer's Influence and Reception', in Lerer (ed.) (2006), pp. 297–323.

Tuck, Anthony (1985) *Crown and Nobility 1272–1461: Political Conflict in Late Medieval England* (London: Fontana).

Tupper, F. (ed.) (1968) *The Riddles of the Exeter Book* (Darmstadt: Wissenschaftliche Buchgesellschaft).

Turville-Petre, Thorlac (2005) 'Political Lyrics', in Duncan (ed.) (2005), pp. 171–88.

—— (1977) *The Alliterative Revival* (Cambridge: D. S. Brewer).

Tydeman, William (1986) *English Medieval Theatre, 1400–1500* (London: Routledge & Kegan Paul).

Utley, Francis Lee (1972) 'Dialogues, Debates, and Catechisms', in *A Manual of the Writings in Middle English, 1050–1500*, vol. 3, ed. J. B. Severs and A. E. Hartung (New Haven: Connecticut Academy of Arts and Sciences), pp. 669–745 and 829–902.

Veldhoen, N. H. G. E. and Aertsen, H. (eds) (1995) *Companion to Early Middle English Literature*, 2nd edn (Amsterdam: VU University Press).

Vinaver, Eugène (1971) *The Rise of Romance* (Oxford: Clarendon Press).

Vinaver, Eugène (ed.) (1990) *The Works of Sir Thomas Malory*, 3rd edn rev. by P. J. C. Field (Oxford: Clarendon Press).

Voigts, Linda (1989) 'Scientific and Medical Books', in Griffiths and Pearsall (eds) (1989), pp. 345–402

—— (1982) 'Editing Middle English Medical Texts: Needs and Issues', in Trevor H. Levere (ed.), *Editing Texts in the History of Science and Medicine: Papers given at the Seventeenth Annual Conference on Editorial Problems, University of Toronto, 6–7 November 1981* (New York and London: Garland), pp. 39–68.

Voigts, Linda and Kurtz, Patricia (2000) *Scientific and Medical Writings in Old and Middle English: An Electronic Reference* (Ann Arbor: University of Michigan Press).

von Kreisler, Nicolai (1970) 'Satire in *The Fox and the Wolf*', *JEGP* 69, pp. 650–8.

Wada, Yoko (ed.) (2003) *A Companion to Ancrene Wisse* (Cambridge: D. S. Brewer).

Waite, G. (2000) *Old English Prose Translations of King Alfred's Reign*, Annotated Bibliographies of Old and Middle English Literature, no. 6 (Cambridge: D. S. Brewer).

Walker, Greg. (2005) 'Medieval Drama: the Corpus Christi in York and Croxton', in Johnson and Treharne (eds) (2005), pp. 370–85.

Wallace, David (1985) *Chaucer and the Early Writings of Boccaccio* (Cambridge: D. S. Brewer).

Wallace, David (ed.) (1999) *The Cambridge History of Medieval English Literature* (Cambridge: Cambridge University Press).

Wallace-Hadrill, J. M. (ed.) (1988) *Bede's Ecclesiastical History of the English People: A Historical Commentary* (Oxford: Clarendon Press).

Watson, Nicholas (1999) 'Middle English Mystics', in Wallace (ed.) (1999), pp. 539–65.

—— (1991), *Richard Rolle and the Invention of Authority* (Cambridge: Cambridge University Press).

Webb, G. (1956) *Architecture in Britain: The Middle Ages* (Harmondsworth: Penguin Books).

Webster, L. and Backhouse, J. (1991) *The Making of England: Anglo-Saxon Art and Culture AD 600–900* (London: British Museum Press).

Wenzel, Siegfried (1986) *Preachers, Poets, and the Early English Lyric* (Princeton: Princeton University Press).

Whitelock, D. (trans.) (1996) *English Historical Documents, c.500–1042*, 2nd edn (London: Routledge).

Wilcox, J. (2005) ''Tell me what I am': the Old English Riddles', in Johnson & Treharne (eds) (2005), pp. 46–59.

—— (2001) 'Transmission of Literature and Learning: Anglo-Saxon Scribal Culture' in Pulsiano and Treharne (eds) (2001), pp. 50–70.

Williamson, C. (trans.) (1983) *A Feast of Creatures: Anglo-Saxon Riddle Songs* (London: Scolar Press).

Williamson, C. (ed.) (1977) *The Old English Riddles of the Exeter Book* (Chapel Hill: University of North Carolina Press).

Wilson, D. (1992) *Anglo-Saxon Paganism* (London: Routledge).

—— (1984) *Anglo-Saxon Art: From the Seventh Century to the Norman Conquest* (London: Thames and Hudson).

—— (1981) *The Archaeology of Anglo-Saxon England* (Cambridge: Cambridge University Press).

Wilson, R. M. (1970) *The Lost Literature of Medieval England*, 2nd edn (London: Methuen).

—— (1951) *Early Middle English Literature*, 2nd edn (London: Methuen).

Wimsatt, James I (1991) *Chaucer and his French Contemporaries: Natural Music in the Fourteenth Century* (Toronto and London: University of Toronto Press).

Windeatt, B. A. (1992) *Troilus and Criseyde*, Oxford Guides to Chaucer (Oxford: Oxford University Press).

—— (1982) *Chaucer's Dream Poetry: Sources and Analogies* (Cambridge: D. S. Brewer).

Winterbottom, M. (ed. and trans.) (2002) *Gildas: The Ruin of Britain and Other Works*, Arthurian Period Sources, 7 (Chichester: Phillimore).

Wogan-Browne, J. (2002) 'The Hero in Christian Reception: Ælfric and Heroic Poetry', in Liuzza (ed.) (2002), pp. 215–35.

Wogan-Browne, J., Watson, N., Taylor, A., and Evans, R. (eds) (1999) *The Idea of the Vernacular: An Anthology of Middle English Literary Theory 1280–1520* (Exeter: University of Exeter Press).

Woolf, R. (1976) 'The Ideal of Men Dying with their Lord in the *Germania* and in *The Battle of Maldon*', *Anglo-Saxon England* 5, pp. 63–81.

—— (1972) *The English Mystery Plays* (London: Routledge & Kegan Paul).

—— (1968) *English Religious Lyric in the Middle Ages* (Oxford: Clarendon Press; rpt. 1998).

Wormald, P. (1999a) *The Making of English Law: King Alfred to the Twelfth Century* (Oxford: Blackwell).

—— (1999b) *Legal Culture in the Early Medieval West: Law as Text, Image and Experience* (London: Hambledon Press).

—— (1991) 'Anglo-Saxon Society and its Literature', in Godden and Lapidge (eds) (1991), pp. 1–22.

Wrenn, C. L. (1973) *Beowulf: With the Finnesburg Fragment*, 3rd edn (London: Harrap).

—— (1967) *A Study of Old English Literature* (London: Harrap).

Wright, C. E. (1960) *English Vernacular Hands from the Twelfth to the Fifteenth Centuries* (Oxford: Clarendon Press).

Yeager, R. F. (1990) *John Gower's Poetic: The Search for a New Arion* (Cambridge: D. S. Brewer).

Yeager, R. F. (ed.) (1984) *Fifteenth-Century Studies: Recent Essays* (Hamden, CT: Archon Books).

Zarnecki, George, Holt, Janet, and Holland, Tristram (eds) (1984) *English Romanesque Art, 1066–1200: Hayward Gallery, London, 5 April–8 July* (London: Arts Council of Great Britain in association with Weidenfeld and Nicolson).

Zeikowitz, R. E. (2003) *Homoeroticism and Chivalry: Discourses of Male Same-Sex Desire in the Fourteenth Century* (Basingstoke: Palgrave Macmillan).

Ziegler, Philip (1969) *The Black Death* (London: Collins).

Zimmerman, G. (1995) *The Four Old English Poetic Manuscripts: Texts, Contexts, and Historical Background* (Heidelberg: Universitätverlag C. Winter).

Freely Accessible Online Resources – a Selection

The following acts as an introductory list to some of the free online resources available in medieval literary studies. This is far from comprehensive and readers are directed to the general resources, many of which contain fuller catalogues.

General

Anglo-Saxons.Net – www.anglo-saxons.net/hwaet/

A Brief Outline of Medieval English Literature – http://accd.edu/sac/english/bailey/medeng.htm

A Companion to Middle English Literature – http://web.phil-fak.uni-duesseldorf.de/~holteir/companion/

HUMBUL –Humanities Hub (general catalogue of reviewed web sites) – www.humbul.ac.uk/

Internet Medieval Sourcebook – www.fordham.edu/halsall/sbook.html
The Labyrinth: Resources for Medieval Studies – www.georgetown.edu/labyrinth/labyrinth-home.html
Luminarium Anthology of Texts – www.luminarium.org/
Medieval Feminist Index – www.haverford.edu/library/reference/mschaus/mfi/mfi.html
The New Chaucer Society – http://artsci.wustl.edu/~chaucer/
Old English at the University of Virginia (P. Baker) – www.engl.virginia.edu/OE/
Old English Pages (C. Ball) – www.georgetown.edu/cball/oe/old_english.html
Online Medieval and Classical Library – www.omacl.org/
On-line Reference Book for Medievalists: The Anglo-Saxons – http://the-orb.net/encyclop/early/pre1000/asindex.html; High Medieval England – http://the-orb.net/encyclop/high/england/engindex.html; Late Medieval England – http://the-orb.net/encyclop/late/england/default.html
Taming the Labyrinth: an Introduction to Medieval Resources on the WWW – http://hosting.uaa.alaska.edu/afdtk/Emporia.htm
Teachers of Old English in Britain and Ireland – www.toebi.org.uk/
Ða Engliscan Gesiðas – www.kami.demon.co.uk/gesithas/index.html

Reference works

Bosworth and Toller's Dictionary of Anglo-Saxon – www.ling.upenn.edu/~kurisuto/germanic/oe_bosworthtoller_about.html#images
Clark-Hall's *A Concise Anglo-Saxon Dictionary* – www.ling.upenn.edu/~kurisuto/germanic/oe_clarkhall_about.html
Fontes Anglo-Saxonici – http://fontes.english.ox.ac.uk/
Old English Corpus – www.hti.umich.edu/english/oec/
Old English Newsletter Bibliography – www.oenewsletter.org/OENDB/index.php
Thesaurus of Old English – http://libra.englang.arts.gla.ac.uk/oethesaurus/

Journals

Anglo-Saxon England – http://titles.cambridge.org/journals/journal_catalogue.asp?historylinks=ALPHA&mnemonic=ASE
The Digital Medievalist – www.digitalmedievalist.org/journal.cfm
Dragons in the Sky – http://users.ox.ac.uk/%7Estuart/dits/
The Heroic Age – http://members.aol.com/heroicage1/homepage.html
Marginalia – www.marginalia.co.uk/journal
Old English Newsletter Online – http://oenewsletter.org/OEN/index.php

Texts/authors

Ælfric's Homilies (Judith, Esther, the Maccabees) – http://users.ox.ac.uk/~stuart/kings/

Ancrene Wisse: A Prototype Edition for the Early English Texts Society – www.tei-c.org.uk/Projects/EETS/

Anglo-Saxon Charters – www.trin.cam.ac.uk/chartwww/

Anglo-Saxon Chronicle (T. Jebson) – http://jebbo.home.texas.net/asc/asc.html

The Auchinleck Manuscript: National Library of Scotland, Advocates' MS 19.2.1 – http://faculty.washington.edu/miceal/auchinleck/

Beowulf in Hypertext – www.humanities.mcmaster.ca/%7Ebeowulf/

The Brut Chronicle Manuscript – www.hti.umich.edu/images/brut/

Camelot Project at the University of Rochester: Arthurian texts, images, bibliographies, and basic information – www.lib.rochester.edu/camelot/cphome.stm

Chaucer Metapage – www.unc.edu/depts/chaucer/

Chaucer Pedagogy Page – http://hosting.uaa.alaska.edu/afdtk/pedagogy.htm

Corpus of Middle English Prose and Verse – www.hti.umich.edu/c/cme/

Electronic *Beowulf* – www.uky.edu/~kiernan/eBeowulf/guide.htm

Entire Old English Corpus – www.hti.umich.edu/english/oec/

Mapping Margery Kempe – www.holycross.edu/departments/visarts/projects/kempe/

The Middle English Collection (The Etext Center at the University of Virginia Library) – http://etext.lib.virginia.edu/collections/languages/english/mideng.browse.html

Old English Aerobics Anthology – www.engl.virginia.edu/OE/anthology/

Old English Coursepack – www.english.ox.ac.uk/coursepack/

Robert Henryson – www.arts.gla.ac.uk/SESLL/STELLA/STARN/poetry/HENRYSON/homepage.htm

Sermo Lupi ad Anglos (M. Bernstein) – http://english3.fsu.edu/~wulfstan/

The TEAMS Middle English Texts – www.lib.rochester.edu/camelot/teams/tmsmenu.htm

The Wanderer (T. Romano) – www.aimsdata.com/tim/anhaga/edition.htm

Online courses

Bibliography and Methods in Medieval Studies – https://netfiles.uiuc.edu/cdwright/www/medsyll.html

First Steps in Old English – www.kami.demon.co.uk/gesithas/OEsteps/index.html

'Hwæt! Old English in Context' – www.georgetown.edu/cball/hwaet/hwaet06.html

Internet Old English (M. McGillivray) – www.ucalgary.ca/UofC/eduweb/engl401/

Learning Old English (T. Jebson) – http://lonestar.texas.net/%7Ejebbo/learn-oe/contents.htm

Old English Aerobics (P. Baker) – www.engl.virginia.edu/OE/OEA/index.html

Email lists

ANSAXNET – To subscribe to the discussion list, you can send an email message to listserv@listserv.wvu.edu.

The message you send should contain just the line 'subscribe ANSAX-L Your Name'. An archive of postings is available at: www.mun.ca/Ansaxdat/

CHAUCER – To subscribe to the discussion list, you can send an email message to listserv@uic.edu.

The message you send should contain just the line 'subscribe CHAUCER Your Name'. An archive of postings is available at: http://listserv.uic.edu/archives/chaucer.html

Index